SEARCHING FOR GOLDEN EMPIRES

Also by William K. Hartmann

Nonfiction

Desert Heart: Chronicles of the Sonoran Desert

The Grand Tour: A Traveler's Guide to the Solar System (with illustrations by Ron Miller)

Out of the Cradle: Exploring the Frontiers beyond Earth (with illustrations by Ron Miller and Pamela Lee)

Cycles of Fire: Stars, Galaxies, and the Wonder of Deep Space (with illustrations by Ron Miller and Pamela Lee)

The History of Earth: An Illustrated Chronicle of an Evolving Planet (with illustrations by Ron Miller)

In the Stream of Stars: The Soviet-American Space Art Book (edited with Andrei Sokolov, Ron Miller, and Vitaly Myagkov)

Traveler's Guide to Mars: The Mysterious Landscapes of the Red Planet

Novels

Mars Underground

Cities of Gold: A Novel of the Ancient and Modern Southwest

Textbooks

The Cosmic Journey (last editions with Chris Impey)

The Cosmic Voyage (last editions with Chris Impey)

Moon and Planets

SEARCHING FOR GOLDEN EMPIRES

EPIC CULTURAL COLLISIONS IN SIXTEENTH-CENTURY AMERICA

———— ⌇ ————

William K. Hartmann

THE UNIVERSITY OF
ARIZONA PRESS

TUCSON

The University of Arizona Press
www.uapress.arizona.edu

© 2014 The Arizona Board of Regents
All rights reserved. Published 2014

Printed in the United States of America
19 18 17 16 15 14   6 5 4 3 2 1

Jacket designed by Leigh McDonald
Jacket illustration by William K. Hartmann

Library of Congress Cataloging-in-Publication Data are available from the Library of Congress.

Contents

List of Illustrations vii

Friends of This Book. ix

Prologue: Simple Tales and Lost Truths. 3

Chapter 1. Cortés and the Gold of Mexico. 11

Chapter 2. Cortés Expands the Frontier. 57

Chapter 3. The Epic Journey of Cabeza de Vaca and Friends. 94

Chapter 4. The New Viceroy Ponders the North. 131

Chapter 5. The Case of the "Lying Monk". 145

Chapter 6. Marcos Races Back to Mexico City. 196

Chapter 7. Cortés and the Viceroy Compete for "Country
Enough for Many Years of Conquest". 214

Chapter 8. To Cíbola by Land and Sea. 222

Chapter 9. Entering the Seven Cities of Cíbola. 257

Chapter 10. Meanwhile . . . on the Colorado River, in Spain,
and in Mexico City 285

Chapter 11. Coronado Fights a War, Reaches Kansas, and
Returns to Mexico 311

Chapter 12. Aftermath. 343

Additional Reading and References 355

Index 363

Illustrations

Figures

Figure 1.   The Plaza of Three Cultures in central Mexico City...... 38

Figure 2.   Canals and gardens of Xochimilco, Mexico City......... 63

Figure 3.   Examples of copper bells commonly found in
            borderland prehistoric sites............................... 110

Figure 4.   House constructed of reed mats, northern Sonora........ 115

Figure 5.   Confirmation of Sonorans' description of Cíbola......... 168

Figure 6.   One of Marcos's "garden-like" valleys,
            southern Arizona.. 186

Figure 7.   Constructions along the Río Sonora. 235

Figure 8.   The Valle de Señora....................................... 241

Figure 9.   Pueblo ruins in the "Chichilticale Province." 247

Figure 10. The arrival of Coronado's army at Cíbola................ 260

Figure 11. Artifacts from the Coronado expedition................... 265

Figure 12. The San Gerónimo II garrison in the Valle de Señora. 299

Figure 13. What Melchior Díaz might have looked like with
            his fateful lance.. 301

Figure 14. The Coronado campsite at Blanco Canyon, Texas. 323

Figure 15. Texas ranch road on the Llano Estacado plains
            adjacent to Blanco Canyon................................ 326

Maps

Map 1. Examples of Spanish explorations. 6

Map 2. The world of Cortés. 23

Map 3. The central section of Motezuma's Tenochtitlan,
ca. 1520. 33

Map 4. The transformation of central Tenochtitlan into
central Mexico City, ca. 1525–1550. 62

Map 5. The northernmost frontier of Guzmán's slave raiding. 89

Map 6. Final stages of the journey of the Cabeza de Vaca party. 114

Map 7. Concepts of the North. 135

Map 8. The first half of Marcos de Niza's journey to the North. 154

Map 9. A crucial region in Marcos's journey, central Sonora. 164

Map 10. Hypothetical reconstruction of the final parts of
Marcos de Niza's northward journey. 181

Map 11. A portion of Domingo del Castillo's 1541 map of
Mexico, prepared for Viceroy Mendoza. 229

Map 12. Reconstructed middle portion of the Coronado
expedition route. 232

Map 13. The region of Coronado expedition activities in
central New Mexico. 280

Map 14. Coronado's expedition to Quivira. 321

Friends of This Book

Special thanks to Gayle Harrison Hartmann for her archaeological and editorial expertise throughout the creation of this book. And to Elaine Owens at the Planetary Science Institute for her expert help in collating my notes on references and resolving problems arising from conversions from one software to another. This book wouldn't have been possible without their help!

Thanks to Allyson Carter and Scott De Herrera and the staff at the University of Arizona Press for their help and faith in this project, to Mary M. Hill for tireless copyediting, and to Ron Beckwith for his talent and patient work in transforming my sketches into the maps published here. Thanks also to various friends and colleagues who offered support, assistance, discussions, and/or enthusiasm, including, in alphabetical order, Agnieszka Baier, Dan Berman, Bill Broyles, Rick and Peggy Boyer, Don Burgess, Bill Doelle, Michael Engs, Richard Flint, Shirley Cushing Flint, Amy Hartmann Gordon, Joe Gordon, Grace and Anna Gordon, Bill Harmsen, Nancy Marble (Floyd County Historical Museum), Ron and Judith Miller, Paula Moskal, Carlos Nagel, Michel Nallino, Elaine Owens, Cal Riley, Matt Schmader, Paul Schwennesen, Carolyn Slaughter, Maria Elena Veliz, and Jannelle Weakly (at the Arizona State Museum). I also thank Tucson's Mexican restaurants, which (like Paris cafés) let a writer hang out and pursue a project: Casa Molina (both the one on Campbell Avenue, with a beautiful mural of Cortés's arrival in Tenochtilan [Mexico City], and the one on Speedway Boulevard, with its lovely patio), La Indita, Guillermo's LL, and Guadalajara Grill, where staffers Reyna, Armando, and others encouraged me during early work on this book—even though I was the eccentric guy with the laptop in the back room.

SEARCHING FOR GOLDEN EMPIRES

Prologue

Simple Tales and Lost Truths

As I grew up in Pennsylvania, we learned stories of the heroes of early American exploration: Christopher Columbus, as he was known to us, followed by Henry Hudson, the pilgrims, and Daniel Boone in the wilderness. When I moved to Arizona as a graduate student, I began to discover a different country. Here, the first explorations unfolded from south to north, several generations before the pilgrims stepped ashore. This history was full of lost civilizations, golden empires, astounding feats, foolhardy courage, idealistic dreams, and self-righteous moral hubris. Here was the epochal first meeting in human history between "high civilizations" of the western hemispheric half and the eastern hemispheric half of humanity—the two halves that had spread around the world for one hundred thousand years, in two directions, and finally confronted each other militarily and culturally in Mexico in 1519. Here were collisions of legal/religious systems, often used as justification to depose rulers, enslave peoples, and occupy lands . . . under the guise of progress. Fascinatingly, written eyewitness accounts exist, not only from the European side, but also in some cases from the Native American side.

These tales, with their larger-than-life adventures and Shakespearean characters, were mostly left out of the story of our country that was told as I grew up around 1950. Columbus the Italian surely sailed the ocean blue in 1492, but we absorbed a zeitgeist that America was colonized mainly by England. Cortés, "Montezuma," and Coronado were part of some distant *alien* history, somehow detached from "real" American history. The idea that Icelandic Vikings had landed in America around A.D. 1000 was considered a tall tale. The discovery of the Icelandic settlement at L'Anse aux Meadows in Newfoundland did not come until 1960. In a 1940s pirate

3

movie, *The Sea Hawk* (showing when I was a kid), the English heroes are dashing Errol Flynn and his jolly crew, and the key villain is a Spaniard played by a wonderfully smarmy and dandified Claude Rains.

Always the problem exists that popular histories are distilled, refined, and simplified—mythologized so as to be more instructive. George Washington could not tell a lie. Such distilled histories can be duller than reality. As North Americans, Central Americans, and South Americans, we need to reboot and go back to the original records.

What I've tried to do here is tell the story in terms of real human beings, both Native Americans and Europeans, who faced challenges and had amazing adventures and left us many personal accounts, some more reliable than others. My intent is to emphasize human stories (both triumphs and tragedies) and the way in which all of us are subject to the political/economic/religio-philosophic paradigms handed down to us at our mother's knee by the cultures we live in.

Take the astounding conquest of Mexico by a handful of Spanish adventurers. According to the myth, the Aztec king, commonly known as "Montezuma," was an incompetent, vacillating fool. But eyewitness accounts from both the Spanish and Aztec sides portray a more complex and subtle man who agonized about the meaning of bearded strangers landing on his eastern shores. Since childhood, he'd heard the legends that a bearded god named Quetzalcoatl might someday return from the east.

Or take Coronado's famous expedition that went all the way to Kansas in 1540–42. According to the story, he was duped into marching north out of Mexico by false stories of gold spread by Father Marcos de Niza, "the lying monk," who proclaimed the news of the Seven Cities of Gold, where riches could be found on every doorstep. Marcos's still-existing notarized report, however, says nothing about gold in the Seven Cities!

To anyone interested in how history is made, all real characters are more interesting than those portrayed by grade-school myths. The stories need desimplification in order to reveal the excitement and pathos of the period. History books talk about battles and dates and travels and destinations, but who were the men and women themselves? It's easy to talk about deeds and/or piously assign Monday morning blame, but can we grasp the sheer physicality and incredible feats of courage on all sides? Can we feel a human connection with these ancestors of ours who knew so much less about the nature of the world than we do but walked in the burning sun and slept through terrifying nights?

In this book, I weave together some historic threads that have rarely been connected. Cortés's conquest of Mexico City around 1520 and Coronado's journey to the Seven Cities in 1540 usually appear in different books. Each tale has been sculpted into a distinct lithic monument, like the statue of a hero in a town square. The fact is that they are intimately tied together, and Cortés was a player in the whole three-decade drama. Cortés ended up as the main competitor to Coronado in the conquest of the Seven Cities of Cíbola in the 1530s. Hugh Thomas's 1995, 807-page book on Cortés relegates his adventures after 1524 to a 13-page epilogue, but, in fact, the initial exploration of the American Southwest was a pivotal race between Cortés and Coronado.

To describe many of the events of the present book, I compared various documents in both old and new translations. Sometimes I encountered cases where translators of individual documents based interpretations of whole journeys on "their" particular document without making interesting linkages to other eyewitness accounts, as I have attempted to do. Clear examples exist in the scholarly literature where early researchers relied too much on a single translation, a mistranslation, or a literal, nonidiomatic meaning of a single word and consequently misinterpreted the larger picture. I reproduce numbers of statements from centuries ago, but I don't claim to be a translator of sixteenth-century handwritten Spanish; thus, when specific word order is important, I quote the best translations. In other cases, as indicated in the text, I paraphrase or abridge and give a "composite translation" based on several different translations.

Just as there is a Heisenberg uncertainty principle that applies to electrons, there is a "Heisenberg uncertainty" that applies to words. The closer you try to look at an electron or a word in its original context, the more you are aware that it comes with a degree of fuzziness. The more you try to act as if words have only one precise meaning, the less you will understand people and their actions. To take an example that will come up later, when the priest Marcos de Niza said he "saw" that the Sonoran coast turned west, most early translators took his statement literally and pointed out that it seemed geographically impossible, and they accused him of lying. I suggest, and other scholars have agreed, that he meant it in the idiomatic sense: he "saw that it was true" after conducting interviews. (As we'll see in chapter 5, he may even have chosen the phrase to be deliberately ambiguous.) My goal here is to place side by side as many eyewitness sources as possible and then try the synthesis with the least number of inconsistencies.

Our modern instant access to information tempts young or poorly educated readers and would-be scholars to accept various web-posted errors, speculations, and even outrageous supernaturalisms as known fact. For that reason, I've tried to integrate into this text as many references to

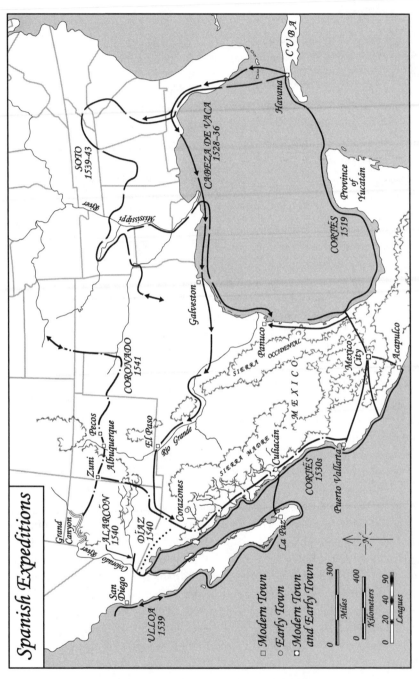

Spanish Expeditions

Grand Canyon

Colorado River

ULLOA
1539

San Diego

ALARCÓN
1540

DÍAZ
1540

CORONADO
1541

Zuñi
Albuquerque

Pecos

El Paso

Rio Grande

Corazones

Culiacán

La Paz

Puerto Vallarta

CORTÉS
1530s

SIERRA MADRE

SIERRA OCCIDENTAL

M E X I C O

Mexico
City

Acapulco

Pánuco

Galveston

CABEZA DE VACA
1528–36

Mississippi River

SOTO
1539–43

C U B A

Havana

Province
of
Yucatán

CORTÉS
1519

□ *Modern Town*
○ *Early Town*
⊡ *Modern Town*
and *Early Town*

0   300
Miles

0   400
Kilometers

0 20 40 90
Leagues

Map 1. Examples of Spanish explorations described in this book. Approximate routes are shown for various expeditions. Map by Ron Beckwith.

fundamental research as possible. Following the University of Arizona Press style, the year and page of the reference are listed, for example, as 1939, 66. Sometimes if the year is already mentioned in the text, the page is listed separately, simply as (66). They are given in the "Additional Reading and References" list at the end of the book. Some of the older books, such as Bernal Díaz del Castillo's eyewitness account of Cortés's takeover of Mexico City, and Cabeza de Vaca's account of his journey across North America, are still thrilling reads.

At the same time I hope to show that scholarly research is not stuffy library work. As I present in some of the sidebars, wonderful adventures are to be had while tracking down and then finding the now-deserted site of some ancient battle or camping under the stars in a lonely spot where your ancient "friends" camped centuries ago.

There is something else intriguing in this research: the research becomes a strange dialogue among fascinating characters from various centuries. It really is a dialogue, because you read what someone said in 1542, and then you say, "But that can't be right . . ." and you scramble to read the report of a historian who visited the site in 1895, and then you rush back to see what one of the other eyewitnesses said in 1540. Then you add your new realization, your tiny bit, and someone else may take it up thirty years later. Many original letters and chronicles of the participants are available from the 1500s, and "waves" of historians have become interested in them. One wave came as Anglo-Americans discovered the West's Spanish roots in the late 1800s, and another wave came in the 1930s and 1940s on the four-hundredth anniversary of the Coronado expedition. You find yourself debating against these long-departed colleagues with respect and affection for them! In a fast-paced world that cares only about the newest version of "now," it's strangely gratifying to be involved in something that has a longer timescale and perhaps even a certain long-term importance to unknown future colleagues and readers.

In Cortés/Coronado research, there is a problem about dates. In the 1500s European astronomers realized that predicted positions of the sun, relative to the stars, were in error, and the calendar dates of equinoxes and solstices had shifted by ten days since ancient times. The first blossoms of spring, for example, were shifting measurably relative to the calendar date. The shift was because the old "Julian" calendar, in effect since Julius Caesar, had assumed that the year is 365.25 days long, whereas more precise measurements show that it is about eleven minutes longer. The error noted in the 1500s was ten days and growing. The Christian Church became involved, partly because its scholars were some of the best educated in such matters, and partly because the date of Easter was tied to the spring equinox and was thus "migrating" through the year instead of sticking to its originally proposed season. After various conferences of astronomers, Pope Gregory XIII decreed in 1582 that an improved calendar should be used and a ten-day correction should be made to keep the seasons matched to the calendar. Thus, in the European world, Thursday, 4 October 1582, was declared to be the last day of use of the Julian calendar, and the next day was decreed to be not Friday, 5 October, but Friday, 15 October 1582. Since then, the new "Gregorian" calendar has been adopted (with various grumblings) virtually worldwide.

Our heroes and villains in this book, in the early to mid-1500s, recorded their dates by the Julian calendar, but their 1 June, for example, would actually correspond to the temperatures and weather patterns that we experience on 11 June in our calendar. This problem can produce wonderful confusion. For example, Coronado scholar Richard Flint noted in 2003 that many dates given by the most detailed chronicler of the Coronado expedition, Pedro de Castañeda Nájera, seem out of sync with dates given by others. He probably wrote in the early 1560s, but the oldest known surviving copy of Castañeda's book postdates 1582, and Flint suggests that a post-1582 copyist dutifully "corrected" Castañeda's Julian dates to the new Gregorian calendar. In this book, I've tried to follow the most common tradition in most studies of Cortés and Coronado, which is to quote the date they recorded in their writings (the Julian date), rather than trying to correct everything by ten days. To reduce possible errors, however, I occasionally mention that a Julian date is involved or cite just the month of events.

There is a similar issue about distances. It's easy today to measure air line distances on maps, but our characters had to travel on the ground. Thus it's more meaningful to estimate trail miles, which are 10 percent to 30 percent longer than air line distances, depending on terrain and winding roads. I try to distinguish between the two, roughly estimating trail miles from terrain or distances along old roads. Worse yet, the Spanish recorded distances in leagues, and, as discussed in the text, the league itself had a range of around 20 percent in possible values, which I try to take into account. So there is a "Heisenberg uncertainty principle" applying to distances as well as words.

Our story needs some introduction.

As schoolchildren know, Cristóbal Colón, sailing under the flag of Isabella I and Ferdinand V, a generation before Cortés and Coronado, found islands sixty-eight days' voyage across the Atlantic from Spain. Contrary to modern myth, the world was not regarded as flat in those days, at least not by scholars. In chapter 7 I point out a case in 1540 in which Spanish mariners, discovering the Colorado River, attributed one of their observations to the curvature of the Earth. Various Greek scholars (who were rediscovered in the 1400s after the so-called Dark Ages) had created globes of the Earth, mapped different climate zones at different latitudes, realized the moon was also spherical, estimated the relative distances of the moon and sun, and measured the approximate circumference and diameter of our planet by 200 B.C.

Columbus knew of some of the old measurements of Earth's size, but he favored too small a value for Earth's circumference and hence underestimated the distance he'd have to go across the Atlantic to reach China. Irony abounded. Had Columbus known the true distance, he might not have dared to sail. Sure enough, when he hit islands at about the right distance, he mistook the island of Cuba for the province of Mangi in China, discussed earlier by the Italian geographer/cosmographer Paulo Toscanelli. During nearly six months in the Bahamas and Caribbean islands in the 1490s, Columbus acquired bits of gold jewelry. Expectations began to build that more gold would soon be found farther west. Till his dying day, Columbus thought he had discovered islands off China.

The generation of Spaniards in this book thus colonized Caribbean islands without knowing whether they were a few days' voyage off the coast of Cathay, where Marco Polo, in the 1200s, had reported a fabulous empire of gold and spice. Marco Polo said the palace of the Great Kahn in Cathay housed a treasure of gold, silver, pearls, and other jewels. Geographer Toscanelli wrote to King Alfonso V of Portugal in 1474, referring to the temples and palaces of Japan as "roofed with massy gold."

Excursions around the Caribbean soon revealed extended coastlines and a huge southern landmass whose shore was mapped by the Italian navigator Amerigo Vespucci. In a popular 1507 book the German mapmaker Martín Waldseemüller described Vespucci's discoveries, and he inscribed Amerigo's first name across what turned out to be the South American continent. To most adventurers in our book, however, it was still known as the Indies. The natives were, reasonably enough, known as Indie-ans. The word "Indian" has come to be tarnished, but I use it occasionally with that sensible original geographic intent—inhabitants of a place that had been named the "Indies."

Why were the earliest Spaniards of the 1500s fixated on gold instead of seeking farmland for rich haciendas or longer-term English-style colonies? Easily transportable wealth, like gold, would allow the explorer/speculator quickly to pay off the investors who financed the quest. Even in the 1500s, capitalism was great for exploiting resources and developing short-term prosperity but less adept at creating the sustainable infrastructure needed to stabilize a civilization.

The first great American gold rush came in 1512, in Cuba, where placer deposits yielded a very brief bonanza. Meanwhile, between 1502 and 1513, sailors passing beyond the west end of Cuba sighted the Mexican coast at various times, in particular Yucatán. In 1513 Ponce de León landed briefly on the Yucatán coast, returning from his fruitless search for a mythic fountain of youth in Florida. (The concept is ridiculed today, yet we spend millions trying to restore youth with cosmetics, drugs, surgeries. . . .) Yucatán attracted more exploration. In 1517 a Spaniard named Hernández de Córdoba sailed along the east coast on a slave-raiding expedition, and he was followed in 1518 by a captain named Juan de Grijalva. Who would be next to explore the new land of Yucatán?

CHAPTER ONE

Cortés and the Gold of Mexico

One day in 1506, young Hernán Cortés stepped off a boat onto a dock in Cuba. It was his first footstep in the New World. He was twenty-two years old, keen to seek fame and fortune.

Cortés had been born in central Spain around 1484. During Cristóbal Colón's four voyages of discovery, Cortés was a youth, growing from eight to eighteen years old. He must have been like a boy growing up in America during the 1960s, the age of astronauts, following the news of otherworldly exploration with growing excitement. Colón had discovered islands thought to be off the coast of China or India — the Indies.

Cortés's extended family included minor Spanish nobles, but that was no guarantee of wealth or respect, because the land was in ferment. The country had been invaded many generations before by "Moors" — Islamic Arabs from Morocco. Spanish Christian, Jewish, and Moorish Islamic cultures were still colliding in Spain, although the Spanish Christians were pushing the Moors out of Granada around the time of Colón's early voyages. Residual skirmishing continued in Spain and North Africa in the 1500s.

At about age twelve Cortés left home to live with an aunt and uncle in the cosmopolitan city of Salamanca. There he followed in his grandfather's footsteps and began to study law, an experience that shaped his handling of many of his escapades in later life.

Cortés liked Latin and gambling. According to the authoritative 1995 biography by historian Hugh Thomas, he did not complete a full law degree, but he did obtain a worldly understanding of how things worked under the dominant Spanish and Euro-Catholic culture. In this political system, the pope in Rome had supreme spiritual/philosophical authority, but the various kings of Europe, armed with divine right and byzantine court procedures, exercised local civil authority. Renaissance humanism was beginning to illuminate, or even compete with, traditional Christianity. Practical empiricism would soon challenge blind medieval appeals to ancient authority figures. Churchmen and philosophers, to their credit, were beginning to debate the nature of the inhabitants of the newly discovered Indies—"Indie-ans." Were they full-fledged human beings with souls, or did they belong to some lesser order, without rights?

In the operative European paradigm of Cortés's day, Earth was thus immovably fixed at the center of the entire universe, created by God in seven days as the home for mankind. Christianity was the one true religion. Europe's Judeo-Christian cultural/economic system was God's gift to the world. Copernicus and Galileo did not move Earth out of its unique position until a few generations later.

The king of Spain after 1516 was Carlos I (or Charles I), but in 1519 he acquired a new name. He was elected to be Carlos V, king of the Holy Roman Empire, a loose confederation of Christian countries that dominated European politics from A.D. 800 until 1806. It was a precursor of the European Union. Cortés and Spanish explorers of the 1500s were thus imbued with the idea that theirs was a special role, spreading civilization and Holy Christianity around the newly discovered pagan world. Some religious orders of the day were convinced that once the pagans had been converted to Christianity, Christ would reappear, and the kingdom of God would be established on Earth.

Cortés, the Man in His Twenties: ca. 1510

During his student years, Cortés picked up some favorite sayings, especially from plays and from volumes of Erasmus. At the top of his list: "Fortune favors the bold." Moved by such a sentiment, he decided to seek his own fortune in the Indies. His style was to calculate his probabilities, then gamble on chance. For a while, it worked.

Arriving in the Spanish territory of Cuba, he ingratiated himself with the governor's circle. As a minor functionary, he pursued several searches for gold, and he witnessed the decimation of the local native population, forced into labor for the Spaniards, and the execution of chiefs for resisting Spanish rule. So convinced were the Spaniards of their right to conquest that resistance by Native Americans was blithely labeled "rebellion" or "treason." This heavy-handed approach sparked outrage among many of the Catholic priests on the scene.

The most important voice on behalf of the indigenous Americans was that of Bartolomé de Las Casas (1474–1566), whose father had been on Colón's second voyage to America in 1493. Bartolomé, at age twenty-four, went with his father on Colón's 1498 voyage to America and in 1502 became the manager of the family's land grants on the island of Española (later Hispaniola). He was known as a very capable young man. Soon he recoiled in disgust at the enslavement and extermination of the native populations. In 1510 he became the first priest ordained in the New World. He became one of the first American historians and an archenemy of the conquistador mentality. He wrote several books encouraging better treatment of the Indie-ans. Las Casas's opponents countered that many native inhabitants were barely clothed and cited Aristotle's argument that certain people were destined by their very nature to be slaves.

To Cortés's credit, he reportedly oversaw the establishment of the first hospital and foundry in Cuba. After eight years, he had accumulated some wealth, built a hacienda, fathered a daughter with a native Cuban woman, and become a secretary to the governor of Cuba. A year or so later, he met Catalina, a young Spanish woman with more or less noble connections. A tempestuous courtship ensued, during which Cortés was briefly thrown in jail by the governor for seduction and breach of promise. In the style of a comic opera, all was saved when he married Catalina in 1516. As we'll see, his marriage was to have a strange fate six years later in a house in the conquered Aztec capital, now Mexico City.

From records of the time, we can piece together a description of Cortés, the man, during those years just before he left for Mexico. He was about five feet four inches tall, in his early thirties, with a broad chest, a slim build, and a pale face. He had longish, red-brown hair and a thin beard of the same color. He had a striking ability to come up with a clever phrase or rationale that would convince men around him. He could be both impetuous and prudent at the same time. After brief reflection, he'd take stunning action. He was attractive to women. He supported the church, good works, and the dominant paradigm. He could get jobs done.

In 1518 the governor of Cuba selected Cortés to be the leader of a new expedition to explore the coast of Yucatán. Spaniards of the time had no concept of the size of North America, and most mariners assumed Yucatán was just one more island of the Indies. Somewhere beyond, to the west and north, lay the coast of Marco Polo's Cathay.

Off to Yucatán: 1518

The Cuban governor could never have imagined what he had set in motion. To him, the Yucatán foray was no more than a fact-finding trip to clarify coastal information from earlier mariners. But to Cortés, it was a chance to explore unknown lands and all they might offer in terms of his own reputation back in Spain. He threw himself into the new adventure. Impetuous but still calculating, he began running up huge expenses to outfit the expedition and began dressing in the fine clothes of a grand leader.

The governor soon had second thoughts about his appointment and began maneuvering to oust Cortés from the job. Sensing danger, Cortés made one of his classic flamboyant decisions. Suddenly he left home and wife, boarded his ships, and prepared to set sail at once instead of waiting for the announced date. Hearing of this move, the governor raced to the dock the next morning in time to ask what was going on. Cortés called back from a small boat, saying that he had thought about this for some time, and then—in a typical gesture—he mimicked cooperation and disingenuously asked for the governor's final orders. Flabbergasted, the governor gave no response. Cortés boarded his ship and sailed away. It was November 1518.

Cortés Lands in Mexico: Early 1519

After several Caribbean stops, Cortés landed near Cozumel, on the coast of Yucatán, in early 1519. By this time he had nine ships and four or five hundred men. As he pushed westward along the coast (see map 2), he found well-clothed Maya villagers with small pyramidal temples and "books" consisting of manuscripts with painted illustrations. He made friends and preached about Christianity. In another of his bold acts, he ordered his men to remove statues of local deities from the pagan temples, replacing them with statues of the Virgin Mary, apparently draped with native women's garments.

The astonished townspeople seemed to accept their guests' behavior. At one point, they brought a "gift" (as the Spaniards recorded it) of twenty young women. Cortés insisted they be properly baptized before being assigned as companions to various officers.

Among the women was an attractive and intelligent young woman whose parents were officials of a nearby town and who was regarded as an important person of royal descent. She was initially the companion of another Spaniard in the expedition, but she soon became not only Cortés's lover but also his trusted assistant and chief translator. During baptism, she was given the name Marina, but she is also referred to in early manuscripts and in Mexico today as Malinche or La Malinche, which was probably a Spanish corruption of some term in the Nahuatl language of the Aztecs. The exact sense of this name Malinche is obscure, as it was apparently occasionally applied to Cortés himself, perhaps alluding sarcastically to their extraordinary relationship.

Marina, with one foot in America and another in the Spanish camp, is one of the most intriguing figures of North American history. Documentary evidence about her is scarce, although linguist Anna Lanyon, after searching for clues in the scanty records, published a fascinating biography of La Malinche in 1999. We have a poignant description of her from one of Cortés's soldiers, a memoirist named Bernal Díaz del Castillo (see sidebar). Díaz talked with her and paints a portrait in many phrases scattered throughout his extraordinary book.

[She was] the daughter of a great chieftain and mistress of slaves, as her appearance clearly showed . . . of good appearance, intelligent, and poised. (Díaz [ca. 1570] 1956, 55)

[She was a person who] knew well how to interpret. (86)

SIDEBAR: The Extraordinary Memoir by Bernal Díaz del Castillo

Bernal Díaz del Castillo was a young, wide-eyed soldier of about twenty-five when he first met Marina. He began writing about his adventures much later, at about age sixty, and kept revising his manuscript over the next decades, from the 1550s to the 1570s. His 1632 book, *Historia verdadera de la conquista de la Nueva España* (usually referred to in English as *The Discovery and Conquest of Mexico*), is a North American classic that has remained in print for several centuries in various Spanish editions and English translations (see Díaz [ca. 1570] 1956). In the present book we will compare many of the scenes he depicts to the Aztec eyewitness accounts, a process that confirms the general consistency and veracity of accounts from the two sides. Díaz, of course, shows proper respect for the authority of Cortés, the king, and the church, while the Aztecs stress their perception of the barbarity of the Europeans. Memoirists from both sides were too full of wonder about what they had experienced to waste time on made-up tales.

Díaz lived perhaps past age ninety without seeing his book published or knowing it would still be in print more than four hundred years later.

[She was endowed with] such manly courage that she never allowed us to see any sign of weakness, although she heard daily how we were all going to be killed. (110)

[She was a helper] after battles when we were all wounded and sick. (110)

[She was] always very shrewd. (137)

Marina seems to have been held in respect by the Spaniards in general, being given the title "doña" (pronounced DÓN-ya, with a long o), usually assigned to noble or respected Spanish women. She is a crucial figure in North American history, because most of Cortés's negotiations with the Native American populace in the ensuing months would be conducted through her. She is also enigmatic; we have no clear records of her own thoughts. From the early 1800s until modern times in Mexico, she's been depicted as a traitor to Native American peoples because of her role in establishing Spanish supremacy in Mexico and Central America. That view would have made little sense to her, however. She could not have seen herself in the context of "Europeans" versus "Native American culture" because her world was not transatlantic. The Mexico she knew was divided into numerous local and/or regional factions, accustomed to complex alliances. The strange, bearded aliens offered an alliance with her people to overthrow the imperialistic Aztec tax collectors from their capital, Tenochtitlan, now known as Mexico City. La Malinche remains a paradox. Was she a gifted champion of indigenous people who may have softened the heart of Cortés against blind slaughter, or was she a collaborator with the enemy? In modern Mexican Spanish, the term *malinchismo* refers contemptuously to the adoption of foreign customs.

Cortés's concerns were different from the mysteries concerning Malinche. He had put a banner on his flagship carrying a Latin exhortation: "Comrades, we follow the cross, and if we have faith, we will conquer in this sign." But was there anything in Yucatán to conquer? The flash of gold was rarely seen among the coastal Maya, but Cortés began to hear tales of a wealthy, gold-splashed empire somewhere inland. The inland empire builders called themselves the Mexica (pronounced meh-SHE-ka). They were the people who eventually gave their name to Mexico itself. Later they came to be called by another name in their Nahuatl language, Aztecs, referring to the ancestral founders of their culture. We'll refer to them as the Spaniards knew them, "Mexica," except when the term "Aztec" may be clearer than the term "Mexican."

The View from Tenochtitlan: 1518

In distant Tenochtitlan,* the fabulous capital of the Mexica—Mexico City—emperor Motezuma was restless. He had a good communication network throughout the region, and for several years his emissaries from the east coast had been bringing tales of strange floating "towers" along the shore. Bearded, light-skinned strangers occasionally made brief landings. A trunk containing strange clothes had washed ashore and been brought to Motezuma's court.

How do we know what Motezuma and the Mexica were thinking during the turbulent months of first contact with the Europeans? By great good fortune, we have fascinating accounts from the Mexica themselves. The survival of these accounts is an epic story in itself. A few years after Cortés's conquest, many of the "first-generation" Spanish priests and governors attempted to suppress and destroy Aztec culture and religion in order to establish Christianity. Some second- and third-generation priests, however, developed curiosity about the ancient Mexican worldviews and began to collect old books and song texts. Today, we are glad they did.

The surviving records came from knowledgeable native residents and from preconquest Aztec books. The books were painted on deerskin or a fibrous paper made from the agave plant. They offer missing-link insight into the origins of written language. Created by educated priests and scribes, they were mostly cosmological, dealing with the calendar, religious rituals, major events in Aztec history, and the Aztec view of the universe and its gods. They combined beautifully rendered, cartoon-like pictures with a sort of protowriting employing ideograms and phonetic symbols.

The most notable example of preservation occurred around the 1550s, when a far-sighted Spanish priest, Bernardino de Sahagún (1499–1590), commissioned historical accounts of Aztec civilization by Aztec eyewitnesses. Sahagún's newly converted young Mexican acolytes, who could write Spanish, were instructed to interview Mexican elders who had experienced the Spanish invasion. The most complete original version of Sahagún's work is a bilingual manuscript preserved in Florence, Italy, consisting of a column of Aztec "text" and a parallel column with a Spanish commentary. Modern printed versions have been available in Spanish since 1829. Sahagún's work was studied by the Mexican historian Miguel León-Portilla in 1959; his account was translated and published in English

---

* Tenochtitlan is often spelled with an accent over the *a*, though Coronado scholar Richard Flint and others point out that the Aztec language, Nahuatl, did not accent the last syllable.

in 1962. The first complete English translation of the Florence manuscript was finally created by historians Arthur Anderson and Charles Dibble in 1969, and here I've used their 1978 version of the final section, along with the León-Portilla translation of various records. León-Portilla, in his introduction, aptly compares what he calls Aztec "literary remains" to Homer's *Iliad*, a semilegendary memory of an epic invasion.

Here, then, is the poignant Mexican counterpoint to the Europeans' version. It's the story of an entire civilization caught in the neck of history's

---

SIDEBAR: The Name of the Aztec Ruler

"From the halls of Montezuma . . ." begins "The Marines' Hymn," referring to the leader Cortés was soon to meet. (The song commemorates the U.S. invasion of Mexico under President Polk in 1846–47, conveniently forgotten in the United States today. Gen. Winfield Scott, like Cortés, landed at Veracruz and marched on Mexico City with officers such as Ulysses S. Grant, Robert E. Lee, and Stonewall Jackson.) "Montezuma" is thus a name familiar to American schoolchildren. But what was the pronunciation that Cortés and his troops actually heard? As with most names in early Spanish documents of the New World, the answer is not certain. Individual eyewitnesses and memoir writers heard local native pronunciations and attempted to render them in Spanish alphabetic characters. As a natural result, there were different spellings by different writers, such as those listed by historian Hugh Thomas:

Mutezuma (ca. 1521, attributed to Cortés himself)

Motecuma (ca. 1541, Codex Mendoza, compiled for the Spanish viceroy, Antonio Mendoza)

Motecuçuma (ca. 1547, Spanish historian Bernardino de Sahagún, writing in 1547 and following years)

Motecucoma (ca. 1576, Codex Aubin)

Motevcçuma (1500s?, early church documents)

Moctezuma (modern Spanish form)

There seems to be no evidence for a prominent *n* sound, as in the common English rendition. Even more uncertainty of sound appears in the second syllable, which seems to be two syllables in some sixteenth-century renditions. Synthesizing, I use "Motezuma" as the best English rendering of what Cortés may have heard in the courtyards of Tenochtitlan.

hourglass. The ancient nation, forced through the nexus, was reduced to a handful of fragile manuscripts from a few survivors. Many of the Mexican eyewitnesses contributing to the Aztec accounts were highly cultured, sophisticated, literate men and women who spoke from the heart about what had happened to them.

The collision of two worlds was thus documented from both sides. Generations of Americans, until the late twentieth century, grew up primarily with accounts based on the writings of the Spanish conquerors—if they learned anything at all about the conquest of Mexico. In our twenty-first century, as the world struggles toward a comfortable planetary culture of mixed roots, the parallel stories of the epic, told from both sides, are much more valuable. For this reason, the present book is devoted to retelling the early explorations of western North America from both sides as much as possible.

There is a caveat to the claim that we have eyewitness accounts from the Mexican side. Historians correctly point out that the Aztec accounts were filtered through translations supervised usually by Spanish priests, so that many of the original Mexican concepts may have been poorly represented or deliberately misrepresented by the Spanish supervisors. Anderson and Dibble, translators of Sahagún, state in their introduction that "we cannot and do not claim that the Aztec account is accurate and dispassionate." Twentieth-century revisionist and contextual scholars go even further, arguing that no ancient writing represents reliable truth because of different meanings attached to concepts in other cultural contexts. Nonetheless, Aztec accounts plainly describe slaughters by the Spaniards, confirmed independently on the Spanish side. These accounts would hardly have survived propagandistic Spanish censorship. Many details, such as Motezuma's anxiety over the Spaniards' arrival, seem ideologically neutral and humanly realistic. In terms of our attempt at a first-order "big picture," the Aztec historical accounts appear to be remarkably frank, heartfelt documents about what happened, full of genuine pathos and drama.

Strangers on the Coast: 1518

The Mexican accounts indicate how their messengers came to Tenochtitlan with news of a strange vessel off the east coast in the Aztec year of 12 Flint Knife, or 1518, the year before Cortés arrived. This ship, which arrived off present-day Veracruz, is believed to have been captained by Juan de Grijalva. Motezuma sent emissaries to the coast to spy on the strangers. Prudently, however, the Aztecs carried gifts—feathered capes in the style allowed only for the emperor, Motezuma, himself. The messengers located Grijalva's ship. Probably through regional interpreters brought by both sides, their story emerged: they had come from the court of the great Motezuma. The feathered capes from Motezuma were exchanged for necklaces of colored Spanish beads. The Spaniards soon departed.

According to the Aztec records, the Mexica began to speculate that Grijalva's ship might be heralding the return of one of their most important gods, Quetzalcoatl. He had an identity as a feathered serpent but also as a man. According to Aztec tradition, he had appeared in Mexico generations earlier. He performed wondrous deeds, bringing the Mexica "all art and knowledge." In his human identity, he was represented as having a beard — unusual among the Mexica except among some elders.

Who was Quetzalcoatl? A cult about him seems to have arisen around the 900s to 1100s among the pre-Aztec Toltec culture in the city of Tula, somewhat north of present-day Mexico City. According to citizens of Tula, Quetzalcoatl was a priest or king. According to one Aztec account, Quetzalcoatl was eventually chased out of Tula, fled to the coast, and threw himself into a funeral pyre. In another account, he departed on the eastern ocean in a special snake-motif raft, asserting that he would "return from the east and resume his rule." (The latter account is reported in the documents collected by Sahagún; see Anderson and Dibble's translation [1978, 11].)

Intrigued by these stories, some modern historians have wondered whether the Quetzalcoatl legends are associated with some errant European or Phoenician boat having crossed the Atlantic, bringing new skills to Mexico, generations before the Aztecs. The idea that Quetzalcoatl constructed a new boat and attempted to return home sounds plausible for a lost Mediterranean stranger in a strange land who transformed himself into a local hero à la Mark Twain's hero in *A Connecticut Yankee in King Arthur's Court*. Perhaps Quetzalcoatl had no second coming because he was lost at sea. Or perhaps he arrived at some African or European port, only to be considered a raving lunatic. How many such incidents must have been lost in the folds of time? Nothing has been proven, one way or the other.

Motezuma's emissaries to the coast, convinced that Quetzalcoatl had reappeared, returned to Tenochtitlan. According to the accounts written by Aztec historians, Motezuma and his court agonized about whether Quetzalcoatl was really returning. Motezuma related the events to "portents" experienced by the Mexica since about 1502. A temple had caught fire. A fragmenting celestial fireball had been seen in the sky, dropping "sparks," as meteoritic fireballs do. Also, if we judge the records correctly, a bright comet had been seen in the morning sky around the year of 12 House, which would be 1517.

The comet is of special interest. Records collected by Sahagún and León-Portilla have minor inconsistencies but indicate something was indeed seen in the eastern predawn sky every morning for months, and it was visible for at least three hours until the "the sun arose and destroyed it." It was described as "a sign like a tongue of fire, like a flame," wider at one end. This beautifully matches the appearance of a bright comet with a prominent tail. Any given comet is visible across much of the world, so a modern astronomer's natural reaction is to see if a bright comet was recorded by other cultures around that time. Modern astronomical historians have collected such records, notably Gary Kronk in his 1999 comet catalog, *Cometography*. Frustratingly, nothing quite corresponds to the Mexican reports. Chinese records document a notable comet with a tail as long as 10° in 1506 and others in 1520 and 1521 that were probably less prominent. Kronk, in a private communication, reminded me, however, that a comet might have been visible only at latitudes from Mexico southward and thus escaped annotation in the better-kept records of Chinese and European observers who lived in northern latitudes.

According to the Aztec chroniclers, speaking with hindsight, the comet, the fireball, the temple fire, and other events were omens of the destruction of Aztec Mexico. Today, we understand that comets, earthquakes, meteorite falls, and so on occur semirandomly every generation or so and that we humans are notoriously prone, *after the fact*, to associate such events with plagues, wars, and the deaths of kings. While the Sahagún and León-Portilla manuscripts start with these events, it's unclear how much Motezuma and his court were worrying about a change in the world order *prior* to the Spaniards' appearance.

Motezuma and his officials, like all of us, were embedded in their own culture. An additional, worrisome interpretation of the strange coastal visitors came, therefore, from their own history. The Mexica conquered the highlands of central Mexico and founded Tenochtitlan around 1325. They held a fatalistic worldview that history was made of inexorable cycles. Just as early Christians expected Jesus to return in their own lifetimes, initiating a new kingdom of God, Motezuma now wondered if the Aztec cycle was nearing its end-time. Quetzalcoatl, hero of Aztec mythology, had reportedly been born in the year called 1 Reed in the fifty-two-year cyclic Aztec calendar, and in some accounts he died or left fifty-two years later, again in 1 Reed. The year Cortés arrived, two years after Grijalva's ship, was 1 Reed, as discussed by Anderson and Dibble (1978, 12).

Motezuma's World: 1518

According to most Mexican accounts, Motezuma was about fifty years old when these events occurred. In European style, he would be called Motezuma II, because he was the second ruler with this name; the first ruled around 1450. Motezuma II seems to have been too contemplative, cautious, and fatalistic to deal with the brash Spaniard who was about to become his "friend," adversary, and downfall. Bernal Díaz later gave us a detailed physical description of Motezuma, whom Díaz perceived to be younger than fifty: "The great Motezuma was about forty years old, of good height, well-proportioned, and slender; he was not very dark, but of the color natural for an Indian. He did not wear his hair long, only long enough to cover his ears. He had few whiskers, dark and well set and sparse. His face was a little long, but pleasant, while his eyes were attractive and he showed in his person and in his glance both affection and, when necessary, seriousness. He was very clean" (Díaz [ca. 1570] 1956, 158).

Motezuma's world was spectacular. His capital, Tenochtitlan, was on a two-by-three-mile island in a bay on the west side of a twenty-by-forty-mile shallow lake. The island was accessed by several mile-long causeways stretching from the nearest mainland shores to the city. The lake and causeways are gone today—filled in, century by century, to create land for modern Mexico City. The streets and plazas through which Motezuma and Cortés walked now lie in the crowded heart of one of the largest urban sprawls in the world. Motezuma's city, however, had splendid palaces, exotically ornamented pyramids, court entertainers, gardens, canals, markets, and a sophisticated culture that admired gold primarily for jewelry, important ornaments, and utensils. Like many of history's "advanced" cultures, the residents were supported by a flow of commandeered resources from other provinces. Their concept of war was non-European. They held what they called "wars of flowers," in which competing statelets sent armies whose soldiers pursued not lethal destruction but rather the capturing of enemy soldiers. The captured opponents had the "honor" of being sacrificed on the pyramid-temples to propitiate the gods and thus maintain the cycles of history and nature. The rest of the defeated armies returned home and paid tribute and taxes to the winners.

These words are not intended to promote a romanticized view of Native American culture in the sense of Rousseau's "noble savage." The Mexica were as capable of bloodletting and oppression as any modern society, yet the Mexica seem to have avoided the all-out bloody wars that have marred European and American history. To the Mexica, all-out killing of too many

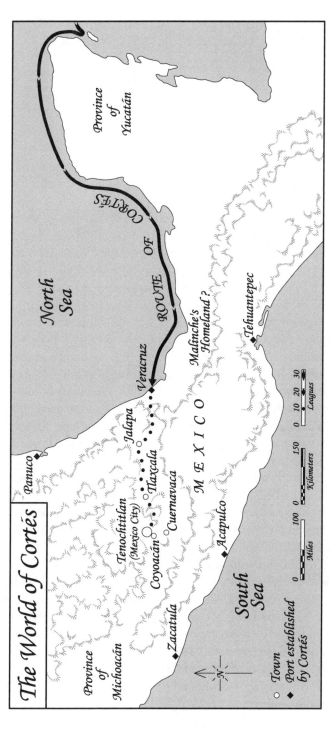

Map 2. The world of Cortés. After Cortés's army marched to Tenochtitlan in 1519 and conquered the city in 1521, Cortés and his men discovered additional gold in Michoacán, explored the "South Sea" coast, and established ports such as Acapulco. Map by Ron Beckwith.

enemies had a counterproductive side because the gods would be deprived of their sacrifices. As the Mexica were soon to learn, the Europeans had a different idea.

Cortés on the Coast: 1519

By April, having learned about the powerful and wealthy inlanders called the Mexica, Cortés had headed west and north, up the Mexican coast to the area of present-day Veracruz (see map 2). From here, Tenochtitlan lay only about 170 miles directly inland.

Motezuma's scouts on the coast reported Cortés's moves. The Mexican leaders conferred in their palaces and gardens. How could they find out if the bearded lord on the eastern coast was Quetzalcoatl himself, returning to establish his rule? Motezuma sent a new contingent of emissaries chosen from his jaguar warriors. They contacted Cortés's entourage on the coast on Easter weekend of 1519. Following Motezuma's policy, they made friendly overtures, offered to build huts to protect the Spaniards from the rainy season, and presented the most valuable and impressive gifts their society could offer: featherwork cloaks, cotton cloth, and decorative objects of gold. They explained that the gifts came from the great lord Motezuma, who wanted to learn more about the new arrivals. Included among the offerings were complete sets of clothing and jewelry associated with four of the highest gods, including Quetzalcoatl, since the Mexica speculated that the strangers might be these gods returning. The Quetzalcoatl materials included a jade neckpiece with a disk of gold, a shield decorated with bands of gold, black obsidian-decorated sandals, and a snake mask of turquoise mosaic (suitable for his feathered serpent identity).

The Aztec accounts describe how Cortés allowed the Mexican emissaries aboard his ships and received the gifts. The Mexican emissaries themselves apparently dressed Cortés in the Quetzalcoatl trappings (Anderson and Dibble 1978, 14; León-Portilla 1962, 25). Cortés/Quetzalcoatl now played his power card: he explained that these gifts were not good enough and had Motezuma's emissaries bound with iron collars. He then provided a demonstration of his might by firing one of his cannons. The emissaries fainted dead away and had to be revived with wine and food. Cortés explained to them that he wanted to know if the Mexica could really fight. Therefore, he would shortly stage a combat between them and his own men.

The terrified messengers countered by saying that this was not what they were sent for and that if they died, they would not be able to deliver news to Motezuma. Cortés then released them, having sized up their reactions about fighting. The messengers sped back to Motezuma. The Aztec documents include detailed descriptions of the Spanish cannon and the Spaniards themselves:

> A thing like a ball of stone came out of its entrails, shooting sparks and raining fire, and the smoke that came out had a sickening odor. It can crack a mountain, or shatter a tree into splinters and sawdust as if it had exploded from within! The strangers themselves are completely covered with trappings of iron. Only their faces can be seen. They have deer as tall as the roof of a house, and these deer carry the strangers on their backs. Some of the strangers are pale and have yellow hair, and some have black hair. It is curly hair, with fine strands. There were other strangers who were black with kinky hair. As for their food, it is like human food. Some of it is white, something like straw, with the taste and pith of a cornstalk. They have enormous dogs, tireless and powerful and spotted like an ocelot. (adapted from León-Portilla's translations [1962, 30])

At one point during the early exchanges, a religious ceremony was held upon the return of Motezuma's ambassadors from the coast. Two captives were sacrificed, and the ambassadors were sprinkled with their blood because "their eyes had looked upon the gods, and they had even conversed with them" (León-Portilla 1962, 29).

The Aztec accounts give us a wonderful sense of how the "aliens" from Europe were perceived. The aliens were reported to be crafty, grasping, hairy, and smelly. They spoke in a strange tongue that sounded coarse to the Mexica's ears. The emissaries from Tenochtitlan included artists who sketched the strangers, prudently including their weapons and horses, never before seen in Mexico.

On the Spanish side, Cortés made deliberately disingenuous inquiries about gold. Did the Mexica have much of it? Yes. Could they, um, send some more? Cortés explained that he knew it was of value, but he wanted to study the Mexican gold to see if it was like that of Spain. Gifts flowed both ways. Cortés sent items such as Spanish silk coats, glassware, a fine chair, and tools such as scissors. He also sent a gift of a metal Spanish helmet to Motezuma with the gentle suggestion that Motezuma might send it back full of granulated gold.

Motezuma reportedly grew depressed about all this. He couldn't sleep. As recounted in the documents collected by León-Portilla, "He thought everything he did was in vain, and he sighed at every moment and could enjoy nothing." Still, he tried to be careful. He did not want to anger these possible gods, nor did he want to anger an invading army from some distant king. One of his responses was to send magicians and sorcerers to cast spells on the strangers and confound them. That strategy failed.

Perhaps, instead, Motezuma could pursue mutual respect. He sent more gifts and more gold, and he continued to consult his soothsayers.

Cortés Establishes the Port of Veracruz: Summer 1519

On the coast, Cortés also considered his options. What he was supposed to do, as an official sent by the Cuban governor, was to return home with the intelligence he had gathered along the coast. But the New World seemed made for heroes, scoundrels, and robber barons—not meek bureaucrats. As generations of later immigrants also found, adventurers in this place could get rich quick. Fortune favored the bold. Cortés's big chance came from a discovery he made by interviewing coastal villagers, presumably with the help of his translator, Marina. Various coastal tribes were not happy taxpayers. They chafed at having to send tribute to the Mexica. Ever pursuing his own interests, Cortés concocted a dicey strategy, conceivably during pillow talk with Marina. He would ally his troops with the disaffected vassal states and march with them to Tenochtitlan to "free" them from their Mexican overlords.

How to implement this plan? Marina could play a key role in cementing the alliances, but how would Cortés defend himself against the inevitable later charge that he disobeyed the governor's order to return to Cuba? His legal training kicked in. Even in Cuba there had been talk about creating a colony if the expeditionaries found a good site. In his Machiavellian way, Cortés did not order such a colony outright. Instead, he subtly fertilized the seed of this idea among his men. Sure enough, as the seed germinated, he "allowed" the men to come to him to suggest establishing a colony. According to later accounts, Cortés demurely pretended to argue against it. To obey his orders, he should really return to Cuba! So skillfully did he prepare sham plans to return to Cuba that some of his men allegedly begged him "in the name of God and king" to establish a permanent foothold in the new land. The issue among the men, of course, was that if they stayed, they would be key players in a potential conquest of Motezuma's wealthy empire, but if they returned to Cuba, the governor would take over the whole enterprise, perhaps with a different army.

Cortés pretended to be converted to his men's wishes—the goal he wanted all along. He "allowed" his men to form a town council and elect him, the modest and reluctant leader, to be mayor and captain general. Thus was founded the town still known today as Veracruz (*vera cruz*, "true cross") on the east coast of Mexico.

Cortés knew that in the Spanish system, major officials and operatives faced occasional reviews of their performance and the legality of their decisions. On the other hand, he knew also that success is a marvelous defense against pesky law. If he could pull off a conquest of the mysterious inland golden empire and present it to the king, he would have not only prestige and wealth but insurance against meddlesome prosecutors. "My men made me do it" would be his line of legal defense, if needed.

Cortés Marches on Tenochtitlan: August 1519

Cortez now began a program of rigorous exercise and discipline among his men in preparation for a march on Tenochtitlan. Meanwhile, he built his "international coalition," which would join in the noble march to free the downtrodden provinces. When he encountered recalcitrant villagers, he easily defeated them in various skirmishes and issued orders instead of requests.

In midsummer 1519 a boat arrived from Cuba with about sixty troops and some horses, presumably sent to check up on Cortés. Within weeks, the newcomers tried to turn Cortés's men against him, but Cortés arrested them and hanged two of the leaders, consolidating his authority. According to at least some of the early chroniclers, he now undertook another of his famously brash acts. To end any indecision on the part of his army, he ordered most of his ships to be run aground and burned. This cut off any hope of escape if the enterprise turned sour. His men would have to conquer or die. In a later investigation of Cortés's acts in 1529, the lawyer for his defense expansively claimed that this act of burning the boats was "one of the most outstanding services to God since the foundation of Rome" (Thomas 1995, 223).

In early August 1519 Cortés and his men turned their backs on the beaches of Veracruz and marched inland. The Spanish contingent numbered about three hundred. Some forty were armed with the primary weapon of those days, the crossbow. Another twenty had newfangled arquebuses — crude early muskets. Many carried swords. Some had metal armor, but most of the troops apparently wore the lighter padded and quilted cotton "armor" favored by the Mexica themselves. It was capable of fending off severe blows from the obsidian-edged Aztec clubs. The company also had several small cannons. Importantly, they also had about 800 Indian allies along with about 150 Indian servants and bearers from Cuba.

Still, what an absurd gamble! A few hundred Spaniards, surrounding themselves with local native allies of uncertain allegiance, were marching over unknown roads toward a great, wealthy city that had already conquered all lands for hundreds of miles around. Their hope was that they could somehow prevail over a population estimated by historians at 60,000 to 250,000. What was Cortés thinking? "Better to die in a good cause than live in dishonor" ran a line he liked from a medieval play. Nice words—but if we could hit a reboot button and run Cortés's bizarre adventure over and over, like a video game, the Spaniards would surely have been wiped out almost every time, and Cortés would have ended up in history-book footnotes as an overly ambitious, bungling maniac.

In the end, his sheer gall, combined with the Aztec beliefs in a second coming of Quetzalcoatl and the end of a calendric cycle, was his major weapon in keeping Motezuma defensive and uncertain. Fortune favored the bold.

Motezuma continued to monitor the peculiar activity on the coast and kept sending gifts of gold. A semipersonal correspondence developed between the two leaders. It was the spookiest political dialogue in North American history. The two men, seemingly from different planets, professed friendship and interest in each other. Cortés explained that he represented a greater lord than himself, the king of Spain. Motezuma said he would be willing to acknowledge the rule of such a king and send a yearly tribute of gold, jade, and jewels if Cortés would just return home and tell his king the good news. No, Cortés wanted to come in person to see his new friend and bring personal greetings from the king.

Motezuma repeatedly begged the strangers to go back and delay their approach. Food and other resources in his city were limited, he said, and he wouldn't want his esteemed guests to be uncomfortable. He would send the desired tribute, so they didn't have to come and collect it. Day by day, as new messengers came into Tenochtitlan, Motezuma faced a deeper and deeper mystery. Why did Cortés keep coming, fighting his way through unfriendly towns when necessary? Who was he? Was he human or god? What was he after?

Motezuma vacillated about whether to attack the newcomers. He had apparently covertly arranged a few attacks against the Spaniards by outlying vassal cities while he, like Cortés, feigned innocence and claimed the collegial friendship of great leaders. His strategy didn't work. Cortés defeated all comers. In the end, Motezuma concluded that resistance was futile. The eyewitness Mexica accounts, recorded by Sahagún some thirty-five years later, described how, in spite of arguments among his advisors,

Motezuma did nothing. He ordered no war against them, because no one was to able to resist them in battle. He commanded only that they be cared for.

Hearing this, Tenochtitlan lay stunned. Nobody went out of doors. Mothers kept their children inside. The roads were wide open and deserted, as if it were early morning. People entered their homes preoccupied with the news. "So be it," they said. "Let us be accursed. What more can we do? We are bound to die." (Sahagún account, adapted from Anderson and Dibble 1978, 27)

The Meeting of Two Worlds: November 1519

Finally, on 8 November 1519 (Gregorian date as reported by Thomas 1995, 276), a stupendous moment in American history took shape. The Spaniards and their coalition army arrived at the end of one of the causeways leading across the lake into Tenochtitlan. Both sides put on their best front. Cortés began a colorful procession across the causeway toward the city. Motezuma and his court, at the other end of the causeway, moved forward with similar gravity to carry out their part of this first formal contact between two worlds.

Many classic science fiction stories and films have tried to imagine the first contact between a mysterious alien spaceship arriving above an earthly capital city where citizens anxiously wait to see what strange beings will appear—and what they will do. That scene has already occurred in human reality, in November 1519 in Mexico City.

Various Spaniards, including Cortés himself, wrote later letters and memoirs about the events of the next days. Best of all is Bernal Díaz's detail-filled account, mentioned earlier. The causeways, Díaz tells us, extended for more than a mile across the swampy water. Díaz described the roadway as eight paces wide along much of its length. On that fateful day, he said, it was jammed with Mexican onlookers. Additional Mexican spectators crowded together in canoes on either side of the causeway, waiting to see what would happen.

At the front of the Spanish procession were four horsemen in armor, then a standard-bearer, then ranks of soldiers with swords drawn, crossbow men, and so on. Toward the rear of that group rode Cortés himself with a small bodyguard and more standard-bearers. Then came the Spaniards' Indian allies. Bernal Díaz gives voice to the strange blend of awe and fear experienced by the Spaniards. (This quote and quotes below from Díaz are abridged from Díaz's volume, which is listed in "Additional Reading and References." Page numbers are omitted, partly to avoid repetitious interruptions and partly because Díaz describes the events in sequence, so that the relevant passages are easily found.)

> Gazing on the wonderful sights, we did not know what to say, or whether it was even real. On the land side, there were great cities. In the lake were causeways with one bridge after another. In front of us stood the grand city of Mexico—Tenochtitlan. We were fewer than four hundred soldiers, and we remembered the warnings we had heard, that we should beware of entering Mexico, where they would kill us all once they had us inside the city. Imagine it, curious readers: What men in the whole world have ever had such a bold adventure!
>
> We came to a point where a smaller causeway branched off to the city of Coyoacán, where there were buildings like towers. [We will reencounter Coyoacán.—WKH] Here, many chiefs appeared, dressed in rich mantles, each differing from the others'. They were Motezuma's advance party, and the causeway was crowded with them. When they came before Cortés, they welcomed us in their language, making the characteristic Mexican gesture of peace and respect, touching the ground with their hands, then kissing the earth through their hands. We paused as these lords went to meet the great Motezuma, who was now approaching, carried in a rich litter, surrounded by still more lords and chiefs. Then we approached to where they were, closer to the city of Mexico. As Motezuma descended from his litter, the great chiefs supported him with their arms, beneath a marvelous canopy of green feathers, worked with gold and silver.

Motezuma perhaps hoped that the strangers really were returning gods, including Quetzalcoatl himself, arriving to redeem Mexico. He must have begun to feel he had the advantage. If they weren't gods, then they were merely human and might be dealt with once they were surrounded in the heart of the city. It was an old principle: it's better to do obeisance to the gods, because if they are real, you come out ahead, and if they aren't, you've lost nothing.

Chroniclers on the Mexican side gave their view as the great cultures of America and Europe made contact for the first time:

> Motezuma dressed in his finery, as did his princes and nobles. They all went out together to meet the strangers, bringing trays heaped with the finest flowers—the flower that looks like a shield and the one shaped like

a heart. In the center were the flowers with the sweetest aroma. They also brought flowery garlands, ornaments, and necklaces of gold and rich stones. In this fashion, Motezuma . . . presented many gifts to Cortés and his commanders . . . who had come to make war. He showered gifts on them and hung flowers around their necks. He put garlands of flowers on their heads, hung gold necklaces on them, and gave them presents of every sort. (León-Portilla 1962, 63)

Bernal Díaz also describes the scene:

Motezuma was richly dressed according to his style. He wore sandals with golden soles, and with precious stones decorating the upper part. The four officials who supported him — his nephews — were also richly dressed. . . . Four others held the canopy, and still more walked in front, sweeping the ground where he would tread and spreading cloths on it so he wouldn't have to step on the earth. Not one of them dared even to think of looking him in the face; they kept their eyes lowered with great reverence.

When Cortés saw him coming, he also dismounted, and when he was near Motezuma, they paid great reverence to each other simultaneously. Motezuma offered his welcome, and Cortés replied through doña Marina, wishing him good health. It seems to me that Cortés offered his right hand, and Motezuma did not wish to take it, but did so, and then Cortés brought out a necklace which he had kept ready, made of glassy stones with diverse colors, strung on a cord of gold, sweetly scented with musk. He placed it on the neck of Motezuma, and when he had done so, he was going to embrace him. But the lords of the Mexica, who accompanied Motezuma, held Cortés back by the arm, because they considered this a great indignity.

So Cortés said that his heart rejoiced at having seen such a great prince, and that he felt honored that Motezuma would come out in person to meet him, and had been showing him such favor in their previous correspondence.

Motezuma replied with other polite words, and then told two of his nephews, who had been supporting him, to go with us and show us to our quarters. . . . Space was made for us to enter the streets of Mexico without being crowded. But who could count the multitude of men and women and boys who were in the streets and balconies, and in canoes on the canals, who had come out to greet us? It was truly wonderful, and now that I am writing about it, it all comes back before my eyes as though it happened only yesterday.

According to the Aztec chronicles, Motezuma gave an additional speech.

"You must be tired, but now you are here in your own city, to sit on your own throne. Our kings who went before, who were your representatives, have preserved it for your coming. If only they could see us now! If only they could see what I see! It isn't a dream! I am not walking in my sleep. I really have met you face to face at last. I was in agony for many days, staring into the mists with my eyes fixed on the Realm of Mystery. But now you have come out of the clouds and mists to sit on your throne. This was foretold by the kings who governed your city, and now it has taken place. Rest now, and take possession of your royal houses. Welcome to your land, my lords." (Motezuma's speech is here synthesized from Aztec accounts quoted by Anderson and Dibble 1978, 33; and by León-Portilla 1962, 64)

Ancient Mexican sketches of this scene almost always show Marina standing between the two groups at this point, handling translations. Mexican eyewitness sources describe the next moments.

When Motezuma finished, Marina translated for Cortés, and Cortés spoke to Marina in his barbarous tongue. "Tell Motezuma to be at ease. We love him. We are truly satisfied and pleased. For a long time we wanted to see him and meet him face to face. Now we have come, and whenever he wishes, he can hear our further words."

Then the strangers took Motezuma by the hand, stroking him with their hands to express affection. They boldly looked directly at him, some of them mounting or dismounting their horses to get a better look.

Motezuma now led his visitors to the great plaza that still marks the heart of Mexico City, known today as the Zócalo. He housed them in a palace that had belonged to his father, across the square from his own compound and close to the base of a great pyramid with a double temple structure on the top. The Spaniards gazed in wonder at their new quarters, which, as Díaz described, were

coated with shining cement plaster, swept, and garlanded. Motezuma had been awaiting us and as soon as we entered the great court, Motezuma took our captain by the hand and led him to the apartment where he was to lodge — richly adorned. He brought a very rich necklace made of gold crabs, a marvelous piece of work, and he himself placed it around the neck of our Captain Cortés, greatly astonishing his own lords and

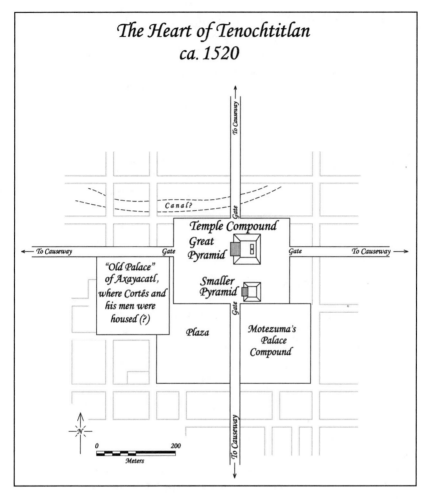

Map 3. The central section of Motezuma's Tenochtitlan, ca. 1520. The temple compound had a number of smaller structures, and the exact layout, as well as the placement of streets and the "Old Palace," is still debated by archaeologists. Map by Ron Beckwith.

captains by the great honor he was bestowing. When the necklace had been fastened, Cortés thanked him, and he replied, "You and your brothers are now in your own house, so rest a while."

We divided our lodging by companies and placed the artillery pointing in a convenient direction, and it was clearly explained to us that we were to stay very much on the alert.

Conversations with Aliens: November 1519

Neither side was sure what would happen next. After dinner on the first day, Motezuma and his upper-class courtiers came across the plaza to the Spanish quarters. What ensued was the first in-depth conversation in the history of the world between leaders from a sophisticated European civilization and a sophisticated urban civilization of the Americas. The Nahuatl language, in which Motezuma expressed his thoughts, was at least as nuanced as Spanish. Florida scholar Viviana Díaz Balsera in her 2005 book, *The Pyramid under the Cross*, notes that the Nahuatl speakers of Tenochtitlan gave great respect to the art of rhetoric, because, as they noted, artful rhetoric can convert listeners' feelings and emotions into belief and action. For this reason, the dynastic governor in a town or neighborhood was known as *tlatoani*, the "speaker." Moreover, while some European languages (e.g., the old English still used in religious services) retain a few pronoun forms of special reverence, such as "thee" and "thou," Nahuatl had those reverential forms for nouns, verbs, adjectives, and adverbs, so that conversation could be loaded with gracious respect for the hearer. Díaz Balsera comments that Nahua rhetoric sought primarily to placate. Even today, Mexican and Latin American letter writing emphasizes phraseology that seems overly flowery to business-like Americans, who likewise seem blunt and brusque to Latin Americans. The Tenochtitlan leaders' emphasis on flowers and gracious interaction may explain the Spaniards' perception that Motezuma was weak.

In keeping with the apocalyptic moment, both sides seemed strikingly preoccupied with their most profound religious and traditional beliefs. Motezuma was still concerned, from his own religious tradition, that these visitors might be gods themselves, such as Quetzalcoatl, though Cortés may not have grasped all the implications of this during the first conversation. At the same time, Motezuma set the stage in order to fish for their reactions so he could measure what to do next. As Bernal Díaz described it, "Motezuma took Cortés by the hand. They brought some seats, richly decorated and embroidered with gold in many designs, and Motezuma asked our Captain to sit, and both of them sat down on their chairs. Motezuma then began a very good speech." He said that two years earlier he had heard of other Spanish ships off the coast and strangers who had landed briefly on the coast. He had been puzzled and concerned, he said, but now he was very happy to meet the strangers. Perhaps it was true, he ventured, that his guests were "those of whom his ancestors had spoken in ancient times—men who would come from where the sun rose, to rule over these lands. Motezuma added that for this reason, "he was at our service and would give us all he possessed."

Cortés answered through Marina and other interpreters, emphasizing that the great lord, don Carlos, king of Spain, had heard of the peoples of this New World and had sent Cortés's army to visit and "to beg them to become Christians." ("Don," rhyming with "loan," is a Spanish title of high respect.) Cortés said he would explain more about the one true god at some appropriate time. At the end of the conversation, Motezuma responded with still more gifts. Díaz says:

> He gave some valuable jewels to Cortés, and in the same manner he gave trifles of gold and three loads of mantles of rich featherwork to each of our captains, and then to each soldier he gave two loads of these mantles, and he did it cheerfully and in every way he seemed to be a great Prince. . . . After he provided servants and food supplies for us and the horses he took leave of all of us with the greatest courtesy, and we went out with him as far as the street. Cortés ordered us not to go far from the quarters, however.

On the next day, the Spaniards went across the plaza to the palace of Motezuma, who advanced to the middle of his hall to meet them. Motezuma insisted they should all sit and be comfortable, placing Cortés at his right hand. Cortés apparently launched into a lecture on religion. It was wonderful to complete their journey, he said, and visit such a great ruler. "But what he had chiefly come to say" (as reported by Bernal Díaz) was that "we were Christians and worshiped one true and only God . . . but that the ones they worship as gods were not so, but are devils, which are evil things." To support this, he argued that the Mexican gods had a fearsome, bad appearance, so "one could see that they were evil." Where the Spaniards had set up crosses, the Mexican gods "dared not appear, through fear of them." Spain, he said, would soon send many priests, "who live better lives than we do, and who will explain all about it. . . . For the present, we came merely to give them due notice, and we hoped he would do what was asked."

Was Cortés naively and sincerely witnessing for his religion—the cultural tradition he absorbed as a young man being raised in Spain?

Or had he calculatingly judged that the Mexica were dominated by religious symbolism, which he could manipulate by invoking his own god to weaken their resistance while at the same time creating a record to ingratiate himself with the Spanish king and priests? By attacking Native religion and announcing a New Order of Christianity, was he cunningly laying out a legal justification he would need in the future if he chose to pursue a policy of regime change? Spanish law, in the wake of the Moorish occupation of Spain, insisted that all peoples be given a chance to embrace Christianity . . . but also authorized what appears today as unchristian punishment for those who, after the offer, chose what the Spaniards called "treason" (i.e., rejection of the Europeans' True Religion).

Whatever the atmosphere that day in the Aztec palace, Motezuma replied with a reasonable and plaintive speech, reported by Díaz.

> Lord General, I've understood these arguments already [from your messages sent from the coast], and I understand about your three Gods [father, son, holy spirit], and your cross. We have not answered yet, because throughout all time we have worshiped our own gods. We thought they were good, as no doubt yours are. So let's not trouble ourselves by speaking more about this for the time being.
>
> Regarding the history of the world, we in Tenochtitlan have held the same belief for ages, and take it as certain that you are the ones whom our ancestors predicted would come from the direction of the sunrise. As for your great King, I feel indebted to him, and I will give to him from what I possess. As I've already said, two years ago I heard similar messages from those who also came in ships from the same direction in which you came. What I want to know is whether you are all one and the same people.

Motezuma may have been fishing (as Cortés had already done on the coast) for indications of ethnic divisions that he could exploit. Cortés replied that his people were indeed one people.

> Motezuma indicated that, while he had earlier sent messages asking the Spaniards to stay out of his city, it was not of his own will, but because his advisors and officials had been afraid. They had heard how we shot flashes of lightning, and killed Indians with our horses, that we were angry lords, and other childish stories, but now that he had seen us he knew we were of flesh and bone and had good sense. So he held us in higher regard now than when he was trying to understand the reports he had received.

Cortés thanked him. Then, as Díaz reported,

> Motezuma replied laughingly, for he was very merry in his princely way of speaking. "I know you've been told that I am some sort of god or supernatural lord, and that everything in my houses is of gold, silver, and precious stones, but I know you're wise enough not to believe it. Just

look! My body is of flesh and bone like yours, and my palaces are made of stone and wood and lime. I'm a great king and I inherited the riches of my ancestors, true, but the nonsense you've been told is not correct, and surely you treated it as just a story, just as I treated the stories about your control of thunder and lightning."

Cortés answered, also laughing, that people always say evil things about those who they think might be enemies.

Getting to Know the City: Late 1519

The Spaniards began to record observations about Motezuma's daily life and his city. Perhaps with official disapproval but secret envy, they noted that Motezuma had two women of noble birth as his official wives, along with many mistresses. He was very clean and bathed not just once but twice a day. He was cheerful and showed tenderness but also, when appropriate, gravity. His government and royal city contained jesters, books of accounts, two buildings full of royal weapons, a treasury, an aviary of rare birds, and beautiful "gardens of flowers and sweet-scented trees." He had meals of thirty different dishes, from which he picked what he wanted; thousands of plates of food were served to his court.

After a few days, the Spaniards were given their first tour of the amazing city. One temple complex contained a zoo with "tigers, two kinds of lions . . . wolves and foxes . . . poisonous snakes whose tails have things that sound like rattles or bells." Bernal Díaz was enthralled, commenting on "the infernal noise when the lions and tigers roared and the jackals and foxes howled and the serpents hissed. It was horrible to listen to and it seemed like a kind of hell."

Nearby was the great market of Tlaltelolco, still a named district in Mexico City today (see fig. 1). Merchants traded in gold, silver, jewels, featherwork cloaks, cloth, ropes, sandals, skins of deer and other animals, vegetables, herbs, pottery jugs from great water jars to small jars, firewood, axes of copper and tin, biscuit snacks, bread, and captured Indian servants and slaves to be sold or traded—men and women, some attached to long poles with collars, and others walking free.

To get a better look, the Spaniards climbed the great pyramid, 114 steps, according to Bernal Díaz (see map 3). The Indians tried to help Cortés in the same way that they assisted Motezuma, but Cortés brushed them off. On top were the shrines and stones where prisoners from the flower wars were sacrificed.

Figure 1. The Plaza of Three Cultures in central Mexico City, marking the site of the great marketplace of Tlatelolco and the final battle between the Mexica and Cortés's troops. The three cultures are marked by pyramid foundations and steps (*left center*), a Spanish colonial church, and modern commercial buildings. Photo by the author, 1970.

"You must be tired from your climb up our pyramid," Motezuma said.

"We never tire from anything," Cortés replied.

Motezuma pointed to the incredible vista of the city and distant towns dotted on islands and around the lakeshores. Díaz says that as they looked down on the market, soldiers who had been to Constantinople and Rome and "all over Italy" agreed that "so large a market, so full of people and so well regulated, had never been seen before." The Aztecs had a greater public market than any in Europe.

Díaz says that Cortés then turned to one of the army's priests who had come with him. "It would be good," he said, "to test whether Motezuma would let us build our church here." Cortés then asked Motezuma if they would be allowed to see the shrines and idols of gods. Motezuma consulted with his priests and then took the Spaniards into "a small tower or apartment where there were two altars with two figures like giants. One was the god of war, covered with precious stones, gold, and pearls . . . surrounded by snakes made of gold. . . . The face was monstrous with terrible eyes." The other altar held a god of Hell, with similar appearance. Everything around them was "clotted with blood. [Even] in the slaughterhouses of Spain there is not such a stench." Five hearts had been offered to these gods during the day's sacrifices. Moved by the scene, Díaz reports, Cortés now lectured Motezuma:

> "Señor Motezuma, I don't understand how a wise man like you cannot see that these idols of yours are not gods, but the evil things we call devils. In order that you and all your priests may know this, do me the favor of letting me place a cross here on top of this pyramid, and in one part of these shrines let us divide off a space where we can set up an image of Our Lady [an image Motezuma had already seen]. Then you will see by the fear in which these idols hold it that they are deceiving you."
>
> Motezuma replied half in anger—and the two priests with him also showed great annoyance. "Señor Lord, if I had known you would say such defamatory things, I would not have shown you our gods. We consider them very good. They give us health and rains and good seed-times, and seasons, and as many victories as we desire, so we are obliged to worship them and make sacrifices. I pray you not to say another word dishonoring them."
>
> When our Captain heard that, and saw the angry looks, he didn't refer to the subject again, but said with a cheerful manner, "It is time for your Excellency and us to return." Motezuma replied he needed to stay to offer prayers because of the sin he had committed in letting us see the gods and speak evil of them. Cortés said, "I ask your pardon if it is so." Then we went down the 114 steps. Some of our soldiers were suffering from abscesses, their legs were tired by the descent.

Cortés himself wrote a description of the city in the second of several long letters he sent back to Carlos V, king of Spain, in October 1520, apparently based on the same tour. (The quotes from the letter given below are abridged; the original five letters can be found in Cortés [1519–26] 1991.)

> The city has many open squares, where markets offer continuous trade. One plaza is twice as big as that of Salamanca. It has a portico all the way around, where thousands of people come to buy and sell all sorts of goods. . . . Each product is sold in its own lane, and the people maintain excellent order. They sell everything by the piece or by measure of size, but I've never seen them sell anything by weight. In the plaza is a large

court-house building where ten or twelve judges are always seated to
settle any market-place disputes and have the guilty punished.

In various quarters of the city, many temple groups and buildings are
set up for their idols, all of beautiful architecture. The greatest temple
can't be described adequately by words. It is so large that within the
surrounding wall of the complex, a settlement of 500 people could be
established. Inside this area, around the edges, are fine buildings with
large halls, where the priests live. There are at least 40 pyramids, tall and
well made. The largest has 50 steps leading up to the main body of the
pyramid itself, which is taller than the tower of Seville's cathedral. The
stone masonry and woodwork couldn't be bettered anywhere.

There are many beautiful, large houses in this city. All the lords of the
surrounding land, Motezuma's vassals, have houses here and reside in
them part of the year. Many rich citizens also have good houses here,
with fine, flowering gardens of various styles.

Along one of the causeways to the city are two conduits made of mortar,
each two paces wide, and almost two yards high. Through one of them
moves a stream of good, fresh water, which flows across bridges over the
salty canals, bringing good water into the center of the city. Everyone
drinks from it. The other conduit is empty so that when they want to
clean one, they divert the water into the other. The whole city is thus
supplied, and they also deliver the water for sale from canoes in the
canals along the streets.

The people's activities and behavior approach the level of those in Spain.
They are just as well organized and orderly. Considering that these people are barbarous, lacking knowledge of God and without communication with other civilized nations, it is astonishing to see all the things
that they have.

Tenochtitlan is all the more impressive when we consider that the
Mexica, astoundingly, hadn't developed the use of wheeled vehicles and,
of course, had no horses. Because of its exotic buildings and canals, the
Spaniards called it the "Venice of the New World." Cortés fell in love with
the city and determined to present it intact to the king.

Nonetheless, the Spaniards were not exactly thrilled by ideals of tol-
erance and cultural diversity. Ensconced among people they regarded as

infidels, they began in the next day or so to look for a spot to create a chapel within their own quarters, with Motezuma's permission. This led to a new discovery. During the search for the right spot, they noticed a wall where a door had been plastered over. Having heard a rumor that Motezuma kept a treasure of his father in that palace, they broke through the door secretly. An astounding room lay on the other side. "Such was the number of jewels and slabs of gold and other riches that they were speechless!" exclaimed Díaz. "[I] had never seen such riches in my life." The Spaniards secretly walled up the room again and covered it over.

What Do We Do Now?: Late 1519

Hard reality soon set in. The Spaniards were in an indefensible position. Their main Indian allies were still outside the island city, across the causeways. Cortés's army was far outnumbered by Motezuma's guards. They were literally sitting on a golden treasure, which is what they wanted, but what could they do about it? More and more, they felt as if they were in a trap. Then came news that some of the captains and soldiers who had been assigned to stay behind in cities that had been conquered along the way had been killed by disaffected locals. In some towns, the people were in revolt. Díaz wrote ruefully that it was "the first disaster we had suffered in New Spain."

In response, they decided on a desperate ploy. They would seize Motezuma, knowing he was revered as a god. "All that night," says Díaz, "we prayed to God that our plan might support His holy service."

After the sun rose on the fateful day, Cortés took five captains, along with Bernal Díaz, doña Marina (as she was now being called), another interpreter, and a group of horsemen across the plaza to Motezuma's palace (map 3). Cortés announced that they were upset that Motezuma would order his distant allies to revolt against the Spaniards in their town and that Cortés would forgive this if the emperor of the Mexica would come quietly across the plaza to the Spanish quarters—"but if you cry out or make any disturbance, you will be killed by my captains, whom I brought just for this eventuality." Motezuma, says Díaz, was dumbfounded and terrified. He protested that he hadn't ordered any such thing. He would send for his own captains to verify this truth and would berate his officers for this situation. Furthermore, he said, "he was not a person to whom such an order could be given. He would not go."

The argument went on for an hour. One of the Spanish captains excitedly yelled out, "What's the good of all these words? Let's either take him prisoner or stab him! Let's settle this by either saving our lives or losing them!" Motezuma, startled, asked doña Marina what they were saying, and she, "being clever," advised him to go with the Spaniards because they would show him honor—otherwise, he was a dead man. Motezuma offered a son and two legitimate daughters as hostages. It was not good enough. In the end he agreed to go. "Cortés and our captains bestowed many caresses on him, and asked him not to be annoyed, and to tell his men that he was going of his own free will."

So Motezuma moved into the palace of Cortés. A bizarre, make-believe coregency ensued. Across the plaza, Motezuma's generals and court, generally more hawkish than their ruler, debated the strange events. His relatives and various nobles came across to visit him and even asked if they should attack. Motezuma answered that he was happy to be there of his own free will for the time being. The official line was that Cortés and Motezuma had developed a friendship and were attempting to set up a joint, peaceful government.

The Aztec accounts, collected by Sahagún, illuminate the situation. They say that after Motezuma was taken hostage, many of the Mexican nobles "went into hiding, not only to get away from the Spaniards, but to express their disgust and anger with Motezuma." As for Motezuma, he brought with him many nobles and a retinue of women servants. He kept up appearances, exhorting his people to remain calm. Even the personal relations between the two leaders remained, perhaps artificially, cordial. Both men seem to have been highly skilled and intelligent regarding diplomacy and human nature. At some level, they were really trying to find a sustainable way out of the crisis, and at another level they were doing an intricate dance around each other, probing for possibilities and options. One day, according to Díaz, Motezuma delivered a speech to the Spaniards:

> "I want you to know that I still feel indebted to your great King, and bear him good will for having sent you to make inquiries about me, and the thought that impresses me most is that he must be the one who is to rule over us, as our ancestors told us. What I have ready for the emperor is the treasure I inherited from my father, and I knew well enough that as soon as you came, you opened the chamber and beheld it all, and sealed it up again. So when you send it to him, tell him, 'This is sent by your true vassal, Motezuma.'"

> When Cortés and all of us heard it, we stood amazed at the great goodness and liberality of the Great Motezuma, and with much reverence, we doffed our helmets and returned to him our thanks.

Cortés and Motezuma really seem to have held each other in some respect, if for different reasons. Cortés repeatedly told Motezuma how much he liked him as a man and as a fellow leader, but, as always, he kept his own long-term strategy close to his vest. Díaz says that Motezuma was "so frank and kind that we [soldiers] treated him with respect . . . and he behaved in the same manner toward us" ([ca. 1570] 1956, 191).

Negotiations: January 1520

The situation grew more and more untenable. About two months after the Spaniards' arrival in Mexico City, with some of Motezuma's nobles now being held literally in chains, Cortés and Motezuma and their top aides met in Motezuma's room in the now-Spanish palace. Motezuma reportedly told his officials that because Cortés seemed to be the one prophesied in the old legends, they should all pledge homage to the king of Spain, and Motezuma himself would embrace Christianity. Cortés, for his part, promised to treat the Mexica well. He proposed that, as allies, they would be able to search for even greater empires to conquer in this new world. The discussions were said to be so touching that some of the Spanish witnesses wept—as did Motezuma. Historians have debated the actual mood at this time and what words were actually spoken. Did Motezuma weep for the end of the civilization he knew, for new friendship, or for some imagined vision of a peaceful future? Was Cortés simply scheming to find the safest way out?

A few days later, Cortés announced that if the Mexican leaders were accepting the role of vassals of Spain, it was only fitting that taxes of gold should be brought in to support the expenses Spain had incurred in coming to Mexico. To make things convenient, this gold could be brought directly to the Spaniards in their palace. In the streets the crowds muttered.

An Unexpected Challenge: April 1520

In April 1520 came word that new Spaniards had appeared on the coast. Was this good news for Cortés? Were they reinforcements? They turned out to be troops sent by the outraged governor in Cuba to arrest Cortés for exceeding his authority and marching on Mexico City instead of reporting back to the king's officials. Motezuma received this news even before Cortés and immediately realized that the Spaniards were, after all, not a monolithic entity. A glimmer of hope now flickered before him. Through his contacts with his nobles, he was able to make a few secret overtures to the newcomers, and he even suggested to Cortés that the Spaniards might now wish to withdraw from the city and that all problems could be equitably resolved.

That was not Cortés's style. His was a personality that had to confront any potential disaster. Fortunately for Cortés, the "police force" from Cuba was led by a competence-challenged Spaniard named Pánfilo Narváez, a man destined to appear, ill-fatedly, several times in our story of New World explorations. Cortés reacted to Narváez by applying the golden rule of New World get-rich-quick schemers: do unto others what's necessary to outflank them. If you win and become rich, all will be forgiven, but if you are timid, your enemies will bring charges and destroy you. So, in early May 1520 Cortés took part of his army out of Mexico City, led his force toward the coast, and made a surprise attack on the other Spaniards at night. In a fabulously cinematic battle atop a pyramid, Narváez not only was trapped and arrested by Cortés's men but lost an eye. Many of Narváez's men then converted to the cause of the very man they had come to arrest, dreaming of riches and glory under the charismatic master of Tenochtitlan. Cortés thus augmented his own army with some hundreds of new Spanish troops plus food and supplies from Narváez's ships. Now the problem was to get back and take possession of Tenochtitlan.

Disaster in Tenochtitlan: May 1520

Back in Tenochtitlan, things were not going well. Cortés's dream of presenting the fabulous city to King Carlos V, thus assuring his own prestige in the Spanish court, began to collapse.

When Cortés had left to attack Narváez, he left a reduced force in the Tenochtitlan palace under the command of a ruthless officer named Pedro de Alvarado. He was known to the Spaniards and Mexica alike for his fair hair and radiant good looks. The Aztecs called him Tonatiuh, "the Sun."

Naturally, Alvarado and his troops were nervous, having been left as a small band holed up in the midst of an increasingly hostile city. Alvarado decided to take action. Mid-May was the scheduled time for a major spring festival of music and dances in Tenochtitlan. Rumors began to fly among the Spaniards that this would be a pretext for massing Mexican warriors and staging a revolt. Chronicles from the Mexican side record that some of Motezuma's generals did propose hiding arms in the temple in order to protect the dancers, but Motezuma responded to them that they were not at war and that they should remain optimistic. As a result, no arms, defensive or offensive, were assembled at the dances. As for the impending ceremonies, some of the Mexica counseled that if the participants could perform their music and dances with enough beauty and dignity, it would convince the foreigners that Tenochtitlan was a city of culture and peace, thereby engendering respect from the Spaniards.

Alvarado, however, saw the festival as the time for a decisive strike.

The day of the celebrations arrived. Alvarado, under the pretext of wanting to observe the ceremony, marched with some soldiers and Indian allies into the courtyard of the great temple, where the main dances were traditionally held. Suddenly, after the dancing started, his men blocked the entrance to the courtyard. Then they commenced one of the greatest stains on the Euro-Christian interaction with America: a gruesome slaughter of the best of the city's young men. According to Mexican eyewitnesses, arms were severed, heads flew across the courtyard, and victims of sword slashes were seen staggering with their own entrails spilling into their arms. Killing as many spectators as they could, the Spaniards then retreated swiftly to their palace, Alvarado celebrating his doctrine of a preemptive strike. In the palace, his remaining troops had also carried out their horrendous assignment: they murdered many of Motezuma's nobles who were being held there.

In a single disastrous day, Alvarado thus destroyed any possibility of collaboration or diplomatic pretenses of friendship. The Spaniards set up defensive perimeters. The Mexica cut off food supplies and closed the market. The streets filled with armed men. At night, cries and lamentations were heard across the city.

Urban Warfare: June 1520

Five weeks later, Cortés and his augmented troops approached the island city on their return from the coast. No one came out to greet them. Crossing the causeway, they found a catastrophe in progress on both sides. Alvarado and his troops were hiding in their palace, desperate for lack of food.

Bernal Díaz reports that Cortés angrily charged Alvarado with making a stupid mistake and even wished that Motezuma had escaped. Nonetheless, Cortés never really punished "the Sun" for the disaster but instead stretched the truth and blamed it on secret conniving between Narváez and envoys from Motezuma. Ironically, Bernal Díaz quotes Alvarado's soldiers as testifying later that it was Motezuma's pleas for calm that saved the small Spanish garrison from being overrun while Cortés was away. Motezuma, far from being the spineless weakling that is often portrayed, may have been the only actor on the stage with enough vision to realize that more Spaniards would come and that some accommodation was needed in order to salvage a decent future. Moderates, however, are rarely crowned with glory. Historian Crane Brinton, in his 1938 book, *The Anatomy of Revolution*, noted that in serious social conflicts, moderates are often the first casualties, since they are seen as threats by both sides.

Now began a famous siege. The day after Cortés returned, a brother of Motezuma, released from the Spanish compound to get the market reopened, helped instead to organize a more potent resistance, a revolt not only against the Spanish but also against the authority of Motezuma. In the following days, the Mexica openly attacked any Spaniards who ventured out, tried to set fire to the Spanish compound, and amassed stones and arrows on the tops of their houses to control the streets. The Spaniards had a well in the middle of their courtyard, but stones lobbed into the yard from nearby houses made access to water difficult. In the next days, the Spaniards set out in the mornings to gain control of the nearby buildings, only to be driven back. Eighty of Cortés's men were wounded within a day or two.

Then came an even worse disaster. According to the Spanish accounts, a group of Mexican nobles gathered in the plaza outside the Spanish compound. Cortés proposed that Motezuma go up to the roof to address the people. Díaz says the plan was to sue for peace in exchange for a chance to leave the city. Motezuma at first refused to participate. "What more does he want from me?" he reportedly said. "I don't want to listen to his plans; I no longer want to live."

Spanish priests were sent to reason with him. Motezuma responded, "I can't end this war. My people have already proposed another leader. They've made up their minds, and now I believe you will all have to die as a result of what's happened."

Finally, Motezuma relented and went out on the roof along with bodyguards, a few soldiers, and doña Marina as a translator. At first the crowd fell silent. Eyewitnesses from both sides are inconsistent on what happened next. Motezuma may have begun to speak, saying something to the effect that if everyone would calm down, things could be settled, as long as he himself remained on peaceful terms with Cortés. The Spaniards could then leave, and that would be the path of least bloodshed, giving a chance for Tenochtitlan to have a future. At some point, however, the outraged citizens began to shout in derision. In the confusion, Motezuma and the rooftop party were reportedly showered with stones and arrows. Spanish soldiers allegedly raised their shields to protect the emperor, but Motezuma was apparently hit by several stones. It's uncertain whether these were chance hits in a shower of stones or if the Aztecs were targeting their own former leader in order to remove him from the Spaniards' chessboard. The wounded Motezuma was taken down into the Spanish quarters, where Cortés's men began to treat him. He resisted aid, however, perhaps due in part to his overall depression. He lingered on. The Mexica were outside, shouting that this war would be fought to its end and that Cortés and his men would die.

Cortés had one more trick up his sleeve. Around 16 June (Julian calendar), while Spanish doctors tried to nurse Motezuma back to health, Cortés organized his men to build three rudimentary "tanks." They were massive mobile wooden structures that could enclose about two dozen soldiers, some of whom carried the structure while others shot their crossbows through the ports. Early on 18 June they set out with three of these war machines, but the scheme failed. Díaz reports how the Mexica taunted the Spaniards during these forays, saying they were cowards, hiding in their boxes like babies, and that their blood would soon flow on the sacrificial stones.

In the next days the Spaniards set out yet again on an even more striking venture. Stones had been flung into their palace grounds from the top of the large pyramid next to their quarters, so the Spaniards launched an attack on the pyramid. All of this was not the impersonal, aerial-drone combat of today's warfare but face-to-face sword-and-club combat. A legendary battle ensued in which the Spaniards, including Cortés and Bernal Díaz, fought their way up the pyramid, step by step, to attack the priests and shrines reestablished on the summit. In retrospect, this enterprise seems insane! Who else but Cortés, besieged in a fortress-like palace, would sally forth into the streets to fight to the top of an open pyramid that could be easily surrounded? However, as historians Arthur Anderson and Charles Dibble point out in their introduction to their 1978 edition of Sahagún's collection of Aztec memoirs, the Spaniards were "the best trained practitioners of the art of war as it was waged in the 15th and 16th centuries."

"Oh, what a fight it was," Díaz says. "What a memorable thing, to see our men covered with blood and wounds." The Spaniards reached the top, set fire to the temple compounds, threw the idols down from the summit, and then threw the priests down after them. Cortés, looking out on the chaos, was aghast at the impending mayhem. He tried to address the throng in a loud voice, calling for an end to the violence. Perhaps he thought the destruction of the Aztecs' main temple would dishearten his enemies. He was hardly in a good position to call for peace, however, after desecrating the Aztecs' primary religious shrine. History shows that societies' most violent reactions involve insults to religious traditions.

Years later, veterans of the two sides, like many graying soldiers, looked back with grudging respect for their adversaries. Díaz reminisced that in later years, he often saw paintings that the Aztecs had made, "showing the battle as we ascended the great pyramid. They show us streaming with blood. They saw it as a courageous deed." Correspondingly, as for the valor of the Mexica, Díaz, in his chapter 26, wrote:

> I don't know how to describe their tenacity. . . . In spite of cannons, arquebuses, and crossbows, and our ability to kill 30 or 40 at a time with one of our charges, they'd fight on with more energy than at the start. If we'd gain a little ground in the street, they'd fall back and pretend to retreat, to entice us into a trap. . . . Three or four of our soldiers who had fought in Italy against the king of France or against the Great Turk, declared they'd never seen such fierce fighting, nor adversaries who showed such courage in closing up their ranks.

A few days later, the situation changed. Motezuma died inside the Spanish stronghold, which had been his own father's palace. Estimates by historian Hugh Thomas place the death on the morning of 20 June by the Julian calendar the Spaniards were using (30 June by our modern calendar). According to the Spanish accounts, death came from the wounds received at the hands of the crowd. Díaz said he'd been hit by three stones, including one to the head. Aztec accounts tell various stories. One version discussed by León-Portilla (1962, 90) affirms the Spanish account, saying that on the third day after Cortés returned, Motezuma appeared on the roof and "tried to admonish the people," but they cursed him as a traitor, and he was killed by a stone propelled from the crowd by someone with a sling. That same account, however, quotes palace servants as declaring that, in the end, Motezuma was killed by his Spanish captors, who stabbed him "in the abdomen with their swords." Other Aztec witnesses (Sahagún, in Anderson and Dibble 1978, 46 ff.) say that it was one of the Mexican nobles who addressed the crowd from the roof and was declared a traitor by the Mexicans, and that this noble, along with Motezuma and other nobles, was ultimately stabbed or strangled by the Spaniards. Each side seems to have developed its own official version of the truth. Motezuma, in any case, was dead.

Díaz asserts that Cortés and the captains wept over his death "as though he were our father, and it is not to be wondered at, considering how good a man he was."

The Spaniards then placed Motezuma's body outside their walls, proclaiming that the leader had died at the Mexica's own hand and that the carnage should stop. At least one Aztec account says Motezuma's body, along with bodies of other murdered nobles, was simply thrown out into the streets. The Mexica, outraged at both Cortés and Motezuma, spirited Motezuma's body away. They reportedly burned it without the normal ceremonies befitting a royal death.

Thus passed one of the most striking and enigmatic leaders in North American history. Motezuma is often dismissed as a vacillating prisoner of his own religious belief in a fated arrival of departed gods. A real leader, the implication goes, would have marshaled his overwhelming troops and defeated Cortés long before he ever reached Tenochtitlan. Yet from a different perspective, Motezuma is a tragic hero. He was right in his suspicion that the Spaniards could never really be stopped by direct conflict—even if he made this judgment partly for superstitious reasons. What good could come from slaughtering Cortés and his troops? Thousands of others would have followed within a generation and decimated Tenochtitlan in revenge. The macho thing might have been for the Mexica to fight for their honor, but honor is rather pointless if it means that your people and your culture all get wiped from the earth and from the history books. Motezuma followed a different course, aiming for a one-on-one relationship with his alien visitor.

Cortés, the alien visitor, began hatching desperate plans for a midnight escape the very next night.

The Night of Sorrows: 20–21 June 1520 (Julian)

During the next twenty-four hours in the halls of Motezuma, the biggest issue was what to do with the treasure the Spanish pillagers had amassed from Motezuma's treasure room. The troops had already melted down many of the golden Mexican masks, plates, and other artworks into bars. In the afternoon of 20 June (Julian), not quite a week after Cortés had returned from the coast, the Spaniards began secret, desperate packing. All the gold and jewels were piled up in one of the main halls. Spanish law required that a certain fraction of all treasures belonged to the king. At least one good horse and perhaps several wounded ones were loaded with gold and assigned to trusted guards as the king's share. In the evening, says Díaz, Cortés (always careful about his legal trail) called in the notaries and proclaimed, "Bear witness that I can do no more with the gold. We have here more than 700,000 pesos worth, and there is no way to weigh it or hide it. I now give the rest to the soldiers—as much as they care to take."

What was the actual value of the treasure? A sword and a crossbow at that time each cost fifty to sixty pesos, according to Hugh Thomas (1995, 547). If we imagine that investment as equivalent in buying power to the cost of a three-hundred-dollar rifle today, we could say that the booty piled in the hallway was worth perhaps $4 million in equivalent buying power. If it were being split four hundred ways, the average share would have been around $10,000 per soldier.

The value may have been even higher. Plausible rumors surfaced later that Cortés significantly underreported the total value—partly in order to keep a large share for himself. He cleverly stated that there was no way to weigh it. Why leave a notarized account of the real total? Who would know?

Each man now began a tragic search for a literal golden mean. If he took nothing, he'd come home broke; if he tried to take too much, he'd bog down in flight and be killed. Díaz says he himself took four jewels—and tells us that this treasure served him well later . . . but only to pay for food.

Much self-serving testimony surfaced in later inquiries. Some witnesses said Cortés spent his time packing his own gold, assigning it to be carried by his own horses and native allies. Then, as things went badly during the escape attempt, he ordered the king's horses to be left behind. Cortés himself, however, claimed that he put all his efforts into preserving the king's share.

Whatever the division of spoils, the men struggled to prepare for the secret midnight escape from the city. Cortés reportedly slept with a new Indian woman that evening, the daughter of one of the ally chiefs.

In the first moments after midnight on Julian date 21 June 1520 (Gregorian date 1 July), the Spaniards crept out of their quarters. The total number of escapees is uncertain, but the number seems to have been well over a thousand Spaniards and their allies (Thomas 1995, 408–12). First into the streets was an advance party of about two hundred men, followed by the bulk of the army, followed by a rear guard. Some of the Spaniards were mounted.

Cortés was toward the front—not a bad place to be. The plan was to escape the city over the nearest causeway, which began about a mile and a quarter west of their compound. Everything hinged on whether they could traverse that first urban distance, then race across another mile of causeway to the mainland lakeshore.

The Spaniards got two breaks. First, the fateful night was "somewhat dark, cloudy, and rainy," according to Díaz. Second, through another unbelievable quirk of history, the Mexica had no tradition of military operations at night. Hundreds of Spaniards and even more Indian allies were able to slip into the streets without being seen by the sleeping Mexica.

For their part, the Mexica had cleverly destroyed the bridges over the canals within the city and over the causeway gaps that were built to allow canoe traffic on the lake. Just as cleverly, the Spaniards carried wooden planks that allowed the creation of makeshift replacement bridges.

Through drizzle and darkness, the Spaniards covered a number of blocks. Near the end of the first mile, as they approached the causeway, they were spotted by a woman who had gone to get water. She raised the alarm. Drums soon sounded on the pyramids. Warriors of Tenochtitlan leaped from their beds, ran into the streets, and launched an enormous fleet of canoes onto the lake.

As the Spaniards and their Indian allies entered onto the narrow causeways, the Mexica attacked from both sides. Cortés and his advance party spurred their horses across the Spanish plank bridges. Many of the Spaniards' Indian allies, bearing some of the gold, also got across.

The makeshift bridges, however, soon collapsed into the lake. Rain continued, horses slipped in the mud, and many men at the rear of the column fell into the water. Many were drowned by the weight of the gold they had hidden in their now sodden, quilted-cotton Mexican "armor." So many died that, in the words of Díaz, "the water in the gaps soon filled up with dead horses, Indian men and women, servants, baggage and boxes." Gold and cannons were jettisoned into the lake. A few of the rear guard, seeing escape cut off, tried to race back to the Spanish compound, where some of Narváez's (least reliable?) men had not even been told about the escape plan. Those ill-fated troops held out for a day or so but were captured and ritually sacrificed. Alvarado the Sun had been put in charge of the rear guard and was later accused of having abandoned his men, fleeing to the front to rejoin Cortés. As for losses to Cortés's army, Thomas (1995, 412) cites conflicting accounts but favors an estimate that the army lost most of the gold, around six hundred of the Spaniards, and possibly as many as "several thousand" of Cortés's coastal Indian allies. The night became known in Mexican history as La Noche Triste, "The Night of Sorrows." The citizens of Tenochtitlan thought they had won. They had driven the Spaniards away, but no complete victory was in store for either side.

The Second Assault: 1520–1521

Cortés was a man obsessed. In the next months, he retreated a third of the way toward the sea, regrouped his army, and started building boats so that he could command the lake and avoid the infernal plague of canoes that had cost him many of his men.

Next, in exhortations to his troops, he spelled out a four-part legalistic rationale for a new conquest. First, the Mexica had now revolted against the Spanish king, and it was the army's moral duty to redress this situation. Second, it was also their moral duty to bring Christianity to these people and remove the pagan idols. Third, they could achieve honor in European history books. Fourth, they could achieve fantastic profit. Cortés added an oft-quoted remark: it was a special opportunity because moral honor and fantastic riches "are rarely found in the same bag."

Meanwhile, in Tenochtitlan, the gods hurled another calamity at the Mexica. In the autumn of 1520, a year after the Spaniards' arrival, an epidemic of European-introduced smallpox swept through the Mexican population. The Mexica, with no immunity, died by the thousands. One of the casualties was an Aztec leader who emerged just before Motezuma's death and who led the final days of fighting against the Spanish invaders. To the Mexica, the fact that the disease killed Mexica but spared Spaniards seemed further proof that the gods favored the Spaniards.

Why weren't Mexican diseases ravaging the Spaniards in equal measure? As Jared Diamond emphasized in his 1997 best seller, *Guns, Germs, and Steel*, ever since Marco Polo in the 1200s, various Europeans had been to China and back, and Africans were common in Europe. So the Europeans had already developed a resistance to most of the world's potpourri of germs. Native Americans, however, had been isolated on their continent with low population densities for at least thirteen thousand years and had limited resistance. The European invaders brought the world's medley of nasty microbes and viral molecules to an innocent America. Estimates, for example, by researchers Henry Dobyns (1983) and Daniel Reff (1991) suggest losses of at least 30 to 50 percent of Native American populations in many areas. (According to at least some archaeological and medical accounts, Americans got their revenge by introducing syphilis to Europe.)

This circumstance raises another interesting aspect of the Spanish accounts. The first generation of Europeans in the 1500s, whose accounts you are reading, was the only generation to see the pristine New World as prehistory ended and recorded history began. The wave of disease and depopulation swept north with the conquistadors, perhaps even jumping ahead of them due to trade among the Indians, so that by the 1600s, eye-witness accounts no longer gave a true picture of pre-European, American life. This is why the descriptions by the *first* explorers are so important in linking eyewitness accounts to archaeological data.

By the spring of 1521, everything was ready for Cortés's second conquest. Thousands of Indian allies were enlisted. In April the new boats were launched into the lake, and a blockade of the city began. The Mexica of Tenochtitlan amassed weapons and took defensive positions on the causeways. Their main problem was maintaining food supplies. In May Cortés divided his land forces and blocked the outer ends of the causeways. For the first ten days of June, a standoff prevailed. The Spaniards advanced onto the causeways each day, only to encounter destroyed bridges, defensive breastworks, and enraged defenders who drove them back.

In early June 1521 Cortés coordinated attacks along several causeways into the city, with instructions for the Spaniards to meet at the central plaza, which they'd abandoned a year before. With cannon fire, Cortés's division forced the Mexica to retreat, but his was the only Spanish group that reached the plaza. As the afternoon grew late, he was forced to retreat. His troops were pummeled by rocks and arrows from rooftops along their way out of the city.

For days, the two sides continued a ludicrous, deadly game. In the daytime Cortés's Indian allies moved forward on the causeways, filling in the breaks, and then the Spanish armies advanced across them . . . but by late afternoon they were forced back. In the night, the Mexican defenders tore new gaps into the causeways. During all these engagements, the Spanish troops destroyed houses, starting at the end of the causeway, so that they could advance farther each day into the city without being attacked from above.

On about the fifth day, Cortés again reached the central plaza but again had to abandon it. More houses were destroyed to make the streets passable for the attackers.

Eventually, Cortés recognized that if his troops were to take Tenochtitlan, the city would be destroyed in the process. "This weighed on my soul," Cortés said later, "and so I tried to find a way to frighten them [into submission]." From the first time he saw the "Venice of the New World" he'd dreamed of taking its pyramids, temples, gardens, waterways, and flowers intact. Now, finally, he began to pay the price of conquest and occupation: devastation. Merely to remove hiding places where defenders hid in the night and attacked in the day, he destroyed many of the buildings. Cortés ordered some of his boats up one of the canals into the city to a point where they could set fire to the palace of Motezuma's father—the Spanish compound of the previous year—and also to the great aviary that housed the royal collection of rare birds. Surely this would convince the citizens to surrender! For neither the first nor last time in history, the devastation merely shocked the citizenry into more determined, destructive defiance.

On 20 June, one year after Motezuma's death, a major assault by a divided Spanish army turned into disaster. In a chaotic retreat, about twenty Spaniards were killed and another fifty captured. Surviving Spanish troops met Mexica carrying the severed heads of their Spanish friends. The Aztecs shouted taunts that all Spaniards would end up that way. That evening, Mexican drums sounded, and Spaniards could only watch helplessly from the causeways as their comrades were pushed up the pyramid steps and sacrificially executed.

SIDEBAR: Of Monuments and Inscriptions

Although the original temples and monumental architecture of Mexico City were destroyed, a modern visitor in the midst of urban bustle can still approach the main plaza along boulevards that lie atop the avenues, causeways, and canals where Cortés and the Mexica fought.

The experience is marred by the current state of Mexico City. Those of us who grew up in the twentieth century were accustomed to being told that ours was the century of progress, the triumph of technology and free-market economies. Today, this view is debatable. Superb at extracting natural resources and building fortunes in the short term, the twentieth-century system was less successful in the long term. Mexico City exemplifies the problem.

In the 1920s the city was a cultural Mecca, full of flowered parks and a magnet to creative personalities such as the much celebrated Frida Kahlo and Diego Rivera. New museums and a magnificent subway system appeared in the 1950s and 1960s. By 2000, however, the population explosion had produced one of the largest urban metro-messes on the planet. Bright, flowery charm faded into the pervasive smog.

Amidst the hubbub, echoes of the ancient city and the vivid events of 1521 persist. My favorite marker is an obelisk in the Plaza of Three Cultures, which was the site of the great market called Tlatelolco. The "three cultures" are exemplified nearby: the remains of one of Tenochtitlan's pyramids, an adjacent Spanish cathedral, and modern office buildings (fig. 1). The inscription on the obelisk, using the Gregorian date, tells the story.

Week by week, Spanish attackers penetrated farther and farther into the ruined city. Street fighting continued for another month, with occasional ineffectual overtures for surrender. By the first week of August, a newly elected emperor, Cuauhtémoc, met with his aides and discussed outlines of a Mexican surrender. They concluded that Cuauhtémoc himself should leave the city. He slipped away across the lake in a canoe with a few aides. On 3 August 1521 (by the Julian calendar) the end came. The remaining Mexica surrendered amidst the ruins of their city. Spaniards, exploring the streets, found such "piles of the dead [that] we were forced to walk over them."

On 13 August 1521, Tlatelolco,
heroically defended by Cuauhtémoc,
fell to the power of Hernán Cortés.
It was neither a triumph nor a defeat.
Rather, it was the painful birth of our multicultured nation,
which is the Mexico of today.

I like the wistful wisdom of this inscription. The climax of Cortés's invasion was not a glorious victory but the solemn inheritance of Mexico. In my novel *Cities of Gold*, I compared that thoughtful Mexican inscription with the bombast of an American inscription on an obelisk in a once-Spanish town, Santa Fe, New Mexico. It reads as follows:

To the heroes
who have fallen in the
various battles with the ——
Indians of the territory
of New Mexico

The blank is a missing word, chiseled out of the original inscription some years ago. I'm told the word was "savage." The other side of the obelisk says it was erected in 1866–68 by the people and legislature of New Mexico. It exemplifies the dangerous, age-old process in which aggressors with self-justifying philosophies claim a moral right to impose themselves on other peoples. Of these two worldviews, the Mexican inscription's tender and wise view of humanity seems to me to be the one we need to pass on to our children if we hope to move beyond Earth's cycles of violence and revenge.

Lost Treasure: Late 1521

The next generations of Spaniards, both in the New World and at home in Spain, were raised on tales of the fabulous wealth that could be amassed by godly conquistadors like Hernán Cortés. All that was needed was pluck and daring. Cortés was, however, only partly right: fortune may favor the bold—but only in the short term.

The short term was ending. Gossip in Mexico City turned from political policy to the question of treasure. Where was the gold that had been left behind? Fortunes had been successfully removed by Cortés and others during La Noche Triste, but more had been lost. What happened to it? Mexica informants claimed vaguely that their people had carried it away. Who, precisely?

Remnants of the treasure were found on Mexica fleeing the city. Perhaps the governing council on the Aztec side had succeeded in spiriting the most culturally valuable pieces out of the city. The rest was missing.

In the end, Cortés had conquered a burnt-out ruin and lost much of the gold he had claimed to have amassed in the first months of his arrival. His reputation began to be questioned among Carlos V's courtiers and the royal governors in the New World.

CHAPTER TWO

Cortés Expands the Frontier

Cortés showed that cities of gold really did exist in the New World. But the fall of Tenochtitlan was only the first act in Hernán Cortés's dramatic life. As mentioned in the prologue, few history books follow the rest of Cortés's story or reveal that he became a major player in the drive to discover more rich lands in what is now the southwestern United States. That story has many twists and turns.

Setting Up a Government: 1521–1522

Cortés's first step after gaining control of ruined Tenochtitlan was to establish a government. In addition, he wanted to chase down the lost gold of the Mexica. He set up headquarters at Coyoacán, an Aztec town across the south causeway from Tenochtitlan on the southwest shore of the lake. At that time Coyoacán was a town of beautiful estates belonging to families of various Aztec nobles. Cortés requisitioned some land, built his house and outbuildings, installed doña Marina and a retinue of servants and retainers, and created a governing center.

Cortés tried—or at least pretended—to include Motezuma's successor, Cuauhtémoc, who had been intercepted and captured on the lake. He set up Cuauhtémoc as a puppet governor of postconquest Mexico City but in practice kept him sequestered in Coyoacán. One of Cuauhtémoc's cousins became the actual leader on the Mexican side, interfacing with the remaining noble families.

In the first months after the fall of Tenochtitlan, Cortés's captains went on rampages to get back "their" treasure, lost during the Night of Sorrows.

They spread out to neighboring towns, often torturing local leaders in a frenzied search for information about gold that might have been recovered from estates, hidden vaults, or even the shorelines of the causeways and then moved into hiding places outside of Tenochtitlan.

At the same time, the conquerors, slaves to their own inherited belief systems, began a centuries-long struggle to eradicate the various Native American religious ideas they encountered, or at least obtain superficial allegiance to Christianity. Obsessive efforts were made to obtain allegiance to their own concept of God, seen by the Mexicans as a curious three-faceted divinity, a father, a son, and an invisible spirit, all linked by a mother who'd been divinely impregnated but remained a virgin. The Aztecs' ritual human sacrifices soon ended on Tenochtitlan's pyramids, but the governing army did not have enough priests or theologians to begin a massive conversion of a whole civilization. The old gods were still worshiped in secret, and sacrifices reportedly occurred in the surrounding provinces.

Eight months after the defeat of the Mexica, Pope Adrian VI consented to a request from Cortés to send priests, who would teach the Christian cosmology and begin the mass conversion of the Mexica to Christianity. Bureaucratic wheels turned as slowly in the Vatican as elsewhere. The delegation of twelve priests arrived in 1524, two years later.

In the sacristies and streets of Europe, a different kind of religious crisis was under way. Martin Luther in 1517 challenged the Roman Catholic version of Christianity. In the summer of 1520, as Alvarado the Sun slaughtered the Mexican dancers, Rome declared Luther a heretic. About the same time, King Carlos V went on a tour of European capitals, taking some of the treasures that Cortés had shipped back from the first days in Mexico, including a spectacular gold disk of the sun and matching silver disk of the moon, each said to be "the size of a cartwheel." The tour caused philosophic upheaval in Europe. An unsuspected alien civilization shared the planet with Europe and China! In today's terms it was like finding fabulous cities on Mars. Alas, the Mexican artisans' gold and silver disks were reportedly melted down to produce bullion for Spain.

Cortés continued sending back letters and messengers to explain his triumphs in hopes of securing royal favor and generous patronage. As the Spanish court absorbed the news, they set up a governing body for the new lands, the Council of the Indies. The king reportedly used the term as early as 1519. Cortés knew of the planned council by 1522, and it was set up formally in 1524. Regulation, law, and bureaucracy—the enemies of get-rich-quick entrepreneurs—were the inevitable handmaidens of civilization. The council's influence was to grow.

Back in Spain, Cortés's supporters painted an image of wonderful conquest on behalf of the king, but historian Hugh Thomas goes so far as to portray Cortés in 1522 as "neglected and ignored" (1995, 541).

Worse yet, troublesome questions were being asked in Mexico. Exactly how much gold had Cortés sequestered for himself during and even before the Night of Sorrows? Of any treasure found in Spanish explorations, a 20 percent tax was supposed to go to the king for the benefit of the country as a whole—the so-called royal fifth. Cortés's partisans insisted that the king's share had been set aside, but, oddly enough, the horses carrying it were the very ones that fell off the causeways. New rumors charged that Cortés was continuing to squirrel away gold found during exploitation of the surrounding Aztec cities.

As in all enterprises after the first goal has been achieved, cliques and factions emerged. Cortés had his circle of loyal officers, but many of the ordinary troops felt cheated out of their role in the glorious conquest. In public, Cortés claimed he was trying to find enough gold to pay the soldiers and enlarge the royal fifth, but, just as publicly, soldiers kept petitioning him for their back pay. Hadn't they been the victorious army? Where was their reward? In the dark hours of night, scurrilous graffiti were scrawled on the walls of Cortés's compound in Coyoacán, demanding better treatment for his men.

What was the truth? During later inquiries, various witnesses testified that they had seen chests full of treasure and equipment for melting gold in the conqueror's home, and rumors circulated about how Cortés had arranged for mysterious masses of material to be buried at hidden locations. Various captains and soldiers in Cortés's inner circle, who were officially recorded as receiving modest official payments, were said to have received much larger amounts under the table. It's not hard to imagine the benefits for a conqueror who might report only a fraction of his captured treasure, send a fifth of that to the king, and keep much larger amounts as a slush fund.

As early as 1521 the first inspector arrived on the Mexican coast to look into Cortés's operations. In an echo of Motezuma sending messengers to learn about the Spaniards on the coast, Cortés now sent his own messengers to the coast to learn about the inspector and his staff. Armed with arguments and papers (and a few bribes?), Cortés's henchmen managed to send that party back to royal headquarters on the Caribbean island of Hispaniola. Officials in the New World, annoyed with what they saw as interference by meddling factions back in Spain, began to perceive Cortés as a winner with largesse to distribute. By mid-1522 the pendulum of Cortés's reputation seemed to swing back in a positive direction.

Dividing the Land: April 1522

As he set up a government, Cortés had to decide how to divide conquered lands among his men. He applied a medieval system known as encomienda, already in use in Cuba and elsewhere in the Indies. Under this system, a Spaniard favored at court was granted a baron-like status over a town or region—an encomienda. The role was like that of a baron in medieval France, England, and Russia. It involved noblesse oblige, the aristocrat's obligation to be a benign governor, taking care of his people and overseeing his lands to increase productivity and wealth. The encomienda system thus included the Spaniards' right to draft the indigenous population into productive work for the benefit of the nation—such as mining, farming, and construction—but did not give them formal ownership of land or people. Natives who happened to be living within an encomienda were supposed to be fairly governed and reimbursed for their labor. In practice, however, the system led to exploitation to benefit the new governors, who had done nothing more than arrive with a paper title in hand, issued within the prevailing political-religious framework.

This old European notion of "highest and best" land use is still found in American zoning and taxation laws under the principle that highest use generates local profits and thus handsome tax revenues for the community. A good enough rule, except that a productive farm field is suddenly more "valuable" if a "higher" use such as a shopping center is established on adjacent land; thus, the field is likely to be taxed at a higher rate, often driving the farmer off the land. An unintended result is that some of America's most fertile land has been lost after being sold off for suburban "development."

Many encomiendas, pursuing "highest and best use," came to resemble the most repressive "company towns" of nineteenth- and early twentieth-century mining conglomerates. Workers might be paid on paper, but after deductions for food, housing, and other services, they owed more than they earned. Overnight, they became slaves. Bartolomé de Las Casas and other reform-minded priests railed against the excesses of the system but had limited influence.

More Golden Empires: 1522

As Cortés's captains fanned out from Tenochtitlan, they learned that they had conquered the richest empire of the region but that other wealthy cultures existed nearby. A smaller, but significant, golden empire was found in 1522 in Michoacán, a province about 200 miles west of Mexico City (see map 2). Today, the name survives as the name of a Mexican state.

A report prepared in 1541 apparently by a Spanish friar named Martín de Jesoes de la Coruña (translated and edited by Ohio historian Eugene Craine and Georgia linguist Reginald Reindorp [1970, 68–69]) described the entrance of Spaniards into Michoacán in the early 1520s. The local governor placed "wreaths of gold on [the Spaniards'] heads" and gave each of them "a round, golden shield." Two of Cortés's officers soon led separate follow-up armed forays into the area, and each came back with hundreds of disks of gold and silver.

Alvarado the Sun, the notorious officer who had ordered the disastrous slaughter of dancers that led to the Night of Sorrows, sent back additional gold to Mexico City from another nearby locale. Cortés had never been able to bring himself to blame Alvarado for the massacre, but the two quarreled over this golden shipment. In a 1528 lawsuit, Alvarado claimed Cortés kept it all for himself. The charge, whether true or not, gives another clue about Cortés's reputation, since Alvarado thought others would find it believable.

Another expedition under Cortés himself resulted in the creation of a new eastern port, Pánuco, on the Gulf of Mexico coast (see map 2, top). As we'll see later in this chapter, Pánuco would soon produce rumors of additional rich provinces.

Meanwhile, in 1522 Cortés ordered the rebuilding of Tenochtitlan. The Spaniards were now referring to the city not by its original name but as Mexico in reference to its occupants, the Mexica. We will use the modern name, Mexico City, to avoid confusion with the nation as a whole.

Cortés overruled some of his own captains who thought it would be better to continue the new government in some less-devastated lakeside town, like Coyoacán. Tenochtitlan, however, had been Cortés's dream. With its symbolic importance, it would be the new capital. This explains why the Zócalo, the central plaza of modern Mexico City, is exactly the same central plaza over which Motezuma had ruled (map 4). The ancient palaces and pyramids, forlorn monuments to a dying civilization, were dismantled to provide stones for the new Spanish palaces and the imperial-scale cathedral that now dominates the space. In succeeding generations, the lake, canal, and gardens were filled in and leveled to provide land for buildings (see fig. 2).

Tens of thousands of regional artisans were drafted to work on these projects. Then, as today, Mexicans were amazingly skilled craftspeople, masters of ancient but still important trades. In 1524 the Franciscan priest Motolinía described armies of the native construction workers singing and gossiping as they swarmed over the new civic projects. Their voices

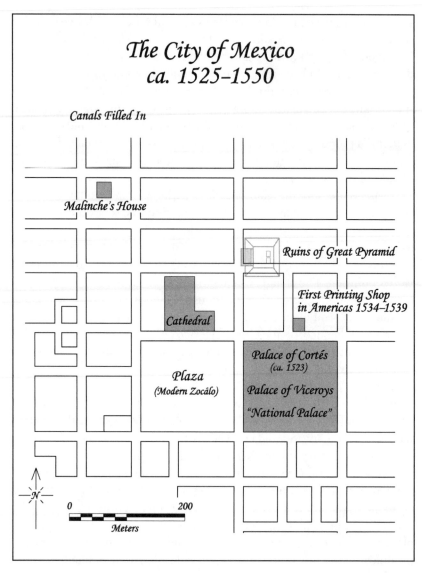

**The City of Mexico
ca. 1525–1550**

Canals Filled In

Malinche's House

Ruins of Great Pyramid

First Printing Shop
in Americas 1534–1539

Cathedral

Plaza
(Modern Zocálo)

Palace of Cortés
(ca. 1523)

Palace of Viceroys

"National Palace"

N

0   200

Meters

Map 4. The transformation of central Tenochtitlan into central Mexico City. The Great Pyramid was torn down to provide building blocks for the new cathedral. Motezuma's compound became the viceroy's palace and the modern-day National Palace. The modern Zócalo, or plaza, overlaps the original plaza. Map by Ron Beckwith.

Figure 2. The canals and gardens of Xochimilco on the south edge of Mexico City, marking some of the last remnants of the canal system and ancient lakeside gardens of ancient Tenochtitlan. Photo by the author, 1970.

could be heard day and night. Motolinía estimated that there were more of them than could have worked on the temple in Jerusalem. Historian Hugh Thomas (1995, 563) estimates that this civic reconstruction in Mexico City was greater than any construction project in Europe at that time.

Reaching the Southwestern Shore of Mexico: 1522

As Cortés's officers ventured farther west and south from the newly rising Mexico City in search of gold, they mapped a new seacoast lying in that direction. Its closest point to Mexico City was due southwest, about 200 miles as the crow flies. Cortés's officers first saw the sea at Zacatula in 1521, and the coast was explored as far as Acapulco by early 1522 (Thomas 1995, 558; see map 2). (The sea had already been sighted in 1513 by Balboa after he crossed the Isthmus of Panama.) Today we know this "new" sea as the Pacific Ocean, and Americans tend to think of it as lying west of Mexico.

To Cortés's generation, however, it lay south of Mexico City and south of Panama and was known as the South Sea.

After locating several sites suitable for ports, Cortés sent a troop of forty carpenters and blacksmiths to start construction of two ships at the port of Zacatula in May 1522 (see map 2, left side). According to naval historian W. Michael Mathes (2000), this was at the small town now known as Peta-calco about halfway between present-day Acapulco and Puerto Vallarta.

The discovery of a new coastline fired Cortés's imagination with new visions. He soon sent several ships southward to look for a passage around the south end of the Mexican "island" that would connect the South Sea with the Caribbean. His interests lay in other directions as well. The discovery of a southern coast encouraged speculation that Mexico was yet another island in the Indies, perhaps lying off the east coast of Marco Polo's vast empire of Cathay, that is, China. As early as 1522 Cortés wrote to King Carlos V about his ideas that by sailing the South Sea his officers would make discoveries "greater than anything else in the Indies." Restless for new adventure, Cortés speculated that if he could be first to get ships into the South Sea, he would be the one to complete Columbus's dream of discovering an oceanic route to Cathay. He would lay at the feet of the king "more kingdoms and lands than we've heard of so far" (Thomas 1991, 558). In 1522 it was a plausible dream.

Back in Tenochtitlan, Cortés was proving himself an able civic administrator. In addition to hankering after new horizons, he promoted commerce. He imported European livestock and urged his officers to bring their wives and families. He also started manufacturing armaments in case of serious revolt or possible conflict with technologically advanced armies or navies from China.

Defining Cortés's Authority: 1522–1523

By late 1522 Carlos V was fully aware that Cortés had made important discoveries, regardless of his shortcomings. At the urging of Cortés's supporters, Carlos granted the conqueror positions as captain general and governor of the Mexican lands, now called New Spain.

The king also addressed Cortés's jurisdiction over Indian laborers. As we've seen, Cortés, in his usual freewheeling style, had already started granting encomiendas to his men. In New Spain such actions by conquistadors often came a few years ahead of any actual official permission, but conquistadors gambled that the permission would arrive after the deed. For

Cortés, the gamble didn't pan out. Cortés's communications from the king in 1523 included an order prohibiting the encomienda system.

Cortés essentially ignored the order. Historian Charles Gibson emphasized that this "refusal to obey [was] the first act of defiance by the Mexican *encomienda* interests against the king"—not unlike certain frictions that arose between property-"owning" American colonists and the king of England two and a half centuries later. Cortés justified his position with several arguments: (1) he needed to be able to offer rewards to his men for their service; (2) the encomiendas would free the Indians from local native despots; and (3) as a strategic matter, encomiendas would bring the Indians into the Spanish legal system. Besides, Cortés was intent on defending the encomiendas he had granted to himself, such as the beautiful suburb of Coyoacán and several other towns. He apparently expected that the reconstructed Tenochtitlan would eventually be added to his own landholdings.

A Son for Cortés and Marina: Family Problems, ca. 1522–1523

Cortés had been living in his Coyoacán estate not only with doña Marina, his primary mistress, but reportedly with a procession of other Mexica women, including the one surviving daughter of the now-dead ruler, Motezuma. A few Spanish ladies were reportedly also involved. In the summer of 1522 his footloose lifestyle was impacted by a slight problem. His program to domesticate Mexico City brought the arrival of none other than his own legal wife, Catalina, and her family, maids, and various family friends! Cortés was amply warned and altered his social arrangements. Doña Marina was hastily moved to a nearby location, and doña Catalina moved into the hacienda. The official family settled into domestic bliss.

This was about the time that Cortés's first son was born—not by Catalina but offstage by Marina. The American historian Henry Wagner, writing in 1942, estimated that the birth occurred between July 1522 and July 1523. Linguist Anna Lanyon, in her 1999 biography of Marina, places it in 1522, closer to Catalina's arrival. The new son, named Martín after the conqueror's father, was much loved by Cortés. Young Martín, an interesting character in his own right, thus became the first (known) mestizo, a person of joint Spanish and Native ancestry. Today, Mexico is primarily mestizo—a nation built from the blending of the Old and New World DNA.

After an uncertain period, possibly as long as two years, according to Lanyon's 2004 biography of Martín, Cortés arranged for Martín to be removed from Marina to be raised by the family of Cortés's cousin Juan Altamirano. Cortés was relatively open about the situation. Eventually, as we'll see, he arranged for the pope to legitimize Martín. (Cortés later gave the same name, Martín, to a "legitimate" son, born in 1532 by his second wife, Juana de Zúñiga, causing some confusion for historians.)

Murder in the Hacienda?: Autumn 1522

About four months after Catalina arrived (and probably a few weeks after Marina gave birth to Martín), around All Saints' Day and Halloween, 1522, a grand fiesta was held at the Coyoacán estate, complete with a banquet and dancing. The event was described in later testimony from eyewitnesses. During table talk about the Indian servants, doña Catalina made a comment about her plans for "her" Indians. Cortés upbraided her, implying that relations with the Indians who worked in this house were his concern, not hers. She fled the room, probably mortified. Sometime later she was seen in her chapel. The party continued.

Late that night, Cortés called his treasurer and majordomo to his room. His wife was dead.

People have argued about the death from that day forward. Did Cortés kill his wife in an argument over his mistresses and her "property" rights? Many people of the time openly said so, and much of the evidence is damaging to Cortés. For example, messages about the death were sent that same night to Catalina's maids and her brother but with the proviso that the brother would not be allowed into the room. Why was the brother excluded?

Cortés must have realized that he himself was the leading suspect. He claimed that friction among Catalina, her brother, and himself had agitated his wife and contributed to her death. The maids, however, rushed to the room and testified that Catalina had bruises about the neck and that beads from her broken necklace were scattered on the floor. Some of them also said she had been unhappy with her husband and that on past occasions he had been known to throw her from their bed. Cortés's priest reportedly proposed an examination of the body with a lawyer, but Cortés is said to have insisted that the body be put in a coffin that should be nailed shut and buried. According to reports of the time, no one else saw the body.

On Cortés's shaky side of the case, testimony was gathered that Catalina was known to be sickly, with a heart condition. Reportedly, she had suffered heart problems in Cuba, and two of her sisters had died abruptly in a similar way. One witness said she had fainted during a visit to a farm two weeks earlier. A friend of Cortés recalled a time when Catalina had appeared to be dead and had to be revived with a dash of cold water. Cortés himself claimed she might have been bruised that night while he tried to revive her by shaking her. Others pointed out that a serious fight between them would have roused others in the house. Character witnesses said Cortés was a good Christian, grieving over the loss of his wife. Still . . . Cortés was the sort who could always bring forth some associates to testify in his favor. Hugh Thomas, taking a middle ground, speculates that when Cortés went to Catalina's room, she criticized his mistresses, and he started shaking her by the neck, as he been seen to do in altercations with other people, and she had a heart attack and died (1995, 582). Whereupon Cortés realized how things would look and ordered the body quickly sealed in a coffin and buried. The true story of that night will probably never be clear.

SIDEBAR: Living in the House of Cortés

In 1981 I was working with my friend, artist Ron Miller, on the first edition of a book titled *The Grand Tour* about the various worlds of the solar system. After the book came out, Ron got a call from the Hollywood producer Raffaella De Laurentiis, who said she was working on the big-budget film based on the famous science fiction novel *Dune*. One of Ron's paintings of Mars matched their concept of Dune, the desert planet. Could Ron come out to Hollywood and work on pre-production art with them?

It was every illustrator's dream! Ron agreed. Production moved to Mexico, and by March 1983 Ron found himself working at the famous Churubusco studios in Mexico City in almost daily contact with the well-known surrealist director David Lynch. Ron and his wife, Judith, invited me to come down for a few days to meet Lynch and talk with him about some astronomical concepts for the film.

During Aztec times, Churubusco was a lakeshore suburb of Tenochtitlan, southeast of the island city. Ron and Judith were renting a house in nearby Coyoacán, the town where Cortés made his headquarters after the fall of Tenochtitlan. At the time, I knew only a little about Cortés's adventures, but Ron claimed the house had been built by Cortés, so I made some notes about our own experiences in Cortés's domain:

"Gayle, twelve-year-old daughter Amy, and I arrive at Ron's house in Coyoacán, which sits on the town-center plaza and turns out to be part of the estate built by

continued

Cortés Squeaks through Again: 1523–1524

Following the scandalous death of Cortés's wife, not to mention his liaisons, a cloud hung over his reputation. Much of the original Tenochtitlan gold had been lost during La Noche Triste, there were questions about how much Cortés had hidden away for himself, his men were complaining about not being paid, and his behavior was being questioned.

In September 1523 he was delivered from disaster once again. News arrived from Spain affirming his royal backing and his titles as captain general and governor of the conquered region. At about age thirty-nine, his authority over New Spain seemed complete. By 1524 he was dressing in

Cortés himself! It's an old, thick-walled, two-story edifice set immediately along the sidewalk, across a dimly lit plaza from a wonderful old church with lighted towers, looming in the evening among the trees. The house has unusual reddish exterior walls patterned with interlocking, embellished rectangles.

"Behind the heavy, multiply locked and bolted front door is a narrow entry hall. To the right, off the hall, is a large living room with a fireplace. All rooms have high, 10- or 12-foot ceilings. The front window is indented in the 3-foot-thick wall, making a nice little shelf under the window, divided in the middle to form two window seats—a great place to sit and write.

"We set out promptly for a delicious dinner. I have filet mignon, tender, juicy, and delicious, for about $2.50.

"Later in the evening, the wind knocks loose a power line to the house. The lights flicker red and dim. By candlelight, we play Parcheesi with Amy in what I call 'Cortés's living room.' Perhaps this was the original lighting. We can't be sure, however, how the rooms we inhabit relate to the original layout or use of the rooms in Cortés's day. Amy beds down on the floor of 'Cortés's living room,' and Gayle and I share a narrow bed in a side bedroom.

"The next day arrives, a sunny March morning, on the plaza in front of Ron and Judith's house—I mean Cortés's house. Inside, the house is cool; we wear sweaters. The sun comes in warm and bright through the white, gauzy, lacy curtains. The steady light is welcome after a night of candles.

"In addition to our electrical problems yesterday, the water was shut off yesterday morning, ruling out evening baths. It came on again this morning, briefly, just long enough for me to flush a toilet, draw some more pans of cooking water, and get about two inches of hot water in the tub before it shut down again. After I black silk, befitting his exalted status, and was surrounded by servants and aides. When he traveled around the countryside, he usually took a retinue of Aztec nobles with him.

Cortés the Man in Middle Age: 1522–1530

It's hard to grasp Cortés the man. Like Motezuma, he was an enigma. We can't claim that he was sincere or honest, yet he passed himself off as devout by the standards of the 1500s. He was clearly an "alpha male," set on dominance, wealth, and respect. He was also a visionary. He had goals

had an unsatisfactory bath, it came on again in fits. Ron and Judith said they were used to such problems—this is life in modern Mexico City."

Years after recording the above notes, I realized that I had been so enthralled by meeting director David Lynch and the star of the film, Kyle MacLachlan (also Lynch's star in his surrealistic *Twin Peaks* series), that I foolishly failed to find time to appreciate Coyoacán. By the 1920s through the 1940s it had become the "Paris of the New World," famous as a center of artistic and intellectual ferment. A few blocks away from Ron and Judith's historic house was the famous Casa Azul, or "Blue House," of Frida Kahlo and muralist Diego Rivera. Around a few corners from the Blue House was the house where Stalin's exiled rival, Leon Trotsky, lived after visiting Frida and Diego—and getting a bit too involved with her. In that fatal second house, Trotsky was assassinated in his study in 1940 by a Stalinist extremist with a pickax. Our house had its share of death, too. Somewhere on the property, some say in one of our very rooms, Cortés's wife, Catalina, died under suspicious circumstances—possibly strangled by the conqueror himself during an after-dinner argument.

While working on the present book, I asked Ron for some of his memories of the house of Cortés. Ron affirmed that he and Judith rented it from a lady who lived upstairs and that the property was quite extensive, including some nearby buildings on the same side of the plaza. He located a 1997 *New York Times* article about the house by journalist Clifford Krauss. Krauss confirmed that it was known as "La Malinche's house," the house where Marina and Cortés had lived before Cortés's lawful wife, Catalina, arrived on the scene. Krauss stated that it was where Catalina met her mysterious fate. Krauss also reported that the owners,

continued

and dreams. In basic human terms, he was robust and intelligent. He was a schemer, but the difference between schemer and dreamer is only a few letters—at least at the beginning.

Shouldn't he be presented as a dishonest scoundrel? Wasn't he a brutal, cynical, and legalistic hypocrite who invaded Mexico on make-believe orders of his "town council," used torture to extort gold, and perhaps murdered his own wife while playing the upright innocent? Yes. He was playing the sixteenth-century game with sixteenth-century cards. That is to say, he grew up within the paradigm of medieval conquest. By those standards he was an industrious, brave, pragmatic, lusty "success." By twenty-first-century standards he was an amoral plunderer. Perhaps it does no good to rail against individuals such as Cortés, Columbus, Alvarado, or the despoiler of Peru, Francisco Pizarro. Or to rail against nations. Better we should spend

presumably Ron's landlords, were Rina Lazo, a prominent muralist, and her husband, the painter Arturo García Bustos. Both had been students of Diego Rivera and Frida Kahlo. Small world!

According to Anna Lanyon, biographer of Marina, Motezuma's daughter, with whom Cortés had reportedly been sleeping, had been installed along with three stepsisters in the Coyoacán estate. Her name was Techuichpotzin. She was duly baptized by the Spaniards, given the name Isabel, and treated as a young woman of nobility under Cortés's dubious "protection." During Cortés's invasion, she had been married (at about age twelve, consistent with Aztec traditions) to Motezuma's ill-fated successor, Cuauhtémoc, who was now Cortés's captive, held separately in the Coyoacán area. Thus, if all the stories are true, Cortés was sleeping with the wife of Cuauhtémoc, his official coregent over postconquest Mexico City.

During a 1529 judicial review of Cortés's actions, a priest and other witnesses testified that Cortés had sexual relations with all of the young indigenous female servants and "protected guests" on his Coyoacán estate (Lanyon 1999, 140). The idea that Cortés had native mistresses was hardly news by 1529; indeed, Cortés made public provision not only for Marina's son, Martín, but also for a daughter who was later born to the daughter of Motezuma. The witnesses were distressed, however, about the fact that several of the mistresses were related to each other. Before we *norteño* Americans are too shocked, we should recall that DNA testing and oral tradition support the claim that Thomas Jefferson and Sally Hemings, a black slave on his estate, had children together.

our time examining the overall philosophic/economic/religious/political framework of their times and then examine our own.

Many elements of that sixteenth-century framework still linger in our twenty-first century, and we, too, will be judged by future standards. We're likely to be judged guilty of accepting a *framework* that has endorsed invasions of foreign lands under false pretenses and exploitation not of gold but of Earth's last easily accessible resources. Few of us have the ability or opportunity to step entirely out of the framework we are taught at our mother's knee, and when we do, we may be made to suffer for it by our compatriots. Like all interesting characters, Cortés was thus a Shakespearean mixture of flawed hero and outrageous villain, shaded toward the latter. He was a classic case of the robber baron who makes a billion "within the system" and then buys respect with public works. As humanity is still

As chronicled by *New York Times* journalist Krauss, Cortés's house in Coyoacán continued to have a colorful history. After Cortés's day, it was occupied by Indian weavers. By the 1600s it was more or less in ruins. In the 1800s it was refurbished as a secret convent. This was an anticlerical period, and when the convent was exposed, the inhabitants were driven off, and the complex was used as a prison. According to Krauss, artists Rina Lazo and Arturo García Bustos bought the house in the 1930s. On the grounds of the property, they found jade pieces and other artifacts from the Aztec period. Their renters have included not only my illustrious friend, Ron Miller, but also Diego Rivera's daughter.

In spite of the property's history and a special listing on a National Geographic Society map, the house was virtually anonymous by the time Ron and Judith rented there. Why? In Mexico of the twentieth century, reminders of Malinche and Cortés were not popular. A monument to them erected by the city council of Coyoacán in 1982 was greeted by anti-Malinche demonstrations, then removed and stored in obscurity. Krauss quoted Ms. Lazo: "For Mexico to make this house a museum would be like the people of Hiroshima creating a monument for the man who dropped the atomic bomb." She made a prediction. "It will take another century before this house could become a museum." So far, her prediction is on track.

And yet . . . such colorful places are part of our human heritage. We'll never learn anything from our multiply-great-grandparents if we suppress currently uncomfortable parts of their stories. Wisdom is created by awareness, not by blindness.

discovering, the boundary between good and evil lies within individuals, not just between good guys and bad guys.

To conjure alternative histories is perhaps pointless . . . but fascinating. But for the blunders of Alvarado the Sun, Cortés might have been able to work with Motezuma as puppet leader of a vassal state of Spain, not unlike puppet leaders propped up by the Soviets in eastern Europe or by Americans in Latin America or the Near East in the twentieth century. In such a scenario, Mexico City might have been preserved more nearly as Cortés found it. Could Cortés and Motezuma jointly have maintained order? In support of such an idea, various Aztec noble families were living only blocks from the new Spanish lordly families in the rising new city of Mexico during the later 1520s and 1530s. Cortez himself took three sons of Motezuma into his retinue, and when Christian names were doled out, one of them became Martín Cortés Nezahualzolotl.

Would Cortés and Motezuma have used Mexican armies to create an expanded Spanish/Mexican/Christian empire in New Spain? Probably. As evidence, we note that Coronado's 1540 expeditionary army, which traveled from Mexico City into what is now the United States, was mostly composed of Native American allies from the region around present-day Mexico City. On the other hand, Cortés's true attitude toward Motezuma may have been revealed by his later relationship with Cuauhtémoc, to whom he made similar promises of joint conquest, only to throw him in jail, have him tortured to reveal locations of gold, and, eventually, as we will see, have him hanged in 1525 for contesting Spanish rule.

When Religious Worlds Collide: 1524

In the early summer of 1524 a delegation of twelve Franciscan friars arrived from Europe, sent by the pope in answer to Cortés's request in 1522. These twelve were to become famous in Mexican history; their number was a deliberate echo of the twelve apostles appointed by Jesus of Nazareth.

Cortés, ever devout (at least in public), met the twelve on his knees and kissed their hands one at a time. Then captains and gentlemen of the new city rising from the ruins did the same. After that, nobles from among the conquered Mexica followed suit. The scene was remembered decades later as the effective beginning of the religious conquest of Mexico. This conquest had its own history, parallel to Spain's civil conquest of Mexico. Now began what was arguably the most intriguing philosophic collision in world history.

The European priests were intent on dismantling the pagan religion. To their credit, they began the process without violence by setting up an extraordinary series of pathos-tinged conferences with the Mexican political and religious leaders of Tenochtitlan. According to the best surviving records, the first colloquium occurred over a number of days in 1524, soon after the Franciscans arrived.

The intercontinental philosophical/political/religious conference was only sketchily recorded at the time. Some forty years later, in 1564, the Spanish priest and record-collector Bernardino de Sahagún gathered the few surviving notes, written in both Spanish and the Nahuatl language of the Aztecs, to produce a book about the priestly conversations, *Libro de los Colloquios* (*Book of the Colloquies*). Sahagún himself is believed to have written much of the text of the book. To translate the Aztec accounts, he utilized four Nahuatl-speaking Christianized Mexica who had been trained

SIDEBAR: The Mexican Conquest as a Unique Moment in the History of the Human Species

Let's step back for a moment and consider the colloquium of the Aztec and Spanish priests in the big-picture context of human history. Our humanoid ancestors appeared a few million years ago in Africa and eventually migrated outward in several directions, creating two halves of humanity, as noted in the introduction. About twelve to fifteen thousand years ago (and perhaps earlier), *Homo sapiens* from the eastern branch wandered from Mongolia to Alaska on a temporary land bridge exposed by low ice-age sea levels. They saw it, of course, not as a bridge, but simply as a new, hospitable unpopulated area—perhaps the source of the mythic "happy hunting ground." Both North and South America were rapidly populated within a few thousand years. Meanwhile, the other half of humanity moved north from Africa, around the Mediterranean, and into Europe. Humanity had spread almost around the world.

In many parts of the planet, including the Mediterranean, South and East Asia, and the Americas, civilizations rose within the last five thousand years, producing massive stone architecture, sophisticated religion, and urbane culture. Mostly, they disintegrated within a few centuries or a millennium.

An epochal moment, unique in all human history, occurred within a few years of A.D. 1000. This was the first known moment when the two halves of humanity finally met, like long-lost cousins. Members of the European branch—the Vikings,

continued

in a Spanish-founded college for bright young sons of the Mexican nobility. The Nahuatl and Spanish versions vary only somewhat, betraying wonderfully different spins on the events. Academic arguments about the details abound, but the bottom line is that the Spanish and Nahuatl accounts, taken together, give an extraordinary portrait of religious and philosophic inquiry as the two halves of humanity collided in 1524.

In 1577, however, before Sahagún could publish his material, King Felipe II (Philip II), only son of Charles V, of Spain prohibited publication of *any* material about the religion of the pagan Indians for fear it would perpetuate false beliefs. In that very year, Sahagún's manuscript was confiscated by the Council of the Indies, the body governing Spain's New World. By a quirk of history recounted by Florida scholar Viviana Díaz Balsera in 2005, Sahagún's documentation of the conference resurfaced in 1924 when a Franciscan priest discovered most of it intact in what Díaz Balsera calls "secret archives of the Vatican." A German translation appeared in 1949, then Spanish and English versions in 1985. Scholarship, though fundamental to human progress, moves at a pace of centuries in the face of public disinterest and political suppression. . . .

who had already sailed west to settle Iceland—sailed farther west to Greenland and then to North America. It was probably in the 990s that they first sighted Native American Inuit peoples in North America, whom they called "Skraelings." The Icelanders had no global map to make them realize the significance of the event. To them, it was just another contact with strangers in a strange land. The epochal moment is described in a few passages in the thousand-year-old manuscripts of Icelandic sagas, but it remained largely unknown around the rest of the world.

Instead, that encounter should be recalled in every school in every land of planet Earth as the moment when the two streams of humanity completed the settlement of planet Earth. Only a thousand years ago, it marked the beginning of the end of "frontier" on our little world.

The climate turned colder over the next few generations, increasing the hazards of the North Atlantic sea lanes, and the Vikings abandoned the settlement they had made in Newfoundland. Even their colony in Greenland died out. Oscar Wilde, the Irish-English writer and wit, toured the United States nine hundred years later and quipped that we should admire the Icelanders because they were brave enough to sail off and discover America and smart enough to go back home and forget all about it.

According to the *Libro de los Colloquios* and related sources, as discussed by Díaz Balsera, the twelve Franciscan priests of 1524 were especially enthused because of the Franciscan idea that Christianization of the New World marked a new phase of human history. Mexico and the Indies offered opportunities to organize perfect communities in accord with Christian principles. Years earlier, Bartolomé de Las Casas, the priestly defender of the Native American peoples, had already circulated ideas about establishing such societies among the "Indie-ans." Soon thereafter, in 1516, the English writer Thomas More wrote a description of a hypothetical perfect society in his much more famous book, *Utopia*. Historian Victor Baptiste, in a little-known 1990 monograph, cited intriguing evidence that More's famous book was a mere embellishment of ideas from Las Casas's writings, which had been sent from the court of Spain to Prince Charles in England.

In that utopian atmosphere, the colloquium proceeded. A series of presentations occurred, as in any scholarly conference. The Franciscans opened the colloquium, speaking to the educated nobles of Aztec society. They expressed love and fellowship for their noble and educated colleagues from Tenochtitlan and then presented the Spanish worldview of that time:

It hasn't been ruled out that the Quetzalcoatl legend in Mexico might represent another such contact between Eurasian humanity and Asian American humanity around the same time but less well recorded.

Columbus made the second known contact between the two branches of humanity. Cortés's adventures—only three decades later—occurred halfway between the Viking age and the present.

An astonishing aspect of all this is that the two branches, as represented by the Mexica and the Spaniards, were as similar technologically as they were. After ten thousand years of independent social development, both branches of humanity had stone architecture, agriculture, canals, metalworking, archery, urbane kings, religious priesthoods, and astronomy. One has to wonder what would have happened, if—with a slightly different roll of the cosmic dice—the Mexica-Maya complex had invented guns and ships first. Suppose, in a mirror image of real history, the Aztecs had invaded medieval Europe, taken over London, Paris, and Rome, demanded obeisance to Motezuma, and sent in their priests to abolish the old religions of Judaism, Christianity, and Islam?

No one was thinking in such cosmic terms in 1524 when the priests and nobles from the two sides came together to talk about their worldviews.

the kings of the world, such as the king of Spain, ruled over civic matters but yielded authority over spiritual matters to the pope in Rome, who was described in the Nahuatl version as "the great speaker of divine things" (Díaz Balsera 2005, 24). The Franciscans avowed that they themselves were not motivated by gold or material wealth but only by a wish for brotherhood with their new friends. They added, however, that they had seen their Mexica colleagues worshiping false gods, and the plan of the Christian god must have been to send Cortés and the Spaniards "to punish and afflict" the Mexica because of this. The Franciscans went on to note that the gods of the Mexica, like the ancient Greek gods, were capricious, dealing in blood and filth, sometimes playing tricks on the people. The Franciscans explained that such trickster gods had been superseded by Christianity. They listed the superior attributes of their own single god, who manifests only love and care for his human creations.

Their argument must have seemed logically inconsistent to the nobles of Tenochtitlan, since the new god who loved his Mexican subjects had sent the Spaniards to destroy their city. The Aztec nobles replied, probably a day or so later. In the polite and flowery style of Aztec rhetoric, they said that they had pondered the Christians' words, which were pure and as beautiful as turquoise and jade. However, the Aztecs explained, they were lords over civic life, and they needed to summon their own priests, who devoted their lives to studying such matters.

The Aztec priests welcomed the Christian priests as great speakers, agreeing that a true god must have sent them to bring sacred texts and to help govern the Mexica. They felt that the Catholic god, or perhaps the three gods of father, son, and holy spirit, had wonderful attributes and that these attributes overlapped attributes of their own gods. They argued that all such gods, who go back beyond human memory, inhabit a divine realm and bestow grace, dignity, and wealth on humans. The Aztec priests argued that the Mexica's hearts were already committed to these ideals. Thus, they suggested, the colloquium itself risked some danger, because the Catholic priests seemed to be pursuing a course that might interrupt traditional Mexican practices and anger the gods who identify with the Mexican people. This might cause more harm than good to the Mexican land.

Now it was the Catholic priests' turn to answer. They argued that, no, their own god was clearly superior, and this could be proved by logic. First, their god was already known around the world, whereas the gods of Tenochtitlan were known only locally. Second, whereas the Mexica did not know about the Christian god, the Christians said they knew all about where the Mexican gods came from. They were like the old, failed gods of

Greece, Rome, and Mesopotamia. The Franciscans said they'd be happy to explain more about this later. Eventually, the Franciscans unleashed their ultimate argument. The Christian god conquered the Mexica, not vice versa. Furthermore, the Christian god had so far punished only Tenochtitlan for its pagan practices, but those practices could be forgiven, since the Mexicans hadn't known yet about the true, Christian god. Now, however, things were different. The Mexica had now been told about the true god. If they chose to reject the true god, they would be completely destroyed, and, moreover, the Spaniards would be justified in destroying them. Historian Díaz Balsera aptly refers to this speech as "discursive terror."

Not surprisingly, the Mexican priests responded that they would be happy to learn more about the Christian god. The Catholic priests then began what the accounts call a "long performance" about the nature of the Christian religion. Their god was eternal, having created the heavens, the angels, the sun, and the world for the benefit of humans. However, according to the ancient book of Genesis, one of the angels, Lucifer, rebelled, setting up himself and other angel-followers as additional gods. Lucifer was defeated by the true god and archangel Michael and was cast into the dark lower world. This event proved that there was only one true god, not many. It enabled the Franciscans to explain the origins of the Mexican religion. The many gods of Tenochtitlan were merely examples of the fallen angels who had set themselves up as false gods.

In this context, the intercultural colloquium devolved into a military argument. The conquest by Cortés proved that the Spanish Christian god had been able to defeat all the Mexican gods in spite of overwhelming odds.

At this point, the differences between the Spanish and Nahuatl accounts in Sahagún's book become especially instructive. Sahagún's preface reported that "the twelve" emerged triumphant and that, through their work, the Mexica accepted Christianity—end of story. The Nahuatl text, prepared by Christianized sons of Tenochtitlan nobility, is more nuanced. Díaz Balsera and other scholars infer that the Mexicans were struggling to find similarities between the European view and their own capricious, Greek-like gods, who combined the inevitable positives and negatives of human life. The Aztecs needed to find some way to absorb the new religion but salvage their culture. In one memorable conversation, recorded in the colloquium records and quoted by historian Hugh Thomas, the Mexican priests responded in despair to the Christians' demands that they give up their gods: "Isn't it enough that we've already lost, and that you've destroyed our way of life?" (1995, 587).

One outcome was clear after the conference. The next generation of conquered Aztecs tried to maintain a mixture of public Christianity to please the Spanish overlords but, in the privacy of their homes and secret shrines, offered obeisance to the old gods. Sahagún, in pursuit of the truth, interviewed many informants from the Mexico City area in the 1560s and confirmed that—no surprise—the old religion was still practiced in private.

If the twentieth century taught us one clear lesson, it is that old cultures die hard. I visited Russia both before and after the collapse of the Soviet system and heard discussion among writers and artists that what Russia needed after the traumatic collapse was a return to assumed spiritual principles of the czarist days. Sure enough, Orthodox Christianity, previously suppressed, surged in post-Soviet Russia. In the same era, Sunni-Shiite conflicts sprang back to life as soon as oppressive dictatorships fell. Governments come and go, but religions are transmitted from ancestors. Governments fall first, religions fall last. At one point in Sahagún's book we find a frank and prescient assessment of this truth, apparently by Sahagún himself: "We can consider as well understood, having preached to them for more than 50 years, that if today they were left on their own . . . in less than another 50 years there would be no trace of what has been preached" (Díaz Balsera 2005, 50).

European Christianity in the 1500s wasn't notably forgiving about the universal human trait of resistance to imposed cultural change. During the decades after 1524, numbers of conquered Mexica were executed for pretending to participate in Catholic ritual yet privately worshiping the old gods. Even during Catholic ceremonies, many Spanish priests felt their parishioners were, secretly and simultaneously, invoking the old religion. The supposed "conversion" was really a slow process of assimilation. Still today, the blanket of Mexican Catholicism contains rich threads of the old Mexica-Aztec religion, from Day of the Dead ceremonies to the ornate folk art of flowers, vines, and skulls.

Even the preeminent Mexican religious icon, the Virgin of Guadalupe, is linked by some scholars to an Aztec goddess, Tonantzin, who was considered the mother of the Aztec people, associated with healing, and possibly viewed as a virgin in some traditions. For these reasons, as the Mexica struggled to fit the Christians' tripartite god and saints into their religious cosmology, they linked Tonantzin to the Virgin Mary. Thereby hangs an interesting sociological tale. Sahagún noted in 1576 that a Catholic church, dedicated to the Virgin Mary and named after the Guadalupe region in Spain, had been built in Mexico City on the site of an Aztec shrine to Tonantzin. Sahagún complained that the native Mexica who came to "Guadalupe" in droves to worship were really worshiping Tonantzin by proxy.

Sahagún's claim is not well documented by other records, but it seems credible, according to an important study by the historian and Roman

Catholic priest Stafford Poole (1995, 78ff.). According to the modern Mexican legend, the Virgin Mary, dark-skinned, appeared to a humble, recently converted local Indian named Juan Diego at "Guadalupe" in 1531. Her image then miraculously appeared on his cloak, which he took to Mexico's first bishop, Juan de Zumárraga (whom we'll meet again later), and the fame of this incident spread.

The problem with the legend, as discussed by Roman Catholic investigator Poole, is that no known records from Zumárraga or others of that time mention this extraordinary incident, and the earliest known version of the story was not published until 1648, after which the tradition spread like wildfire, especially among Catholics born in the New World, who now had their own New World Madonna. As a result, the figure of the Virgin of Guadalupe is still venerated throughout Latin America.

Rumors of Amazon Women, Lost Bishops, and Cities to the North: 1524–1527

As the Spaniards began to learn more about the history and culture of the people they had conquered, they took more interest in recording myths dating from before the 1520 conquest. Some of the stories suggested an intriguingly detailed legend about the unknown North. One such tale was preserved around 1580 by a Dominican friar, Diego Durán, in his book, *Historia de Las Yndias de Nueva España y Yslas de la Tierra Firme* (*History of the Indies of New Spain, and the Islands of Terra Firma*): "The only story I have of the origins of these people, and the Indians know more than they relate, tells of the Seven Caves where their ancestors dwelt for a very long time, and which they abandoned in order to seek this land. Some came first and others later, until those caves were deserted. The caves are in Teocolhuacan, also called Aztlán, which we are told is found toward the north and near the region of La Florida." The Mexican tradition, in other words, was that their founders had come generations earlier from the unknown North. "La Florida" referred not just to the area known today as Florida but to the whole terra incognita north of Cuba, including much of the Gulf of Mexico coastline as far west as Texas. "Florida" loosely means Land of Flowers, and the name was given by Ponce de León not only because of modern Florida's tropical vegetation but because he had landed there during the Easter season, known in Spanish as Pascua Florida, the Easter season of flowers.

To some sixteenth-century Spanish ears, the story of Aztlán could be stretched to connect with a European legend about the supposed Seven

Cities of Antilia. According to this legend, seven bishops escaped the invasions of the Moors between the 700s and 1100s and traveled west across the Atlantic. Somewhere in the New World, they founded seven cities, which had grown wealthy in the interim. Many conquistadors thought they might, at some point, stumble on these wealthy "Seven Cities" in the lands they were encountering. Were the Aztecs saying, perhaps in veiled language, that they had a connection with seven great settlements in the North? Did this explain why the people of Tenochtitlan seemed so much more sophisticated and wealthy than the other Indie-ans encountered so far?

To add an additional magnetic pull to the north, a 1508 edition of old tales about a fictional chivalric action-hero, Amadis of Gaul, had included a new tale, *Las sergas de Esplandián* (*The Adventures of Esplandián*) about the hero's son, Esplandián. In this adventure yarn, Esplandián fought an army of Turks allied with Amazon warrior women from an island ruled by an Amazon queen named Califia. The island, lying "at the right hand of the Indies," was said to be called California. As recounted by historians Jane Walsh (1993, 75–76), Hugh Thomas (1995, 61), and others, many conquistadors suspected the legend might be based on some reality. In a comic twist, our own Golden State inherited the name of the imaginary Queen Califia—the equivalent of naming a state after Princess Leia or Wonder Woman. But then, California has long been reputed to have a certain affinity for fantasy.

Conquest of an island of Amazon women, no matter how unrealistic, offered an attractive prospect. It couldn't fail to be interesting, and perhaps the land of Amazons, and Marco Polo's Cathay, *and* the legendary wealthy cities founded by seven escaping bishops all lay ahead somewhere to the north and west.

Hernán Cortés sought more information about such lands. His letters to the king recount his results. As early as October 1524, one of these letters described how he ordered one of his captains to found the town of Colima in the province of that name 300 air line miles west of Mexico City near the coast, where evidence was found to support old Euro-fantasies:

> When [the captain] returned, he brought a report, along with certain samples of pearls. . . . He likewise brought me an account of the chiefs of the province of Ceguatan, who affirm that there is an island inhabited only by women without any men. At certain times, men from the mainland come to be with them, and if they conceive, they keep the female children to which they give birth, but the male babies they cast away. They say this island is ten days from that province, and many of them

have been there and seen it, and told me that it is very rich in pearls and gold. I shall strive to ascertain the truth of the matter, and, when I am able to do so, I shall make a full account to your Majesty. (synthesized from translations of Cortés's fourth letter by MacNutt 1908, 177–88; Pagden 1986, 298–300; and Morris 1991, 253)

It's interesting that Cortés regarded these ideas as credible enough to include in a letter to the king. It signals why Cortés thought he might have found something important and why shipbuilding was one of his most serious pursuits.

Still more rumors of interesting lands in a different direction filtered in. As recounted by geographer Carl Sauer (1937b, 271–72), a naval pilot, Luis Cárdenas, wrote a letter to the king in August 1527 describing cities where metal was used. These cities were supposed to be 200 leagues to the north of Pánuco, the city Cortés had started as a northern outpost on the Gulf of Mexico coast. The distance, somewhere between 500 and 620 road miles, would place this locale along the Rio Grande, around the Big Bend country of Texas. This, indeed, was an area where copper bells were traded, as we'll see in the next chapter. Roughly another 400 road miles north were the multistory Pueblo Indian towns along the Rio Grande near present-day Albuquerque. In other words, there was some basis in truth for rumors of interesting provinces 500 to 1,000 miles to the north.

Fortune No Longer Favors the Bold: 1524–1526

In 1524 Cortés received word of renegade Spanish soldiers operating in the area of what is now Honduras. The news seemed to challenge his authority. He decided on a punitive expedition that turned into disaster. In October 1524 he left unreliable aides in control of his conquered capital and departed with horsemen, foot soldiers, Aztec lords, Franciscans, his own household staff, musicians, dancers, jesters, and Marina, setting off across the swamps of Yucatán toward Honduras. Hugh Thomas describes it as a party of several thousand, the greatest such procession that Mexico had ever seen, a happy band, apparently, of brothers of all races (1995, 596). Cortés and Marina left their son, Martín, in the care of the Altamirano family. The expedition lasted two years and saw a serious decline in Cortés's fortunes.

Thomas calls the whole trip "a pretext" to resolve certain problems—out of the public eye (1995, 596). Certainly, the expedition saw a succession of unexpected personal developments. Probably mindful of gossip in

Tenochtitlan, Cortés seems to have decided to relieve himself, legalistically at least, of the embarrassment of his relationship with Marina. Only a week or two into the journey, he arranged for her to be officially married to one of his loyal officers, Juan Jaramillo de Salvatierra. The first biographer of Cortés, a contemporary named López de Gómara, repeated stories that Jaramillo was drunk at the ceremony, though this story was later disputed by Bernal Díaz (who was not present but who joined the expedition in December). In short, Cortés seems to have "married Marina off" to clean up his own messy affairs. As a wedding present, he apparently granted her lands where she'd been born, between Mexico City and Yucatán. What were the true emotions of the players? Marina's biographer, Anna Lanyon, wisely comments that the interpretation of this striking development requires historians and readers to "steer a path between romance and cynicism" (1999, 144ff.).

On the trip through this area, Marina had a chance to meet her own mother, from whom she'd been separated (traded?) about a decade before.

Another development on the ill-fated march involved the captive final ruler of Tenochtitlan, Cuauhtémoc, who had been brought on the trip, along with several Aztec nobles. During the trip they were accused of "rebellion" against the Spaniards. Cortés had them executed in late February 1525 somewhere in the Yucatán peninsula. Bernal Díaz says that many of Cortés's own officers were dismayed at this decision. According to Lanyon (1999, 150–51), a Maya document discovered in 1933 records that Marina prayed for Cuauhtémoc at the moment of his execution— in Nahuatl.

To cast more gloom over the trip, some of Cortés's troops died from the hostile climate and lack of food during the Yucatán crossing. All of this seems to have weighed heavily on Cortés. Díaz reported with horror that Cortés began drinking heavily, starting sometimes before breakfast. Was he drowning romantic sorrows as Marina stayed with her new husband? Or fleeing his other misfortunes?

By the time the expeditionaries arrived on the Honduras coast, their opponents had mostly died from disease and fighting among themselves. Cortés's party obtained ships from the survivors, but by the time they sailed north around the Yucatán peninsula and arrived in Cortés's colony-town of Veracruz in May 1526, Cortés had grown "corpulent with a great belly," in the words of plain-speaking Díaz. His beard had turned gray. He was now forty-one years old. During that period Marina had become pregnant by her new husband, Jaramillo, and her daughter was born probably in 1526 during the voyage back to Veracruz, according to Lanyon (2004, 153).

The Fate of Marina: 1527–1530

Upon the return to Mexico City, Juan and Marina Jaramillo settled in a house a few blocks north of the famous Zócalo in Mexico City. As described by Lanyon (2004, 11ff.), Marina's son by Cortés was still being raised in the Altamirano family household only a few blocks south of the plaza, and we have no direct testimony of the relationship between Marina, Martín, and the Altamiranos. In Mexico City of 1527, she was well known and respected as a Christian woman, doña Marina, with lands and some wealth. She was especially esteemed by many of the troops who had witnessed the conquest. A house where tradition placed her late in life was sought out by Lanyon (1999, 17ff.) only a few blocks from the modern central plaza of Mexico City. It was a school when Lanyon visited in 1994.

Marina disappears from most accounts a year or so later. According to documents cited by Lanyon, Marina's daughter by Juan Jaramillo testified in a 1548 legal proceeding that her mother, Marina, had died about twenty years earlier. Independent records of a land grant petition from Marina and Juan Jaramillo in Mexico City indicate she was alive in early 1528 (Lanyon 1999) but suggest she might have passed away by mid-1532, when Juan Jaramillo remarried (Lanyon 2004, 68). Marina's date of death is controversial, however. Hugh Thomas (1995, 769, footnote 31) cites a letter by her son, Martín, indicating a house where she was supposedly living in 1551 and a second letter from her son-in-law indicating she had died at an undisclosed time prior to February 1552.

Cortés Makes a Journey to Spain: 1528–1530

In March 1528, the very year in which Lanyon suggests Marina died, Cortés left Mexico for Spain with their son, Martín. To go with them, Cortés organized a triumphal party, outdoing the gold-deficient triumphal returns staged by Columbus. Cortés brought three sons of Motezuma, about another forty Indians, including other lords of central Mexico, jugglers, acrobats, dwarfs, and hunchbacks, not to mention jaguars, pelicans, Aztec featherwork, and treasures of gold, silver, turquoise, and jade (Thomas 1995, 597). Cortés wanted to make a splash in Spain.

To understand the human situation between Marina and Cortés, we yearn to know how this trip relates to her death. Did she die a few months *before* Cortés took her son to Spain? Was Cortés trying to escape his own grief over the loss of his most faithful companion? Or did Marina die in grief *after* Cortés disappeared with her son to Europe? Or did she really live on until 1552? Perhaps a box in the archives in Mexico City, not fully cataloged, or a strongbox in the attic of some Mexican colonial hacienda will one day reveal news about the public and private life of the enigmatic couple, Cortés and "Malinche."

The roots of Cortés's trip to Spain seem to go back several years. In the summer of 1526 his past began to catch up with him. Because of his appointed position he was subject to performance reviews, which involved a commission of appointed magistrates known as the *juicio de residencia*, or, more commonly, the *residencia*. The system was Kafkaesque. Magistrates gathered a list of charges that were circulating—from hard evidence to gossip. The reviewee was a defendant; he was expected to provide evidence to refute any damaging charges. In other words, in this antecedent of the Napoleonic legal system, the defendant was supposed to prove he was innocent—the opposite of the current American system, where the prosecution has to prove the defendant is guilty.

That summer, in 1526, the residencia arrived with their list of questions. Shortly after they arrived, the chief judge died—reportedly after having dinner with Cortés. Then, oddly enough, a second magistrate died. Rumors circulated. Weren't these deaths of inconvenient critics remarkably like the death of Cortés's inconvenient wife? Cortés's situation was growing precarious.

During those same years, 1526 to 1528, gossip from Spain indicated that Cortés now had more enemies than friends in the court of King Carlos V. Cortés's bold return to Spain was thus an attempt to reinstate himself with the king and plead for authority to explore the South Sea. Thus he arrived in Spain in May 1528 with his favored son, Martín.

King Carlos V, in his role as head of the Holy Roman Empire, was holding court in various European cities, and Cortés had to chase him about, seeking an audience. Finally, a triumphal procession was held. The king was fascinated by the spectacle, and Cortés was able to present his case.

The results were mixed. On the up side, the king greeted him warmly, being intrigued by Cortés's glowing promises about the benefits of exploring the South Sea and searching for undiscovered lands that it might contain. Cortés suggested that these lands would surpass anything that had been seen so far. To Cortés's delight, King Carlos eventually granted him rights to explore and colonize such territories and appointed him "governor of the islands and lands that he might discover." Cortés was also granted the title marqués del Valle de Oaxaca, assigning him and his descendants baronial rights over large land grants in the general vicinity of Tenochtitlan. (Oaxaca, pronounced wa-HA-ka, is a Zapotec name now applying to a state of Mexico, southeast of Mexico City, with ports on the Pacific coast.)

On the down side, Carlos V prudently appointed a royal governing authority, or *audiencia*, to govern Mexico City in the future. Worse yet, he placed at its head an opponent of Cortés, Nuño de Guzmán, who was to have a notorious career in the next few years, as we'll soon see.

These developments left Cortés with a murky role vis-à-vis his own conquered city. In short, Cortés had grand titles and a mandate to make more discoveries, but he was shunted off to the sidelines, no longer with practical political power over the lands he had plundered.

Cortés took care of some other business while in Spain. He placed his favored son, Martín, who was now about seven years old, in a good position as a page in training at court and a member of the august Order of Santiago. More importantly, he arranged for the pope, Clement VII, to remove Martín's "stain of illegitimacy" and declare that Martín was now legitimate. The pontiff may have had a special sympathy for Martín: he was also illegitimate and had his own much beloved illegitimate son.

Perhaps mindful of appearances and social connections, Cortés also acquired a well-connected new wife in July 1529. She was Juana, daughter of a powerful family in Spain. The marriage was blessed by the king himself. She was to be the first *marquesa* of the Valley of Oaxaca. Historian Hugh Thomas (1995, 598) says Cortés was now the seventh-richest noble in all of Spain.

The Slave Raider of the Northern Frontier: 1530–1535

In Mexico the newly appointed governor, Nuño de Guzmán, began consolidating his new authority. The audiencia was initially supposed to be run by Guzmán himself, but it was soon reorganized under a group of ecclesiastics, leaving Guzmán free to pursue his fortune in the New World. By 1529 or 1530 Guzmán was governor at Pánuco, Cortés's northern outpost on the coast of the Gulf of Mexico. Here he was told by an Indian, Tejo, about seven cities in the North that Tejo had visited. This seemed to fit the report Cortés had received from his naval pilot, Luis Cárdenas, about prosperous northern cities. Tejo was probably speaking about the multiple Pueblo communities along the Rio Grande near modern Albuquerque or perhaps about smaller pueblos scattered downstream on the Rio Grande. Modern archaeological finds confirm that those communities traded for shells and other goods from the Gulf of Mexico and that such trade routes stretched south along the Rio Grande, bordering modern Mexico. Guzmán also apparently heard rumors of metal use inland toward the mountainous spine of Mexico. The rumors always seemed to indicate that the wealthy population centers were "más allá, más adentro" (farther on, more toward the interior).

All such rumors aroused Guzmán as much as they had aroused Cortés. Guzmán soon organized a large expedition to probe north and west. He found a way across the sierras, and in 1531 he founded the town of Culiacán on the Pacific coast, at the south end of the Gulf of California, where Cortés had already plied the waters. Historian Herbert Bolton pointed out that this Pacific coastal town was thus founded a full century before the city of Boston. It was the northernmost Spanish settlement on Mexico's west coast. From this post, Guzmán saw a get-rich-quick opportunity and raided north across the virgin frontier to capture Indians who would become servants and slaves to the Spanish. The present city, thriving with a population around 700,000, is located about 30 miles north of its original Guzmán site. Culiacán is a tourist destination for its marvelous colonial-era architecture, but since the 1990s it has suffered from wars between the new get-rich-quick conquistadors—the drug cartels.

The Return of Cortés: 1530–1532

Cortés, his mother, and his new wife returned to Mexico in 1530 with a retinue of four hundred, landing in mid-July at the port he had founded, Veracruz. His now-legitimate first son, Marina's son, Martín, was left in Spain to be trained at court. In Mexico City, the worst of the agitation against his personal life seems to have been defused by his new respectability. Reinvigorated, and with his new title of marqués del Valle de Oaxaca, he began to reestablish himself as a player in the race to the North.

On 16 January 1531, however, Guzmán wrote to the king in a confident style not unlike that of Cortés. His letter, quoted by historian A. Grove Day (1940, 372), mentions that he had heard rumors of the Amazon country, and he planned to go north up the coast as far as the fortieth parallel searching for it. He promptly began by probing a few days' travel north of Culiacán. Soon frustrated at finding neither golden glitter nor warrior women, Guzmán turned to a different plan: vicious slave-raiding forays that might not only pay his bills but also turn up new evidence of the rumored northern cities. Guzmán and Cortés were the primary names in a growing list of conquistadors who were betting heavily that a new fortune could be found beyond the northern frontier. A race was on.

Cortés's personal life took a new turn, as well. In 1532 he had a fully legitimate and proper son, whom he named after his father. In other words, there was now a third Martín Cortés, if we count the son of Motezuma who had already been named Martín Cortés Nezahualzolotl—much to the consternation of record keepers and future historians. That son of Motezuma was now out of the picture, as far as Cortés was concerned. He had been murdered by fellow Aztecs soon after his 1530 return from Cortez's trip to Spain, where he had taken a Spanish wife. Probably the murderers saw him as a traitor, as he had begun putting on the airs of a Spanish gentleman.

Cortés's love for his first son had not abated, even if Martín number one was back in Spain being educated. Late in 1532 the first Martín was temporarily ill, and Cortés wrote an anxious parent's letter to a cousin in Spain (Lanyon 2004, 70). Cortés begged for news about his son and confessed, "I do not love him less than the child God has given me through the marquesa, and . . . I therefore desire to know everything of him, always" (70). (These details are discussed further by Lanyon in her 2004 biography of Martín.)

News from Peru: 1531–1533

While Guzmán chased rumors of the seven northern cities in the early 1530s, a new story from the south spread like wildfire. Francisco Pizarro, along with his brother and various followers, had invaded Peru in 1531 and found another golden empire as spectacular as Tenochtitlan. They had captured the ruler, Atahualpa, called by the title "the Inca." Pizarro briefly spared his life in exchange for the greatest treasure ever, in excess of a million pesos' worth of gold and silver, in 1532–33. Later, he was sentenced to be burned alive, but a priest, claiming mercy, offered to reduce the sentence to garroting if Atahualpa would convert to Catholicism. The Inca ruler was duly strangled in 1532. By 1534 Pizarro, who by happenstance was a cousin of Cortés, sent a much appreciated "royal fifth" of gold to the king of Spain—larger than Cortés had managed to collect either in Tenochtitlan or in Michoacán. This not only pushed Cortés into a lower position but also seemed to prove once and for all that the New World was dotted with golden kingdoms. Where was the next empire waiting to be discovered?

News from Guzmán: 1532–1534

Guzmán, riding north on his sinister forays, pursued a profitable trade in human beings. He expanded his operation north along coastal plains and inland valleys, reaching the south end of modern Mexico's beautiful

northwestern state, Sonora. Here, around the Río Mayo, he and his henchmen rounded up hapless villagers and sold them as slaves to compatriots
farther south in New Spain. The local inhabitants abandoned their fields
and fled into the hills, leaving the area a deserted shambles by the mid-
1530s. Guzmán rode ever farther north for fresh victims. Soon he began
to hear additional vague but repeated rumors from local Indians about
wealthy cities to the north.

How far north did Guzmán's men reach? This is an important question
in interpreting the events of the next few years. Surviving documents suggest that the northernmost latitudes were reached by slave-raiding parties
led by Nuño de Guzmán's nephew, Diego de Guzmán, from August to
December 1533. One journal of the trip was written by Diego himself, and
a second "anonymous account" probably was written by another participant, Jorge Robledo, according to linguist-historians Rolena Adorno and
Patrick Pautz (1999, 2:347–48). The Spaniards were crossing unmapped
coastal plains and rivers, so their accounts are unclear about exact locations. Several rivers run southwest out of the foothills of the Sierra Madre
toward the Gulf of California (see map 5), and scholars argue about which
one is the northernmost river reached. Adorno and Pautz think that Diego
de Guzmán's troops got as far north as the lower Río Yaqui, but, as we'll
see (in chapter 5), Indians interviewed on the Yaqui in 1539 apparently
did not know much about the Spaniards and did not have specific information about the northern cities either. Plausibly, Guzmán's troops didn't
have much contact with Indians beyond the Río Mayo and heard only the
vaguest rumors about northern cities.

Cortés's First Naval Expedition North into the Gulf of California: The Lost Ships of June 1532

Meanwhile, Cortés was armed with his new assignments from the king, and
his plan was to discover the northern prize by using his ships to leapfrog
ahead of Guzmán. Cortés had already set up several ports and shipbuilding
facilities on the coastline south of Mexico City, including the now-famous
port of Acapulco, as mentioned by his biographer Francisco López de
Gómara ([1552] 1964, 396ff.).

His original goal in the 1520s had been to discover a rumored strait by
which ships could sail from the Caribbean, around the south tip of the
supposed island of Mexico, and then into the South Sea, thus supplying
the Spanish coastal settlements south and west of Mexico City. By 1532

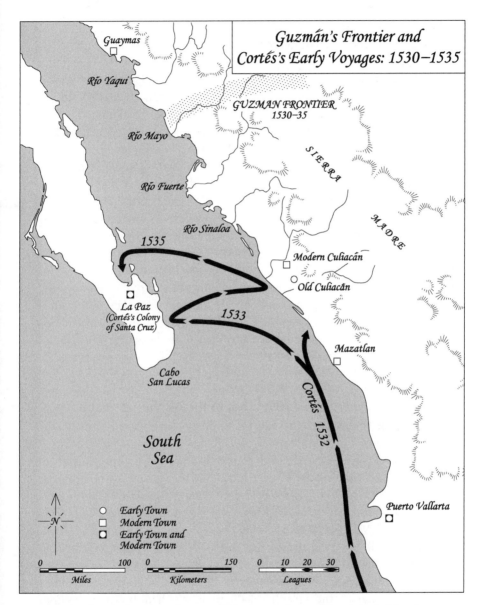

Map 5. The northernmost frontier of Guzmán's slave raiding (stippled band at the top). Guzmán operated out of Old Culiacán some miles south of the modern city. The arrows show the early naval explorations of Cortés, probing into the Gulf of California, which became known as the Sea of Cortés. Map by Ron Beckwith.

hopes for a naval route from the Caribbean to the Pacific were fading. (The problem was not solved until the building of the Panama Canal, opened in 1914.) Still, Cortés had a good shot at using his ships to win the race to the North, thus redeeming himself in the king's eyes . . . and perhaps in his own.

No one really understood what lay beyond the southwest coast of Mexico in the "South Sea." The inland arm of the Pacific, known as the Gulf of California, was not yet fully understood. Rumors persisted that Baja California, on the west side of the gulf, was an island, perhaps inhabited by the mysterious Amazons and Queen Califia. Cortés's troops set about to explore the gulf, hoping to find the source of the pearls that had been seen among the coastal Mexican Indians. Mightn't the pearls have arrived by trade from Cathay? Because of the voyages Cortés promoted, the Gulf of California is sometimes called by an old, alternate name: the Sea of Cortés.

In June 1532 Cortés ordered two ships built and sent northwest up the Mexican coast under the command of a cousin. This first attempt met an ignominious end when the ships arrived only at a part of the coast already controlled by Cortés's nemesis, Nuño de Guzmán. The fate of the ships themselves is uncertain. Diego de Guzmán's expedition in 1533 discovered what seems to have been the wreckage of one of them, apparently near the mouth of the Río Fuerte (Reff 1991, 35) (see map 5).

Cortés's Second Naval Expedition to the North: Mutiny and Murder in 1533

By October of the next year, 1533, Cortés had two more ships ready to go. He appointed captains and officers, journeyed to the shipyard, boarded the lead ship, and gave a rousing speech to the crew, explaining that the fleet would go in the service of His Majesty to discover new lands. California historian W. Michael Mathes quotes a description by one of the 1533 witnesses: "In his presence, all took a solemn oath that we would be faithful to the said service and obey the captain. After this, when we swore loyalty to him with the affection and good will he inspired in us, he embraced most of the men and left the galleon" (2000, 6). Cortés had shown many times that he was no slouch when it came to inspiring his men.

The ships set sail on 29 October 1533, but they were doomed to an even darker fate than that of the first expedition. As if to set the tone for the voyage, the smaller ship got stuck on a shoal while leaving port and was unable to free itself for several days. The two ships then sailed off together, but on the second night out in the gulf, a storm came up, and the ships were separated. The Gulf of California is notorious for unexpected squalls that, even today, can be life-threatening for fishing boats and pleasure craft. Probably the storm was to blame for the separation, although there has been speculation that the captain of the smaller ship took advantage of the situation to escape tensions that were already building among the crews. At any rate, the smaller ship went on to discover some islands and then returned to Mexico without incident in January 1534.

The larger ship, a galleon, sailed on toward disaster. The seeds of discontent seem to have come from the makeup of the crew. While most officers were from various parts of Spain, the important post of pilot-major was filled by a Basque named Fortún Ximénez. Most of the ordinary sailors were also Basque, so ethnic conflicts may have been at work. After a month of sailing, strange events ensued in the gulf on the night of 28 November 1533. The captain and various officers were sleeping. Shortly before midnight, Pilot-Major Ximénez (who was supposed to be on watch), his brother, and several sailors attacked the sleeping officers, bludgeoning them with clubs and swords. A few sailors, marooned after a few days, survived and gave testimony three weeks later in a special inquiry. Naval historian Mathes cites their vivid accounts, which I synthesize here:

> During the voyage, Ximénez showed the captain great courtesy and honor and never quarreled or fought with him or anyone else. . . . [But that night the captain slept] without thought of disturbance and without weapons, undressed to his shirt, and they attacked him with broadswords, daggers, and other weapons, slashing him on his head so severely that his brains came out, and giving him other stab wounds in his right arm and on his thigh. He fell off the chest on which he had been sleeping and they left him for dead, chained with irons on his feet. . . . They stabbed and wounded the other officers as they lay in their beds, undressed and unarmed. They were crying "Death to the traitors of the sea! Death to them! Long live the King and Señor Fortún Ximénez!" (2000, 7–8)

The officers would all have been killed on the spot except that three Franciscan friars, assigned to the expedition, interceded. The mutineers relented but bound and imprisoned the officers. The captain lingered in pain for three days and then died, and his body was thrown overboard. Ximénez announced that he was now captain. The galleon sailed along the coast for at least eleven days, and finally Ximénez put the officers and priests ashore at a desolate spot on the coast of Michoacán, a place known even today as Motines, the Mutinies. They were marooned with poor clothes and no equipment, not knowing how far it was to civilization. One friar and one sailor set off along the coast, trekking 15 to 20 miles before finding Indians, who led them to a Spanish settlement. The wounded survivors on the beach were then rescued, and their testimony was taken during an inquiry on 17 December 1533. At least one died soon after.

The mutineers, for their part, took the galleon northwest and hit the south tip of Baja California between La Paz and Cabo San Lucas (see map 5). Ironically, Ximénez and twenty-one mutineers were then killed on that desolate coast by local native inhabitants. The remaining hapless crew sailed back across the gulf to the mainland coast, where they were met by Nuño de Guzmán, who imprisoned them and kept the ship.

At the legal inquest, no firm conclusions were reached about motivations. Since the mutineers called the officers traitors and claimed to be for the king, one wonders if they perceived that Cortés and his officers once again were pursuing riches more for themselves than for the Crown. Ximénez hardly seemed a crusader for king and country, however. He did not set sail for Mexico with a list of charges against Cortés's officers but rather sailed in the other direction, away from the coast. Perhaps, like Cortés, he wanted to discover new wealthy lands in his own name and sort things out later.

An insight comes from the testimony of an envoy that Cortés sent to the inquest. He warned that if Ximénez had found "good lands," he would likely have reported them to some other nation, because he would have had neither means nor authority to conquer or settle the new lands himself. Such actions, by Ximénez or later pirates, would create a threat to further Spanish exploration, not to mention, of course, Cortés's considerable personal aspirations.

Cortés's Third Naval Expedition: Claiming Baja California in 1535

Confiscating Ximénez's property, Cortés now set out to get his ship back from Guzmán, taking personal command of a new expedition. He recovered the galleon and in 1535 sailed it across the gulf to the south end of Baja California, where he found the good harbor at La Paz and claimed the region for Spain on 3 May 1535. He tried to start a colony there, calling it Santa Cruz (map 5). The land, however, turned out to be exceedingly barren, harsh, and dry—except when hurricanes passed over. There was no exotic tribe of Amazon women, no Queen Califia, no gold.

Cortés's men did find modest numbers of pearls on the Baja coast. Also, he had already written to the king in his letter of October 1524, telling of "certain samples of pearls" found on the mainland coast and the rumors of an offshore island that "is very rich in pearls and gold" (Cortés [1519–26] 1991, 253). The actual numbers of pearls could not support a colony, however. Cortés's Baja California enterprise never attracted much interest and was soon defeated by the harsh desert environment. Cortés had to disband the colony in 1536.

By this time Cortés had gambled a fortune on exploration of the west coast of Mexico and still had little to show for it. In his mind, however, it was a long-term investment. He still nourished hopes that a new Tenochtitlan or Michoacán or Peru would be found to the north. If he could conquer such a place, he could not only replenish his personal treasury but also ship enough gold back to the king to make up for the Night of Sorrows. His dream of wealth in the North was about to be revived in a most unexpected way.

CHAPTER THREE

The Epic Journey of
Cabeza de Vaca and Friends

Because of the successes in Tenochtitlan, to the west in Michoacán, and southward in Peru, Spanish explorers competed not just to push north from Mexico City but also to branch out *northward* from Caribbean bases in Cuba and Hispaniola. One of the explorers from Cuba was an old enemy of Cortés—Pánfilo Narváez, the captain who had been sent from Cuba to the coast of Mexico to arrest Cortés for his unauthorized conquest of Mexico, only to lose an eye in his battle with Cortés's men on a pyramid. Narváez had managed to return to the good graces of officialdom. He had a red beard, a deep voice, one remaining eye, and poor leadership skills. Already he had participated in a massacre of Indians in Cuba and then joked about it in front of Bartolomé de Las Casas, the priest who fought for Natives' rights. Now he had a charter to explore La Florida, where he and other Spaniards still hoped to find another golden empire, or at least a rumored fountain with mineral waters that restored youthful vigor. It was still not known whether La Florida was an island or a new continent, nor was it fully understood what east–west distances separated La Florida from the discoveries in Mexico. North–south distances, or latitudes, could be measured within a hundred miles or so by observations of the stars, but, as recounted in Dava Sobel's 1995 best seller, *Longitude,* there was still no way to make reliable measures of longitudinal east–west distances.

Narváez's expedition, with several hundred men, set out from Cuba to explore Florida in 1528—the same year in which Cortés had sailed back to Spain to try to gain new authority in America from the king. His expedition was a disaster. After eight years of adventuring, only four participants survived to reunite with Spanish society. The four survivors' journey from modern Florida through Texas and then along the present U.S.-Mexico border (either north or south of it) and into Mexico is known mainly through writings associated with one of them, Álvar Núñez Cabeza de Vaca, who started out as the royal treasurer of the expedition. In 1528 he would have been somewhere between thirty-six and forty years old, the oldest of the four survivors. His strange family name (which translates as "head of a cow") was handed down from a famous ancestor who had used a cow's skull as a coded warning to alert Spanish troops to an unguarded pass in a famous Spanish victory over the Moors in 1212.

Cabeza de Vaca was involved in three slightly different written versions of the journey. The earliest version is known as the "Joint Report." It was apparently prepared in 1536, just after the ordeal, by Cabeza de Vaca and the three other survivors, who will be introduced in a moment. The original is lost, but a good summary exists, probably made between 1543 and 1547 by a later Spanish writer named Gonzalo Fernández de Oviedo y Valdés (see Hedrick and Riley 1974). Also in 1542 Cabeza de Vaca circulated his own personal memoir, which he followed with a revised edition, published in 1555. This memoir is still internationally in print today, more than four centuries later (Adorno and Pautz 1999; Covey 1961; Krieger 2002; Pupo-Walker 1993). Not a bad showing for a memoirist! Scholars still argue over which of the three versions is most accurate. In the quotes below, I will usually offer my own synthesis to avoid laborious comparisons of the three versions.

The documents of the Cabeza de Vaca party are not just a record of adventure; they provide a unique record of what I call the last days of prehistoric time across much of the southern United States. History begins, by definition, with writing, and the Narváez survivors produced the first written account of life in that region. Furthermore, as we'll see, their report motivated the Spaniards in Mexico City to expect, more than ever, another gold-laden city in what is now known as the American Southwest.

Ill-Fated Travels to Florida: 1528

Narváez's expedition involved one fiasco after another. After an initial loss of two ships and fifty men to hurricanes in Cuba, Narváez arrived on the west coast of Florida near Tampa Bay in April 1528 with several ships and an army of around four hundred men. Against strong arguments from Cabeza de Vaca, Narváez decided to split his men into a land party and a sea party, leaving about one hundred men in the ships with orders to sail along the coast, north and west, parallel to the troops. With some three hundred men and some horses, however, Narváez plunged inland, marching north to check out reports of "Indie-an" settlements. As we know today, this is one of America's most inauspicious coastal regions. It's hot. It's muggy. It has swamps full of mosquitoes, snakes, and alligators. The Spaniards found neither golden cities nor fountains of youth.

Cabeza de Vaca related that the troops were totally unprepared for an inland march in such country, and he describes how, in the first weeks, they found themselves struggling through "water up to the middle of our thighs, and stepping on oyster shells that gave us severe cuts on our feet." The ship captains, meanwhile, having lost contact with the army, gave them up for lost and returned to Cuba.

SIDEBAR: Problems with Reading the Old Documents

Readers of English translations of sixteenth-century Spanish documents (not to mention biblical-era and other ancient sources) need to be aware of the pitfalls in transforming the old reports into modern language. It's not just a simple matter of translating one word at a time into a modern equivalent. First of all, word meanings are mutable over multicentury timescales, and old idioms may not be clear today. As for distances, the Spaniards reported their estimates in leagues, but even the usage of "league" differed somewhat with time, person, and place (see the sidebar "How Long Was a League?" later in this chapter). Worse yet, sixteenth-century Spanish texts had few paragraph breaks, little punctuation, and many run-on sentences linked with innumerable "ands"—not to mention ambiguous pronouns and antecedents. Here's an imaginary example, constructed to illustrate some of these sins: "The captain and his guide met the people from that village and on the next morning they gave them news that a ship ran aground two days before on the coast and they saw it was true and they prepared a reception for them." It's often hard to be sure about the who, what, when, and where of the story. Written literature was still being created in the 1500s. Divisions of the old texts into modern paragraphs and distinct topics have been introduced by modern translators. In a few key cases, however, one translator favors a meaning different from that of another translator. Scholarly arguments abound.

Scattered in the forests were modest agricultural towns, remnants of the mound-builder cultures of the Southeast. Like many indigenous American cultures, the mound builders peaked around the A.D. 1200s, with large, well-planned towns, trade networks, and earthen pyramids. By the 1400s and 1500s they had reverted to smaller villages. Narváez's army soon encountered stories of a major Indian town called Apalachee and thought it might be a ticket to their own private Tenochtitlan. When they reached the town, near modern Tallahassee at the east end of the Florida Panhandle, they found no more than a few trinkets of gold, along with maize, deerskins, and about forty houses of straw-like brush, "built low and in sheltered places because of the fear of the great storms that occur all the time in that region." After reaching a second similar town, they gave up hope that Florida had anything to offer and realized they were stranded in what we would call the Florida Panhandle. "We saw how little possibility there was of going forward, for there was nowhere to go," says Cabeza de Vaca in a forlorn statement. "Even if the men had wanted to continue, they couldn't, because most of them were ill."

In a daring decision, Narváez ordered construction of five boats. The expedition would sail west along the coast until they came to the Spanish settlements they had heard about, such as Pánuco. They couldn't know that Pánuco was about 900 miles away around the curve of the Gulf of Mexico coast.

"Everyone thought it was impossible," Cabeza de Vaca says, "because we didn't know how to make boats, nor did we have the tools, iron, forges, or pitch or rigging." They decided to sleep on it. Next day, "Robinson Crusoe creativity" kicked in.

> God willed that one of our company came forward to say that he could make some wooden tubes and rig a bellows with deerskins . . . and we decided to make nails and saws and axes and other tools out of the stirrups and spurs and crossbows and other bits of iron that we had. To get food, we made four forays to the [nearest] town, and every third day we'd kill a horse. . . . A Greek, don Teodoro, made a kind of tar-like pitch from the pine trees. From palmetto fiber and the horses' tails and manes we made cords, and from our shirts we made sails.

In six weeks they finished five boats, each thirty to thirty-five feet long and big enough to hold about forty-eight men. It was a feat beyond most modern adventurers.

A Desperate Voyage: Autumn 1528

On 22 September, having eaten nearly all the horses, they sailed west along the coast, running out of water in about thirty days. Trying to get water and food, they skirmished along the way with coastal Indians who came out in canoes. In the midst of one such fight, Cabeza de Vaca relates,

> my boat, which was ahead of the others, came to a point formed by the land, and on the other side was a very wide river. I gave orders to drop anchor on a little island. The governor [Narváez] refused to join us and put into a bay with more little islands. So we gathered there and were able to take fresh water out of the sea, because there was a strong current of fresh water where the river emptied. We went ashore to roast some of our maize, which we'd been eating raw. Since we found no firewood, we decided to go around the point to the river. As we moved the boats, the current became so strong that it carried us away from the land, even though we struggled to reach it. The north wind coming off the shore swept us farther out to sea against our will. We tried to drop anchor but could find no bottom. For two days we sailed, trying to reach land.

Cabeza de Vaca's account marks the Europeans' 1528 discovery of the Mississippi River. Carried seaward by the mighty flow, the boats were now separating. Cabeza de Vaca's crew caught sight of only two others. Catching up to the closest one, they found it was captained by Narváez, who called out to ask what Cabeza de Vaca thought they should do. Cabeza de Vaca counseled catching up to the third boat, but Narváez said it was too far ahead, and that he wanted to land, and that they would have to row for it. "Since the governor's boat had the healthiest people among us, we could not keep up. I asked him to throw us a line, but he answered that they'd be lucky to survive themselves. I asked what his orders were for us then, and he said, this was no time for orders; it was every man for himself." Such were the last words of Narváez in the history books. The rest of his story would emerge later.

After four days in a storm, Cabeza de Vaca's party lost sight of the one remaining boat. In the dim light of dawn, Cabeza de Vaca heard waves breaking on a shore, and they turned toward the shoreline: "A wave tossed the boat out of the water, and with this great jolt, the half-dead men came to their senses, began to slip over the side, and crawled on hands and knees onto the land, where they found some protected gullies with water. We made a fire, cooked some of our maize and found some rainwater, and with the heat of the fire the men began to revive and their spirits picked up."

It was the sixth of November. Seven months after they had landed in Florida, they were marooned on or near Galveston Island, south of modern-day Houston, Texas.

Among the Texas Coastal Indians: 1528–1533

Various groups of half-starved Spaniards washed up on this coast in different locations. They soon encountered unclothed, barely fed bands of Indians, who lived on the flat, green, humid Texas coast amidst pine and deciduous woodlands. After bartering beads and bells for food, Cabeza de Vaca's group tried to launch their boat and sail on, but waves capsized the boat. Several men were drowned, and the survivors were thrown onshore essentially naked. They were cold and wet, and the weather was stormy. Cabeza de Vaca remarked that "firewood was scarce and mosquitoes plentiful." More survivors died, but in the first days, the Indians were helpful and took some of them in. Soon they heard stories that other Spaniards were stranded nearby.

The surviving Spaniards were thus assimilated into different villages, but their treatment deteriorated, and they were forced into servitude. Cabeza de Vaca said, "They worked me so hard, I couldn't bear the life I led, and decided to flee to some people who lived in the forest on the mainland. My fingers were so worn from pulling roots that a light brush with some straw would make them bleed." After some months he moved to the mainland group and established a role as trader with various other tribes. In this role, he made various journeys of 40 leagues (100 to 124 miles) and more.

Cabeza de Vaca, though unhappy, was lucky. From the viewpoint of the local inhabitants, captured enemies were the lowest social caste and were assigned to various menial tasks. Some were killed at once. Regarding this period, the Joint Report commented, "No one [of us] could count on staying alive from one day to the next." Cabeza de Vaca went inland with his own captors on their summer migrations to pick the seasonal fruit of prickly pear cactus, still a food staple today in many parts of Central and South America, where it is known as "tuna fruit."

From time to time, news arrived about other survivors in the region. Amidst one group stranded in the fatal November storm, the starved Spaniards ate the flesh of the ones who had died. The last of them, named Esquivel, survived until March 1529. According to this report, the friars in that group thought (incorrectly) that their boats had already gone past Pánuco. Esquivel, when last heard from, had planned to escape and backtrack toward the east. In another group, four hikers and strong swimmers were sent off to try to reach Pánuco and organize a rescue, but nothing came of that either. Some of those four were later reported killed. (Interestingly, unbeknownst to Cabeza de Vaca, two other Spaniards survived and were encountered in 1539 by the expedition of Hernando de Soto.)

News of Narváez finally surfaced. His boat had reached some of his soldiers and friars stranded on the coast. He picked them up and helped them across a river that interrupted the coastline. The men camped onshore, but Narváez decided to stay that night on his boat with the mate and a page. In the middle of the night, the wind blew the boat out to sea without anyone realizing it. Narváez and his "crew" had no water, no food, and no anchor. They were never seen again.

Cabeza de Vaca hung on to his life in this region for five years. News of other Spaniards diminished. One day, during a trip to a region where various villagers converged to harvest the prickly pears, he suddenly found himself reunited with three other survivors: Andrés Dorantes, who was a

---

SIDEBAR: How Long Was a League?

Spanish travelers of this period reported distances in terms of leagues. To deduce where they were requires us to know the length of the league as used by Spaniards at that time. The term was often just an estimate based on travel time and refers to distance along a trail, not the air line distance. In the larger expeditions, like Coronado's, participants were often assigned to keep a count of the number of paces, giving a somewhat more reliable distance estimate. Still, the league could vary somewhat from one writer to another and from generation to generation. In the case of Cabeza de Vaca, the uncertainty is compounded by the fact that he and his friends were trying to recall their experiences much later. Published studies suggest a range of possible values. Among my sources, George Undreiner in 1947 favored about 3.0 miles; Cleve Hallenbeck ([1949] 1987, 46, 98, 100), 3.1 miles; and Madeleine Turrell Rodack (Bandelier [1886] 1981), 2.6 miles. In the Spanish colonial period (1700s), the league was closer to 2.5 miles (Ives 1975; Chambers 1975, citing Gilbert Sykes, who cited Pedro Font in 1775); Roland Chardon (1980) infers that it may have had two different values, about 2.6 miles and 3.5 miles. Based on all this, for our interpretations in the 1500s, I attempt prudence by using a range of values, 2.5 to 3.1 miles. For example, if a traveler reports a journey of 10 leagues, I allow that the distance was likely in the range of 25 to 31 trail miles.

captain under Narváez; Estevan de Dorantes (Estevan of Dorantes), who was Dorantes's black Moorish servant; and, from a different Indian village, an expeditionary named Alonso Castillo. They hadn't seen each other for nearly five years. "That day," reported Cabeza de Vaca, "was one of the happiest of our lives."

Dorantes told how he had been isolated with an Indian group for ten months, digging roots for them. He recounted how they would sometimes run toward him with bow and arrow, fiercely pulling the bow back to their ear with the arrow aimed directly at him . . . and then laugh and say, "Were you afraid?"

The four made secret plans to meet during the next summer's prickly pear harvest and escape inland. Anything would be better than what they had experienced so far.

The year was now 1533, the same year in which Diego de Guzmán was probing north toward Sonora, and mutiny was ending Cortés's second expedition northward into the Gulf of California.

Wandering across West Texas: 1534

The intrepid four escaped in the late summer or fall of 1534. Sneaking away from their respective tribal groups, they rendezvoused in the cactus country of southeastern coastal Texas, probably dozens of miles inland, somewhere between Galveston and San Antonio. Now began one of the epic adventures of North American exploration. It was not a grand crusade with flags flying and armor glinting but a desperate walkabout by shipwrecked castaways. They had no chroniclers, no logbooks. They did not know where they were, except for local informants' descriptions of the regional trade routes to unfamiliar places. They did not know which way to go, except to start toward the west. They had no Spanish weapons or survival equipment. Nonetheless, they were able to cultivate the goodwill of people they encountered and find their way to New Spain.

Their written account was prepared after the journey, and even then, there were no maps for them to trace where they had been. They could describe the trip only in terms of a river here, a mountain there, the practices of peoples they visited, and numbers of days between landmarks.

Today, the problem for historians is to try to figure out where they went by matching their descriptions with modern landmarks or archaeological sites. Every generation or so, new scholars take a crack at this intellectual treasure hunt, utilizing the latest historical information. Reconstruction of the early routes is not just an amusing pastime but a quest for a priceless missing link: eyewitness reports of American life in specific places during the last days of prehistoric time. Only by combining all the Spanish descriptions of Native American towns, people, and behavior in the 1500s can we fill in the gap between archaeologists' mute arrowheads, bones, and pottery sherds, on the one hand, and the much better records kept in the 1600s and 1700s on the other.

Of our four "reporters," Andrés Dorantes was perhaps the best known at that time. He was an officer of the Narváez expedition, and, after the ordeal, he was the one most often mentioned in the records from Mexico City. He'd be the first one tapped in Mexico City to try to establish a route back to the north. Cabeza de Vaca was the one who became famous by virtue of his memoir. Alonso Castillo, who had been a captain in Narváez's army, soon faded into obscurity after the journey. The most intriguing personality, however, was the dark-skinned Moorish servant of Dorantes, Estevan de Dorantes, sometimes called Estevan the Black or Estevanico. As we'll see, he played a later, ill-fated role in the subsequent European discovery of the American Southwest. His exact racial background and appearance are uncertain. Oviedo, who edited the surviving version of the Joint Report, says that Estevan was born in the Moroccan coastal town of Azamor, which is about 40 miles southwest of Casablanca and about 250 miles southwest of Gibraltar and Tangiers (Hedrick and Riley 1974, 80). Morocco is a melting pot of lighter-skinned North Africans and darker-skinned groups from the south. Since he was known to the Spaniards as Estevan the Black and remembered in Indian legends as dark skinned and thick lipped, he may have had at least some sub-Saharan heritage. He seems to have been the most charismatic and outgoing of the wandering group. As the party approached new villages, he was the one who usually went ahead and established rapport in the next village. He was described at least once in the Cabeza de Vaca records as always chatting with the local people.

Ever since the old Spanish records became well known in the late 1800s, historians have argued about the route of these four. We can hardly blame the castaways for imprecise information. If you drove across Texas without a map, primarily on back-country roads, keeping no day-by-day log, would you be able, a year later, to give a clear description of where you went? Modern scholars' proposed routes for the castaways' journey across Texas look like a tangle of strings tossed casually on a map of the state. Generally, the strings wander from Galveston to the western tip of Texas.

There are two broad categories of routes. The more popular ones go inland from the coast, then bend west toward the Rio Grande and upstream to El Paso, about 300 miles inland. The others follow the coast southwest toward Pánuco, crossing the Rio Grande near its mouth, and then finally turning northwest into Chihuahua. All routes converge, more or less, where the castaways crossed the Continental Divide somewhere near the southwest corner of New Mexico. Then they headed south across what is now the Mexican state of Sonora in search of other Spaniards.

To a modern reader with a map such as our map 1, the decision to head west across the mountains may seem odd. Why didn't they simply follow the Gulf Coast all the way to a Spanish colony such as Pánuco? The answer is that they had no such map. They were especially unsure of their position in the east–west direction because of the problem of uncertain longitudes in those days. More importantly, they'd heard that earlier attempts to reach Pánuco had failed, with some of those involved killed by coastal Indians.

Becoming Shamans: 1534–1535

The four Spaniards had been slaves to coastal villagers, but their status changed once they got "on the road." After spending some months regaining their physical strength among the first group they reached, they pressed on to another group who regarded them with awe and brought people to be touched by them. In one of the towns, Cabeza de Vaca says,

> the very night we arrived, some Indians came to Castillo, saying their heads hurt, and begging him to cure them. After he made the sign of the cross and commended them to God, they said their pain was gone. They went back to their huts and brought him many prickly pears and a piece of venison. News of this spread among them, and many people came that night to be cured. Each brought a piece of venison, and soon we had so much we didn't know where to put it! After the healings, they began to dance, and the festivities lasted until dawn. This merrymaking, caused by our arrival, lasted three days.

After a couple of weeks of further wandering and a narrow escape when Cabeza de Vaca was lost without any supplies, they moved into lands with more prickly pear cacti for food. They were already known as mysterious traveling shamans.

> Many Indians gathered, and they brought five people who were crippled, and in poor condition. They wanted Castillo to heal them. At sunset, Castillo made the sign of the cross and commended them to God, and

as best we could, we all asked God to restore their health, since He knew it was the only way those people could help us escape from this miserable life. God was so merciful that on the next morning, the patients awakened well, and departed as if they had never been sick. This caused great astonishment among the people, and it made us thank our Lord enthusiastically for showing us His kindness, and giving us hope that He would get us out to a place where we could serve Him. As for me, I can say I always had faith in His mercy. Many times I said to my companions that He'd bring us out of captivity.

These scenes are reminiscent of nothing less than the New Testament. Villagers invested great faith in the marvelous new teachers who appeared in their midst. For their part, the Spaniards seemed to struggle with the role imposed upon them, having some trepidation about dealing in possible dark arts. But for the first time in years, they were beginning to allow themselves optimism that they could survive among the unknown peoples of the uncharted interior—survive long enough, that is, to reach other Spaniards. One occasion of healing was especially noteworthy:

Castillo was a timid physician, especially when the cases were extreme. He thought his sins would prevent a successful healing. The Indians told me to heal them because they liked me and remembered an earlier time when I had helped someone feel better. . . . When I got to their huts, along with Dorantes and Estevan, I concluded that the sick man we were supposed to heal was already dead, because many people were weeping, and his lodge was dismantled, as the sign of his passing. When I got to him, I saw his eyes were turned back, and he had no pulse. It seemed to me that he showed all the signs of death. Dorantes agreed. I removed a mat that covered him and beseeched our Lord to restore his health and grant health to all who needed it.

After I made the sign of the cross and breathed on him many times, they took me to cure others who had the sleeping sickness. Then we returned to our dwellings. The Indians who had come with us remained behind.

The translation as "sleeping sickness" is interesting because that is known today as an African disease, spread by the tsetse fly, in which the victim experiences fever, headaches, apathy, and profound sleepiness. In the worst cases, it can be fatal. The concept may have been known to the Spaniards and may give an idea of the symptoms they witnessed, but is not likely to have been present in Texas in 1534–35. Whatever the sickness was, the villagers returned to us later that night, saying that the man who seemed dead had gotten up, walked, eaten, and spoken with them and that the others had gotten better too and were very happy! This caused great wonder and awe, and throughout the land people spoke of nothing else. Our fame spread. People who heard about it came looking for us so we could heal them and bless their children.

We remained with this group for eight months (noting the time by the moon's phases). People came to us saying we were children of the sun. Until then, Dorantes and Estevan the Black had performed no healings, but finally we all did it because so many people insisted. We never treated anyone who didn't later claim to be cured, and they were so confident about our cures that they believed none of them would die as long as we remained among them.

Some rationalists of the nineteenth and mid-twentieth centuries tend to ignore or reject these accounts of healings as impossible. Anthropologist Daniel Reff, known for his work on the rapid spread of European diseases among Native Americans in the 1500s and 1600s, suggested that the various peoples met by Cabeza de Vaca's party had heard about Motezuma's fall a dozen years earlier, so their illnesses were associated with stress and terror. This idea may apply later, as we'll see, but there is no evidence in this part of the trek that the local informants knew anything about fearful Spanish invaders. Rather, Cabeza de Vaca's account emphasizes joyful greetings in this region.

As mentioned earlier, other twentieth-century scholars applied theories of contextual analysis to the fifteenth-century records. This involves the idea that an individual's words cannot be understood without analyzing influences from his or her culture and role in society. The methods are valuable but problematic because they can devalue simple, direct observations as useless reflections of cultural bias. Historians in this camp "explain away" the reported healings by portraying Cabeza de Vaca and his friends as hopeless victims of their own cultural imagery, unwittingly creating pale imitations of Bible stories. If this approach is adopted without common sense, plain sentences can be dismissed as symbolic smoke and cultural mirrors. In extreme cases, such work ignores the need to reconstruct what actual events, if any, triggered the descriptions. It ignores, too, what might be learned by relating the descriptions to similar reports at other times in other cultures.

The practical application of contextual analysis to our explorers remains unclear. The method tends to produce relatively impenetrable academese. Even Reff, an important researcher, concludes his 1996 article about "text and context" in the Cabeza de Vaca report as follows: "The challenge facing the reader is to determine how inter-textuality, broadly defined, articulates with cultural-historical contingencies, fueling text-formation processes. The issue is an empirical one that can be resolved only by affording research priority to literary as well as cultural-historical contingencies, broadly defined." I think this means that in order to understand the Spaniards' accounts, we should consider their cultural background while evaluating their observations.

My own conclusion is that the castaways' accounts are more plain-spoken, sober, and significant than admitted by many contextual critics. The authors were trying to report what they experienced. What may be important in the stories of healings is the deep role of human suscepti-bility to suggestion and naive faith. If biblical accounts, Cabeza de Vaca's accounts, and TV evangelism are viewed as anthropological documents (as they must be), then we have repeated indications that naive onlookers, with little sophistication about modern psychology, can be enthralled when a charismatic teacher or healer comes to town. Individuals suffering certain kinds of maladies may declare themselves improved or cured. Even in the twentieth century, certain Native American communities divided maladies into "white man diseases" and "Indian diseases." A compound fractured leg may benefit from Western medicine, but a problem rooted in psycho-logical stress may respond better to shamanic practices familiar within the community. Cabeza de Vaca is very clear in describing the villagers' faith in the alien healers; the body's capability to cure itself (at least temporarily) is still a realm of mystery not fully clarified by either Western, Eastern, or Native American medicine. The Joint Report, prepared by all four travelers before Cabeza de Vaca wrote his memoir, wisely and wittily puts the whole case much more succinctly than most moderns might: "If the Christians did not cure all of them, at least the Indians believed they could cure them."

At the same time, Cabeza de Vaca's group dealt with bloodier maladies. For example, Cabeza de Vaca in a later village gives a vivid description of removing a bone arrowhead that was lodged in one man's chest; he made incisions, removed the point, "stanched the blood flow with scraping from a hide," made two stitches, and removed the stitches later.

How Far Inland?: 1535

The big controversy about the route in Texas is whether Cabeza de Vaca and friends traveled through the center-west part of the state or stayed near the coast. This affects where they traveled once they got into Mexico, which, in turn, affects our understanding of later explorations by other Spaniards. A three-volume 1999 study of the Cabeza de Vaca party by linguist-historians Rolena Adorno and Patrick Pautz argues for an extreme southern route, following the Gulf Coast and curving west and south well into Chihuahua in an aborted effort to reach Pánuco. However, the Joint Report of the four travelers says that

> the natives tried hard to take the Spaniards [south] toward the sea . . . but the Spaniards refused to go there. They preferred going inland [north and west] because they were disillusioned by the coastal Indians. Also, they had always been told [in order to cross the mountains and reach the supposedly richer provinces on the South Sea] to go not toward the sea but toward the sunset. They were afraid to try it and preferred to go further inland. . . . And in that manner they advanced 80 leagues [about 200 to 250 miles], traveling by way of the mountain foothills, and entering the interior of the land, going directly toward the north.

A subsequent document by an eyewitness chronicler of the Coronado expedition named Pedro de Castañeda recorded an incident that happened in 1541, giving a clue about their route. In 1541 Coronado's army camped at a site called Blanco Canyon, south of Amarillo at the base of the Texas Panhandle. (We'll see more details in chapter 11.) Castañeda says that near here they were told that "Cabeza de Vaca and Dorantes had passed this way" (Flint and Flint 2005, 409). The Indians piled up hides and other gifts for the Spaniards, and when Coronado arrived with his soldiers, the troops fell on the pile voraciously and stripped it to the ground in fifteen minutes. Castañeda then describes how, among the Indians, "the women and some others cried because they had believed that [the members of the expedition] would not take anything from them, but would bless [their things], as Cabeza de Vaca and Dorantes had done when they passed through this place" (409).

These accounts suggest that the Cabeza de Vaca party traveled into west-central Texas instead of following the Gulf Coast south toward Pánuco. Castañeda's wording makes it sound as if the Indians had seen the castaways at this very location but does not rule out the possibility that the castaways had been seen during the Indians' peregrinations farther south. As we'll see in a sidebar, Indians in 1583 at the confluence of the Rio Grande and the Río Conchos, about 450 air line miles inland from the coast, also told stories about Cabeza de Vaca's party passing through that area. That locale is about 340 air line miles southwest of Blanco Canyon, but the Rio Grande itself passes as close as 280 air line miles south of Blanco Canyon. Since the castaways said they initially spent some time traveling due north before turning west, they may have reached points within 200 to 300 miles of Blanco Canyon.

The Last Day of Prehistory in Texas: 1535

The Cabeza de Vaca party's reports give invaluable anthropological views of Native American life at the end of prehistoric time. In the whole region from the Galveston coast inland, a man lived with a woman "until there was a disagreement, then they marry whoever else they please." This was remarkable to the Spaniards, because proper sexual relationships in Europe had to be legalistically confirmed and thus required legalistic action to dismantle. Relatively casual associations persisted among these people until children were born, but "those who have children remain with their wives and do not leave them." In cases of spousal disputes, fistfights could erupt, and then "women separate them by coming between them, but the men won't do this. Afterward, the men go to their lodges and the wives go live in the wilderness until their anger subsides, after which they behave as if nothing had happened."

As for child raising, "all through this region, men don't sleep with their wives from the time they notice they are pregnant until the child is two years old. Children nurse at the breast until age twelve, when they can forage for food for themselves. They said it was because of the great hunger in that land."

As for other aspects of life,

these people don't have any system to count time by the sun or moon, nor do they keep track of the month. They keep track of time by the different seasons when fruits ripen or fish die, and they are very skilled at knowing when the different constellations appear. We all walked naked with them, covering ourselves at night with deerskins. We were hungry for six of the eight months!

When the prickly pears ripened (summer, 1535), we moved on, to another group of Indians. . . . We still went naked all the time. Since we weren't used to it, we shed our skins twice a year like serpents. The sun and air cause large sores on our chests and backs, which hurt especially because the ropes of the loads we carried cut into our skin.

As the Spaniards trekked across Texas and became famous, the custom was that a group from village A would lead them to village B. Villagers at B, having heard of the wondrous strangers, would meet them with gifts. Cabeza de Vaca's party then gave the gifts to the villagers from village A, who returned home "the happiest people in the world." Then, after a day or so, guides from village B would lead them to the next town. In this way, the Spaniards soon found themselves traveling from town to town with crowds of two or three hundred enthused followers.

To put these events in a larger context, Cortés's ships in these years had been plying the waters of the Gulf of California, trying to find out more about the same lands that Cabeza de Vaca's group was approaching.

The Bell Heard round the World: ca. 1535

Somewhere, probably in west Texas, after trekking 50 to 80 leagues (125 to as many as 250 miles) north upstream along one or more rivers and into the interior, according to both the Joint Report and Cabeza de Vaca's later report, the Spaniards came to a community of forty dwellings. Here they met people who, following the custom, gave the travelers so many of their possessions that the Indians in Cabeza de Vaca's party could carry only half of them. "We told the Indians who had given these things to take back the remainder so it would not go to waste, but they replied they would certainly not do it, because it was not their custom to take back something they had given away"—the exact opposite of the cliché of the "Indian giver."

According to the 1542 and 1555 memoirs of Cabeza de Vaca, another gift soon appeared. (This quote and the following quote are synthesized from translations by Favata and Fernández 1993; Pupo-Walker 1993; and Krieger 2002.)

> Among other things they gave us, Andrés Dorantes received a big, heavy copper bell, with a face engraved on it [see fig. 3]. The Indians valued it highly. They said they had acquired it from other Indians who were their neighbors. When we asked them where such a thing had come from, they said it had been brought from the north, and that there was much of it there, and it was greatly esteemed. And we concluded that in the places where it came from there were foundries, and that they cast metal in molds.

A day later they crossed some mountains and came to another small village, this time "on the banks of a very beautiful river," possibly one of the

Figure 3. Examples of copper bells commonly found in prehistoric sites. Small bells (from "Snaketown" site in southern Arizona) are about the size of a quarter, and the larger bell, with incised decorations, is similar to the description of the one given to Dorantes in west Texas. It was found in a site in the San Pedro River valley near Mammoth, Arizona, northeast of Tucson (see map 10). From site context, archaeologist Emil Haury suggested this bell dates from about 1300 to 1400. Copper analysis suggests such bells were made west and south of Mexico City and traded northward into the American Southwest (see map 1). Photo courtesy Arizona State Museum.

turns of the Rio Grande. (Because of its famous "big bends," the Rio Grande could have been crossed three times by travelers moving west—first flowing south, then north, then south again.) The villagers gave them buffalo hides, beads, and bags containing shiny mica and kohl, which the women used for painting their faces. Cabeza de Vaca's memoir tells us: "We showed them the bell we were carrying, and they said that in the region where it came from, there were many sheet-like plates of that metal buried in the ground, a thing held in much esteem. They also said that the houses there were permanent. We think the area must be on the South Sea, because we always heard that the South Sea is richer than the one in the north."

These statements are much more important than they may seem at first glance, because they triggered in the minds of the Cabeza de Vaca party (and their later listeners) a vision of the geography just north of their route. Thus, it's useful to be as clear as possible about what Cabeza de Vaca meant. Fortunately, we can compare his statements above to the text of the Joint Report, prepared by the castaways months after they exited the wilderness and available in Oviedo's copy. The following quote is synthesized from translations by archaeologist Alex Krieger in 2002 and historians Basil Hedrick and Carroll Riley in 1974, with additional discussions about terminology from Coronado scholar Richard Flint (private communication, 1999).

> [The Indians] gave [them] a copper bell and some blankets of cotton. They said these came from the north, traversing across the land toward the South Sea. The next day [Cabeza de Vaca's party encountered other Indians, who] told them that the people who gave them the bell had a lot of them (or a lot of that metal), even if they hadn't given them more. The travelers deduced that [in the place] where this bell came from, though it was not gold [or "though there exists no gold"?], there was a mining settlement, and the people there did smelting (although by our deduction that place must have been on the coast of the South Sea).

This somewhat opaque passage contains crucial roots of the soon-to-come Spanish expeditions of exploration and conquest from Mexico into the American Southwest. The logic is decipherable by combining the Joint Report with Cabeza de Vaca's memoir. The bell came from a trade center north of the Cabeza de Vaca route in a land of permanent houses. Sources of copper were available to those people in some form, presumably mines. Therefore, some major city in the North must have metalworkers. This was no shadowy myth of seven bishops' cities but direct information. The copper bell was the proof. It was probably about fist sized and spheroidal, with an engraved image, a design popular at the time (fig. 3). Bells of this type and, even more common, sleigh bell–like designs about an inch across have been found by modern archaeologists in late prehistoric village sites throughout wide areas in New Mexico, Arizona, and Sonora, as described by archaeologist Victoria Vargas, 1995.

Combining the accounts above with what we know today, we infer that Cabeza de Vaca's party was in west Texas when they were given the bell and that the bell came from one of the pueblos to the north, in New Mexico. Furthermore, the Indian testimony that the metal was easily found in the ground was not far-fetched. As was to be discovered by later Spaniards in the 1700s, the Southwest was full of various ores that in reality were mostly unexploited by the Native Americans. The state of Arizona was named for such a mine at "Arizonac," on the Sonora border, where silver was found in 1736 lying in large pieces on the ground. Similarly, as we'll see in a sidebar in chapter 4, pieces of raw copper were probably known at Casas Grandes, a multistory pueblo from the 1200s that is now a very impressive ruin just south of the New Mexico border in Chihuahua.

The next step in the castaways' logic was their belief that the coast of the South Sea (the Pacific) had towns richer than the miserable villages along the coast of the Gulf of Mexico. (This was true in Michoacán.) If the copper bell came from a prosperous area to the north, then the Pacific coast itself, or some inlet of it, must curve around to the north of where they were located. This seemed not unlikely. After all, if Mexico was another Caribbean island off the coast of Cathay, like Cuba and perhaps La Florida, then the seacoast must curve around to the north. Hence, Cabeza de Vaca's party deduced that some wealthy metalworking urban center lay near the Pacific coast, north of their route. As we'll see in the next chapters, their deduction (although highly incorrect) had important consequences.

Along the Rio Grande: 1535

Cabeza de Vaca claims that they soon had three to four thousand people traveling with them, but due to the apparent sixteenth-century idiomatic Spanish exaggeration of large numbers, we might guess the numbers were closer to three or four hundred.

The travelers reported crossing several large rivers in the next days, and, as usual, it's hard to tell exactly what river is being described in any given instance. They were apparently in the vicinity of the Pecos River and the Rio Grande, approaching the mountainous country (probably the Fort Davis Mountains; see map 6). In this area, they encountered new tribal groups, one of whom, unlike the celebrating villagers who greeted them in west-central Texas, were downcast about their arrival. "So great was their fear that during the first days we were with them, they were always trembling, without daring to speak or raise their eyes." These people seem to have been close to the Rio Grande, so that in this case we can adopt Reff's 1996 hypothesis that they may have heard through the Rio Grande grapevine about the Spanish invasion to the south. Guzmán's men in Pánuco had heard rumors of the Rio Grande pueblos, and it's likely that news traveled both ways along the river (see map 1). Thus, villagers along the Rio Grande valley may have heard alarming news about aggressive strangers to the south.

Nonetheless, these people guided them on through 50 leagues (125 to 155 miles) of empty plains and across rugged mountains until they eventually reached a village on what seems to have been the Rio Grande. From that point on, some of the people who had come with them began to fall ill from hunger and the difficulties of crossing the rugged mountains.

> We told [the villagers] we wanted to go toward the sunset, but they said there were no people in that direction for a long way. We told them to send messengers [along the best route] to announce we would come, but they declined, because, as best we could understand, those people were their enemies. Still, they didn't want to disobey us, so they sent two women, since women can negotiate even during a war. . . . After they were gone five days, the local Indians said they must not have found anyone.
>
> We proposed they might lead us north, but they said there were no people in that direction either, except far away, and there was no good food or water on that route. We insisted, they refused, and we became angry. One of those nights I went out to sleep on my own, and they became very fearful, and came out to spend the night where I was, begging us not to be angry anymore, and saying they'd take us, even though they thought they might die along the way.

Cabeza de Vaca says the Indians who were to lead them (perhaps already weakened by hunger) became so upset that many fell ill, and at some point, eight died. After relations improved, those who were still ill recuperated.

Regarding the travel directions, we can make sense of the Indians' reluctance to go west or north. A journey west would take them into the rugged mountains of the Sierra Madre in Mexico, as shown in map 6. And if they tried to go north to the big pueblos north of modern Albuquerque, they would encounter a stretch along the southern New Mexico Rio Grande so barren that later Spanish colonial settlers called it the "Journey of Death."

"Permanent Houses": Late 1535

As the travelers prepared to leave, the women scouts returned with news of permanent settlements, as opposed to seasonal hunting-gathering campsites. The new settlements were on a river where people had beans, squash, and buffalo-skin blankets, though many of them had gone to hunt buffalo. Estevan and Castillo set out to investigate: "Castillo came back and said

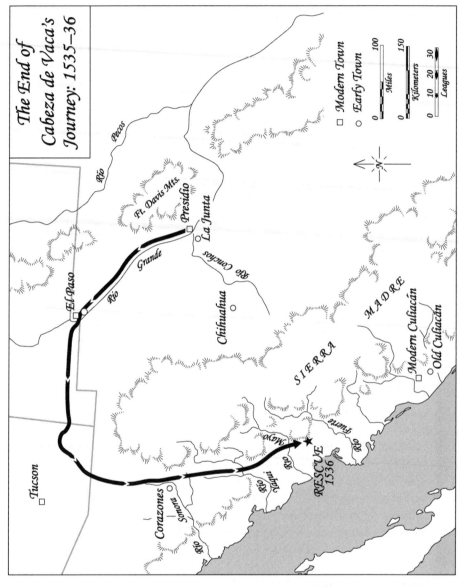

The End of
Cabeza de Vaca's
Journey: 1535–36

□ Modern Town
○ Early Town

Miles
0   100

Kilometers
0   150

Leagues
0   10 20 30

Pecos
Río

Ft. Davis Mts.

Presidio

La Junta

Río Grande

El Paso

Río Conchos

Chihuahua

SIERRA   MADRE

Modern Culiacán

Old Culiacán

Tucson

Corazones

Río Sonora

Sonora

Río Yaqui

Río Mayo

Río Fuerte

RESCUE
1536

Map 6. Final stages of the journey of the Cabeza de Vaca party. The heavy line indicates the highly uncertain route in central Texas, converging toward La Junta. The travelers had to ascend the Rio Grande to cross the Continental Divide and turn south into Sonora. Map by Ron Beckwith.

Figure 4. House of "mat construction," resembling a construction style described by Cabeza de Vaca's party along the maize route in Sonora. It is more substantial than what they had seen on the plains of Texas. Mats of woven reeds, cactus ribs, or similar material were attached to a framework of posts, and the houses typically had flat roofs, as in this example. "Permanent" houses that impressed Cabeza de Vaca's party were similar but plastered over with adobe. 2002 photo by the author, showing an indigenous example in northwestern Sonora, south of San Luis on the communal farm Ejido Johnson. Modern mat construction often uses scrap plywood, sheet rock, and even cardboard.

he'd found real and permanent houses, with people who ate beans and squash, and that he had seen maize. In the whole world, this was the thing that made us the happiest, and we gave infinite thanks to our Lord."

The castaways moved on to join these people. Cabeza de Vaca reported, charmingly, that they had "the first houses we saw that really looked like houses" (fig. 4). The discovery of "permanent houses" was important. In this locale, "permanent houses" probably referred not to multistory pueblos, as in central New Mexico, but to simpler, one-story, flat-topped structures, often with mud-plastered or adobe walls, as opposed to the simple, thatch-like brush huts they had seen earlier. "Permanent houses" signified to the Spaniards that they were reaching lands with more cultured people. Perhaps they were getting closer to the lands conquered by Cortés.

The inhabitants lived not in transient camps but in relatively fixed settlements, growing corn and communicating with the buffalo hunters of the plains. The castaways were now in an area later called La Junta (the junction or meeting area) near modern Presidio, Texas (see map 6), where the Río Conchos flows out of Chihuahua into the Rio Grande, which forms the Texas-Chihuahua border. Archaeological and historic evidence confirms that La Junta was an area of villages with more substantial structures than the travelers had encountered so far (see the sidebar "Confirming the Cabeza de Vaca Route from Records in 1581 and 1583"; see also Hammond and Rey 1966, 73, footnote 2). In that area, the castaways said the people were the "liveliest and most skilled, with the best physiques we had seen; they understood and answered our questions best."

As we read Cabeza de Vaca, first ethnographer of the American West, we see his growing interest in the range of different human living conditions. He reported that in the first of these riverside villages, the men walked around totally naked, as in earlier villages, but the women and some of the older men covered themselves with deerskins. "Their way of cooking is so novel I want to record it here." They were "too primitive to have cooking pots," but they put water in a large gourd, heated rocks in the fire, dropped the rocks into the gourd with wooden tongs, and cooked in the gourd. "It can be seen," says a marveling Cabeza de Vaca, "how diverse and strange are the devices and methods of different human beings."

The travelers referred to these people as the "Cow People" because they hunted "cows" on the plains and gave the castaways many "cowhides." In these passages, the Spaniards used their word *vaca*, or "cow," since they had no better word for the animals they were hearing about.

Having hit the Rio Grande, the castaways were now encountering settlements on a river that, upstream, bordered the buffalo country (see map 6). The people grew corn in agricultural fields and traded with the more nomadic buffalo hunters on the plains to the east of the Rio Grande (perhaps also to the west). In lean years these riverside villagers themselves went out on their own forays to hunt buffalo that approached the river. Cabeza de Vaca reported that for 50 leagues (125 to 155 miles) northward along the river, there were people who lived that way. This might refer to a stretch from the La Junta area to modern El Paso or Las Cruces (see map 6).

The people were not growing corn that year. They explained that they had been through two years without good rain and had to save their seed supply until they were assured of a rainy year with good planting prospects. They asked the Spaniards to intercede with the heavenly powers and bring them rain. The castaways noted that the villagers *did* have *some* maize.

Where did they get it? The answer was that the closest sources were toward the west—the direction the travelers now wanted to go: "We asked them the best way to get to the western maize country. They described the route, but said they didn't want to go themselves. First we would need to go up the river to the north, for 15 to 17 days, when we would find nothing to eat except a fruit they called *chacán*, which you had to grind between stones, and even after this treatment it was barely edible." The lack of food along the way was probably aggravated by the recent drought.

> We stayed there two days, discussing what to do. Finally we decided to go look for the maize, because we didn't want to go farther north into the buffalo country, which seemed out of our way. . . . The fears they tried to instill in us were not enough to deter us from the difficult journey.

SIDEBAR: Confirming the Cabeza de Vaca Route from Records in 1581 and 1583

To help confirm the location of Cabeza de Vaca's party, we apply our rule that any document is best interpreted after comparison with other, related documents. In this case we can do some sleuthing with accounts from later expeditions. The first known expedition into the La Junta–El Paso area (map 6) after Cabeza de Vaca's party was led by a priest named Agustín Rodríguez, who came north from Mexico in 1581 with eleven other Spaniards and about sixteen Native American servants. Documents of this expedition were published and analyzed by Berkeley historian George P. Hammond, working with Indiana linguist Agapito Rey, in 1966. The expedition left a Spanish frontier outpost and traveled through Chihuahua, downstream on the Río Conchos to the Rio Grande at La Junta, then upstream and north-northwest past El Paso to the Pueblo country near Albuquerque (which had already been reached in 1540 along a different route by Coronado, as we'll see later).

One chronicle of the expedition describes "permanent houses" in the area of La Junta. They were square, apparently one story high, built with forked posts supporting a flat roof with "timbers the thickness of a man's thigh," and staked walls plastered with mud. (Imagine a structure like that in figure 4, but plastered over with a thick mud, or so-called puddled adobe.) The inhabitants stood on the rooftops to welcome the Spaniards (Hammond and Rey 1966, 75). Such houses, and the reference to "fields," flesh out the nature of the "permanent" settlements

continued

First we walked nine days up the river, walking all day, very hungry. We found very few people along the trail; we were told most of the people had gone to hunt buffalo. As we traveled up the river, the few people gave us many buffalo hides and a kind of seed or fruit picked from trees ground between stones into a splintery, poor meal. It was very poor and we did not eat it, sticking instead to our own rations—a handful of deer fat that we tried always to keep on hand for emergencies.

described by Cabeza de Vaca around La Junta: stable communities raising modest crops but also dependent on buffalo products.

The Rodríguez expedition then proceeded upstream on the Rio Grande, probably following the Cabeza de Vaca route and then going beyond it to the north. Their account indicates they went twenty days up the river through about 80 leagues (200 to 248 road miles) of deserted country, past El Paso, perhaps to the region of modern Truth or Consequences, averaging 10 to 12 miles a day, an easy, plausible rate. The empty country matches what the locals had told Cabeza de Vaca. "Farther up the same river" the Rodríguez party came to what seems to have been the southernmost multistory pueblo. It was only an abandoned ruin but a complex three stories high. It was identified by Hammond and Rey (1966, 171, footnote 35) as a ruin still known today, about halfway between Socorro and Truth or Consequences. The next day they finally came to the southernmost active three-story pueblo, near Socorro. The inhabitants had fled, however, no doubt recalling the problems with the Coronado army of 1540–42, as we will discover in later chapters. Cabeza de Vaca's party turned west before reaching the multistory pueblos.

A more provocative account of this area comes from an expedition in 1583 led by Antonio Espejo, a wealthy explorer from Mexico City. Espejo led a small band including fourteen soldiers and a priest along roughly the same route as the 1581 Rodríguez expedition, following the Río Conchos to La Junta and then north along the Rio Grande (see map 6). They described La Junta clearly as "the junction of the rivers called Del Norte and Conchos, along which we were traveling" (Hammond and Rey 1966, 160). Interestingly, they regarded the Rio Grande as a tributary of the Río Conchos rather than vice versa. After all, if we arrive where two major rivers join, how do we define which one should be called the "tributary"?

For the first twelve days north along the Rio Grande they found Indians settled both in grass huts and in more substantial-looking flat-roofed houses—confirming the "permanent houses" of the Cabeza de Vaca and Rodriguez parties in that area.

At the end of about 15 or 17 days, we crossed over to the west side and set out in the direction of the sunset, traveling another 17 to 20 days or more through plains and high mountains [map 6]. On the way we found some people who, for four months of the year, have nothing to eat but powdered straw-like meal [mesquite flour?]. We had to eat it too, until the end of that westward journey, because we passed through during the difficult season.

One chronicler mentioned that some of the houses were "half under and half above ground" (Hammond and Rey 1966, 162). Twelve days could cover about 150 to 210 miles, which would bring them from La Junta upstream to the region of El Paso or Las Cruces. Here, people came out to greet the Espejo party, bringing food and hides. Espejo himself recorded that "the hides are from hump-backed cows, which they call civola, whose hair is like that of cows in Ireland. The natives dress the hides of these cows . . . making shoes of them [and] using them for clothes. These Indians appear to have some knowledge of our holy Catholic faith, as they point to god our Lord, looking up into the heavens. They call him Apalito. . . . Many of them, men, women, and children, came to have the priests and other Spaniards bless them, which made them very happy" (Hammond and Rey 1966, 217).

We don't have to speculate about the source of these Christian ideas, and it was not just the Rodríguez party. Espejo hands us a smoking gun! "They told us, through the interpreters, that three Christians and a Negro had passed through there, and by the indications, they appeared to have been Álvar Núñez Cabeza de Vaca, Dorantes, Castillo Maldonado, and the Negro who all [had come] from Florida" (Hammond and Rey 1966, 217). Here is direct proof that Cabeza de Vaca's party passed along this stretch of the Rio Grande upstream to the area of El Paso. As Espejo's party left this area on the river, they remarked on the friendly inhabitants: "We met many Indians [who] brought us many things made of feathers of different colors, and some small cotton mantles, striped with white and blue, like some they bring from China."

Even in the 1580s belief persisted that if explorers could travel far enough to the northwest, they would connect with China. Eventually, the Espejo party reached not China but what would become Albuquerque, which was then the area of prosperous multistory pueblos that had been explored by Coronado in the 1540s.

These accounts, four decades after Cabeza de Vaca, confirm not only the castaways' location on the Rio Grande south of El Paso but also the trade in prized items made in the pueblos, such as cotton fabrics.

Finally, we came to another land with permanent houses where much maize was stored, and they gave us great quantities of it, and its flour, along with squash and beans and cotton blankets. We gave it all to the people who had brought us here, and they returned to their lands, the happiest people in the world. We gave thanks to God our Lord for bringing us there, where we found so much food.

Once Cabeza de Vaca's party left the Rio Grande near El Paso and headed west, they went (in one version) "more than a 20-day journey . . . across hunger-stricken country," where they "rested sometimes" and had herb flour and "many jackrabbits" for food. That journey, west from the river, is indeed difficult. To modern travelers by auto or train it is a flat, wide-open, and poorly vegetated stretch along Interstate 10, past Deming and Lordsburg, New Mexico. In one traverse by car, I was stopped for half an hour or so by a dust storm opaque and gritty enough to force traffic off the road.

SIDEBAR: Checking Cabeza de Vaca's Mileages

As usual, we want to compare Cabeza de Vaca's reported travel times with mileages on today's maps. For example, their fifteen- to seventeen-day trek up the Rio Grande from La Junta to El Paso would cover roughly 225 road miles, only 13 to 15 miles per day, a relatively easy rate. If we start them from farther south, in Big Bend National Park, the modern road mileage would be about 280 miles, giving a still reasonable travel rate of 16 to 19 miles per day on average. El Paso got its name, of course, because it was "The Pass"—the best way to cross the Rio Grande and proceed west across the Continental Divide.

The second stretch lasted seventeen to twenty days, or "more than a 20 day journey" (Joint Report), west from the Rio Grande to the beginning of what they called the "maize road." As documented in chapter 8, this maize road was almost certainly a north–south route, perhaps including part of the north-flowing San Pedro River in southern Arizona and then along the south-flowing Río Sonora through the northern half of the Mexican state of Sonora. (Here, in 1539–42 the Coronado expedition found not only a long-used north–south trade route but also a town that had been visited by Cabeza de Vaca.) The road mileage on the modern I-10 route, west from El Paso to the San Pedro Valley and then a few miles south to the headwaters of the Río Sonora, is about 290 miles. Allowing seventeen to twenty-two days of travel from the Rio Grande to the maize road would thus imply an average travel rate of 13 to 17 miles per day—very reasonable.

Turning South along the Maize Road through Sonora: Late 1535

Now the castaways were finally moving south, in the fertile valley of the south-flowing Río Sonora between pine-topped, six- to eight-thousand-foot mountain ridges on either side. This beautiful valley still defines a major route through central Sonora. Here they found villages with irrigated, corn-producing fields, dotted along an idyllic river, shaded by cottonwood trees. Villagers raised abundant maize and lived in brush houses, along with a few more permanent earth-plastered structures, the most substantial that the Spaniards had seen.

Combining the description of this route in the Joint Report with Cabeza de Vaca's later memoir and synthesizing several translations, we have the following account of what the castaways saw:

> Among the houses some were made of adobe-like earth, and all the others were made of reed mats. From this point we went on for 80 to 100 leagues [200 to 310 miles, south], and we always found permanent houses and good supplies of maize and beans. Every two or three days we arrived in a town and would rest a day or two in each one. They gave us meat from many deer, along with cotton blankets finer than those of New Spain. They also gave us beads, corals from the South Sea, and fine turquoises that they have, which come to them from the north. People came from 10 to 12 leagues [25 to 36 miles] to see us.

In 1890 the Swiss American archaeologist and ethnologist Adolph Bandelier described many ruins in the Río Sonora valley, and nearly a century later, in 1988, Texas archaeologist William Doolittle published the first detailed survey of archaeological sites along the Río Sonora. Studying village sites thought to date from the 1400s and 1500s, Doolittle concluded that the numbers of small villages and several major towns in the valley and the construction styles of buildings matched the descriptions of the Cabeza de Vaca party and the later Coronado expedition.

As Cabeza de Vaca's party moved south from town to town, they were still being accompanied by crowds of local villagers, numbering a hundred or more.

> All these people came to us to be touched and signed with the cross. They were so insistent that we found it hard to cope with them. Sick or well,

they all wanted us to make the sign of the cross over them. Occasionally, the women who were traveling with us gave birth, and they would bring us the baby as soon as it was born, to have us touch it and sign it with the cross. They'd go with us until they turned us over to others (from the next villages). They were all convinced we had come from heaven.

For our part, we behaved toward them with much gravity. To preserve their impression, we spoke little. When we were with them, we'd march all day until evening, without eating, and we ate so little that they were astonished. They never observed us to get tired, because we were so used to hardships that we didn't feel any fatigue. Estevan the black talked with them incessantly, finding out the routes we wanted, and what towns were there and whatever we wanted to know. We found many languages, yet we always managed to understand each other. Indians who were at war would quickly become friends so they could come and greet us and bring us things, so that we left the whole land at peace.

We explained to them that there was a man in heaven whom we called God, who had created heaven and earth, that He was our lord and provided all good things, so that we did what He commanded—and that if they too would do this, they'd be better off. They had such a disposition to believe, that if only we'd had a language to understand each other perfectly, we'd have left them all Christians. From then on, when the sun rose, they held up their joined hands to heaven and then passed them all over their bodies. They'd do the same at sunset. They are a well-disposed people, intelligent, and apt to follow any doctrine if it is well prepared.

Discovering the Gateway Settlement of Corazones: December 1535

Toward the south end of the maize road, somewhere in central Sonora, the travelers came to a prosperous community that was to become a key to later northern exploration. It was often referred to by a single name, but the Joint Report says that it was a cluster of three villages, presumably in a localized segment of the river valley. In this community, says Cabeza de Vaca, "they gave me five arrowheads made of emerald-like stone; with such arrows they perform ceremonies and dances. Since they seemed so fine, I asked where they got them. They said they were brought from high mountains toward the north, where they bought them in exchange for parrot feathers. They said there were towns there that had many people and very large houses." (This quote and the next quote are a synthesis of translations from Krieger 2002, 225; and Pupo-Walker 1993, 104.)

Cabeza de Vaca goes on to describe the dress and habits of the people. The accounts revealed two exciting things. First, the earlier indications of a large urban trading center in the North were true. Second, the informants knew a trade route that led to that province. They said they traded bright-colored macaw feathers, which came from the south, to the northerners, who prized them for ceremonies. Describing the community where they were staying, Cabeza de Vaca wrote:

> In the same village, they gave Dorantes more than 600 opened hearts of deer, which they always have in abundance for their food. So we called this town *Corazones* [Cor-a-ZONE-ace, with a slight roll of the *r*, meaning "hearts" in Spanish].
>
> Among the Indians along this maize route we saw women more modestly dressed than in any other part of the Indies we'd seen. They wear cotton shifts that reach to their knees, and over them a tunic with half-sleeves, with skirts of dressed deerskin that touch the ground. They soap these with a kind of root that keeps them clean, and they are very well kept, open in front and tied with thongs. They wear shoes. . . .
>
> Corazones is the gateway to many provinces on the South Sea. If those traveling toward the provinces on the South Sea do not take the route through here (or try to travel along the coast instead), they will be lost, for there is no maize on the coast. As for food on the coast, they have only flour made from rushes and grasses, along with fish they take from the sea in rafts. They are too primitive to have canoes. The women along the coast cover their private parts only with grass and straw. They are very timid and dejected. But along the maize route that we found, we believe there are more than a thousand leagues of populated country with good supplies of food, for the people sow beans and maize three times a year. There are permanent houses as well as three kinds of deer, and those of one kind are as large as yearling bulls in Castile.

The fact that Corazones means "hearts" is useful to know. According to my not-quite-scientific survey of the popular music played in the Mexican restaurants that I colonized during the writing of this book, *corazón* is the most important of all words. Everything is about *mi corazón* (mee cor-a-ZONE)—my heart.

Locating Corazones, and Why It Matters: ca. 1535

The location of Corazones is critical to the rest of our story. In accord with Cabeza de Vaca's report, it was a significant locale, or junction, on the prehistoric trade route through Sonora to the mysterious trade center in the North. This is the very route on which Coronado's grand army would march a few years later into the western heartlands of what is now the United States. Coronado's expedition considered Corazones such a key locale that they established a base camp there. If we could locate Corazones, we'd have a fulcrum that could give us leverage to reconstruct not only the prehistoric trade route but also Cabeza de Vaca's whereabouts and Coronado's garrison. The location is a controversial mystery. We'll postpone further discussion about the location until we describe the arrival of the Coronado expedition in chapter 8.

Another View of Corazones: 1535–1550s

The crusading priest, Bartolomé de Las Casas, collected additional information about northern Mexico in his massive historical volumes, *History of the Indies* and *Apologetic History of the Conquest of the Indies*, finished (when he was in his eighties) around 1557–62. The second title did not refer to an apology for the European invasions but rather to a theological/literary mode of defending the truth of Christianity against other belief systems. The books were based on his interviews with the explorers themselves, along with documents he collected, as described in a 1967 biography of Las Casas by Henry Wagner and Helen Rand Parish. Certain passages of the *Apologetic History* indicate that he got information about Corazones from Cabeza de Vaca or someone in his party and also from Marcos de Niza, who was the next European explorer to reach the area, as we'll see in chapter 5. It was apparently from these interviews that Las Casas reported that Corazones had about eight hundred houses constructed of a framework of thick cane that was covered with mats of "delicate palm." Some of these were "adobe houses" built not as dwellings but for storing maize (Las Casas, quoted by Riley 1976, 19).

Being a priest, Las Casas was especially interested in religious practices and gives us a vivid picture of ceremonial life in Corazones:

> Although Cabeza de Vaca does not mention it in his account, when they arrived at that town, the inhabitants were holding a fiesta. They had a great number of animals: deer, wolves, hares, and birds, and carried them before a great idol, [and] accompanied by much flute music, which they played, they split the animals down the middle [and] ripped out the hearts, and with the blood . . . they bathed the idol, and then they

hung the hearts around the idol's neck. When they made this sacrifice, they threw themselves on the ground before their idol as a sign of great reverence. . . . In this region of the valley of Sonora, only the hearts of animals are sacrificed. They hold two fiestas in which, amidst great singing and music-making, they make their sacrifices with great joy, pomp, and devotion. The first fiesta is at the time of sowing, and the other at harvest time.

They must have other ceremonies, but those were not to be witnessed in such a short time, because Cabeza de Vaca's party was just passing through. It appears that they have some indication of those [ceremonies], which [people] of [the northern trade center] Cíbola carry out in honor of the Sun.

Next, Las Casas implies that it was the later explorer Marcos de Niza (see chapter 5) who learned of these Sonoran customs, inspired by practices in Cíbola:

When Marcos de Niza entered the principal village and governing center of the region the chief of the entire valley came out to meet him and, extending his hands to the Padre, then rubbed him all over his body. Then, in another town in the valley, 6 leagues from there toward Cíbola, a very tall stone and adobe temple was found with a bloodied stone statue [with hearts around its neck]. Near the statue were also many dead, desiccated, disemboweled human bodies leaning against the walls. They must have been the past lords of the valley, and that was their sepulcher. (adapted from the translation of Las Casas by Riley 1976, 20)

From later evidence (chapters 5, 8), we know Cíbola was a group of pueblos at Zuni, New Mexico, where ethnographers in the 1800s documented a sun "priesthood." These "priests" were not so much worshipers of the sun as trackers of it. They observed the solstices and equinoxes in order to set important calendar dates and ceremonies. Las Casas's report gives us an intriguing clue that people in central Sonora relied on the Zuni sun priests' observations. Consistent with this, Cabeza de Vaca's report, quoted above, indicated active trade between Corazones and Cíbola, with parrot feathers going north and turquoise products going south. The distance from Corazones to Zuni was 520 to 540 trail miles, based on my proposed location of Corazones on the lower to mid–Río Sonora (see chapter 8). Here, then, we have direct evidence of active networks of trade, travel, and religious-cultural influence over distances of at least 500 miles in late prehistoric Sonora, Arizona, and New Mexico.

In the same way, Las Casas's report of ritual excision of animal hearts as sacrifices to idols in bloody temples sounds like a northern provincial echo of the human sacrificial practices of mighty Tenochtitlan, around 1,350 trail miles to the south. The fact that Cabeza de Vaca's party was given deer hearts, perhaps considered sacred, may indicate that the native Sonorans did not regard the travelers as ordinary mortals.

Moving South from Corazones: Christmas 1535

Cabeza de Vaca, Dorantes, Estevan, and Castillo did not realize, when they feasted in Corazones, that they were within days of their journey's end. After three days in Corazones, they set out, guided by their usual crowd of adoring locals. The Joint Report says it was "around Christmas."

Somewhere beyond Corazones a rainstorm caused a local river to rise so high that they couldn't cross. Cabeza de Vaca implies that this was about a day beyond Corazones, but the Joint Report says it was a journey of 30 leagues (75 to 93 miles) to the new river. Cabeza de Vaca surmised that the people in the Corazones province were influenced in architecture and dress by the people from the northern trade center. He also noted that at the new river they had just reached, the housing style changed to flimsier mat-sided housing, and the style of dress among women was less modest, with "mantillas" reaching only to the waist or knees. This suggests that the next river valley south of Corazones lay south of the zone where people had contact with the northern trade center. The Joint Report implies (somewhat vaguely) that exhausted scouts of the slave trader Nuño de Guzmán (or from one of Cortés's boats?) had recently reached some point along this river. These descriptions suggest that the party could have reached the Río Mátape, or more likely the Río Yaqui (see map, p. 164).

Here they stopped for fifteen days to wait out the high waters, presumably having arrived at the best point to ford the river when the waters subsided.

Rescued at Last: Spring 1536

While they waited in this area, Castillo came upon a stunning sight. A local Indian was wearing a pendant made from the buckle of a Spanish sword belt with a horseshoe nail sewed to it! Asked what it was, the Indian replied that it had come from heaven. Affecting nonchalance, Castillo asked, Who brought it from there? The answer, as related by Cabeza de Vaca, came back through the translators: "Some men with beards like ours, who had come from heaven, had reached that river. They had horses, lances, and swords, and had wounded two of the coastal people with their lances. Feigning as much indifference as we could muster, we asked what had become of these strangers. The Indians said they had gone to the seacoast and floated away in the direction of the setting sun." This coastal sighting of Spaniards in ships probably referred to a landing party from one of Cortés's naval forays of 1532–35 or perhaps Guzmán's men in a ship they captured from Cortés.

The castaways thanked God, eventually crossed the river, and raced south, hoping to find the "Christians," as Cabeza de Vaca referred to the Spaniards ahead. The events of the next few weeks are difficult to reconstruct in detail, since the Joint Report and Cabeza de Vaca's memoirs mention various distances that are difficult to reconcile into a coherent narrative or itinerary. Suffice it to say that they reported following the coastline south and east, staying 10 to 12 leagues (25 to 37 miles) inland, near or somewhat inland from the modern coastal highway and railway. They reported the "Christian border," or Spanish frontier, to be "100 leagues or more" (at least 250 to 310 trail miles) from where they had been stopped by rain. In our reconstruction, this Spanish frontier (where Guzmán's troops were known) would thus be well south of the Río Yaqui, probably in the region of the Río Mayo or Río Fuerte. Such a trip may have taken twelve to twenty days. To Cabeza de Vaca's horror, they did not find Spaniards living in harmony with local villagers but a region devastated by Nuño de Guzmán's slave-raiding parties.

> We traveled over much territory and found all of it uninhabited because everyone had fled to the mountains for fear of the Christians. The people dared not have homes or cultivate the fields. It made us sad to see how fertile and beautiful the land was, while all their places were depopulated, deserted, and burned. The few people there were thin, ill, and scabrous. They lived off bark and roots of trees, since they could not sow their fields. We also suffered this hunger, since they couldn't feed us. The people were so unhappy they wanted to die.
>
> We told them that we were seeking the Christians in order to tell them not to kill Indians, or make slaves of them, or remove them from their lands, or harm them in any way, and they rejoiced greatly to hear this.
>
> So they brought us blankets they had hidden, and told us all about the several occasions when the Christians came and destroyed and burned their villages, and carried off half the men and all the women

and children. They had been thinking that to die was better than waiting around to be treated so cruelly.

Cabeza de Vaca, having traveled with the Native Americans and having been treated as a slave, a shaman, and a divine visitor, had a strikingly modern attitude toward these peoples. In a statement that would foreshadow five centuries of future arguments over military and geopolitical strategy, he argued for kindness over combat: "All these people, if they are to be brought to be Christians and into obedience of Your Imperial Majesty, must be *led* [emphasis added—WKH] by good treatment. This way is guaranteed, and no other will succeed."

The castaways were now led to a secret village or gathering spot atop the crest of a knife-like mountain ridge where many refugees had fled to escape the Spaniards. The Joint Report places it 40 leagues (100 to 124 miles) north of Culiacán, which would be near the Río Sinaloa. Collecting as many of the local people as he could find, Cabeza de Vaca assured them they would be safe. Bravely, the party, now numbering in the hundreds, pushed on toward the Spaniards. Within a few days they encountered a spot where Spanish horsemen had camped on a river named Petatlán. Located roughly 60 to 90 miles north of Guzmán's settlement at Culiacán, the river "Petatlán" and an adjacent village of the same name would play an important role in the activities of the next few years (see chapter 5).

The horsemen, Guzmán's slave raiders, had passed by, planning to attack the very area where the castaways had recently "left the land at peace." Cabeza de Vaca and eleven Indians rushed back up their trail, in search of the Spaniards, covering 10 leagues (25 to 31 miles) that day—a good indication of the distance that could be covered on a long day's march. Next morning, they came upon four Spanish horsemen. What a meeting this must have been! As Cabeza de Vaca describes it: "The four Christians on horseback were thunderstruck to see me so strangely dressed and traveling with Indians. They stared at me for a long time, so astonished that they couldn't speak or manage to ask me anything. I asked them to take me to their captain."

Arguing with Guzmán's Men: March 1536

Guzmán's men were led by a captain named Alcaráz. After an ecstatic reunion, Alcaráz and Cabeza de Vaca sent for the rest of Cabeza de Vaca's entourage. Some six hundred joyful Natives gathered, anticipating liberation from the slavers. "They brought us all the maize they could lay their hands on, in pots sealed with clay, which they had previously buried and concealed" (an interesting insight into late prehistoric food preservation techniques).

Guzmán's men, however, still viewed the regional villagers as commodities. To Alcaráz, this was an opportunity to take all the Indians captive on the spot. Cabeza de Vaca recounts:

> As long as the Indians were with us, they feared neither the Christians nor their lances. The Christians were angry about that friendship. They had their interpreter say that we were men of their race who were unlucky, cowardly people who had gotten lost, whereas *they* were the true masters of that land. The Indians should obey and serve them!
>
> The Indians paid no heed to this. They talked among themselves, saying that the Christians were lying about us being the same, since we came from where the sun rises, and they came from where it sets. Not to mention the fact that we cured the sick, whereas they killed the healthy. We came naked and barefoot, while they came on horses and carried lances. We coveted nothing, and whatever was given to us, we gave back to the Indians who helped us. The Christian soldiers, however, never gave anything to anyone but tried to steal whatever they liked. The Indians discussed this and told it to the Christians' interpreter by means of a common language they used, which we didn't understand. They have a special name for those who use this language, and we found it in use over a region of 400 leagues.

Here is another interesting bit of "prehistoric ethnology." The tribes had special interpreters who could speak a "universal" language, facilitating interregional communication. The 400-league distance (1,000 to 1,200 trail miles) over which such communication was possible would stretch all the way back to Texas: "We never could make the Indians believe we were related to the other Christians, but we finally convinced them to return home and reestablish their villages. We had intense arguments with the Christians about it. We were so angry that when we departed, we forgot about many bows and arrows we had collected, and numerous pouches, including the one with the five emerald arrowheads. They were left behind and lost."

Such was the return of the shipwrecked wanderers to the glories of civilization. Soon they had to reacquaint themselves, as well, with the wonders of bureaucracy. Cabeza de Vaca had enough presence of mind to request a notarized statement about the date when he first contacted the Spaniards.

After we left the Indians in peace, the Christians delivered us under guard to a certain justice of the peace and two other officials, who led us through forests and empty lands [toward the Spanish outpost of Culiacán]. The route was chosen to keep us from conversing with local Indians and from seeing or hearing what the Christians had done.

How often are men's thoughts frustrated! We sought only freedom for the Indians, yet just when we thought we had achieved it, we had accomplished the exact opposite! The Spaniards had secretly agreed to fall upon the Indians that we had reassured and sent away! So they planned and so they acted. Meanwhile, we were led through forests for two days, without water, lost and unable to find a trail. We thought we'd perish of thirst, and seven men in the party died. After 25 leagues [62 to 75 miles], we reached a town of friendly Indians, and the justice of the peace went another 3 leagues onward to the town of Culiacán, where the mayor was Melchior Díaz.

Happily, Mayor Díaz, unlike regional governor Guzmán, was a capable and enlightened official. He would play an interesting role in the next few years, as we'll see. Díaz traveled several miles out of the town to greet the lost Spaniards and their Indian supporters. Upset by the actions of Alcaráz, Díaz asked Cabeza de Vaca to send messengers back up the trail to reassure the Indians north of the Río Petatlán that Díaz would support their cause. Most of those Indians had escaped Alcaráz's attempted onslaught by disappearing into the hills. The messengers persuaded some of them to come to Culiacán, where Díaz tried to encourage them to adopt the sixteenth-century Spanish principles of Christianity and the legal structure by which Europeans justified their entry into the New World. The Indians answered that they already believed in a spirit in heaven—known to them by the name Aguar—who had created the world and provided water and health.

Díaz ordered that no more slave raiding would be allowed on the frontier, and the Indians agreed that they would do whatever Díaz asked. Fifteen days later Alcaráz came back from his slave raiding, reporting dumbfoundedly that the Indians had returned to their towns and come out to meet his slave raiders with crosses. Sheepishly, Alcaráz had backed away from confrontation.

Díaz now tried to get Cabeza de Vaca and the other three travelers to settle in Culiacán, saying that the province needed such capable men. The castaways, however, decided to return to true civilization: Mexico City. The date was early May 1536, and their tale was not yet ended.

CHAPTER FOUR

The New Viceroy Ponders the North

The miraculously resurrected castaways—Cabeza de Vaca, Andrés Dorantes, Estevan de Dorantes the Moor, and Alonso Castillo—planned their departure from Culiacán toward Mexico City. The distance along the old trails, according to historian Cleve Hallenbeck in 1949, was about 830 miles. The first half of the trip led to Compostela, a settlement where Guzmán, as governor of the Northwest, maintained his headquarters. The country between Culiacán and Compostela, however, was in revolt against the Spanish overlords because of the depredations of men like Guzmán. As a result, Cabeza de Vaca's party had to wait ten or twelve days until an armed guard could be organized. It included twenty horsemen and several hundred local Indians. Cabeza de Vaca wrote that they finally left Culiacán on 16 May 1536.

In Compostela, Guzmán gave them a hardy welcome, providing their first fine Spanish clothes in eight years from his own supplies. Cabeza de Vaca says the clothes were so strange on his skin that he could not wear them for many days, and during the same time he found it easier to sleep on the floor than in a bed. In spite of the welcome, Cabeza de Vaca's party regarded Guzmán as no friend, and they pressed on. According to historian Cyclone Covey (1961, 135), they arrived in Mexico City on 24 July 1536. If Covey's date is right, the trip from Culiacán to Mexico City took them sixty-nine days, for an average of only 12 miles per day, including their stopover in Compostela. Allowing two weeks of down time, perhaps mostly in Compostela, the average travel rate would be about 15 miles per day. The rates will be useful in our later tests of reported travels.

Mexico City: 1535–1536

In Mexico City, two important changes had occurred during the castaways' odyssey. First, in the early 1530s, as already mentioned, sensational news of Francisco Pizarro's discovery of a golden empire in Peru had arrived. To young Spaniards in the streets of Mexico City, this was glorious proof that the New World was dotted with empires of stupendous wealth. Such empires could be conquered by any handful of disciplined Spaniards who believed that fortune favored the bold . . . or the ruthless. These young men, already drawn to America by tales of Cortés, chafed to see what New Spain's next northern frontier had to offer.

A second new development in Mexico City was that in 1535 the governing council, or audiencia, had been augmented by a viceroy (*vice-roi*, i.e., vice-king—the king's direct representative), who served as president of the audiencia. Cortés was thus even more marginalized.

The viceroy was Antonio Mendoza. According to Mendoza's 1927 biographer, Arthur Aiton, he arrived in Mexico with great ceremony in November 1535. He was an interesting man. Born in 1490 or 1491, he was about forty-five years old when he arrived to govern Mexico for the king. He came from a distinguished family (an important criterion in those days). His father had shown not only military ability against the Moors in Spain until their expulsion in 1492 but also administrative ability as governor operating from the Alhambra, which had been the palace of the Moorish kings in Granada, a city with an interethnic population of Muslims, Christians, Jews, and others. Young Antonio showed similar military and diplomatic skill. He'd been with Cortés in Mexico and was sent by Cortés in 1521 to carry the first eyewitness news of Tenochtitlan back to Spain. Ironically, as noted by Hugh Thomas (1995, 539), Mendoza had left New Spain before the final fall of Tenochtitlan, so he was enthralling Castile with awe-inspiring descriptions of the city, but at the same time the city itself was, unknown to him, being destroyed, first by Cortés's final attack and then by the dismantling of the Aztec structures to provide building materials for the Spanish cathedral and other structures.

Still, by 1528 Mendoza was well known to King Carlos V, who was pondering how to shift governance in Mexico from Cortés to more direct royal control. By 1529 there was talk of Mendoza being sent to rule New Spain. His actual appointment as the first viceroy did not materialize until April 1535.

Mendoza thus headed the "second generation" in Mexico City. As viceroy in Mexico, he displayed substantial vision in managing New Spain, creating a reputation for justice and generosity toward Native Americans and Spaniards alike. He supported the first printing press in the New World (set up by Bishop Zumárraga; see map 4), minted coins, and helped set up a university teaching European liberal arts and theology to the sons of Aztec nobility. At the same time, he violently resisted regional rebellions in the 1540s. One way or another, his name should be in the list of important early North American political leaders. Our histories, however, tend to favor colorful conquerors over capable governors.

Cortés probably assumed he would have an "in" with his former subordinate. Remember that Cortés already had ships probing north into the Gulf of California. Such an alliance was not to be. Mendoza (with coaching from the Spanish court) probably viewed Cortés as a loose cannon.

As Mendoza consolidated his authority over New Spain, he and Cortés maintained formal, oh-so-cordial relations, but they emerged as rivals in the coming conquest of the North. Mendoza's goal was to see that further exploration proceeded according to Spanish law, with the king receiving accurate reports, along with his designated share of whatever treasures were found. Cortés's goal was profit for Cortés.

Into this unstable political situation, in the summer of 1536, walked the four castaways, who had actually seen the much-discussed northern country. Mendoza set up an interview. The travelers began the discussions by lodging a complaint about Nuño de Guzmán's treatment of the Indians, which was alienating the Native American communities throughout the northwest frontier. Mendoza, working with a newly appointed law-enforcement magistrate, responded by having the notorious Guzmán arrested and thrown into prison. A prompt inquiry removed Guzmán from power in January 1537. Guzmán appealed his treatment from a Mexico City jail cell but was sent to Spain in July 1538 and held in detention. Any conquistador who found gold could always fall back on his secretly sequestered wealth to escape or prolong legal inquiries, as Cortés had shown. Guzmán, however, as the historian Arthur Scott Aiton remarked in 1927, "had been cruel, rapacious, and self-seeking, but worse than that, had failed to discover new stores of ready-made wealth, and this failure extinguished any hope of hiding his shortcomings" (26). Guzmán thus died in poverty in Spain, probably around 1544, though Covey (1961, 143) places the date as late as 1550.

Cortés, for his part, was no doubt happy about Guzmán's arrest. His primary rival on the frontier was now out of the way. His open path to the north was suddenly threatened, however, by the 1537 alliance of Mendoza, Cabeza de Vaca, Dorantes, and their friends. Why should the viceroy waste time with newcomers and their gossip about the indelicate tactics employed by bold men who, after all, had achieved patriotic success by adding new lands to the Spanish Empire?

Back in the viceroy's palace, Cabeza de Vaca and his colleagues emphasized to Mendoza that throughout their route in northern Mexico, they had found the Indians to be intelligent people of goodwill. The tone of their conversation is conveyed by comments that Cabeza de Vaca made in his book years later. While he criticized the Indians over some of their practices, he also remarked that they "see and hear more and have the sharpest senses, I believe, of any people in the world. . . . They are well-disposed, intelligent people, able to follow any doctrine if it is well presented. . . . In the lifetime of His Majesty it will be possible to subject these people to the true Lord . . . because in the 2,000 leagues that we traveled by land and sea, we found no sacrifices nor idolatry."

The last lines are interesting, since Las Casas later claimed that Marcos de Niza had reported animal sacrifices and bloody shrines with hearts draped around idols, just 6 leagues (12 to 19 miles) from Corazones. It's possible that Cabeza de Vaca did not see such things during his brief visit or that Las Casas exaggerated or in some way was misled.

Mendoza interviewed the travelers with great care about societies, cities, towns, and routes. Most exciting of all was their report of the metalworking center of commerce somewhere north of their route. Could this be, at long last, the direct confirmation of the earlier rumors about another golden empire beyond the northern frontier? Mendoza, as well as Cortés, was aware that in the days when Guzmán ran Pánuco, Guzmán had interviewed Indians who described a great trade center in the North. One Indian had claimed to have seen a street with silversmiths or metalworkers.

Interpreting Señor Dorantes's Copper Bell: 1536

Mendoza assembled his evidence methodically. In his conceptual edifice, one item stood out like the keystone in an arch. It was the copper bell given to Andrés Dorantes (see fig. 3). The castaways had been told it came from a land with large, permanent houses north of their route. Here was physical proof that the distant northern metropolis not only existed but traded in metals.

Map 7. Concepts of
the North. (a) The
Mendoza-era vision,
based on the best infor-
mation and rumors,
available in 1538.
Cabeza de Vaca's report
suggested a wealthy
trading center near
the north coast. Baja
California was thought
by some to be an island
occupied by Amazons.
(b) Reality. Maps by
Ron Beckwith.

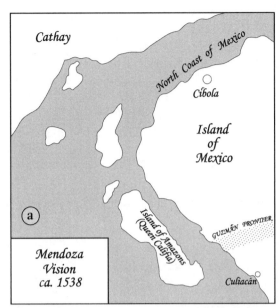

Mendoza
Vision
ca. 1538

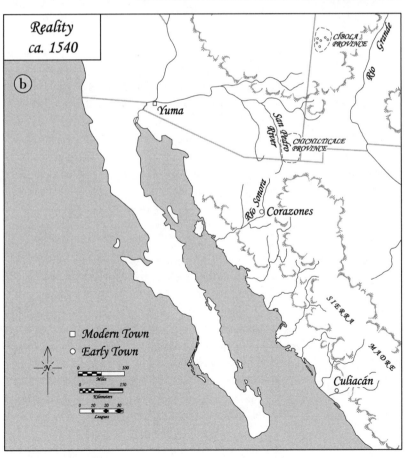

Pedro de Castañeda, the memoirist who wrote two decades later about that era, may or may not have exaggerated when he said the castaways gave the viceroy "marvelous news of some wealthy . . . pueblos" (translation by Flint and Flint 2005, 379, 387; see also discussion of the conversation between Mendoza and Cabeza de Vaca in chapter 5).

Viceroy Mendoza was impressed by another report from the castaways. We saw in the last chapter how Cabeza de Vaca and his friends "deduced" that the prosperous metalworking trade center, though north of their route, was near what we now call the Pacific coast (see map 7a). This idea thrilled

---

SIDEBAR: The Irony of the Copper Bell

Modern research has revealed a stunning irony about Dorantes's copper bell. As mentioned in chapter 3, archaeologists have found numbers of copper bells in the southwestern United States comparable to Dorantes's bell. The large, incised bell shown in figure 3 is an example. It was found amidst prehistoric trash in a room in one of the "Salado era" pueblos (built typically around A.D. 1300). The ruin that produced this bell was near the San Pedro River, a river likely on the route of the Cabeza de Vaca party. Based on the context, the dean of Arizona archaeologists, Emil Haury, in 1947 estimated this bell's date as 1300–1400. Another bell in a similar style was reported in 1907 from a site on the Tularosa River in west-central New Mexico. In 1995 archaeologist Victoria Vargas published a major study of 622 bells from 93 sites in the American Southwest and in northwestern Mexico. She confirmed her suspicions, based on bell design, age, spatial distribution, and chemistry of the copper, that these bells did not originate in the North. Instead, the chemistry revealed copper ore sources in Michoacán, 200 miles west of Mexico City, and in other coastal provinces only as far north as Sinaloa. The bells were traded from there to the northern pueblos.

Interestingly, archaeologist Charles Di Peso and his coworkers in 1974 had announced that copper was being smelted and fabricated into bells at the huge pueblo of Casas Grandes, just south of the border in Chihuahua. That would have confirmed Cabeza de Vaca's conclusion that metalworking occurred in urban areas near their route, but Vargas reviewed Di Peso's data and refuted his result from the chemical evidence. In another example, Di Peso presented four copper pieces he called "ingots," a word that implies smelting and shaping. Vargas and her consultants concluded they were not ingots but pieces of raw copper shaped merely by hammering. Such raw copper masses were probably examples of the "plates" of copper, or "sheets buried in the ground," that Indians had described

Mendoza. If the northern empire were on the coast or perhaps on an inlet from the sea, it meant that the proposed northern cities might be reachable by ships.

This important idea, which has been underappreciated by modern historians, influenced many actions in the next four years, as Mendoza and Cortés jockeyed to organize the first grand conquest of the North. Mendoza proceeded with plans for an expedition by land, but both Mendoza and Cortés now also expected to reach the northern wealth by sea, or at least place their ships within striking distance.

to the castaways. Furthermore, Di Peso found no smelting furnaces during his excavations of Casas Grandes. Vargas's bottom line was that no good evidence exists for production of the copper bells in the northern provinces, corresponding to the current borderlands.

Herein lay the great irony: Mendoza and Cortés were preparing to travel nearly 2,000 miles to chase the implications of a bell that came from Mexican provinces only 200 miles away from their starting point!

How, then, did Mexican bells reach the North? Today we know that villages in Mexico and the American Southwest were loosely linked by broad, informal regional networks involving trade and information flow. The degree of that trade is still controversial, but trade items clearly went from one village to another along well-known routes. Individual Native American traders traveled hundreds of miles along these routes, as confirmed in eyewitness testimony from Marcos de Niza (see chapter 5) and also from Mendoza's naval captain, Hernando Alarcón (see chapter 10). From such commerce, specialized trade goods from Mexico diffused, village by village, all the way from central Mexico to Arizona and New Mexico and perhaps beyond.

Irony piles on irony! The Indians who gave Dorantes the bell may have actually been trying to explain the existence of that trade. As referenced in chapter 3, the castaways' Joint Report contains a garbled statement quoting the Indians as saying the bell "came from the north, traversing across the land toward the South Sea." Cabeza de Vaca's group seems to have taken this to mean that the sources were cities on the South Sea coast (map 7a), but the Indians may have been trying to explain that such bells came to them from the north but that the bells had first traveled from southern Mexico to the New Mexico pueblo trade centers, then south along the Rio Grande to the region around modern El Paso. They "came from the north" but "traversed lands extending toward the South Sea."

Viceroy Mendoza Makes Plans with Dorantes: 1536–1537

Viceroy Mendoza was a prudent planner. He knew he needed better information. Where were the mysterious cities? What routes reached them? What metals were worked there? How big were the cities? Were they well defended? Did their metalworkers work in gold, like the Mexica and the Incas? Could the cities be reached by sailing up the coast?

Mendoza knew that Cortés was already trying to get his ships far enough north to learn about the cities or perhaps even reach them. No doubt this increased Mendoza's own interest in a naval route. Cortés could not be trusted to play by the rules; if he made the discovery, wasn't he likely to launch a conquest, claim the lands, send the king less than the royal fifth, and keep the extra for himself?

Mendoza picked one of the castaways, Capt. Andrés Dorantes, to help him get better information. Here, we recount what happened next in 1536 and 1537 by paraphrasing the viceroy's own words in two letters Mendoza wrote to King Carlos V. One was written on 10 December 1537 (discussed by Hartmann and Flint 2003, 27–28) and another on an uncertain date in 1539 (translated by Flint and Flint 2005, 45–48):

> After Cabeza de Vaca's party arrived in Mexico City, one of the castaways, named Andrés Dorantes, joined my court. I consulted with him many times. I realized it would be to the King's service to send people to that northern land to learn for certain its nature. I engaged Dorantes close at hand, supposing he would be able to do great service for Your Majesty. I employed him to take a party with forty or fifty horses and search out the secret of the northern regions. To outfit Dorantes and these people, I estimate it would cost 3,540 pesos. Even though I provided all things necessary for his journey and spent money to that end, I [eventually] found that the matter had been broken off. I don't understand why this happened, but the enterprise collapsed [in 1537]. I previously wrote to you, asking permission for exploration, but I have received no reply, so I am petitioning again for this permission.

Why did the plan with Dorantes fall through, and why did Mendoza seem so vague about it? The movements of Dorantes and Cabeza de Vaca give some clues. They left Mexico City during the spring of 1537 to sail to Spain from Cortés's colony of Veracruz. Cabeza de Vaca's ship made it, but Dorantes's leaky ship had to turn back to Veracruz, arriving probably in May 1537. That's when Viceroy Mendoza offered him the northern expedition.

According to historian Cyclone Covey, writing in 1961, Dorantes held back, waiting for a royal joint command to be obtained by Cabeza de Vaca in Spain. A commission direct from the king might give Dorantes and Cabeza de Vaca much greater authority than a mere viceroyalty commission. They might gain rights to return to the North on their own, search for wealth, and establish new settlements. The royal command from Spain never materialized. Mendoza may even have known about their plan but may have diplomatically pretended not to understand why Dorantes withdrew in order to avoid becoming entangled in the Dorantes–Cabeza de Vaca court intrigue.

Dorantes remained in Mexico but retired from exploration, married a rich widow, and fathered at least fourteen children, including three sons who became well-known figures in New Spain. Mendoza had to start over.

The *Requerimiento* and a Proclamation from the Pope: June 1537

Mendoza had another problem. How should justice be extended toward the Indians if new Tenochtitlans or Cuzcos were discovered in the North? In the face of wildcat conquistadors wanting to enslave the Indians at every turn, what legal tools did Mendoza have to regulate the treatment of Native peoples?

One answer already existed, a document called the *requerimiento*. It had been hammered out by European legal and religious scholars and enumerated the rights and duties of peoples in lands being claimed by Spain. Interestingly enough, its roots went back to decrees that Islamic Arabs had read to peoples they were conquering. Based on that tradition, a royal order issued as early as 1512 required that the requerimiento be read to newly discovered peoples during any formal "acts of possession." This was one small step but hardly a great leap forward for humanity. On the enlightened side, it spelled out Native Americans' rights and summarized the entire cosmic reality as understood in those days. Also on the side of enlightenment, it was not some secret legal justification penned by an attorney-general's henchmen in case of legal challenges; it was public, and explorers had to read it in person (and have it translated as well as possible) in front of the natives of all new lands they discovered. On the negative side, it endorsed astonishing despotism. As pointed out by the Flints, various versions existed, and the specific versions used by various Mendoza-era explorers, such as Coronado, are not known. Below, I have adapted and combined various versions. Flint and Flint (2005, 616–18) translate a specific version dating from 1514 or 1515.

Imagine an explorer, then, accompanied by a few semieffective translators, reading this document to villagers somewhere in Guatemala or Sonora:

> On behalf of the King, Don Carlos V, and his Queen, subduers of the
> barbarous nations, I, ——, his servant, inform and make known to you,
> as best I can, the following. The Lord God created heaven and earth,
> and made one man and one woman, of whom we are all descendants.
> But because of the multitude that sprang from this original man and
> woman, during the five thousand years and more since the world began,
> it was necessary for some men to go one way and some another, dividing
> themselves into many provinces.

So far, so good. The explorer was explaining the European view of the
world. The estimate of Earth's age had been obtained by adding up all the
generations mentioned in the Bible since Adam. It was fine-tuned more
famously a century later, in the 1600s, by Bishop James Ussher in Ireland.
(He put the date of creation at 23 October [Julian] in 4004 B.C.) Of course,
this calculation is too short by a factor of a million and has been abandoned
in most of the educated world, except in the United States, where funda-
mentalists try to insert it in public school science classes.

Now came the next most important part of the requerimiento—the
sociotheological structure of things.

> Over all these nations, God appointed one man, called Saint Peter, to
> be superior to all men in the world, so that everyone should obey him.
> ... God commanded [Saint Peter and each of his successors] to put his
> seat in Rome, the spot most fitting from which to rule the world. From
> there he should judge and govern all Christians, Moors, Jews, Gentiles,
> and all other sects. This man is called the Pope. The men who lived in
> the time of Saint Peter regarded him as the most superior person of the
> universe. People have regarded all the others who have been elected to
> serve as Pope, after him, in the same way.
>
> One of these Popes has given all these islands and mainlands—all the
> Indies and Mexico—to the aforesaid King and Queen, and to all their
> successors. This is recorded in certain legal writings, which you can see
> if you wish.

Even this was a step forward—compared to Attila the Hun. A certain
absurdity hung over the scene, however, as an expeditionary or priest read
the document in Spanish or Latin, through translators, to astonished Native

Americans. Still, like many legal documents, it salved consciences by giving conquerors an answer to their critics. Everything was legal and proper. Now came the important part:

> Therefore, their highnesses, the King and Queen, are lords of these islands and this mainland. . . . Many of the inhabitants of these lands, once informed of the aforesaid facts—indeed nearly all to whom this proclamation has been read—have accepted their highnesses as their lords, in the way that subjects of a king ought to do, with goodwill and no resistance. They also received and obeyed the priests whom their highnesses sent to preach to them and teach them about our holy faith. They have all become Christians, and their highnesses have joyfully received them, commanding that they be treated as subjects of Spain.
>
> Thus, as best we can, we ask and require that you think about what we have said, and take whatever time you need to deliberate about it, and that you acknowledge the Church as the ruler and superior organizer of the whole world; and the Pope as high priest; and the King and Queen of Spain as our lords and as the lords of these lands, since the Pope has designated these lands to belong to the King and Queen of Spain.

Here is a bit of becoming modesty: "As best we can, we ask . . . that you think about what we have said." At least the writer of that sentence recognized that there might be difficulties in understanding between the reader and the listeners. Did that writer have to fight with members of some committee in some European palace to get that sentence into the document? Did debate occur about whether the whole document was a farce? The language continued in a soft vein.

> If you do so, you will do well, and we will receive you in all love and charity, and we will leave you your wives and children and lands, free without servitude, that you may do with them as you think best, freely. The King and Queen will not compel you to become Christian unless you yourselves, when informed of the truth, wish to be converted to our holy Catholic faith, as almost all the inhabitants of the other lands have done. Furthermore, their highnesses will award you many privileges and benefits.

After the velvet glove came the iron fist:

> But if you do not agree to this, or maliciously delay in doing it, I certify that with the help of God we will forcefully enter your country and attack

you in every way we can, and subject you to the yoke and obedience of the Church and of their highnesses. We will take you and your wives and children and make slaves of them, and will sell and dispose of them as their highnesses may command. Also, we will take away your goods, and do you all the harm and damage that we can, as befits vassals who do not obey, or who refuse to receive their lord, resisting and contradicting him. Further, we state that the deaths and losses that you will suffer from this are your own fault, and not that of their highnesses, or ours, or any of the soldiers that may come.

In spite of its harshness, the requerimiento was a legal tool intended by at least some of its authors to advance the cause of fairness — it was a sort of sixteenth-century *Miranda* clause. On the freewheeling American frontier, however, it was not very effective. In early 1537 Bishop Zumárraga and Bartolomé de Las Casas met with other clerics in Mexico City and then sent a letter to Pope Paul III urging a clearer edict. Thus, in June 1537 Pope Paul III issued another small step on the Renaissance road out of the Middle Ages, a papal proclamation called *Sublimis Deus*. It presented the "infallible" opinion that "the Indians are truly men and they are . . . capable of understanding the Catholic faith. . . . The said Indians . . . are by no means to be deprived of their liberty or . . . their property."

Word of this probably reached Mendoza toward the end of 1537 and probably influenced his next steps. In one bold move, he proclaimed freedom for the northern Indians from the slave raiding conducted by Guzmán. No doubt he was encouraged not only by the pope but also by Cabeza de Vaca's insistence on the friendliness and intelligence of the Native Americans along most of his party's route. In this act, Mendoza foreshadowed by some 326 years Abraham Lincoln's Emancipation Proclamation. Lincoln had precious little control over the situation he confronted, and Antonio Mendoza had even less. In the haciendas, mines, and construction sites of New Spain, many overseers were not about to have their profitable practices cramped by proclamations from distant cathedrals, universities, and viceroys.

The King Supports Mendoza: April 1538

The requerimiento, the *Sublimis Deus*, and Cabeza de Vaca's testimony were only three of the tools that Viceroy Mendoza inherited to deal with governance. On 17 April 1538 King Carlos V gave him another tool, an authorization to pursue exploration of the North. It meant that the viceroy, not the marqués del Valle de Oaxaca (Cortés), had the right to explore the northern lands. News of this authorization may have reached Mendoza in the summer of 1538.

Armed with this proclamation, Mendoza tried a new tack in his attempt to learn about the North. He turned to a highly recommended Franciscan priest, Marcos de Niza, who had recently arrived in Mexico City. Marcos agreed to attempt a northern reconnaissance. Again, Mendoza tells the story in his own words in his 1539 letter to the king. He relates that after the Dorantes plan collapsed, "a black who came with Dorantes remained with me. [Also there were] some slaves I had bought, and some Indians I had recruited [who were] natives of those [northern] regions. These [people] I sent with Fray Marcos de Niza and a companion of his, a [Franciscan] ecclesiastic. [I chose them] because they are men who have been in this part of the world a long while, accustomed to labor, [having] experience with matters in the Indies" (Flint and Flint 2005, 47).

The simple comment "a black . . . remained with me" hides a dramatic tale. Viceroy Mendoza is usually described as simply having bought Estevan as a servant from Andrés Dorantes. But a chronicle written in 1584 by a historian named Obregón reveals that Estevan was a valuable commodity. It says that Dorantes "was very grieved at being asked that Estevan should serve the viceroy. He would not release him for 500 pesos, which the viceroy sent on a plate of silver, but then said he was willing for Estevan to serve the viceroy in the name of His Majesty, without payment, because of the good that might be done for the souls of the native peoples of those [northern] lands and also because of the good that might accrue to the royal estate" (see Aiton 1927). So Estevan the Moor seems to have been "on loan" to the viceroy's proposed expedition. Estevan was a crucial player, since he had already traveled in the mysterious northern lands and had proved his worth as he established rapport among the northern villages.

The viceroy's plan finally materialized. Marcos would depart quietly, not only with Estevan the Moor, who had already traversed much of the country, but also with some of the Indians who had come south with Cabeza de Vaca's party. Marcos's miniexpedition also included a lay brother named Onorato and, almost surely, a handful of other unnamed assistants, messengers, and servants from Mexico City. They would travel north, assure the Indians that the slave raiders were gone, reconnoiter the lands, and find out if there really was another wealthy empire and, if so, how to get there. The viceroy also ordered them to investigate the configuration of the coast and to send reports back along the way by messengers. Finally, they were to return and report in secret only to Mendoza.

Secrecy was essential, because the race to the north was heating up. Stories of the Cabeza de Vaca trek were circulating, along with the earlier rumors of northern cities obtained by Guzmán and Cortés. Various parties, not to mention Cortés, with his shipbuilding yards on the coast, were organizing to explore the North on their own. Cortés had already side-stepped official orders. Who would get there first?

By August 1538 Mendoza had his plan ready to go. To maintain order on the northern frontier and fill the gap left by the arrest of Guzmán, Mendoza appointed a promising young friend, Francisco Vázquez de Coronado, as the new governor of the northwest frontier, a province then known as Nueva Galicia (New Galicia, named after a province in Spain). Nueva Galicia included Guzmán's headquarters town of Compostela and the even more distant northwest coastal outpost of Culiacán.

Francisco Vázquez, known later simply as Coronado, has an uncertain early history. His biographer Herbert Bolton estimates that he was born in 1510, making him twenty-eight years old when he assumed the governorship (1949, 19).

In September 1538 the young governor left Mexico City for his new post, taking with him Marcos de Niza, Onorato, Estevan de Dorantes, the crowd of northern Indians, and probably various unnamed servants. They headed first for the governor's headquarters in Compostela and then continued to Culiacán. The 1538 departure date from Mexico City is important in terms of later events. This date is known from a letter written in the next month by an obscure priest named Ximénez, quoted by the historian Henry Wagner in 1934. From the point of view of Spaniards in Mexico City, therefore, 1538 was the date of departure for Marcos's expedition to explore the North. When Marcos submitted his final report on this effort, however, he began it with his departure from Culiacán in 1539. Thus, while contemporaries saw his journey as a 1538 expedition, later historians associated it with 1539—a point that led to spurious later accounts of a separate 1538 expedition (Nallino and Hartmann 2003).

The first deliberate reconnaissance of the fabled North (the future United States) was now under way. If a golden empire really existed, Viceroy Mendoza, Governor Coronado, and their inner circle would soon know.

But would Marcos de Niza learn something before Cortés's ships came back with a rival claim on the northern lands? Whose claim would the king honor? If Cortés did get there first, would he proceed with military conquest and slaughter, as happened in Tenochtitlan and Peru?

CHAPTER FIVE

The Case of the "Lying Monk"

Now we come to the heart of the strange story of the man whom Viceroy Mendoza picked to explore the northern frontier: Fray Marcos de Niza, which is to say, Friar Marcos from Nice, the beautiful city on the French Mediterranean coast. According to all the viceroy's sources of information, he was a good choice. He'd already served in Peru, where his fellow priests elected him as *custodio*, or manager of his local order. He was willing to criticize conquistadorial outrages there. He had visited the first bishop of Mexico, Juan de Zumárraga, in April 1537, and the bishop promptly wrote a glowing testimonial, saying that Marcos was "a great religious person, worthy of credit, of approved virtue, and of much religion and zeal" (quoted by Wagner 1934, 198). The minister provincial of New Spain also recommended Marcos for the trip north, saying he was "esteemed by me and my brethren of the governing deputies . . . and held suitable . . . for making this journey . . . because of the aforesaid sufficiency of his person [and also] for being learned—not only in theology, but also in cosmography [the art of navigation]" (Flint and Flint 2005, 67).

Nearly a year after Marcos left Mexico City, he returned to report good lands and the first European sighting of a multistoried trading community. Cíbola, it was named. As a result of this discovery, which confirmed Spanish dreams, Marcos gained immense popularity. By late 1539 he was touted as heir apparent to become the second bishop of all of Mexico. In 1540 he helped lead the mighty Coronado expedition back to Cíbola.

Then disaster struck. Late in 1540 Marcos came back from the Coronado journey in disgrace. Soldiers of the expedition insulted him to his face, and he went down in the history books as a liar, a fraud, the first Great American Con Man. He had lied to everyone about Cíbola, according to the gossip. In the 1800s, however, a few investigators came to his defense. As early as 1886, the historian-archaeologist Adolph Bandelier wrote that "Fray Marcos . . . has been treated as an exaggerator, even, to put it bluntly, as a liar, an impostor. . . . [Yet,] as for those of his writings that remain to us, their facts are surprisingly accurate" (Bandelier [1886] 1981, quoted by Rodack 1981, 98–99). American historian George Parker Winship, in a 1904 book about Coronado (republished in 1990), offered criticisms of Marcos but agreed that "Friar Marcos was not a liar" (1990, 21).

Later in the twentieth century, however, three major historians shot back with prodigious rhetoric, creating the dominant twentieth-century view that Marcos was a charlatan. Here is University of California geographer-historian Carl Sauer touching off the argument in 1932:

> The paucity and confusion of data as to terrain, as to direction, distances, and . . . latitude, make [Marcos de Niza's *relación*, or report] easily the worst geographic document on this frontier, and indicates either that Brother Mark was an amazing dunderhead or that he indulged in deliberate obfuscation. . . . If we subscribe to the old theory that he was an arrant swindler, it is perhaps more charitable to leave him in that role, rather than have him also a fool who had no business to wander about in strange places. (1932, 30)

University of California historian Henry Wagner followed Sauer's lead with his blistering critique of Marcos in 1934, writing that "such people . . . are simply victims of their own imaginations or hallucinations" (227). Self-described "free-lance" New Mexico historian Cleve Hallenbeck followed with a key book about Marcos in 1949. He wins the "Malign Marcos" prize with his talk about Marcos's "whopping falsehoods" ([1949] 1987, 70), "mendacity" (76), and "disregard for most of his instructions" (85). His index includes "Marcos . . . hallucinations of" and "sanity of" (113). Hallenbeck's final sentences: "I confess that I have been harassed by the suspicion that the friar's more recent defenders have espoused his cause . . . as a 'comedy relief' from their staid work as professional historians. . . . It is difficult for me to believe that any careful student of the twentieth century would *seriously* defend Marcos. . . . So let us pigeonhole 'The Lying Monk' with the other Munchausens of history" (95).

The basic objection of these three historians was that Marcos de Niza did not have time to complete the trip he reported. Therefore, they said, he reached only as far north as the modern Arizona-Sonora border, turned back, and made up the rest of his story by exaggerating information he'd received from local people along his route.

The "Case of the Lying Monk" is complicated by the fact that most twentieth-century popular accounts said Marcos came back to Mexico reporting vast treasures of gold in Cíbola and single-handedly motivated the Coronado expedition under false pretenses. The reality is that we have notarized copies of Marcos's official report, and they never mention gold in Cíbola! From what we know now, the descriptions that Marcos recorded in his relación—people, coastline, turquoise jewelry, even the multistoried towns of stone construction—were essentially correct.

This chapter is thus different from the other chapters because we have a mystery on our hands. Can we trust our sources? Did Marcos really run out of time and make up his tale? Did the discovery of the Seven Cities of Cíbola involve a colossal hoax? If not, then how did a widely respected priest end up in history books as a conniving liar? In this chapter, we're trying to understand not only Marcos the man but the vicissitudes of how history is made. In my citations, I rely mainly on the definitive translation by New Mexico scholars Richard and Shirley Flint and cite some of their page numbers; however, I have been influenced also by other translations and occasionally synthesize (combine) the various translations or abridge them to get a clear, concise meaning of what the author was saying. Marcos's narrative, in particular, is so linear that interested readers will be able to find the passages in Flint and Flint (2005) or in any other translation they may have.

Marcos the Man: 1495?–1558

What a life Marcos lived! He grew up in Europe but was uniquely related to all three of the major American conquests. He arrived in recently conquered Tenochtitlan and was sought out by Cortés, he traveled with Pizarro in Peru, and, finally, he led Coronado into what is now the United States. (Viceroy Antonio Mendoza is another member of this small club. He served with Cortés, organized the Coronado expedition, and then briefly served as viceroy in Peru in 1551–1552, about two decades after Pizarro's conquest.)

Not much is currently known about Marcos's early years, although still-undiscovered documents may exist in Mexico, Spain, or France. My colleague Michel Nallino, who lives in Nice, is Marcos's primary modern biographer and has assembled the known information in a magnificent

Web-based multivolume biography in French (Nallino 2012). A Franciscan priest and historian, Pedro Oroz, around 1585 collected some sketchy, early notes about Marcos (as referenced in a 1584 book cited by Wagner in 1934), saying that Marcos was born in Aquitaine, a province in the south of France. As for Marcos's birth date, the *Encyclopedia Britannica* and Nallino (2012) cite the year 1495, but I've found no other confirmation of that. Marcos said in a 1546 letter that he was an orphan. He was educated in a monastery named Sainte-Croix in Nice, perhaps having been left there, hence "Marcos de Niza." While Nice is now in France, it then belonged to the province of Genoa, in Italy. As a boy, he experienced the exciting years when the idea of a New World was being born in European minds.

SIDEBAR: The Novel as a Tool for Understanding History

Curiosity about the Marcos mystery led me to study the Marcos-era documents for some years in the 1990s and publish a number of papers in scholarly journals. Eventually, I succumbed to temptation and wrote a novel about the case (*Cities of Gold*, 2002). The experience changed my view of history.

I see a novelist not just as an entertainer but as a scientist of the human psyche, trying to synthesize all that we know about our sometimes messy, all-too-human behavior. The process of writing a historical novel, in particular, puts the novelist more directly in the shoes of the historical figures than does the traditional process of historical analysis. A historian may be concerned foremost with what happened, but a novelist is equally concerned with why it happened, facing questions about thought processes, motivations, and relationships. For example, a personal letter is one thing when read at face value as a record of names, dates, and stated events, but it may turn into something else if we start asking personal questions. What did the writer know at the time? What did he or she leave out? What did the recipient know? What were their attitudes toward each other? Was the writer conscious of a possible third reader? My best analogy is that some historians may act like prosecuting attorneys who try to assemble the known facts in a version that will get a conviction. The novelist is more like the cop on the beat at an earlier stage in the case, perhaps worried about arresting the wrong man and trying to figure out what really happened among all the "persons of interest." I was particularly happy, therefore, when western environmental writer Craig Childs (2002) remarked in reviewing my novel that it dealt not only with history but with "the formation . . . of history"—which is the real issue in the case of Marcos de Niza.

The monastery no longer survives, but Michel Nallino took me to the site, located amidst the modern bustle of cars on the Rue de France.

Oroz recorded that Marcos left Europe for America in 1531. The young priest arrived, likely thirty-something years in age, in a world as alien as Pluto or Purgatory. Oroz said he landed in the Spanish colony on the Caribbean island of Española and then proceeded to Peru. French historian Michal Nallino confirms that Marcos arrived in Peru in 1531, the year before Pizarro's third, best-known expedition. He was regarded well enough to be elected commissary, or manager of supplies. According to documents published in the mid-1500s by the priest-historian Bartolomé de Las Casas, Marcos was aghast at the behavior of the conquistadors and testified a few years later about their atrocities against the Incas and their leader, Atahualpa:

> I, Fray Marcos de Niza, of the order of St. Francis, commissary in Peru over the friars of that order . . . speak out in order to give a truthful account of certain matters which I saw with my own eyes in that country. Through various experiences I found out that the Indians of Peru are among the most benevolent people that have been found among all the Indians. . . . They are friendly toward the Christians and I saw that they gave the Spaniards an abundance of gold, silver, and precious stones, and everything asked of them, whatever they possessed or could be helpful. Their great lord, Atahualpa, gave these Spaniards more than two million in gold and all the country in his possession very soon after the Spanish entered that country.
>
> Yet, soon after Atahualpa gave the Spaniards his gold, and without provocation from the Indians, the Spaniards executed him. . . . They also burned the feet of another lord of Quito, Aluis, and tortured him in other ways, to force him to reveal any additional gold of Atahualpa, a treasure of which it seems he knew nothing.
>
> I also know of an incident where the Spaniards collected a number of Indians and shut them up in three large houses . . . and then set fire to them and burned them all. . . . One of our priests, Ocaña, rescued one boy from the fire, but along came another Spaniard, who threw him back, where he was reduced to ashes like the rest. . . .
>
> In God and my conscience, so far as I can understand, the only reason that the Indians of Peru rose in revolt was because of the bad treatment—a fact that is clear to everybody. . . . They determined to die rather than to suffer such treatment. (abridged from Las Casas [1552] 1992; see also Hartmann 2002)

Las Casas quotes additional Marcos reports from Peru in this vein. Such reporting was hardly popular among the conquistadors. Marcos moved from place to place amidst those years of carnage. In 1534 he was with a side expedition in Ecuador led by none other than Pedro de Alvarado, "the Sun" of Cortés's army in Mexico, who, fourteen years before, had ordered the disastrous slaughter of the dancers in Tenochtitlan, arguably leading to the destruction of the whole city. Alvarado, for his troubles, had been appointed governor of Guatemala. According to Nallino (private communication, 2012), Marcos probably headed to Guatemala in a party with Alvarado in 1535. By September 1536, Marcos showed up at legal inquiries in Guatemala, testifying against the conquistadors' outrages.

Nallino notes that Marcos probably crossed paths at that time with Bartolomé de Las Casas, but they may even have met as early as 1531 in Peru, allowing chances for Las Casas to collect Marcos's comments. Later, around 1560, Las Casas confirmed (in his massive *Apologetic History* of the Indies) that he had known Marcos well (see Wagner and Parish 1967). Las Casas may have been the one who recommended Marcos to the elderly bishop of Mexico, Juan de Zumárraga.

When Zumárraga heard the good reports about Marcos, he invited Marcos to Mexico City. A few months later, Zumárraga's April 1537 letter noted that Marcos had visited Zumárraga "in my house." There, Marcos was surrounded by the bustling transformation of the ruined Aztec city into a Spanish city only sixteen years after Tenochtitlan's destruction by Cortés. At the bishop's urging, Marcos signed another testimonial against the "crimes and cruelties" of Peru. Zumárraga said they wanted to "put a stop to these conquests, which are opprobrious injuries to our Christianity [because] there have been . . . as many butcheries as there have been conquests" (Wagner 1934, 196–97). Zumárraga says he also took Marcos to see Viceroy Mendoza.

Marcos was thus visiting Viceroy Mendoza in 1537, just at the time when Mendoza was hatching his plan to get Andrés Dorantes and Estevan de Dorantes to lead a party to explore the North before Cortés could gain the upper hand. After Mendoza gave up on sending Dorantes north, he turned in 1538 to Marcos as the man who could do the job.

Marcos Gets the Viceroy's Orders: Autumn 1538

Marcos was now probably in his early forties—older than many conquistadors, but not too old for more adventures. As described in chapter 4, Mendoza's proposition was that Marcos would lead a quiet expedition and report back in secret. Marcos agreed, and the expedition left Mexico City in September 1538.

On 20 November, far from prying eyes in Mexico City, Governor Coronado handed Marcos a set of sealed instructions from Viceroy Mendoza. This bit of stealth was presumably designed to keep information about the expedition from reaching Cortés and the excitable young adventurers swarming the streets of Mexico City. The secret instructions have been preserved in Spanish archives and are usually appended to Marcos's relación. They form a crucial document, because they reveal Mendoza's vision, interests, and suspicions about the North, including lands of the future United States:

> Tell the Indians that I send you in the name of His Majesty, to see that they are treated well. And say that he grieves because of the wrongs they have suffered. Anyone who does evil to them will be punished. Assure them they will no longer be made slaves or removed from their lands, but will be free, and that they should put aside any fears and recognize God, Our Lord, who is in heaven, and the King, who is placed on earth by God to govern it. . . .
>
> If, with the aid of God, you find a route to enter the country beyond, take with you Estevan Dorantes as a guide, whom I order to obey you in all that you command. If he fails to do so, he shall incur penalties. . . .
>
> Francisco Vázquez de Coronado has with him the Indians who came from the northern lands with Dorantes. If it seems advisable to both of you, take some of them in your company, and employ them as you see fit to the service of Our Lord.
>
> Always arrange to travel as securely as possible. Inform yourself in advance if the Indians are at peace or if some are at war with others. Give them no occasion to commit any violence toward you, which would be cause for punishing them. . . . Take much care to observe the following: people who are there, if they are many or few, and if they are scattered or live in communities; quality and fertility of the soil; climate of the country; trees and plants and domestic and wild animals; nature of the ground, whether rough or level; rivers, if large or small; minerals and metals that are there. If there are any things that you can send or bring as specimens, bring them or send them, so that His Majesty can be advised of everything. (the instructions listed here and below are adapted from the more complete translation by Flint and Flint 2005, 65–66)

Next came the command, underappreciated today, to learn about the coast:

Always inquire about knowledge of the coast, whether north or south, because the land may become narrower [i.e., Mexico might be an island—WKH] or some arm of the sea may run into the interior of the land [see map 7a]. If you come to the coast of the South Sea [the Pacific Ocean], bury letters about noteworthy matters on selected promontories at the foot of some prominent tree, and on such trees make a cross so that it can be seen. Likewise, on the largest trees at the mouths of rivers, and in situations suitable for harbors, make this same sign and leave letters, because if we send ships, they will be advised to look for such signs.

Then came an instruction that would play an important role later in the strange saga of Marcos's future reputation: "Always try to arrange to send information by the Indians, telling especially how you are faring, how you are received, and especially what you find. If God is so pleased that you find a grand settlement, where you think there are good materials to build a monastery, where religious officials could be sent . . . then . . . inform [me] via Indians or return yourself to Culiacán in complete secrecy and inform me, so that appropriate steps can be arranged without [any] commotion." This secrecy, if maintained, would insure that Viceroy Mendoza would receive the news before potential rivals. In an additional instruction, Mendoza tried more explicitly to preempt any rival claims on the northern land, adding a bit of European hubris and Christian exceptionalism: "Though the land already belongs to our lord the Emperor, you should formally take possession of it on behalf of His Majesty in my name. Make the proper signs and ceremonies, and inform the natives that there is one God in heaven and an emperor on earth to govern the land, and that everyone must be his subjects and serve him."

As I've remarked, many twentieth-century historians virtually ignored that Mendoza was considering a two-pronged land/sea expedition and ordered Marcos to investigate the seacoast. For example, Hallenbeck, in his pivotal book on Marcos, stupefyingly *denies* that Marcos was ever urged to explore the coast. Hallenbeck claims that "Marcos was *not* [Hallenbeck's emphasis] instructed to visit the coast" but only to "inquire always for information . . . and if perchance he came to the coast, to leave evidence" ([1949] 1987, 84). This paraphrase disingenuously pretends that any coastal encounter would have been a lucky by-product of Marcos's expedition. In reality, Mendoza clearly wanted such information from Marcos, even instructing him how to leave messages for ships and post signs at potential harbors.

In this same vein, several historians, notably Carl Sauer in 1932, investigated a later, colonial-era northward route that stayed inland. They assumed that Marcos had to travel on that route, even though Marcos, on his way north, recorded islands and often spoke of his attempts to gather coastal information. Marcos was clearly thinking about the coast. A key example is an incident when he was told of an inland region that might have gold. He says in his relación that "as this region is away from the coast, and as my instructions are not to depart from it, I decided to leave that [inland] region for my return" (Flint and Flint 2005, 68). This suggests that Marcos stayed to the west during his northern trip but took a more direct, inland route during his return. In any case, Marcos remembered his instruction to favor the coast, even if reputable historians forgot about it.

Toward the Frontier: December 1538

By December 1538 Coronado, Marcos, and his party were at Compostela, the governance center of New Spain's northern frontier (see map 8). Coronado wrote to the king on 15 December (his Julian calendar dating), saying that he planned to leave for the extremity of Euro-Christian civilization, Culiacán, on 23 December.

Months later (15 July 1539), Coronado wrote another letter to the king, shedding optimistic light on the frontier situation. He told how Indians near Culiacán had "rebelled" against Guzmán in 1536 and that in 1538 they had been

> occupying the mountain ranges because of their uprising. They had no houses nor did they plant crops, but now [mid-1539] they are building houses, and preparing fields. They have returned to their accustomed locations, but with much reduced population.
>
> Into this province I brought with me a Franciscan, Fray Marcos de Niza. Viceroy Mendoza recommended that I bring him inland, as per your Majesty's order to reconnoiter the coast of this New Spain by land, in order to learn what secrets, lands, and people are there.

Note once again that, contrary to Hallenbeck and Sauer, Coronado says that Marcos, as per royal orders, was going there to "reconnoiter the coast." This and the next passages from the letter are abridged and adapted from the Flint and Flint translation (2005, 39–40), with a nod toward the shorter translation by Hammond and Rey (1940), telling how Coronado prepared for the beginning of Marcos's epic journey northward:

> In order that Marcos might travel safely, I sent some Indians from among the slaves whom the viceroy had freed, to the towns of Petatlán [see map 8]

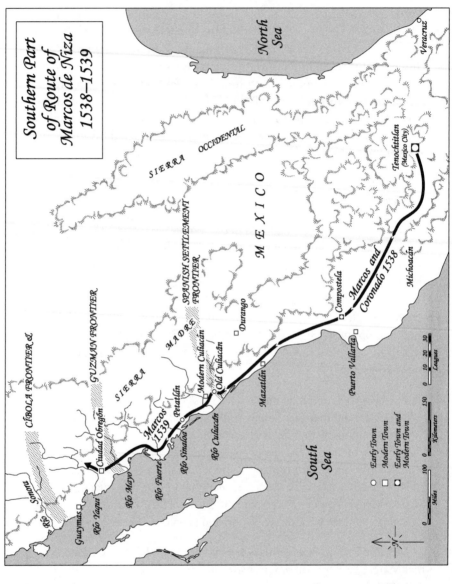

Map 8. The first half of Marcos de Niza's journey to the North. Marcos and Governor Coronado left Mexico City in late 1538 for Coronado's headquarters in Culiacán. Marcos began his explorations from there in 1539. Stippled "Cíbola Frontier" shows the approximate zone north of which Cíbola was well known. Map by Ron Beckwith.

and also Cuchillo, located nearly 60 leagues [140 to 180 miles] beyond Culiacán. I told them to summon natives from those towns and tell them not to be afraid. As a result, and also because the messengers were free men, which amazed them, more than 80 men came to see me.

I explained Your Majesty's royal will (which, for now, is that you want only for them to become Christians and know God and your Majesty as their lord). Then I directed them to take Fray Marcos and Estevan into the interior of the land, in complete safety. They did this just as I asked, treating them most excellently.

Viceroy Mendoza summarized the situation in a letter to the king, undated but also written in 1539. He described the Indians who had come to visit Coronado:

They said they represented all their people, who wanted to learn about the newcomers who were doing them so much good, and allowing them to return to their homes, and letting them plant maize. After all, they'd been in flight in the mountains for several years, hiding like wild beasts for fear of being enslaved. . . .

Coronado comforted them with kind words, fed them, and had them stay for three or four days. During those days the ecclesiastics [Marcos and associates?—WKH] taught them to make the sign of the cross and say the name of our lord, Jesus. . . . Then Coronado sent them home, telling them not to fear, but to remain calm. He gave them clothes, rosary beads, knives, and other such things which I had supplied for this purpose. They departed well pleased, saying that whenever he sent for them, they and many others would come and do whatever I might command.

When the groundwork for the *entrada* [entrance into a region] had thus been prepared, and Marcos and his companions had spent ten or twelve days with the Black Moor and other slaves and Indians I had given him, they departed. (abridged and adapted from the translation by Flint and Flint 2005, 48)

Marcos's Journey and Why It Matters: 1538–1539

Marcos and his companions were now on their way north. The main source of information we have about his journey is Marcos's own *relación*, which was handed to Mendoza and officially notarized in 1539 at the end of the journey. It is chatty, relaxed, entertaining, and seemingly open-hearted and

displays a sense of humor, but it is skimpy on dates or specific place-names—
perhaps deliberately so, as we'll see. It offers challenges. Can we reconstruct
Marcos's route, both northward and southward? Can we solve our primary
mystery: Did Marcos have time to complete his journey? Marcos was in a
hurry to explore the North and get back to Mendoza, so if his story is true,
he needs to accomplish his orders without much excess time left over. One
of my rules has been to follow a Goldilocks principle: His rates of travel
can't be impossibly fast, but they can't be too slow, either. They need to be
just right (see sidebar, "How Far Could Marcos Travel in a Day?," p. 159).

At many points, we can link the relación to consistent information from
the Cabeza de Vaca journey and later accounts from the Coronado expedition. Only by taking all the reports together can we construct a latticework
of clues. Adding recent discoveries of artifacts, we can tie down parts of the
route in ways that were unknown only a few years ago.

First Steps toward the North: 7 March 1539

Marcos, Onorato, Estevan, additional servants, and enthused Native escorts
left Culiacán on Friday, 7 March, according to Marcos's certified relación.
The party headed from Culiacán up the trail toward the Indian villages
of Petatlán and Cuchillo, where Guzmán had raided (see map 8). They
were met at various villages with joyful festivity. The porters, carrying their
baggage, helped them travel fast between villages.

Examples of routing issues arose at once. First, the Culiacán of Marcos's
time was some 30 miles south of the present town (Hallenbeck [1949] 1987,
98, footnote 27). Second, the locations of Petatlán and Cuchillo are now
unknown, even though Petatlán was on a river then called by that name.
How far were Petatlán and Cuchillo from Culiacán? Clues are buried in
several sources, mostly found in the definitive modern translations of Flint
and Flint (2005). They illustrate the range of uncertainty in this kind of
detective work.

* Cabeza de Vaca's reports say the Río Petatlán was 30 or 35 leagues
  from Culiacán.
* A 1533 report by Jorge Robledo, who had traveled with Guzmán,
  cites 50 leagues from Culiacán to the Río Petatlán (as mentioned by
  Adorno and Pautz 1999, 2:367).
* Coronado's letter to the king of 15 July 1539 refers to "the towns of
  Petatlán and Cuchillo, nearly 60 leagues north of Culiacán." The

wording could imply that Cuchillo is "nearly 60 leagues" north, with Petatlán being closer.

* Marcos mentions "Petatlán and . . . Cuchillo, which is 50 leagues from [Culiacán]." The wording again suggests it is Cuchillo that is at 50 leagues, while Petatlán is closer.

* Pedro de Castañeda, the soldier-memoirist with Coronado in 1540, gave two different distances for Petatlán — 20 leagues and 30 leagues.

* Juan Jaramillo, a captain in Coronado's army, says it took them four days to go from Culiacán to Petatlán. At typical rates for the army, this makes it 20 to 28 leagues to Petatlán.

* Jaramillo says they crossed the Río Petatlán after four days and then crossed the Río Sinaloa three days later. Some modern historians assume the Río Petatlán was the river known today as the Río Sinaloa but must then claim the names were shifted in position in later decades. I see no need for this.

Seeking the best fit to all the data, I've assumed that Petatlán was 25 to 30 leagues (62 to 90 miles) north of Culiacán and that Cuchillo was about 55 leagues (137 to 170 miles) north of Culiacán.

To deal with the alleged insufficient time for Marcos to complete his trip, I assume Marcos started with a burst of enthusiasm. Moving at a plausible 21 to 30 miles per day, he'd have reached Petatlán on Sunday evening, 9 March. (Since Petatlán and Cuchillo were known to the Spaniards, and since some of the Indians with Marcos had come from there, it's conceivable that Coronado sent a mounted party at least as far as Petatlán, in which case Marcos might have ridden on a horse or cart and gained as much as a full day ahead of the schedule I have given him.)

Petatlán was named from a local word for the reed mats used to construct lightweight walls of modest homes throughout the warm coastal plains (see fig. 4). To supplement figure 4, I note that Arizona anthropologist Edward Spicer, writing in 1980 about the Yaqui Indians in this region in the 1930s and 1940s, shows a 1942 photo of such a structure, rectangular, with diagonally woven "twilled cane" mat walls and similar mats on the relatively flat roof (his p. 18). His photo shows one such structure plastered over with mud, and Spicer remarks on seeing numbers of these "plastered" structures, which probably explains why Cabeza de Vaca's party and other later Spaniards recorded some buildings as more "permanent houses."

Marcos's relación says that "in this town of Petatlán [map 8] I rested for three days because my companion, Fray Onorato, suffered from sickness. Because of that, it was advisable for me to leave him there" (Flint and

Flint 2005, 67). When Marcos says, "I rested for three days," I propose that he does not mean a full seventy-two hours of downtime but refers to the "three days" he was in Petatlán, namely, Sunday evening, Monday, and Tuesday morning (9–11 March). This may sound like a stretch, but a quirk of history supports the interpretation. Medieval Europeans inherited the Roman numerical system, which lacked the use of zero. They thought of time not so much in terms of true *durations* but in terms of the number of days involved. The most dramatic proof, almost completely unnoticed, lies at the heart of Christianity. How many days did Jesus lie in his tomb? I've asked many people this question, and they virtually always say "three days." After all, various Christian creeds state that "on the third day" Jesus rose from the dead. But the actual duration, *explicitly reported* in the Bible, was from Friday near sunset to Sunday before dawn—about one and a half days. The early counting system included the first and last day. (The medieval method of music annotation offers another example. If you play the note C on the piano and then move up two steps to E, that interval is called a "third," because the conception was to count the C, the D, and the E, even though there are only two intervals. An "octave" has only seven intervals.) Even today, if we pack the car on Monday morning, depart on Monday at noon, and arrive on Wednesday at noon, we may say, "I spent three days getting there," even though the elapsed *travel* time was only forty-eight hours. I have no proof that Marcos reported travel in this way, but such proof may be confirmable in the future from other records.

As for Onorato, he disappears from recorded history, but it's likely that Marcos told him (on Tuesday morning?) to stay there or in Culiacán in order to facilitate the delivery of any of the messages that Mendoza had ordered Marcos to send back to Mexico City.

Marcos tells us he now traveled another 25 to 30 leagues (62 to 90 miles) beyond Petatlán, probably to Cuchillo. He gathered information about off-shore islands, implying that he traveled near the coast. If he departed Petatlán Tuesday morning (after rising to find Onorato still ill) and then arrived on Thursday evening, 13 March, the rate would be about 22 to 32 miles per day—another burst of speed, since Marcos had rested all day Monday.

In a touching comment, Marcos says that the people native to this area had become "more skillful in hiding themselves than in planting." This proves he was still in the zone ravaged by Guzmán. He says he saw nothing worth discussing in his relación—probably because the region was already known to the Spaniards. The distances suggest he had arrived at the Río Fuerte, which I measure at about 141 trail miles from old Culiacán (following prefreeway roads on Mexican road maps; see map 8).

All along this part of the trip, Marcos tells how the newly freed Indians met him "with many hospitalities, and presents of food, roses . . . and huts they built of mats and brush in the uninhabited districts . . . , arranging . . . celebrations and triumphal arches" (Flint and Flint 2005, 67). Celebratory arches were widely observed throughout Sonora in later centuries. In the 1690s the Jesuit explorer of northern Sonora, Eusebio Kino, had a military aide, Capt. Juan Mateo Manje, whose diary repeatedly mentions Sonoran natives carrying arches during joyous welcoming ceremonies in various towns. Spicer says that among peoples native to southern Sonora in the early twentieth century, the arch still connoted "a beautiful part of the setting for a ceremony" (1980, 90). He adds that the arches derived from a symbol for the rainbow and were made from cane stalks, freshly cut to nine-to-ten-foot lengths, bent over, and tied to form an arch six or seven feet high (91, 173). Spicer's page 91 includes a photo of such an arch. The descriptions by Manje in the 1690s and Spicer in the 1980s agree perfectly with Marcos de Niza's account of 1539.

SIDEBAR: How Far Could Marcos Travel in a Day?

As mentioned in the text, the major charge against Marcos is that he could not have completed his trip in the time available. Therefore, a key factor in reconstructing Marcos's case is the distance he could travel in a day. My mentions of 20 to 30 miles per day may sound unlikely to some readers, but Marcos was an experienced walker. Franciscan priests of the day generally walked instead of traveling on horseback, and Marcos's own party surely did so, at least beyond Cuchillo.

Marcos gives a few dates and positions during his trip north, allowing us to evaluate his claimed average rates if we try out various locations for those reports. Today, for example, we know that Cíbola corresponds to the modern pueblo of Zuni, New Mexico, as first identified by the Swiss-American geographer Adolph Bandelier as early as the 1880s (Bandelier [1886] 1981, 85–98; Rodack 1981, 34–35). According to historian Cleve Hallenbeck ([1949] 1987, 46), Marcos covered about 1,029 trail miles north from Culiacán to Cíbola/Zuni. Marcos's report indicates that he required forty-five to fifty-four days of cumulative northward travel (not counting days when he said he had halted). This gives an average of 19 to 23 miles per day for the days when he was actually on the trail. Marcos gives little detail about the return trip, but in one place, as we'll see, he

continued

Crossing the "Guzmán Frontier": Mid-March 1539

Marcos's journey took him across three different frontiers (see map 8). The first was the Spanish settlement frontier at Culiacán—the northernmost Spanish outpost of New Spain. The second frontier was the Guzmán frontier, which was the rough, northernmost limit where the local people knew about the Spaniards and their slave-raiding parties. The third frontier, still farther north, was what we'll call the Cíbola frontier, the zone dividing where Cíbola was known from where it was unknown.

Along river valleys on the Cíbola route, Indian villages were typically dotted a few miles apart. Most people in a given valley would thus share

remarks on fleeing a dangerous situation at 8 to 10 leagues per day on several consecutive days, implying that this was toward the upper end of his normal range. This amounts to 20 to 31 trail miles per day when Marcos pushed himself. Marcos would not have reported these rates if they were considered impossible by his contemporaries.

Are such rates plausible in terms of modern experience? Yes. Hallenbeck ([1949] 1987, 43–44) stated that seasoned walkers can cover 25 to 30 miles per day on a smooth, firm trail. He also asserts that indigenous people of the region covered 30 miles per day on a "fair day" but could "maintain . . . better than 50 miles a day on [their] own trails." Hallenbeck said that on backcountry hikes of a week or more, 20 miles a day was a good rate for him, and 25 miles per day was "exceptionally fast." Hallenbeck tended to portray Marcos as an aged man traveling rough trails, but he ignores Marcos's statement that he traveled on a "road" (i.e., a well-used Indian trail) and had Indian friends guiding him, carrying his supplies, and making camp.

Another historian, George Undreiner, writing in 1947, assigns 25 miles per day as typical for Marcos and supports his claim with the case of the hardy southwestern explorer Charles F. Lummis, who in 1884–85 "tramped" (according to Lummis's article title) from Cincinnati to Los Angeles. Undreiner has him covering 3,507 miles in 143 days, for an average of 25 miles per day. I checked and found a road distance from Cincinnati through New Mexico to Los Angeles, estimated on modern Web-based calculators as 2,180 to 2,370 miles. This is about 3,500 kilometers, suggesting that Undreiner confused the units. My numbers give an average travel rate of 15 to 16 miles per day for 143 days, or 18 to 19 miles per day on the trail, with one day of rest per week—plausible and still impressive.

the same knowledge. Therefore, the transitional zones—particularly the Cíbola frontier—probably corresponded to relatively uninhabited zones between major rivers.

After leaving Cuchillo, Marcos crossed the Guzmán frontier. This corresponded to what he called a four-day *despoblado*, probably traveling on Friday (14 March), Saturday, Sunday, and Monday (17 March). Despoblado is a wonderful Spanish term from the 1500s. It refers to a depopulated area, usually a stretch of upland between river valleys. Despoblados were common landscape features in northern Mexico and the southwestern United States, and even today, a driver along highways in the western United States passes through many despoblados. A three-day despoblado

Other examples support such rates. Bertrand Russell, in his autobiography, refers to a "walking tour of Devonshire." He asked his companion, a "terrific walker," to promise to be content with 25 miles per day, but after some days his companion left him, complaining that now he must really "have a little walking." Another example comes from an account of hiker Bob Payne (1987), who considered himself not particularly experienced but decided to walk from Boston to New York. According to his account, he covered 16 miles per day on his first weekend of practice and 30 miles per day on his last weekend of practice six weeks later. On the actual trip, he covered 259 miles on twelve days of walking, averaging a rate of 22 miles per day. An account of a woman park ranger in Montana refers to her frequent walks of "20 miles in a day" as part of her job, "while a 40 mile trek isn't exactly uncommon" (Marston 2011).

Based on these and other accounts, I assume that Marcos could easily manage 17 to 22 miles per day in rough country, 22 to 25 miles per day for sustained marches in smoother country, and 25 to 31 miles per day for a few days at a time when in a hurry. The maximum rate I assign matches the rate Marcos reported as he fled for his life. These are all "road miles," not air line miles. As an example, the "road mileage" cited by Hallenbeck from Mexico City to Compostela is about 1.35 times greater than the air line mileage, a representative ratio that allows for the twists and turns of a ground route.

Assuming these rates, we need only calculate whether Marcos could have done what he said he did. At various points in the text I offer quantitative tests to show that the dates, assigned locations, and distances indicated by Marcos are consistent with the above travel rates. I believe this kind of test is more rigorous than has been done in other reconstructions and critiques of Marcos's journey.

for Marcos is reduced to a one-hour despoblado for us as we tool along in air-conditioned comfort.

The four-day despoblado of the Guzmán frontier was possibly between the lower Río Fuerte and the lower Río Yaqui (see map 8). In this region, roads are fairly straight and level. The lower Río Mayo would have been in the middle of this stretch, but according to our reading of Cabeza de Vaca's observations in 1536, Guzmán had ravaged this area. The villages were depopulated and burned, and thin survivors "lived off bark and roots of trees." According to Coronado's description of conditions when Marcos left Culiacán, Indians in the devastated zone still "had no houses nor did they plant [anything]" (Flint and Flint 2005, 39). Hence, to Marcos, that zone was a despoblado. I estimate a road mileage from the Fuerte across the Mayo to the lower to mid-Yaqui at 120 to 136 miles, depending on the portions of the rivers considered. With four full travel days until Monday evening, 17 March, Marcos traveled at about 30 to 34 miles per day across this relatively flat area, which is plausible for one of Marcos's fastest marches with his servants and enthusiastic local bearers (see the sidebar "How Far Could Marcos Travel in a Day?").

Arriving on the Río Yaqui on Monday evening, Marcos met "other Indians who marveled at seeing me, because they had no knowledge of Christians, since they have no dealings with those below the despoblado." In other words, he had now crossed the Guzmán frontier. He says these people "tried to touch me on my clothes and called me 'Sayota,' by which they mean in their language 'man from the sky.' . . . Thus I traveled for three days [among] those same people" (Flint and Flint 2005, 68).

Cabeza de Vaca noted that anything the people "do not have or do not know the origin of, they say [came] from the sky" and that the whole concept was widespread (Adorno and Pautz 1999, 2:351, 352). It is similar to our own idiom that anything unexpected comes "out of the blue."

Interesting linguistic clues support our idea that Marcos was now somewhere along the Río Yaqui. Linguists Heidi Harley (University of Arizona), Constantino Martínez Fabián (Universidad de Sonora), and I, in an international project, showed that the term recorded by Marcos as "Sayota" matches a word known to modern Yaqui speakers, so'ita or soita, to refer to vertical movement, including things falling from above. (The paper has been submitted to a professional journal and is under review at this writing.) Furthermore, a modern town on this part of the Río Yaqui is named Soyopa (map 9). It has also been spelled Sayopa, even closer to Marcos's spelling. We consulted two modern Yaqui speakers, and they recognized the word so'ita and the town name as relating to movements such as throwing grain up in the air and letting it fall to separate the wheat from the chaff. The match-ups with Yaqui words support our idea that Marcos was passing along the Río Yaqui. The name Yaqui was first recorded for that part of the river in the following year, 1540, by the Coronado expedition—an indication that the area was associated with Yaqui-speaking people. A tempting speculation is that after Marcos visited a certain village along the river, it came to be known as Soyopa (or Sayopa), associated with the visit of the mysterious "man from out of the blue."

To summarize, it seems plausible that Marcos, aka Sayota, was now moving among Yaqui speakers on the Río Yaqui drainage to the general latitude of the village now called Soyopa or Sayopa. He tells us that local villagers welcomed his party with cheerful receptions and gifts of food. He quickly learned that he was moving inland, which fits the way the Río Yaqui angles north, away from the northwest-trending coast. The three days mentioned could have been Tuesday morning through Thursday afternoon or evening (20 March), gaining perhaps 78 to 93 trail miles upstream at 26 to 31 miles per day.

The first 40 miles (after Marcos encountered the Yaqui speakers on the Río Yaqui) would be mostly due north to a point where the river forks, near the modern town of Cumuripa. Here, Marcos had two choices. The first route would follow the eastern fork (the modern-named Río Yaqui itself), jogging east, then traveling north along the river, where a journey of 40 more miles could bring him directly to Soyopa or "Sayopa" (see map 9). The second and more direct route north would continue about 37 miles on the western fork, now known as the Río Tecoripa or Río Suaqui. (Modern Mexican road maps may disagree on names for some rivers due to local traditions along each river segment. After thousands of years of language use, we are still at the tail end of the era when spellings have not been agreed upon!) By Thursday night Marcos could have arrived at the headwaters of that drainage, and by Friday he could have crossed over from the Río Tecoripa to the next northern drainage, the Río Mátape, as can be seen on map 9. Or he might have continued upstream on what is now called the Río Yaqui to the region of Soyopa.

The Lynchpin Town of Vacapa: 21 March 1539

Marcos's next sentences give one of his rare dates and village names. On Friday, "two days before Passion Sunday," he arrived at "a fairly large settlement they called Vacapa, where they gave me a grand welcome and . . .

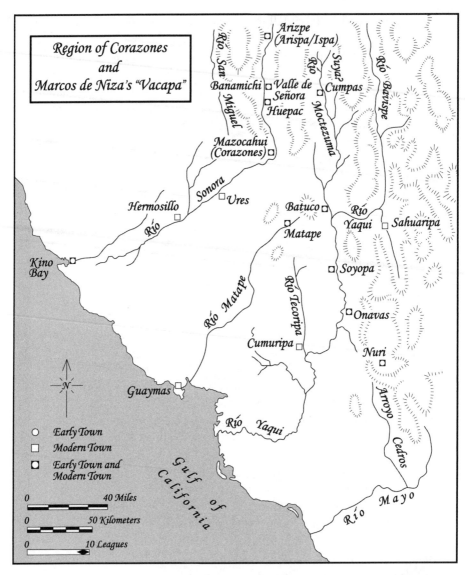

Map 9. A crucial region in Marcos's journey. If Marcos's relación is correct, his town of "Vacapa" and the southernmost towns where Cíbola was known must lie in this area. This map also details important parts of the Coronado expedition's journey (see chapter 8). Map by Ron Beckwith.

much food." Marcos described Vacapa as having abundant food because it was "all irrigated" (Flint and Flint 2005, 68) and lying 40 leagues inland — about 100 to 124 trail miles. Most scholars now consider his Friday arrival date to be 21 March by the Spanish Julian calendar (see the sidebar "A Little Mystery"). This means that he'd been hiking for an exhausting ten days of high-speed hiking since leaving Petatlán. Learning from local informants that he was now moving away from the coast, he decided to rest there until Easter (known to be 6 April) and to use Vacapa as a base from which to send scouts in different directions in order to understand where to go next. First, he sent scouts by three routes to the sea, following Mendoza's instruction to get more reports about the coast. Second, he sent Estevan, his charismatic servant and ambassador, northward to look for news about "the great things we were seeking." Estevan left Vacapa on Sunday (23 March) "after eating" (Flint and Flint 2005, 68–69).

Marcos now waited for his messengers to return or send information from various directions. He probably used this downtime to send his own messages back to Mendoza as ordered. Vacapa thus becomes an important lynchpin in reconstructing Marcos's journey not only because of the known date but also because of some notable news that he received there.

SIDEBAR: A Little Mystery: The Date of Passion Sunday and Why It Matters

The date Marcos arrived in Vacapa is important because it constrains how far north Vacapa could be from Culiacán and Petatlán. The problem is that Marcos reported the date only as "two days before Passion Sunday." That's ambiguous, because Catholic calendars used in different periods put Passion Sunday either one week or two weeks before Easter. What was the date of Passion Sunday as understood by Marcos in 1539?

If Passion Sunday was only one week before Easter, then Marcos had plenty of time—three weeks—to reach Vacapa from Culiacán. In that case, there's no problem with plausible locations for Vacapa. However, if Passion Sunday is two weeks before Easter, then Marcos had only thirteen or fourteen travel days (fifteen full days minus a day and a half downtime in Petatlán with Onorato) to reach Vacapa. That means he had to hustle in order to reach the latitude of Soyopa or Mátape.

Recent research on manuscripts of that period, especially by Coronado scholars Richard and Shirley Flint in New Mexico and Marcos biographer Michel

continued

First News of the Great Northern Trade Center: Late March 1539

Marcos's decision to send Estevan north from Vacapa on 23 March was fateful. It led to success . . . and disaster. According to Marcos's *relación*, his instructions to Estevan were clear and clever. Estevan was to go no more than 50 or 60 leagues (125 to 190 miles, or five to nine days) beyond Vacapa. He was to gather news about the North and then return, or send back his news and wait for Marcos.

Because Estevan could not write, they agreed on a code, recounted by Marcos in his *relación*: "If Estevan got news of a settled and rich land, he should stop and send Indians with our signal: if it was of moderate importance, he would send back a small white cross the size of a hand; if it was great, he would send back a larger cross the size of two hands, and if it was even grander than New Spain, he'd send me a large cross" (abridged and adapted from the translation by Flint and Flint 2005, 68).

Four days after Estevan left, probably on 26 or 27 March, excited messengers came back down the trail to Vacapa, carrying a cross as high as a man! They said Estevan had arrived in a village where he had learned news of "the greatest thing in the world," provinces with big *"ciudades"* only thirty days to the north of Estevan's location. The word *ciudades* had

Nallino in Nice, indicates that Passion Sunday, as then defined, was indeed two weeks before Easter. For example, as pointed out by Richard Flint (private communication), the Wycliffe Bible, from around 1400, when England was Catholic, refers to Passion Sunday as followed by Palm Sunday and Easter. Flint also pointed out to me an account by the 1517 English traveler Richard Torkington, who, while describing a pilgrimage to Jerusalem, referred to Passion Sunday on a date two weeks before Easter. Also, the name given to the Sunday before Easter in some old Spanish manuscripts is Domingo de Ramos, Sunday of the Branches—known in English as Palm Sunday.

This evidence, then, requires Marcos to get to Vacapa, wherever it was, in about thirteen and a half days of actual travel time from Culiacán. My tabulation of road mileage from old Culiacán on Mexican road maps suggests 370 to 380 road miles to a plausible Vacapa location either on the Río Yaqui near or north of Soyopa or near Mátape, giving a plausible 27 to 28 miles per day for his time on the trail in his initial energized march to Vacapa.

a special meaning in Spanish of that time. Flint and Flint note that it denoted a community "among the highest-ranking, most important, and largest settlements" (2005, 12). In Spain, the title had to be assigned by the king. *Ciudad* is thus often translated as "city," even though some examples, from modern hindsight, might better be called "towns" or, more neutrally, "communities." The messengers relayed Estevan's advice: Marcos should leave Vacapa that very hour to catch up.

One of the messengers had traveled to the North in person. He told Marcos about seven towns with "grand houses made from stone and lime, the smallest having one story with a flat roof, and the others, two and three stories" (Flint and Flint 2005, 69). Figure 5 reveals the accuracy of this information. Marcos carefully interviewed this gentleman and learned exciting new information: there was not only one province of seven cities but several other comparable provinces.

> He told me so many magnificent things about [that land] that I stopped believing them until later, [so that] I might see them [for myself]. . . .
> It was thirty days' journey from where Estevan was to the first city of that land, which is called Cíbola. In this first province there are seven very great cities, all under one lord. . . . On the façades of the principal houses [are] many ornaments of turquoises. He said there was a great abundance of this. The people of the cities go about very well dressed. And he told me many other details, both about these seven cities and about other provinces farther on. Each one . . . is much more than these seven cities. In order that I could learn how he knew all this, we had much discussion, and I found him a very keen intellect. (translation by Flint and Flint 2005, 69)

Marcos now had his first *specific* confirmation of a northern trade center. In terms of our analysis, it meant that the third frontier, the Cíbola frontier, lay between Vacapa and the town Estevan had visited, about two days north of Vacapa (map 8).

Marcos was thrilled, but he delayed his departure from Vacapa because he'd promised his coastal scouts that he'd wait for them. "I had determined," he said, "always to behave very truthfully toward the people whom I was meeting" (Flint and Flint 2005, 69).

During the next days, more messengers arrived from Estevan, again with a cross the size of a man. Estevan insisted (through his messengers) that Marcos should hurry, because "the land we sought was the best and greatest thing ever described."

Figure 5. Confirmation of Sonorans' description of Cíbola, as reported by Marcos de Niza. (a) Fragment of a wall at the Hawikku site, matching reports that the cities of Cíbola were built of stone. In the finished pueblos, these walls were often plastered over with adobe. 1994 photo by the author. (b) Zuni Pueblo in an 1873 photo, confirming the multistory structure and ladders, as reported by Marcos. Photo by T. H. O'Sullivan, Library of Congress.

In a crucial development, Estevan now gave up waiting for Marcos. He disobeyed his orders and moved onward. In retrospect, we might well ask why Marcos took the risk of letting him go ahead in the first place. Pedro de Castañeda, the Coronado chronicler, hinted at an intriguing answer. We have to caution that Castañeda didn't really know much about Marcos's trip. For example, Castañeda referred to "friars" in the plural, which tips us off that he didn't know that Onorato had been left behind. So Castañeda was probably repeating what he'd heard as gossip along the trail. Nonetheless, he cheerfully dished the dirt:

> It seems that the Black was not going with the support of friars because he had the habit of taking the women whom the Indians gave him, collecting turquoises, and amassing a quantity of both. Still, the Indians in the settlements through which they passed understood the Black better, since they had already seen him before. For this reason Marcos sent him ahead, to reconnoiter and pacify [the land], so that when Marcos arrived, he could concentrate on collecting reports about what he was searching for. (adapted from the translation by Flint and Flint 2005, 387–88)

A Note about Interpreters: 1530s

How was Marcos able so effectively to interview natives of different areas with different languages? There are three answers. First, as we've seen, Cabeza de Vaca indicated a practice of translators moving among local villages. Second, some kind of simple universal language (or sign language?) existed. Third, Marcos had with him local villagers who had traveled south with Cabeza de Vaca from these provinces.

A Lost Document: April 1539

On Easter Sunday, 6 April 1539, a new group arrived in Vacapa to meet the strange visitor from the sky. They were painted or tattooed Indians from the east. They, too, knew of Cíbola and confirmed many points mentioned by Estevan's emissaries. Marcos's own coastal scouts returned the same day, bringing news of poorer people along the shores and of thirty-four offshore islands, whose names Marcos recorded in "another document where I [was] recording the name[s] of the islands and settlements" (Flint and Flint 2005, 69).

Marcos's onetime mention of this additional document is tantalizing. Was it a day-by-day log of Marcos's journey? Did it contain additional detailed geographic information about settlements and rivers? Probably it was a document for Viceroy Mendoza's eyes only—place-names and associated route information. Recall that Mendoza ordered Marcos to report in secret in order to keep routing information hidden from Cortés and other competitors. Marcos's onetime mention of the second document in the relación may have been a way to record legalistically that he had supplied additional information. Twentieth-century researchers did not agree. Wagner noted that Adolph Bandelier, as early as 1890, had also proposed that Marcos might have prepared an additional document, but Wagner then cavalierly claimed that "this of course is impossible" (1934, 213).

The fact that Marcos refers directly to some geographic details in a separate list not only counters Wagner's "impossibility" but also answers Carl Sauer's 1932 complaint, cited earlier, that Marcos's relación was "the worst geographic document on this frontier." As we'll see, the publicly notarized

SIDEBAR: The Location of Vacapa and Why It Matters

The location of Vacapa is important because it gives us a chance for a consistency check on Marcos's veracity, route, and rate of travel, and it helps locate the Cíbola frontier, as we'll see below. If Vacapa is placed too far north, Marcos doesn't have time to reach it by 21 March. If it's too far south, Marcos can get there easily but won't have enough remaining time to get to Cíbola. Also, it needs to be thirty-two or thirty-three days' travel south of Cíbola, because Estevan (and later Marcos himself) said that Cíbola was thirty days' travel from a village two to three days beyond Vacapa.

Interestingly, in spite of these constraints, Vacapa seems to be one of the most well-traveled villages in Mexico. One group of theories places Vacapa too far south to fit what Marcos said. Carl Sauer (1937b, 279) and Cleve Hallenbeck ([1949] 1987), for example, placed Vacapa in the Río Fuerte–Río Mayo region (see map 8). These theories were based on making it easy for Marcos to reach Vacapa, but they placed it too far from Cíbola and too close to Culiacán to fit the totality of clues. (As a result, Sauer and Hallenbeck argued that their favored Vacapa position proved Marcos a liar.)

Another group of theories places Vacapa too far north. The historian Father Oblasser Bonaventure, writing in 1939, placed it in the northwestern corner of Sonora because the famed Jesuit explorer Father Eusebio Kino, during his relación was never intended as a full disclosure of routing information but was rather a certification that Mendoza's man reached the North before Cortés.

Who knows? Perhaps Marcos's missing geographical document might still turn up in some old box in Mexico City or in the church archives in some village—an idea I played with in my novel about Marcos.

Marcos Gathers His Own News about Cíbola: April 1539

Marcos tells us that he left Vacapa on 7 April, the Monday after Easter, and traveled "that day . . . and the next two days." In those two or three trail days, he crossed the Cíbola frontier and found the people who'd given Estevan information about the seven cities, presumably on the evening of 9 April. Here, probably on the Río Sonora, Marcos excitedly interviewed the villagers:

travels in 1698–1701, recorded a village there called Bacapa, centered at springs in extreme northwestern Sonora between Sonoyta and Caborca (see maps 9 and 10). No later travelers used this name, which now seems irrelevant to the search for Marcos's Vacapa.*

Kino's colleague Juan Mateo Manje said that "Bacapa" comprised six springs and "80 persons, poor and naked, who exist on roots, wild sheep, and deer" ([ca. 1701] 1952, 157), which does not match Marcos's fairly large irrigated town with abundant food. My colleague in Nice, Michel Nallino (2012, private communication), also places Vacapa far north, near Nogales, on the present Arizona-Sonora border. Quitobac and Nogales are both much too far north for Marcos to have

continued

---

* In Piman speech of that region, the syllable *bac* (or sometimes a variant) often referred to a pond, spring, or depression (but reportedly also to reed grass, a house, or a ruined house—see the entry for "Bacapa" by Frederick Hodge in the *Handbook of American Indians North of Mexico* [1910]). A modern O'odham dictionary (Saxton et al., 1983, 61) lists the spelling *wahk*, defined as "entering; sink in," as often referring to where water sinks into the ground. More elaborate meanings depend on suffixes. The Norwegian explorer Carl Lumholtz passed through Quitobac in 1910 and recorded that the O'odham name was "Vapk (the O'odham name for reeds) or Váketa" ([1912] 1971, 392). Kino, knowing of Marcos de Niza's explorations, was probably primed to hear "Váketa" as Vákapa or, as he wrote, Bacapa. Later explorers recorded this tiny settlement as Quitobac, not Bacapa.

They told me that from that place they were accustomed to travel to the city of Cíbola in 30 days. . . . Not just one told me about this, but many. And they told me in great detail about the grandness of the houses and their form, just as the first [messengers] told it to me. They told me that besides the seven cities there are three other *reinos* [kingdoms], called Maratta, Acus, and Totonteac.

I tried to learn why they traveled so far from their homes. They told me that they went for turquoises, [bison] hides, and other things. . . . [I asked what they traded for those things.] They told me [it was] their sweat and their personal service. (adapted from the translation in Flint and Flint 2005, 70)

reached if he left Culiacán on 7 March. Nogales, only twenty days' travel from Cíbola, based on later historical records, violates the constraints listed below.*

Marcos's relación survives as a trustworthy document only if Vacapa is midway between the extremes of north and south in the central Sonora region of Mátape and Soyopa. This follows our Goldilocks principle. It's not too far south and not too far north. It's just right. The clues that narrow down the location of Vacapa can be summarized as follows:

- Vacapa was no more than about fifteen days north of Culiacán (thirteen and a half days of fast march plus one and a half days of rest in Petatlán).
- Since Cíbola was unknown in Vacapa, the village where Estevan learned about Cíbola was probably on a different drainage than Vacapa.
- Vacapa had to be thirty-two or thirty-three days south of Cíbola along the Natives' trade route (i.e., two or three days south of the village where Cíbola had been reported to be thirty days away).
- Vacapa was plausibly two or three days south of some part of the Río Sonora. The logic: Cabeza de Vaca indicated that people in Corazones knew of a northern trade center with big buildings, meaning that Corazones was north

* Nallino solves this by invoking a letter from Governor Coronado in Culiacán to the viceroy, saying that Marcos departed Culiacán on "the seventh of the last month, February" (translation by Flint and Flint 2005, 34). That gives Marcos plenty of time to get wherever we want him to be, but it disagrees with Marcos's own notarized statement of a 7 March departure. Furthermore, Coronado's letter is known only through an excerpt reproduced in a 1556 book by an Italian editor, Giovanni Ramusio, who is notorious for incorrect material and later insertions. (See discussion of Ramusio and the translation of the letter in Flint and Flint, 2005, 31–34.)

Here, then, was the first report of migrant workers from Mexico to "El Norte"—the United States. In those days, it seems not to have been the earth-shaking issue that it is today. Marcos continued:

The people in the town where I was all wear fine turquoises hanging from their ears and noses. They say that decorations on the main doorways of the buildings in Cíbola are made from these stones. They said the men of Cíbola wear a cotton shirt, reaching to the instep of the foot, with a button at the throat with a tassel hanging from it. . . . It seemed to me like a Bohemian outfit. They go around with belts of turquoise. On top of the shirts some wear very good mantles or blankets. Others wear buffalo

of the Cíbola frontier. Corazones was on the Río Sonora (see chapter 8). But Vacapa was two or three days south of the Cíbola frontier, according to the item above.

- Vacapa was probably only a few days from Corazones. Pedro de Castañeda describes the Coronado army moving north from Corazones, and in the next sentence, he mentions passing through a "province called Vacapan." Taken literally, this would put "Vacapan" north of Corazones, which we reject because of the previous two clues. Vacapa/Vacapan, however, could have been a province name for a broad region around Corazones. Alternatively, Castañeda's mention of "Vacapan" (written twenty years after the fact) might have been out of correct sequence due to a lapse of memory.
- Vacapa was about 40 leagues (100 to 124 trail miles) from the sea. Marcos cited the forty-league distance and confirmed it with an anecdote. He sent scouts to the coast from Vacapa with instructions to bring back information, and they came back after thirteen days of travel. Allowing five to six days' travel time each way at 17 to 22 miles per day, we'd have 87 to 132 trail miles. We note also that Coronado described Corazones as being five hard days' travel from the coast. These two sources thus agree that Vacapa and Corazones are both five or six days from the coast, and this fits with them being within a few days of each other.

According to these clues, Vacapa could be located either on the upper Río Mátape near Mátape village or on the upper Río Yaqui (see map 9). Mátape, an obscure village today, was one of the most important towns on Spanish maps

continued

hides, which are considered to be the best clothing. They say there is a great quantity of these in that land. The women also go about clothed similarly, covered to the feet in the same manner. (adapted from Flint and Flint 2005, 70)

Marcos's news that turquoises were worked into doorways in Cíbola is of special interest. Starting as early as 1539, many commentators charged Marcos with exaggerations, this story being one of them. Yet, three and a half centuries later, Marcos's statement was confirmed by anthropologist Frank Hamilton Cushing. Cushing, one of many colorful scholars who came from the east coast to the western frontier in the late 1800s, lived with the Indians in Zuni for nearly five years in 1879–84. At that time, Zuni was still similar to the Cíbola of the 1500s, and Cushing found turquoises embedded in doorways! As summarized by anthropologist Adolph Bandelier in an 1886 article,

from the 1600s and 1700s. The identity of Mátape with Vacapa was suggested as early as 1886 by Adolph Bandelier, who noted that Mátape had been known as Matapa (with no accent, phonetically similar to Vacapa).*

As noted above, if Marcos stayed west toward the coast, he could have taken the western fork of the Río Yaqui (Río Tecoripa/Suaqui) and crossed over hills to the Río Mátape. As for distances, Mátape fits Marcos's report that Vacapa was 40 leagues (100 to 124 miles) inland, because it is about 110 to 120 trail miles up the Río Mátape from the coast. Vacapa must have been somewhere in the central-right part of map 9.

The Soyopa area of the Río Yaqui, mentioned above, is another attractive candidate for Vacapa. Historian-geographer Carl Sauer, in his 1932 paper, "The Road to Cíbola," wrote that Soyopa, during the Spanish colonial period of the 1600s to 1700s, was the major ford across the Río Yaqui on the royal north–south

* The suggested spellings of Mátape are as variable as the suggested locations of Vacapa. The great Jesuit explorer Eusebio Kino shows the name as Matápe on three of his maps (1685–1696), reproduced by Bolton in 1960 (and no accent on a fourth map). Most modern maps spell it as Mátape, but a 1998 book of road maps of Mexico in the respected Guía Roji series shows the river as Río Matapé (the village, like many small towns, is not shown). Many other maps, including the 1981 *National Geographic World Atlas*, which shows all sorts of accent markings, show no accents on Matape. Thus, we have examples with any of the three syllables being accented or none, not to mention Bandelier's "old" spelling of Matapa.

Turquoises and all sorts of green and blue stones . . . were a fairly common ornament among the natives of Zuni . . . as in all the New Mexico pueblos. . . . What the Indian informants told Marcos about the turquoises set in the doorways at Cíbola was absolutely true. This custom persisted from ancient times. As Mr. Cushing discovered during his stay in Zuni, they set small stones of this kind in the wooden frames around the entrances, through which they passed by ladders, especially in the *estufas*, or meeting places. Today the custom is falling into disuse. (see Bandelier [1886] 1981, 99 for a slightly different translation by Madeleine Rodack)

Cushing's testimony adds evidence that what Marcos recorded in his relación from his Native informants was correct. The exaggeration was in the minds of the later readers.

highway. When Sauer visited the area around 1930, he said it was still the best place in this region to cross the Río Yaqui. This would have been an important motivation for pausing in Soyopa for two weeks. Marcos could cross easily to the northwestern bank and could send messengers in all directions on either side of the river. Arizona anthropologist Edward Spicer's 1980 study of the area offers support for either Mátape or Soyopa. His map of the "probable route of El Camino Real" (1980, 33), the main north–south route through Sonora in the 1700s, shows it passing up the Río Yaqui through Soyopa, then crossing west past Mátape and on to the Río Sonora near Ures.

One more clue is linguistic. One day, looking through a dictionary of the Yaqui language (now more properly called Hiaki), I realized that "Vacapa" was probably Marcos's spelling of the Hiaki name for the Mexican palo verde tree (*Parkinsonia aculeata*), vaka'apo. My work with linguists Heidi Harley and Constantino Martínez Fabián supported this. Yaqui/Hiaki was apparently spoken along the Río Yaqui (hence the name) and possibly at Mátape, but not much farther north. Charts of the distribution of the Mexican palo verde by botanist Ray Turner and his colleagues (1995) show the main concentration in the general area of Mátape and along the north–south upper Yaqui/Bavispe drainages. Perhaps the whole area was known as "Vacapan."

The linguistic clues may also explain why the Cíbola frontier occurred in this interval. According to this idea, Pima speakers from the Río Sonora north traded with Cíbola; the Yaqui speakers from the Río Yaqui south did not.

As had been happening a few days to the south, the people at the new location tried to touch Marcos's robe, and as with the Cabeza de Vaca party, "they brought their sick to me so that I might cure them." Marcos responded by reciting the Gospels over the patients. He gives us no comments on the results but says people gave him bison hides from Cíbola, "so well dressed [that] they seemed to have been made by highly civilized men."

Success was within Marcos's grasp. The long-rumored northern trade center was real, thirty days away, and all he had to do was get there.

Mysteries of Corazones: Spring 1539

It's curious that Marcos's relación doesn't mention Corazones, which had been touted by Cabeza de Vaca as a "gateway" to the North. Corazones was important enough that, according to a letter written by Mendoza in October 1539, Marcos and Governor Coronado had discussed a plan by which Coronado would explore the mountains east of Culiacán (in search of a rumored gold-bearing area called Topira) and then rendezvous with Marcos at Corazones. The rendezvous never materialized, but the idea emphasizes the town's importance in their minds.

The town where Estevan (and later Marcos) first contacted people who knew about Cíbola could have been Corazones, which Estevan had visited in 1536 and in which he knew he'd get a friendly reception. Consistent with this, the Coronado memoirist, Castañeda, says that Estevan was known among the Indians among whom he was now traveling.

Marcos's relación, however, never mentions being in *any* town where Cabeza de Vaca had traveled, let alone Corazones. There are three plausible explanations for this. The first is that Marcos, on his way north, didn't pass through Corazones because, mindful of Mendoza's instruction, he stayed closer to the coast, reaching the Río Sonora downstream from Corazones. Marcos may then have crossed the Río Sonora and ascended the major western tributary of that river, the Río San Miguel. A 1978 archaeological survey of the Río San Miguel by Mexican archaeologist Beatriz Braniff showed that it had villages similar to those in the Río Sonora valley and consistent with those described by Marcos. The coastward route up that valley is supported by Marcos's frequent mentions on his way north of his desire to get coastal information.

A second explanation is that Estevan, the only person in Marcos's party who had been to Corazones, had already passed through and gone north, so Marcos had no direct witness to confirm to him which village was the one Cabeza de Vaca's party had called by the *Spanish* name Corazones.

A third explanation is that Marcos (trying to meet Mendoza's orders) recorded all his village names and geographic specifics in his separate, secret document, mentioned previously. When he returned to Mexico City, he turned it over to Mendoza, who then kept geographic details out of the relación to prevent wildcatters from heading north along the trail. As early as 1932, Carl Sauer suggested that "the official *Relación* may well have been dressed up for official consumption" by adding false claims. I'd suggest it was more of a case of "dressing down" by deleting route information. According to this view, Marcos may have passed through Corazones (either when going north or when going south), but Mendoza insisted on no direct references to the position of Cabeza de Vaca's now-famous "gateway to the north."

All three explanations may be simultaneously true. Marcos may have passed west of Corazones up the Río San Miguel on his way north, absent Estevan, and then have returned by the more direct Río Sonora, through Corazones, on his way south.

Why Was Marcos's News Exciting?: April 1539

A curious question arises. The Cabeza de Vaca party, including Estevan, had clearly told Mendoza that in Corazones they heard about large towns with "many people and large houses" (Cabeza de Vaca's phrase) north of their route. Why, then, was the news so exciting to Estevan and Marcos?

The real question is how much Cabeza de Vaca's party had learned about Cíbola and reported to Mendoza. Apparently, not very much. They were not explorers but survivors trying to reach the Spanish colonies and save their lives; their faces and minds were turned south. They didn't know about Pizarro's discovery of Peru or about the race among Guzmán, Cortés, and Mendoza to discover cities in the north. To them, the possible trade center to the north of their route seems to have been more a matter of interesting speculation. Although Cabeza de Vaca's memoir gives evidence that the inhabitants of Corazones knew about the northern trade centers, he didn't even record names for those communities. As mentioned earlier, he said that people in Corazones gave him "emerald" arrowheads, "brought from high mountains toward the north, where they bought them in exchange for parrot feathers. They said there were towns there with many people and large houses." The tone of the original Joint Report, which the castaways gave to Mendoza in 1536, is similar. It says that Indians in Corazones told them about northern places with "very large" houses and turquoises but that the Indians of Corazones "were not able to inform them about gold nor did they have any news concerning mines" (translation by historians Basil Hedrick and Carroll Riley in 1974).

This gives a good sense of what the Cabeza de Vaca party transmitted to Mendoza. Years later, Castañeda said Cabeza de Vaca's party had mentioned "four- and five-storied *pueblos*," but it appears that he conflated Cabeza de Vaca's report with Marcos's discoveries and with what Castañeda himself had seen when he passed through Cíbola with Coronado in 1540.

In any case, Mendoza now had evidence that largish cities existed somewhere in the North, but he knew virtually nothing about their distance, locations, or residents. Success for Marcos and Estevan was thus not so much learning of the *existence* of the "cities" but learning their locations, architecture, and general prosperity relative to towns encountered in Sonora. This helps us understand Estevan's excitement when he was told about northern towns with multistory stone buildings only thirty days away.

One more aspect applies to Estevan's reaction. From his point of view, he had set out with Narváez in 1528 on an expedition to seek wealth in La Florida. For ten years, he'd been associated with the search for grand, wealthy cities in what we now call the United States. This facet of his experience is confirmed in a letter from a financial officer in Mexico City to the royal treasurer on the Caribbean island of Hispaniola written on 18 October 1539, about seven weeks after Marcos got back to Mexico City. It says that "according to the information the Black had obtained, [the Narváez expeditionaries] were going to travel until they reached an exceedingly wealthy land" (Flint and Flint 2005, 89). Finally, a decade after setting out with Narváez, Estevan felt he had found the wealthy land. This explains his giddy message to Marcos that, finally, he had news of "the greatest thing in the world."

Marcos probably harbored a more subtle kind of excitement. As mentioned in chapter 2, the Franciscans saw themselves as agents of a great cosmic plan. They shared a theological dream that conversion of the Native Americans would complete God's plan for humanity and usher in the Second Coming. Thus, if Marcos could assist Mendoza in a peaceful, "apostolic" conquest of the North, God's plan would come to fruition.

Where Was Estevan?: April 1539

Instead of waiting for Marcos as instructed, Estevan planted another tall cross and disappeared up the trail to Cíbola. As a result, he has gone down in history as the unfaithful Moor, ignoring orders from the viceroy and the priest. But it's interesting to put ourselves in his shoes. He was an intelligent fellow, and we can glimpse the possibility of more complex rationalizations. Knowing the Spanish system, he may have calculated that if he could be the first to enter Cíbola and establish good relations, he might reap rewards of royal favor, freedom, and lands. Cortés's example showed that producing new treasure made up for a lot of broken promises along the way.

Perhaps Estevan rehearsed his justifications as he moved along the trail. He'd sent message back to Marcos around 25 March, as instructed. The town from which he'd sent the message was two days from Marcos, and he'd urged Marcos to come at once, so he thought Marcos might appear by 29 or 30 March, even though Marcos had probably announced his plan to stay in Vacapa until Easter, 6 April. Estevan had sent even more messengers a few days later, again urging Marcos to come. But Marcos didn't show up by 2, 3, or 4 April, so Estevan would claim that Marcos was the one who had broken the agreement. Estevan might actually have waited until 8 April in the town where he got the news of Cíbola. From the relación, we see that Marcos didn't arrive there until 9 April.

If Estevan waited to leave until 5–8 April, it would put him in Cíbola thirty days later. Many accounts instead portray Estevan as taking off immediately, between 25 and 30 March, rushing directly to Cíbola and arriving weeks ahead of Marcos in order to claim priority in the "discovery." In reality, there is some evidence that he did wait for Marcos, as we'll see in a moment.

Marcos's Controversial Trip toward the Coast: April 1539

In evaluating whether Marcos had time to complete his own journey, it's important to note that he continued to have help on his journey north. For example, as he passed through villages north of Vacapa, the people "took great care to learn the day I left Vacapa, so they could [estimate my rate of travel] and take food and shelter for me on the road ahead." Later, he remarked that as he crossed a four-day despoblado, the locals were "making me shelters and carrying the food, [and] . . . wherever I needed to dine, I found huts and sufficient food—and at night I found huts and similar food again." Assistance to Marcos from local people along the route, which Cabeza de Vaca also reported, contradicts the impression left by Hallenbeck and others that Marcos struggled through uncharted lands. If you've ever backpacked on wilderness trails, you can imagine what a difference it makes in daily mileage if you are guided and have your gear managed by a support group that sets up camp and prepares dinner for you.

Marcos's itinerary for the next few weeks is hard to unravel because his relación is so cryptic about geography. He describes valleys and well-irrigated villages but doesn't say where they were relative to each other. He mentions erecting two crosses and taking possession of the land in accordance with Mendoza's directions "because it seemed to me that [this land] was better than what I was leaving behind." He also implies at one point that he thought Estevan could be no more than eight or ten days ahead, but his wording (Flint and Flint 2005, 70) is unclear.

The next date Marcos mentions is 9 May, when he entered the final despoblado, only fifteen days from Cíbola. Since 9 May is thirty days after 9 April, however, Marcos could theoretically have reached Cíbola, according to the Sonorans' reports of the travel time from just north of Vacapa. Why was he delayed? He gives a clear answer. In one of the intervening villages, he tells us, "I learned that the coast turns very sharply to the west . . . [whereas] all the way from the beginning of the first despoblado, the coast had been [bounding] the land. Because the turn of the coast is something very important, I went in search of it so it could be clarified and understood. And I understood clearly that at thirty-five degrees [latitude the coast] turns to the west. From this [discovery] I had no less happiness than from the good news about the land. Then I resumed my journey" (adapted from the translation by Flint and Flint 2005, 72). The fact that Marcos tells us he detoured west toward the sea (see map 10) when he was fewer than thirty days from Cíbola reflects the value he placed on Mendoza's instructions to get coastal information.

This side trip to the sea, however, is controversial. One reason is the chatty quality of the relación. I suspect that Marcos dictated it to scribes when he returned to Mexico City (a pre-Xerox way to create multiple copies). He mentions this or that valley, but it's unclear whether he has entered a new valley or is continuing in one already mentioned. Interestingly, he occasionally changes into present tense; for example, his informant "says" that a certain land lies to the southeast. This suggests that he took parts of his text from a present-tense journal or letters sent to Mendoza written in real time when he was in the village of the informant. Piecing together the relación in this way as he dictated it, he failed to make adequate connections between segments of the story, which leaves scholars frustrated about reconstructing his route.

Critics of Marcos say he had insufficient time to do all that he reported and thus that he simply made up the side trip toward the coast. But then how did he correctly report the turn of the coast? My suggestion would be that to get the information, he chose to travel north along a western river, the Río San Miguel, where he heard about the coast. Then, for his side trip, he crossed west toward the Río Magdalena, which runs westward toward

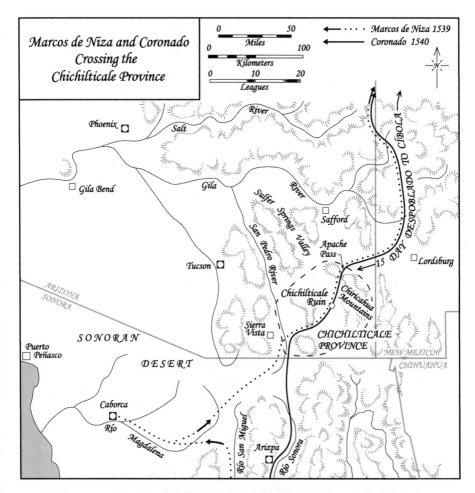

Map 10. Hypothetical reconstruction of the final parts of Marcos de Niza's northward journey, including the controversial side trip toward the sea, his passage through the Chichilticale region, and the fifteen-day despoblado, according to recent data from Nugent Brasher and the Flints. Cíbola lies north of the upper right corner of the map. The Coronado expedition traversed the last part of the same route (see chapter 8). Map by Ron Beckwith.

the coast at this point. He may even have traveled several days downstream on the Río Magdalena toward the ancient community of Caborca (still a prominent town; see map 10), where he confirmed information about the coastline and the latitude. He was happy about getting this information, because it was "hard data," and perhaps he thought it indicated that the coast might yet lead to Cathay. At the same time, his happiness was ironic, since Mendoza was hoping the coast turned *east* in order to provide access to the northern cities Cabeza de Vaca's party had mentioned.

The key sentence about this is rendered literally by most pre-2000 translators as "I saw clearly that at latitude thirty-five degrees it turns west." Critics assert that he did not have time to reach a beach and "see" the sea. Applying our "Heisenberg uncertainty principle of words," I noticed that when Marcos recounted his experiences in Peru, he seemed to distinguish between bearing witness that something was true and his use of a phrase "I also affirm and saw myself with my own eyes . . ." In other words, "I saw" used alone meant "I understood." Even today, we might chat with someone and then say "I saw what he meant." Thus, I suggested in my novel that the phrase "I saw clearly that the coast turns west" might actually have meant "I came to understand clearly, from my interviews, that the coast turns west" (2002, 187). Thus the Flints, in their 2005 translation, rendered the passage as "I understood clearly that at thirty-five degrees [latitude the coast] turns to the west." Their footnote (630, footnote 131) discusses the issue. "Understood

---

SIDEBAR: Who "Discovered" What, and When?

The "discovery" that the coast turns west, that the Gulf of California is really a gulf with a northern end, and that Baja California is not an island has a strange history. We put the word "discovery" in quotes because, of course, all the geography discussed here was well known to local people. Having said that, we note that the first European "discovery" about the north end of the Gulf of California came in 1539, when Marcos correctly reported that the northern coastline of Sonora abruptly turns west and got a crude latitude estimate of 35°. Four or five months later, Cortés's naval captain, Ulloa (pronounced oo-YO-ah), actually visited the head of the gulf and reported the latitude as 34°, as we'll see in chapter 7. Ulloa sailed on to discover that Baja California was not an island but a long peninsula.

Shockingly, these major discoveries were forgotten within a century. This happened because the Spaniards in the late 1500s gave up on finding anything interesting in the North. Thus, by the 1690s, when the Jesuit father Eusebio Kino began his pioneering land-based explorations of the Sonoran Desert, many people once again believed that Baja California was an island. Ironies abound. Kino is mantled in glory even today for inferring that it is not an island in 1698–1706 (Bolton 1960, chap. 106), even though Ulloa had already proved it in 1539. Kino was even moved to write a booklet, *Cosmographical Proof That California Is Not*

clearly" is a subtle but profound difference from asserting that Marcos stood on a beach and observed the coast visually. Mendoza himself may have had a hand in crafting this sentence. He wanted to preempt any claim that Cortés's ship captains were the first to map and claim the north end of the Gulf of California, where the coast turned west, but to do so without an overtly false statement that Marcos had walked and mapped the beaches.

This scenario of learning about the coast may sound like speculation, but it is explicitly supported by events 150 years later, as described in the sidebar "Who 'Discovered' What, and When?"

During the nights of 22–23 April 1539 (by Marcos's Julian calendar), the probable time of the coastal survey, a full moon lit the desert landscape, according to a tabulation by Gary Kronk (1999), and in this region, the bright sandy soil and sparse vegetation make it easy to hike by moonlight. This gave Marcos a chance to cover large distances in this near-coastal region, as he used the pleasant desert evenings to return to his main route toward Cíbola.

an Island but a Peninsula. Meanwhile, Marcos's 1539 more or less correct information about the coastal configuration is written off as fraudulent.

Still more ironic, there is no single beach or mountaintop from which either Marcos or Kino could visually prove that the gulf has a definitive northern end. Marcos had to depend on native informants. Kino climbed to the top of the Pinacate volcanic mountain and claimed to see that Baja connects to the mainland. I've climbed that peak on several occasions, and I'd say that the view reveals the coast turning west but does not prove a continuous land bridge to Baja. Kino, on the summit in 1706, said he could see the sea to the south, but "no sea ascending toward the north . . . and we saw very plainly the connection of this our land with that of the west" ([ca. 1711] 1948, 2:205). Later, he said he thought he could see it, although even his military aide questioned this (Manje [ca. 1701] 1952, 161, 165). In reality, the land bridge to Baja is broken by the Colorado River, which in those days was a mile or more wide at its mouth, and its nature (river? isthmus? oceanic inlet?) is not very clear from the Pinacate summit. Kino, who had already referred to Marcos de Niza's account on another occasion, may have been influenced by Marcos's earlier report that the coast turned west.

In this sense, Marcos has been undercredited (not to mention called a liar) for his basically correct report, while Kino has perhaps been overcredited for what he thought he could see.

Marcos Returns to His Main Journey: April 1539

After leaving the coast, Marcos passed through several prosperous valleys without reporting clear geographic identifications: "I traveled through that valley [location unspecified] five days. . . . It is all irrigated and is like an evergreen garden. The clusters of houses are half a league and a quarter of a league apart [around a mile]. In each of these [villages] I obtained very lengthy reports about Cíbola. [The informants spoke] as people who go there each year to earn their livelihood. Here I found a man, a native of Cíbola, who said he had come [there] fleeing from the governor" (translation by Flint and Flint 2005, 72). From this man, who Marcos said was of "good character," Marcos learned that the "lord" of the seven cities of Cíbola lived in one of the seven towns, called Ahacus, which was allegedly the "most important" town in the Cíbola province. The man of good character wanted to go back to Cíbola with Marcos, who might, he hoped, "obtain a pardon for him."

These pages, both before and after the coastal foray, include cheerfully amusing anecdotes. (This and the next passages are adapted from the translation by Flint and Flint 2005, 71–73.) For example, in a "recently irrigated town,"

> I was wearing a habit of gray, closely woven woolen cloth. The governor and others examined the habit with their hands and told me there was a lot of it in Totonteac [one of the other kingdoms said to be near Cíbola], and that people there were clothed with it. I laughed and said it couldn't be my cloth, because they were wearing cotton. They replied "You think we don't know the difference? In Cíbola, all the houses are full of the cloth that we wear, but in Totonteac they have animals whose fur makes the kind of material you are wearing."

A few days farther along the trail, a local informant described the marvels of the stone-walled buildings in Cíbola.

> I protested that it wasn't possible that the houses were made in the way they said. To help me understand, they took soil and ashes mixed with water, and showed me how they laid the stones and built up the walls, [then] laid down the mixture and placed [more] stones up to the [intended] height. I asked them if the men of that land had wings to reach those upper stories. They laughed and pantomimed a ladder to me just as well as I could have indicated it. Then they took a stick and

held it over their heads and said this was the height between the floors [note the ladders in fig. 5b].

Though we don't know the locations where these anecdotes were told, the accounts themselves have a ring of truth; a good-humored traveler is reporting real incidents. Eventually, Marcos arrived in the last populated valley before Cíbola itself: "I traveled through this valley for three days. . . . Here . . . I saw more than two thousand buffalo hides. I saw a much greater quantity of turquoises and necklaces in this valley than in any of the earlier ones. . . . Here I received messengers from Estevan. They told me that he was already traveling in the final despoblado [the final, fifteen-day unsettled region, south of Cíbola], and was very happy because he was assured of the magnificence of the land."

Marcos had reached the final village before Cíbola, and he stated that the beginning of the final, fifteen-day despoblado was considered to be four days away (see fig. 6 and map 10). The inhabitants of the village asked Marcos to wait three or four days so they could collect food and gather a group to go with him to Cíbola. They claimed that more than three hundred people from villages of the region had already left for Cíbola with Estevan because "they thought they would return as wealthy people."

The location of Marcos's route in southern Arizona and the locale of the last populated valley become clearer as we combine Marcos's relación with later Coronado expedition accounts and modern discoveries. The last valley with settled villages before reaching Cíbola was probably the San Pedro River valley in the southeastern corner of Arizona. The Coronado chronicles (see chapter 8) suggest that the fifteen-day despoblado was considered to begin in the Chiricahua Mountains, 60 to 70 road miles northeast of plausible "last village" locations along the San Pedro. This distance matches Marcos's report of four days' travel from the last valley (the San Pedro) to the start of the despoblado.

When Marcos arrived in the "last village" on 1 or 2 May, he remarked that he had traveled 112 leagues (280 to 347 miles) since he first reached the people who knew about Cíbola (9 April). Elapsed time was twenty-two or twenty-three days. This allows us an extra check on his story. If he had come by the most direct route, without detouring toward the coast (north upstream on the Río Sonora, across the Cananea grassland, and north downstream on the San Pedro to the area of Lewis Spring), he'd have covered only about 200 trail miles at a wildly uncharacteristic rate of only 9 miles per day. In our scenario, however, travel from the Río Sonora, up the San Miguel, across to Magdalena, then halfway to Caborca (during which

Figure 6. One of Marcos's "garden-like" valleys. This scene (in a Conservation Area) along Arizona's San Pedro River a few miles north of the Mexican border, illustrates the beautiful, cottonwood-lined, north–south valleys that Marcos found in the middle portion of his journey. Villages within a few miles of this location were the last that Marcos visited before entering the final, fifteen-day despoblado on the way to Cíbola. Photo by the author, 2005, showing the Southern Arizona Hiking Club.

he learned about the seacoast), and then back to the San Pedro and Lewis Spring is roughly 300 trail miles—just the distance Marcos reported. His average travel rate would then be 300 miles in twenty-two or twenty-three days, or an easy 13 to 14 miles per day, giving him plenty of downtime for the interviews he reports. Even if we allow him seven days of total downtime in various villages, he still needs to average only 19 or 20 miles per day on the trail. In summary, Marcos's reported distances are consistent with his story of a coastal foray.

Theories that Marcos lied about his coastal trip ignore that Marcos reported correct information about the coast. The coast did turn west. His

---

SIDEBAR: Did Marcos de Niza Stop in Phoenix?

A discovery made in the 1920s seemed to pinpoint a spot on Marcos de Niza's path. On a vertical slab of rock near an east entrance to South Mountain Park (on the south edge of Phoenix, west of Guadalupe, Arizona) is a clear inscription.

Fr Marcos
d^e Nisa

Below it on a horizontal slab is an additional description, harder to read, that probably says:

Corona to Doel nuebo
Mexico a su costa
No (or ANo) De 1539

This lower inscription means something like "Crown all of New Mexico at his cost, year of 1539." The last part, on the horizontal slab, doesn't make much sense. Still, the whole thing looks like the smoking gun that fixes Marcos's location.

Not so fast! In 1940 scholarly sleuths Katharine Bartlett and Harold S. Colton proved (from the words and letter style in the second portion) that the inscription is actually a partial copy of a clearer inscription made in 1692 on El Morro, the famous Inscription Rock in New Mexico. The cryptic phrases were part of a statement about the 1692 Vargas expedition, coming from New Mexico in the service of the Crown at their own expense. The copyist probably did not understand Spanish spellings and fused a few words nonsensically. Bartlett and Colton concluded that the Phoenix "Marcos inscription" was a fraud. It may date back as far as the late 1800s or early 1900s, when there was a certain amount of freewheeling boosterism for then-fledgling Phoenix; its intent may have been to prove that Europeans were in Phoenix before they reached Jamestown or Plymouth Rock (see also Dorn et al. 2012).

latitude measurement of 35° was similar to Ulloa's. Both measurements were three or four degrees too high, which sounds suspicious until we realize that Spanish latitude measures in this area at that time were commonly a degree or so too high, as we'll discuss in chapter 7.

For Marcos, everything was coming together. He'd learned about the coast and claimed new lands for the viceroy, and now Cíbola was only nineteen days away.

Sending a Message: ca. 4 May 1539

While waiting three days at that final village on the San Pedro River, Marcos knew that if some accident befell him during this last, crucial phase of his trip, his latest news would reach the viceroy. Therefore, he probably followed Mendoza's instructions and sent one last message back down the trail to the viceroy, summarizing his exciting results. This message would probably have included the kinds of phrases reproduced later in his relación: valleys "all irrigated . . . like an evergreen garden," cities with multistoried stone buildings, well-dressed people with turquoises, the "magnificence of the land."

Since Marcos knew he was nineteen days from Cíbola, he could reason that his new message would arrive in Mexico City at least thirty-eight days before he himself could get back. Based on his elapsed time on his way north plus at least thirty-eight days, his letter may have predicted to Mendoza that he might be back to Mexico City in August or September.

Into the Last Despoblado: 9 May 1539

By 4 or 5 May groups had assembled with food and supplies in the village where Marcos was waiting. Marcos selected about thirty local *principales* (village leaders) to go with him, noting that they were well dressed, some wearing necklaces with as many as five or six strands of turquoise. No doubt others of lesser rank joined Marcos's party to lead the way, carry supplies, and set up camps. The party walked from a village on the San Pedro River east for about two days to the western base of the Chiricahua Mountains, and then two more days to Apache Pass, at the north end of the mountains, and then into the fifteen-day despoblado. According to the route proposed by the Flints (2005, 695–96 footnotes) and supported by finds of Coronado-era material reported in 2011 by New Mexico geologist Nugent Brasher, the route then crossed the higher country along the modern Arizona–New Mexico border to Zuni. The modern road mileage is 270 to 305 trail miles, giving a reasonable average of 18 to 20 miles per day in rough country for what Marcos reported as a "long day's travel." Along this route, Marcos said, "we traveled the first day via a very wide and well-used trail. We reached a water source at which to eat, which Indians had indicated to me, and another source of water at which to sleep. There I found a building which they had just finished putting up for me, and another . . . where Estevan had slept when he passed, [and] old shelters and many signs of fires from the people who had traveled to Cíbola along this trail" (Flint and Flint 2005, 73). Given this information, Marcos now expected to catch up with Estevan at the great metropolis of Cíbola around 24 May. What could possibly go wrong?

Disaster: ca. 21 May 1539

Now came one of the most dramatic scenes in early American history. Marcos tells it very well in his own words. (This and the next two translations are synthesized and abridged from Flint and Flint 2005 and Hallenbeck [1949] 1987.) Around 21 May, three days out from Cíbola, the party ran into

an Indian, the son of one of the important men who were traveling along with me. He'd gone in the company of Estevan [and] he came to us exhausted and sweaty. He told me that one day's journey before reaching Cíbola, Estevan sent his gourd, a talisman rattle, ahead into the city with messengers. He always sent it in advance, so that people in the next town would know he was coming. The gourd had rows of bells and two feathers on it, one white and one red.

When his messengers arrived at Cíbola, they came before the local governor, appointed by the lord of the seven cities. They gave him the gourd. When the governor saw the gourd and the bells, he flung it to the ground in fury, and told the messengers to leave at once, saying he knew what people they represented, and that Estevan's party should not try to enter the city. Otherwise, they'd all be killed.

The messengers returned and told Estevan what had happened. Estevan said it was nothing—the very people who exhibited anger were the ones who usually ended up welcoming him the best. So he traveled on toward Cíbola.

The citizens wouldn't let him in, but placed him in a large building outside the city, and took away all his trade articles, turquoises, and other items he'd accumulated from Indians along the road. He and his party were stuck there that whole night without anything to eat or drink.

Next morning, the Indian who was relating these events grew thirsty, and left the building to drink from the nearby stream. Moments later, from that spot, he saw Estevan beginning to flee. People from the city were chasing him, and they killed some of his companions. As soon as our informant saw this, he hid himself upstream. Later, he entered the despoblado along the trail, where he eventually met us.

After we received this calamitous news, some of the other Indians with me began to weep. I feared all would be lost. I didn't fear losing my life as much as I feared being unable to return to Mexico with information about the grandness of the country, where God, Our Lord, could be so well served, his Holy Faith glorified, and the royal patrimony of His Majesty enlarged.

Given the situation, I consoled my Indian companions as best I could, and told them they shouldn't necessarily believe everything the fugitive said. But they said, through tears, that he wouldn't have described anything he hadn't seen.

So I withdrew to commend myself to Our Lord, and to beg him to guide this situation according to His will, and to enlighten my heart. Having done this, I returned to the others. With a knife I cut the cords of the leather trunks of clothing and trade goods that we had been carrying. Until then I had not opened these bundles, nor given anything from them to anyone, but now I distributed them among all the chiefs, and told them not to fear, asking them to proceed ahead with me. And they did.

It's interesting to note that Marcos does not lament the loss of the chance to find treasure but rather losing the chance to report a grand land where the Christian Spain's "patrimony" could be expanded. Marcos was obsessed less about gold than about the expansion of Christian civilization as he understood it.

Marcos now pushed on toward Cíbola. One day from Cíbola, he encountered two more survivors from the group who had gone with Estevan. The previous story was repeated: "They came stained with blood and with many wounds. I urged everyone to quiet down, so we could learn what was happening. How could they be silent, they responded, when they believed that more than three hundred might be dead among their fathers, sons, and brothers? They added that now they could never again dare go Cíbola, as they traditionally did! I tried to calm them as best I could . . . though I was not without need of someone to rid me of fear myself!"

Marcos went on to describe how the two refugees confirmed the story of the first one: Estevan had arrived at the city of Cíbola just before sunset along with all the people who had gone with him, both men and women. The governor of Cíbola had angrily refused entry to Estevan's party, concluding from the style of the Moor's ceremonial (Texas? Sonoran?) rattle that the strangers were enemies of Cíbola. The officials of Cíbola put Estevan and his friends in an outlying building and confiscated Estevan's possessions. Marcos continues the story:

[The Indians said, "On the] next day, when the sun was a lance-length high, Estevan went out from the building with some of our chiefs. At once, many people came out from the city. When Estevan saw them, he began to flee, and we with him. Immediately, they gave us arrow wounds and gashes. We fell down and others fell on top of us, dead. So we remained until night, without daring to move. We heard loud voices in the city, and saw many men and women watching from the city's terraces. We saw no more of Estevan. Maybe they shot him with arrows like the rest of us. No one escaped but us."

When I heard all this, and realized the poor state of my gear for continuing the journey as I had wished, I couldn't help imagining Estevan's death and my own. . . .

I proclaimed to them that Our Lord, and the Emperor, would send many more Christians to punish that city. They didn't believe me, because they say no one can match the might of Cíbola. I begged them to feel better and stop weeping, and I consoled them with the best words I could find—too many to repeat here.

After this, I withdrew a stone's throw or two to commend myself to God. I spent probably an hour and a half. When I came back, I found one of my own Indians, named Marcos, weeping. He was one of those I had brought with me from Mexico City. He told me, "Father, these people have plotted to kill you, because they say it's your fault that Estevan and their kin are dead. They believe that none of their friends, man or woman, is likely to survive this trip."

At this, I distributed what I had left of the garments and trade articles to calm them. I told them that even if they killed me, it wouldn't really harm me, because I would die a Christian, and would go to heaven. Those who killed me, however, would suffer, because more Christians would come to search for me and kill all of them, even though such a thing would be against my own wishes. These and other words appeased them, though they still felt great resentment over the people who had been killed.

I proposed that some of them should continue with me to Cíbola, to see if anyone had escaped, and to learn what we could about Estevan. No one agreed. So I said that, no matter what, I had to see the city of Cíbola. Finally, two of the native leaders who had come from the last inhabited region, seeing me determined to go on by myself, said they would go with me.

As we'll see in a moment, Marcos next describes how he and a few others crept through back country and ventured within sight of Cíbola. As noted earlier, however, some scholars use the schedule of Estevan's travels to discredit Marcos at this point. The argument was that Estevan could theoretically have reached Cíbola between 1 and 5 May if he left promptly from the village where he learned of Cíbola and if he rushed up the thirty-day trail. This would place Estevan's execution around the first few days of May. Marcos indicates that he met the first survivors of Estevan's murder about 20 May, three days south of Cíbola, implying that Estevan was executed about 17 May. So it has been argued that these dates convict Marcos of lying by his own account.

Estevan's Calendar as Testimony against Marcos?: May 1539

The problem with the above argument is that we have no direct testimony about Estevan's travel. Thus, the best way to test whether Marcos told the truth is to assume Marcos's dates as a working hypothesis and then see if a hypothetical "Estevan calendar" can be constructed that is at least consistent with Marcos's story. The answer is yes. Here is a resulting, possible version of Estevan's calendar as related to Marcos's movements.

* approximately 24–25 March: Estevan reaches villages north of Vacapa where he learns of multistory stone towns thirty days to the north. He sends fast messengers to Marcos indicating he had arrived there in two days, telling Marcos to come at once, thus hoping Marcos will arrive 28–29 March.
* late March: Marcos had already told Estevan that he (Marcos) would like to stay in Vacapa until Easter, 6 April. Therefore, Estevan waits impatiently until 8 April for Marcos to arrive in the village where Estevan heard about Cíbola.

* 8 April: Estevan gives up waiting and leaves that village. (Marcos arrives there on 9 April, as per Marcos's relación.) Initially, Estevan travels slowly north to allow Marcos to catch up, enjoying receptions in villages. Estevan realizes he could claim discovery of Cíbola if he gets there first but dares not get too far ahead of Marcos for fear of being charged later with disobedience. With some time on his hands, his dalliances in the villages may explain his reputation as a womanizer.
* approximately 19–22 April: After eleven to fourteen days, Estevan arrives in the "last village" before the remaining fifteen-day despoblado, on the San Pedro River in southern Arizona. He spends several days organizing his reported party of three hundred people who want to go to Cíbola.
* approximately 26 April: Estevan leaves the "last village" with a large party.
* approximately 30 April: Estevan has crossed the four-day zone from the "last village" to the beginning of the fifteen-day despoblado. A few people from the last village return to it as messengers. Estevan can now expect to arrive in Cíbola around 15 May.
* 1–2 May: Marcos arrives in the "last village" on the San Pedro River, as indicated by his relación. Estevan's messengers report his progress to Marcos. Marcos tells us he was asked by local villagers to wait "three or four" days for the assembly of more people who wanted to go with him.
* 4–5 May: Trailing Estevan by eight or nine days, Marcos departs the "last village," which he said was four days from the beginning of the last, fifteen-day despoblado.
* 9 May: The date specified by Marcos when he entered the fifteen-day despoblado. At his normal rate, he could thus arrive at Cíbola on the evening of 23 May.
* approximately 15 May: Estevan arrives at Cíbola fifteen days after he entered the despoblado. After parleys, he is installed in the house outside Cíbola.
* on the morning of approximately 16 May: Estevan is attacked, and presumably killed. (We'll learn more later.) Natives from San Pedro engage in a skirmish. Many play dead and remain until night, according to their testimony to Marcos.
* on the morning of approximately 17 May: Natives from the San Pedro villages escape from Cíbola in disorganized groups.
* approximately 20 May: Three days from Cíbola (as stated by Marcos), Marcos encounters the first exhausted native from the San Pedro

valley; the escapee gives the first account of the debacle at Cíbola. Marcos's group stops to hear the story, losing about a day of travel time.

* approximately 23 May: One day from Cíbola (as stated by Marcos), Marcos encounters other bloodied stragglers who have hidden in the hills, then reassembled with their friends and are fleeing from Cíbola. Further delay.

* approximately 24 May: Marcos views one of the towns of Cíbola and then flees.

In this reconstruction, there is no catastrophic discrepancy in Marcos's account. A strong point in this reconstruction is that it follows the Goldilocks principle: Neither Estevan nor Marcos is traveling unbelievably fast or unbelievably slow. Each man's travel rates work out to be just right.

Marcos at Cíbola: 24 May(?) 1539

For the remainder of Marcos's description of Cíbola, I quote the translation by Flint and Flint (2005, 75–76). It is the most authoritative in terms of word-by-word rendering from the Spanish, and the precise wording is important in terms of the scholarly arguments about what Marcos was trying to say. He set off with two of the village leaders who agreed to go with him.

> With those [*principales*] and with my own Indians and interpreters, I continued on my way until within sight of Cíbola. It is situated in a plain, on the lower slope of a round hill. As a town, it has a very handsome appearance, the best I have seen in this region. As it appeared to me from a hill where I positioned myself in order to view it, the houses are arranged in the way the Indians told me, all made of stone with their upper stories and flat roofs. The settlement is grander than the Ciudad de Mexico. [Here, Marcos refers to the extent and condition of Mexico City as known to him when he left in 1538.—WKH] A few times I was tempted to go there myself, for I knew I was risking only my life, and I had rendered that to God.
>
> Considering my danger, from the day I began my journey until its end, I had feared that if I were to die, no report about this land could be obtained. In my view, this is the grandest and best of all discovered. When I remarked to the *principales* I had with me how excellent Cíbola seemed to me, they replied that it was the least of the seven *ciudades*

[i.e., the pueblos of Cíbola—WKH] and that Totonteac is much grander and better than all the seven *ciudades*. And that [Totonteac] comprises so many buildings and people that it has no end. Considering the excellence of the *ciudad*, it seemed [appropriate] to me to call that land the Nuevo Reino de San Francisco.

An enthused Marcos was naming the land after the founder of his Franciscan order—the New Kingdom of Saint Francis.

I erected a large mound of stones there with the help of the Indians. On top of it I set a small, thin cross, since I did not have the equipment to make it bigger. I declared that the cross and mound were being erected in token of possession in the name of don Antonio de Mendoza, viceroy and governor of Nueva España, [and] on behalf of the emperor, our lord, in accordance with the [viceroy's] directive. I declared that [by] that act of possession I was there taking possession of all of the seven *ciudades*, plus the *reinos* of Totonteac, Ácus, and Maratta. [I stated] that I was not going on to them in order to return to give a report of what had been seen and done.

At this point, Marcos turned away and fled from the city that he had come so far to see.

CHAPTER SIX

Marcos Races Back to Mexico City

Marcos was refreshingly frank about his concerns as he fled Cíbola. He continues the story with a wonderful sentence: "And so I turned back, with much more fear than food." After two days, he caught up with his former friends, who had abandoned him. He retreated with them back across the fifteen-day despoblado to their villages, which we place on the San Pedro River in southeastern Arizona. Here, he tells us, "the people did not give me as good a reception as before, because both men and women were making a great lament for their friends [apparently] killed at Cíbola. With trepidation, I immediately said farewell to the people of that valley. The first day I traveled ten leagues; then I traveled at a rate of eight or ten, without stopping until I returned past the second *despoblado*" (this translation is based mainly on Flint and Flint 2005, 76).

This gives us intriguing information about his rate of travel. He was racing away from possible mortal danger and so is revealing his peak rates of travel. Eight to ten leagues per day is in the range of 20 to 31 miles per day. If Marcos counted his despoblados from north to south during the return, he traveled at that rate to the headwaters of the Río Sonora in northern Sonora, safe from the angry San Pedro valley natives. If he used his original numbering of despoblados, from south to north, it would mean he traveled this fast to somewhere just south of the Río Sonora valley in the Vacapa area.

From here on, Marcos devotes only the last 7 percent of his relación to his return. This is typical of many travelers; who ever recites the story of their *return* trip? Marcos mentions little about the route south, except that he traveled farther inland than on his northern trek in order to check a rumor he heard on his way north that gold was used in a certain valley to the east. Based on Marcos's relación and statements by Coronado expeditionary Juan de Jaramillo the following year, this valley was in the Sierra Madre foothills, east of the Arroyo Cedros in southeastern Sonora. Marcos resisted the temptation to detour all the way into the valley "because it seemed to me that it was . . . better [to gather information] without putting my person at risk." He surveyed the valley from a distance, noting villages with smoke rising in a "verdant" and "excellent land." He was told again that the natives of this region traded in earrings, jars, and a type of spatula or scraper for removing sweat, all made from gold.

Contrary to popular image, this episode is the only mention of gold in Marcos's relación. We'll see in chapter 8 how the golden valley turned out. As for gold, silver, or other riches in Cíbola, Marcos must have agonized during his return about his lack of proof. Describing the episode of the eastern valley, Marcos reveals that he carried samples of gold and other metals, and he showed them to local people along the way during his inquiries about valuable metals. Surely he used his gold samples to ask the people who'd been to Cíbola if gold existed there. What were the answers? Presumably, the Indians said they hadn't seen significant amounts of that metal, though they might have recognized copper samples. Why doesn't Marcos's relación talk about this? We can speculate that Mendoza did not want that publicly certified document to say that his man Marcos found no evidence of gold. There were three reasons. First, it would open the door to Cortés claiming any gold that *Mendoza's* men might find later. Second, Mendoza had Cabeza de Vaca's copper bell, "proof" of metals in the North. Surely northern treasures would eventually be found. Third, Mendoza and Marcos wanted to encourage the great work of expanding Spanish lands and planting Christianity in the North.

Mexico City: Summer, 1539

From records in Mexico City during 1539, we see the race between Cortés and Mendoza heating up as rumors about Marcos's journey began to filter into the streets. Cortés surely knew by early 1539 that Mendoza had sent Marcos from Mexico City to the North. Cortés then spent the spring preparing his ships to sail north up the gulf. On 8 July, weeks before Marcos reappeared, Cortés made his move. He suddenly dispatched one of his own naval captains, Francisco de Ulloa, up the gulf with three ships to see what discoveries and legal claims they could bring back regarding the northern lands.

Cortes's move was likely precipitated by specific rumors that Marcos had reported good lands in the North. Such rumors could have been based on leaks of information from the letters that Marcos had sent back. Cortés may even have had his own men in Mendoza's court to keep him informed. We have evidence that Marcos sent such letters back; Coronado wrote to Mendoza from Compostela in March or April, stating that he was enclosing "a letter I have received from the aforementioned father," describing Marcos's happy progress in the first days of his journey.*

When did Marcos actually arrive back in Culiacán, Compostela, or Mexico City? He gives no specific arrival dates, probably because Mendoza told him to report in secret. Fortunately, we can develop estimates from various peripheral documents. The sidebar "A Plausible Reconstruction of Marcos's Return Trip: Summer, 1539" presents plausible rates of travel and suggests that Marcos was back at the frontier town of Culiacán by 10–12 July. His relación tells us that he didn't find Coronado in residence there and that he continued southeast toward Compostela, where the sidebar places him about 26 July.

Coronado had already arrived in Compostela sometime before July 15 after his own failed attempt to find the rumored gold-bearing province of Topira in the Sierra Madre. (The rumors may not have been false; as shown on map 8, Durango, a famous modern gold-mining district, lies in the mountains about 300 modern road miles east-southeast of his base at old Culiacán; additional modern gold and silver mining in the Sierra Madre is even closer.) We know Coronado was in Compostela by 15 July, because he sent a letter on that date from Compostela to the king recounting news of Marcos's messages about "the magnificence of the land which Fray Marcos reports." This phrase is similar to phrases Marcos used in his relación. (Here, then, is a hidden clue that Marcos likely used his own letters and notes in compiling the relación.) Another proof that Marcos had been sending letters back is that Coronado's 15 July letter reveals an important fact: Marcos himself had not arrived in Compostela by 15 July, so the news must have arrived by messenger. Coronado tells the king: "I directed [Indians from towns north of Culiacán] to take Fray Marcos and

---

* We don't have the original of Coronado's letter, nor do we have Marcos's letter. Coronado's letter was published by Giovanni Ramusio with a date of 8 March, but from internal evidence in the letter, his date, like certain other details in Ramusio's edition, seems likely to be an error.

Estevan to the interior of the land in complete safety. [They] performed it just as I asked, treating them most excellently" (translation from Flint and Flint 2005, 40).

As pointed out by New Mexico historian Lansing Bloom in 1940, Coronado would never have sent this cheerful report to the king if Marcos had already arrived, because Marcos would have told Coronado, as Mendoza's appointed governor, that the Cíbolans had executed Estevan. Thus, Coronado's letter must have been based only on messages Marcos had sent back on his way north before the disaster happened.

Pedro de Castañeda, in his three-book eyewitness "Narrative," written in the 1560s about the Coronado expedition (book 1, chapter 4), tells us that once Coronado and Marcos reunited in Compostela, "so great was the magnificence" of Marcos's news about Cíbola and "about the Mar del Sur and islands" that they left for Mexico City "without further delay" (Flint and Flint 2005, 389).

Castañeda (book 1, chapter 4) reports an instructive anecdote about that final July/August journey from Compostela to Mexico City. He says that Marcos "made things seem more important because he refused to inform anyone about them, except his particular friends in stealthy, secret talks, until after he had reached Mexico City." Castañeda's source may have been rumors he heard from people in that party. Marcos, of course, was following Mendoza's orders to keep things secret. The air of secrecy (like many attempts at secrecy) was ultimately counterproductive because it enhanced rumormongering among the bystanders.

We know that by 26 July Cortés had already heard the rumors of Marcos's reports of good land and Marcos's impending return. Cortés, who was located near Mexico City at that point, wrote to Mendoza on that date about the news he'd heard, disingenuously offering his help, begging to learn the location of Marcos's discoveries, mentioning his ships, and subtly implying his own priority in the matter.

> I am infinitely pleased . . . with the news about Fray Marcos because although I was certain that a good country would be found, I did not think it was so near. My ships will find out what may be beyond, which I am sure must be something great. God desires that we shouldn't be idle, but act otherwise, because he placed us here for each to use his own talents. As Fray Marcos will return so soon, he will give more news. I beg your worship to order that the details be sent to me, especially about the location where it is, for I firmly believe he will have marked it down. (translation by Wagner 1934, 213–14)

Cortés's 26 July phrase that "Marcos will return . . . soon" proves that Marcos had not arrived in the Mexico City area by 24–26 July (allowing a day or so for Cortés to hear about it). Mendoza answered quickly, requesting Cortés's advice about future explorations. Mendoza's letter has been lost, but the archives contain a follow-up letter from Cortés dated 6 August, sent to Mendoza from Cuernavaca, about 35 miles south of Mexico City.

Today I received great favor and much happiness, when your lordship sent the letter concerning news of Friar Marcos. I had been wishing to receive this news on account of what is being said around here about that country. I hadn't given credence to it until I saw your letter, since your lordship had written to me that you would have me informed of whatever Friar Marcos might say.

It's worth rendering praise to God . . . that in our very own times, He is pleased to reveal to us this knowledge that has so long lain hidden. We may succeed in giving Him thanks for so great a boon by making proper use of it.

If anyone is going to be successful in this affair, surely it is God himself. It was God who wished to reveal this, not by expenditures for huge fleets

SIDEBAR: A Plausible Reconstruction of Marcos's Return Trip: Summer 1539

When did Marcos reach Mexico City? Using various dates mentioned in the text and elsewhere, I developed the following plausible calendar for Marcos's actions on his return. My intent is not to claim precise dates, but only to see if some combination of dates is probable in terms of other evidence. The distances are estimates based on map measurements and also tabulations by Cleve Hallenbeck ([1949] 1987, 46).

- Depart Cíbola 24 May about midday (see text), fleeing for his life. Race about 340 miles to the villages on the San Pedro River in fourteen days through rough country at an average rate of 25 miles per day. Arrive on the San Pedro on 6 June by his Julian calendar.
- Depart village on San Pedro River the same day, 6 June. He says he was still fleeing angry locals and that "with trepidation" he continued from there, 10 leagues (25 to 31 miles) on the first day, implying that this was a high but feasible rate for him. He says he continued at 8 to 10 leagues per day until he reached the second despoblado.

by sea and large armies by land, but through a single, barefoot friar, so that we may better understand . . . that to Him alone the glory is due, and nothing can be attributed to man. (translation by Wagner 1934, 217–18)

Again, there is no proof in this letter that Marcos himself was in Mexico City by 6 August. There is only "news of Marcos." Notice that the letters don't refer to Cíbola or the death of Estevan but only to "good country," indicating again that all this news came from messages that Marcos wrote on his way north, *before* the Cíbola debacle.

When Marcos reached Mexico City—regardless of the exact date—he reported his findings in secret to Mendoza. In courtyards and cantinas, however, friends of Coronado, Marcos, and Mendoza began to leak their versions of what they had heard. Castañeda says the news spread quickly: the rumored northern cities had been discovered! Wagner (1934, 218ff.) remarks on an "entire change in the situation" sometime between 6 August and 2 September, which supports our argument that Marcos's arrival was in that interval. Our sidebar suggests that Marcos reached Mexico City about 22 August, and this is supported by a very dramatic acceleration of events at just that time:

- The distance from the San Pedro River to Culiacán is about 770 miles (allowing for the side trip to the eastern valley). If he travels at an average rate of about 23 miles per day, the trip takes thirty-four days. If he averages 24 miles per day when actually on the road, he could have had two full days of rest on the way. Arrive in Culiacán on 10 July. Coronado not there. Rest about a day and a half.
- Depart Culiacán on 12 July. Travel to Compostela: 307 miles in fifteen days, averaging about 20 miles per day (possibly partly on horses or in wagons?). Henry Wagner (1934, 214) cites 250 miles for this distance. In that case, the rate would be only 17 miles per day. Wagner says that "due to the character of the country this could hardly be negotiated under two weeks at the least," which is consistent with my figures.
- Arrive in Compostela on the afternoon or evening of 26 July. Marcos's relación says that Coronado was already there, which fits with the fact that Coronado wrote from there to the king on 15 July. Assume Coronado required two days to organize the departure to Mexico City. This is generous, since Castañeda says they left "without stopping for anything." It is consistent,

continued

* 23 August: The bishop of Mexico, Juan de Zumárraga, wrote a letter stating that Fray Marcos "has discovered a much more wonderful land" (Wagner 1934, 223). The letter summarizes Marcos's discoveries about Cíbola. The letter doesn't explicitly say that Marcos was back yet, but it contains strong clues. First, it reports details about Cíbola that are not known from any other source, including Marcos's relación. This suggests a private conversation between Marcos and his bishop. For example, it notes that the Cíbolans were "cultured in their wooden edifices of many stories," that they "worship the sun and moon," and that each man had only one wife. Second, Zumárraga made a provocative mistake, saying the buildings were made of wood (instead of stone, as Marcos wrote). This would be a curious mistake if Zumárraga were merely copying letters from Marcos. It fits better a scenario in which Marcos has just arrived, Zumárraga has had a first chat with him, and then, in a flush of excitement, Zumárraga writes about what he'd just heard. In support of this, Wagner (1934, 224) states that Zumárraga wrote hurriedly in order to send the letter "by a messenger then leaving" to catch a ship sailing from Veracruz. The bishop's letter notably

however, with Marcos's comment that he wrote to his superior: "Send me orders what to do." Marcos wrote to his superior, but then after a day or so of downtime, Coronado ordered a precipitous departure. Marcos would get his orders in Mexico City, or on the way.

- Depart Compostela with Coronado on the morning of 28 July in a hurry to report to Mendoza. Travel to Mexico City: 513 miles in twenty-five days of travel at 21 miles per day (possibly partly in wagons or on horses).
- Arrive in Mexico City around 22 August. In this reconstruction, the total elapsed time from Culiacán through Compostela to Mexico City is about forty-two days at about 20 miles per day. Recall from chapter 3 that Cabeza de Vaca's larger party took about sixty-nine days, but they presumably stopped in Compostela for a longer time to parley with Guzmán.

Based on this list, the return from Cíbola to Mexico City took ninety-one to ninety-three days, covering about 1,930 miles at an average travel rate of about 21 miles per day. This average rate is well below the fastest rates that Marcos himself reported, and it seems plausible for an experienced hiker fleeing for his life in the first two or three weeks and anxious to deliver his news.

says *nothing* about gold in Cíbola. If Marcos had told Zumárraga that Cíbola was full of gold, would the bishop have failed even to mention it? Marcos seems to have told Zumárraga only correct information about a cultured group of towns with larger communities beyond.

* 24 August: The very next day, Viceroy Mendoza suddenly issued a proclamation forbidding anyone to leave the country by sea or land without his permission. This was presumably to block Cortés from sending more ships and to stop wildcat expeditions launched in response to the now-rampant rumors. The order was too late. Cortés's ships, launched 8 July, were halfway up the Gulf of California.

* 26 August: A copy of Marcos's relación was certified in Mexico City by the minister provincial of Marcos's religious order and signed by Marcos, virtually proving that *Marcos was in Mexico City by that time.*

* 2 September: Marcos's report was presented to officialdom, as we learn from wonderfully flowery language appended to the existing copies during a formal notarizing process: "The most reverend Father Fray Marcos de Niza, vice *comisario* in this part of the Indies of the Mar Oceano . . . appeared [on 2 September] before the very illustrious lord, don Antonio de Mendoza, viceroy and governor for His Majesty in this Nueva España, and president of the audiencia and royal chancery. . . . Also present were the most excellent lords [such as] Francisco Vázquez de Coronado, governor for His Majesty in the province of New Galicia" (translation by Flint and Flint 2005, 77). Mendoza presumably orchestrated this event to emphasize publicly that it was his man who discovered the good lands to the north. On the same date, Mendoza, still nervous that Cortés might make his own claims, had Marcos make an additional special affirmation "in the sight of God" that "he had received no notice [relating to his discoveries] from Cortés, nor any account whatever of the country from him" (wording from Wagner 1934, 218–19).

* 4 September: Cortés made his own move in public, appearing before the audiencia council with a petition (as described by Wagner). Recognizing that the viceroy was solidifying his royal claim to the northern lands, Cortés challenged Mendoza by enumerating his own alleged discoveries in the Gulf of California.

* 11 September: An answer of sorts came to Cortés from an official known as the *fiscal*, requesting Cortés to verify his signature on his two letters from 26 July and 6 August 1539. Cortés did this.

* 12 September: Mendoza's appointed governor, Coronado, petitioned the audiencia that Cortés should be prohibited from sending any

expedition, by land or by sea, because it was rumored that Cortés was planning such an expedition. Coronado's argument was that he himself had been appointed by the king's representative to govern such northern lands. The audiencia took no action.

* 9 October: A transcript of these proceedings was made. Cortés demanded removal of the case to the higher court of the Council of the Indies.

* 16 October: Mendoza wrote to the royal treasurer in Spain, describing how *he* sent two Franciscans (Marcos and Onorato) "to reconnoiter along the southern coast" (again showing the importance he attached to the coastal configuration) and that they brought back "news of a very excellent and great land, comprising many settlements." Mendoza said his current plan was to organize "as many as 200 horsemen by land and two ships by sea with as many as 100 arquebusiers, some crossbow men, and some priests, to see how they will be received by those natives." Here we see in embryo the plan for the giant Coronado expedition, which soon set out for Cíbola. (Copies of these letters, said to be word for word, are translated by Flint and Flint in their 2005 book, pp. 91–92.)

* 18 October: A financial officer in Mexico City, Rodrigo de Albornoz, known to Mendoza, sent a summary of the situation to the royal treasurer in Spain, telling how a "new land" had been discovered to the north beyond the region where Guzmán had been slave raiding. Albornoz pictures it as "adjacent to the island the marquis del Valle [Cortés] recently discovered [i.e., the peninsula of Baja California], to which he has sent three or four fleets." Albornoz verifies that Marcos returned with news about "seven very populous *ciudades*," with grand buildings, and provided an "eyewitness account" of one of them. That land was called Cíbola, and another land in that area was called Marate [*sic*]. The letter refers also to "another very populous land [Totonteac?—WKH] about which Marcos gave very marvelous news, both in regard to its wealth and . . . the harmony, excellent conduct, and orderliness [of the people], with respect to their building . . . since they have houses made of lime and stone of two or three stories, and at the doors and windows, a great quantity of turquoises" (Flint and Flint 2005, 91–92). Albornoz went on to talk about animals, good clothing, and the "intelligent" people and then concisely reported the gossip about the dispute over the new land: "The lord viceroy says it pertains to him because he has discovered it, and the *marqués* [Cortés] alleges and declares that he discovered it much earlier [having] spent

a great sum of gold pesos in locating it. . . . There have been a great many stipulations and responses from the one party to the other. . . . The *marqués* is going to Spain on the first ships that leave, [and] the viceroy is sending Francisco Vázquez de Coronado [north] to make an extensive report and provide information about the land. . . . Their departure from here will be in a month and a half."

The race between Cortés and Mendoza had clearly spilled into the public arena.

Checking Up on Marcos: Autumn 1539

By mid-October 1539 Mendoza was organizing his own proactive response to Marcos's discoveries and Cortés's provocations: a massive land expedition to be led by his appointed governor of the Northwest, Coronado. His confidence was shaken, however, by the lack of definitive information on the wealth of Cíbola. To make a successful conquest, he needed to find gold or other transportable wealth that could be sent back to Spain, first to pay for the venture, and then to provide profit to the royal treasury. Therefore, he arranged (as cited by Castañeda, book 1, chapter 7) that "the captain Melchior Díaz and Juan de Zaldívar would go forth from Culiacán with a dozen good men." Díaz was the capable mayor whom Cabeza de Vaca's party had encountered in Culiacán—the man who had heard their complaints against Guzmán and ended Guzmán's slave trafficking. Zaldívar was second in command. As recorded by Mendoza, the Díaz/Zaldívar party set out from Culiacán on 17 November 1539 (Flint and Flint 2005, 234, 235).

In December Cortés made his own dramatic move. He left Mexico altogether, taking his case directly to the king in Spain.

Was Marcos a Fraud?: 1930–2000

Was Marcos really a "dunderhead," as charged by Sauer (1932, 30), or a mendacious "lying monk," as charged by Hallenbeck ([1949] 1987)? If we back off and look at the big picture, the charges are puzzling, because Marcos's reports were essentially true. Beautiful irrigated valleys *did* exist in Sonora. The coast *did* turn west at a latitude not far from Marcos's reported value, allowing for the errors typical of that time. Cíbola *did* have well-dressed people living in multistory buildings of stonework with ladders and turquoise in doorways.

But did gold exist in Cíbola? To repeat, Marcos's notarized report did not even mention it.

So why the charges against Marcos? As we'll see in chapters 8 and 9, they started with Coronado and his troops in 1540. These men blamed Marcos for misleading them about the route and the riches. Mid-twentieth-century historians accepted the sixteenth-century complaints and sought supporting evidence. As mentioned earlier, Sauer in 1932, Wagner in 1934, and Hallenbeck in 1949 concluded that Marcos did not have time to reach Cíbola and turned back near the modern-day border. Hallenbeck embellished the charges by portraying Marcos as a doddering old man. He referred to "the aging friar" ([1949] 1987, 44), the "slow plodding pace of the old friar" (54), his "rather leisurely" rate "because of his age" (55), and Estevan's "effort to hasten the laggard friar along" (74). But if Marcos was such an elderly sluggard, one wonders why Bishop Zumárraga and Viceroy Mendoza would have favored him. In fact, his age was not well known to Hallenbeck or anyone else. According to the *Encyclopedia Britannica*'s estimate of Marcos's birth date, he was in his prime, about forty-four years old, and (unlike most of us) had spent a lifetime walking.

The question boils down to this: Why did these historians think Marcos ran out of time? The key is their claim that Marcos arrived in Compostela around the end of June, which would not give him enough time to get back from Cíbola. That date contrasts with our reconstruction, in which Marcos arrived in Compostela around 26 July. Here is Sauer, writing in 1932: "The impossible part of the schedule is the return from Cíbola to Compostela in one month. We are told that he arrived at the latter place at the end of June. That would mean covering 1,200 miles in a month" (28). It would imply a virtually impossible sustained average travel rate of 40 miles per day for thirty days.

Wagner (1934) wrote himself into an inconsistency on this issue. His page 213 says: "No contemporary statement . . . gives the date of arrival of Fray Marcos at Culiacán on his return, or even at Compostela," but by page 215 he speaks of "the almost certain date of his return to Compostela . . . confirmed by contemporary evidence." He puts Marcos in Compostela by 1 July. By 1937, Sauer admitted that "a definite date of return has not been established" (1937b, 286).

Why, then, did Wagner and Sauer insist on the early date? Their supposed proof was the letter from Governor Coronado to the king, dated 15 July 1539 in Compostela, about "the magnificence of the land that Fray

Marcos reports." They said this phrase proved that Marcos himself was in Compostela by 15 July. In other words, they assumed that Coronado could learn Marcos's result only from face-to-face talks. As noted above, face-to-face talks are ruled out, because Coronado wrote a letter from Compostela on 15 July informing the king that the Indians had taken "Fray Marcos and Estevan into the interior of the land" and treated them "most excellently." Not a word about the debacle and death of Estevan in Cíbola! So Marcos was not in Compostela by 15 July, meaning that Coronado based his letter only on messages Marcos sent back on his way north while everything was going well.

Let's test that idea. When Marcos was waiting at the last village in southeastern Arizona in early May, he would likely have sent back a message regarding his news of Cíbola and perhaps a prediction of his return in August or September. Could that message have reached Coronado in Compostela by 15 July? Yes. The time available, early May to 15 July, is about seventy-two days. The trail distance from Marcos's early May position in southern Arizona to Compostela is around 1,045 to 1,113 road miles, based on Hallenbeck's compilations from several sources. This requires only about 15 miles per day for the message's rate of travel—a reasonable, even slow, rate for Native American messengers in those days. Such a message would have described the good country of Sonora, with its prosperous villages and irrigated valleys—exactly what Coronado told the king!

As mentioned earlier in this chapter, the Sauer/Wagner version of Marcos's return to Compostela by 1 July was challenged on these grounds as early as 1940 by University of New Mexico historian Lansing Bloom. Bloom's suggestion seems obvious, in retrospect. In 1941, however, Sauer blasted it: "I see no basis for [Bloom's] interpretation that Coronado had only advance reports brought back by Indians, which seems sheer supposition." Hardly supposition, I'd say, since Mendoza ordered Marcos to send such reports, and Coronado had already mentioned at least one early letter from Marcos. Bloom (1941) attempted an answer, but Sauer was the better-known authority, and Bloom's suggestion gradually sank into obscurity. In 1949 Hallenbeck reinforced Sauer, but with an even more astonishing reaction. Hallenbeck (1949, 85) explicitly stated that Mendoza's instruction to send back messages was "totally ignored in so far as there is any evidence"—in spite of Coronado's statement that Marcos had written to him.

Most books today still say that Marcos did not have time to reach Cíbola. Summarizing the work since the 1930s, however, we can see a gradual unraveling of Sauer's argument. In the 1930s Sauer claimed that Marcos turned back approximately at the present international border (nineteen to twenty-three days south of Cíbola). Wagner (1934, 216) allowed Marcos to get as far as the Gila River in southern Arizona (thirteen or fourteen days south of Cíbola). Hallenbeck ([1949] 1987, 53–54) agreed with these estimates. Michel Nallino's research in the 1990s and my 1997 article favored Marcos arriving within sight of Cíbola, as Marcos reported. The Flints (2005, 62), in an intermediate position, concluded that it "seems improbable that Marcos crossed the last *despoblado* to Cíbola." This allows Marcos to have traversed at least a few days into the despoblado (perhaps ten to thirteen days south of Cíbola). Richard Flint (2008, 35–37) concluded that it is "more plausible" that Marcos "turned around" as soon as he heard the news about Estevan (three days from Cíbola, according to Marcos). Flint added that Marcos's "exaggerations and outright lies were to lead to an extravagant expenditure of effort, life, and wealth" but suggested that Marcos's alleged lie about reaching Cíbola "might have seemed to him only a technical untruth." Once we allow Marcos to have arrived within three days of Cíbola, however, there is little evidence that would convict Marcos of lying about the last three days. It seems plausible that he did spend those last days creeping through the back country to a point where he could get a distant view of one of the outlying Zuni pueblos and its agricultural fields.

SIDEBAR: Lies, Conspiracies, and Solving Historical Mysteries

In my own involvement with historical incidents, I served as a consultant to the congressional House Select Committee on Assassinations from 1976 to 1979, investigating photographic evidence on the Kennedy assassination. I learned a useful lesson. If someone claims to have solved a mystery by hypothesizing lies and conspiracy, the most useful response is not to attack the hypothesis but to assume for a moment that it's true and then see if it would actually make sense from the point of view of the participants.

That principle came back to me as I pursued the issues of Marcos and his journey. Marcos in 1538 was well regarded in Mexico City and seems to have been a candidate to become the heir to Zumárraga's position as bishop. With that in mind, let's assume that he really did turn back at the border or some days into the final despoblado and then decided to lie about the rest of the journey in order to satisfy Mendoza's desire to claim the northern city. Why would he make up a story of traveling with many leaders of the southern Arizona villages, and probably some of his own servants from Mexico, all the way to Cíbola? And once

What Did Marcos Really Say about Gold in Cíbola?: Early Autumn 1539

Mendoza, for his part, surely didn't sit through conversations with Marcos without pressing him: "Didn't any of the Indians say *anything* about gold in Cíbola?" Presumably Marcos told Mendoza the truth—that in spite of the gold samples that he showed to the Indians along the way, he'd not been able to confirm gold use in Cíbola. Mendoza put a good public face on it during October and November, emphasizing that *his* man had found the good new lands while, at the same time, he sent out the Díaz/Zaldívar party to check the reports and organized his new expedition of conquest. He may have been reassured that various independent informants in Sonora and southern Arizona reported a "kingdom of Totonteac" some days away from Cíbola, said to be even greater than Cíbola, with "the grandest in the world, [with] the most people and the greatest wealth" (translation by Flint and Flint 2005, 72, 75).

The usual story about Marcos, in contrast, is that he arrived in Mexico City proclaiming gold in Cíbola so enthusiastically that he convinced the populace of Mexico City to form an army and rush off to Cíbola to acquire the treasure. Because of a curious incident, however, we have eyewitness accounts of what people in the streets of Mexico City were really saying in the early fall of 1539.

he returned to Mexico City in glory, why would he agree to return to the "scene of the crime" as a leader of the Coronado expedition? He'd know that the community leaders in southern Arizona could have told any interviewer in the Coronado army that "this priest never even reached our villages" or "this priest turned back only days before we got to Cíbola."

Worse yet for this theory, the Díaz/Zaldívar party reached southern Arizona in late 1539 or early 1540, as we'll see in chapter 8, and spent weeks there systematically interviewing local villagers. Yet they did not report a single Indian informant who said, "Marcos never arrived in our town" or "Marcos turned back just before reaching Cíbola." Indeed, Chronicler Pedro de Castañeda confirms that Marcos was the one who "found" a famous ruin, which is now known with fair certainty to be in southeastern Arizona, at least four or five days north of the present border (about seventeen days south of Cíbola). This alone disproves Sauer's and Hallenbeck's suggestion that he turned back at the border.

A ship bound from Mexico to Europe stopped in Havana on 12 November 1539. Mendoza had ordered it not to stop in Cuba because he wanted to keep Hernando de Soto from finding out about Cíbola. (Soto was claiming rights to explore that area, since the king had granted him rights to "La Florida," a land that was considered to extend west and north from modern Florida for some undefined distance.) The ship's officers claimed onboard illnesses and insufficient drinking water, so they put in at Havana. Officials there took an interest in the squabbles between Soto, Cortés, and Mendoza, so they recorded testimony from seven passengers about the news that had been circulating that fall in Mexico City.

Five out of seven of the witnesses said they had heard about a friar (only one knew his name) who had discovered good lands about 400 leagues (1,000 to 1,240 miles) to the north. They all used a phrase similar to "a wealthy and populous land," echoing Marcos's relación—implying that Marcos's phrases were circulating on the streets. Some of these reports correctly mentioned multistory stone buildings and intelligent people in the new land. Strikingly, however, none of these five eyewitnesses offered any rumors of the friar talking about gold.

A sixth witness testified that "he had heard it said publicly that a friar had recently arrived from a newly discovered land. . . . He says it is a land wealthy in gold, silver, and other items of trade." The witness added that in this northern land were "grand towns" with buildings of stone, weights and measures, and people riding on animals. Marcos reported nothing about Cíbolans mounted on animals, so the wording suggests not an eyewitness record of Marcos's words but rather a secondhand rumor.

The seventh and last shipboard witness gave an amusing *thirdhand* account, asserting that Marcos himself had talked about gold in Cíbola. The witness said his son-in-law was a barber. While Marcos was being shaved, he told the barber, who told the father-in-law, that after Marcos crossed a "mountain range" and a "river" he came to a land with many walled *ciudades* and *villas* (towns). Here, he said, "there were silversmiths. The women were accustomed to wear golden necklaces, and the men, belts of gold. There were hooded cloaks . . . a meat market, a blacksmith's forge, and weights and measures" (translations from Flint and Flint 2005, 97–101). Who knows what Marcos actually said? Marcos's barber might not have been the first barber in history to embellish a tale. Zunis were never known, in prehistory or history, to wear necklaces and belts of gold. There's an interesting connection, however. Marcos correctly wrote in his relación about Cíbolan "cintas de turquesas" (belts or waistbands made with turquoises; see Flint and Flint 2005, 70, 82) rather than "cintas de oro" (belts of gold). One wonders if the barber or the father-in-law simply transmuted the turquoise into gold through optimism, faulty memory, or blatant rumormongering.

As to the location of the wonderful new lands, the Havana witnesses were divided. One passenger said he heard that good land had been found by Marcos "on the coast of the [Mar] del Sur," that is, the Pacific coast, suggesting rumors about Mendoza's beliefs. Another said he'd heard that the new province "was toward the middle of the land."

In addition to these seven man-in-the-street witnesses, we have four more accounts about what Marcos said, brought forward by Henry Wagner (1934, 222–23). The eighth is the letter we've mentioned, from Bishop Zumárraga, written on 23 August, probably just a day or so after Marcos arrived in Mexico City. As mentioned above, it describes details of Cíbola, even their sleeping arrangements, yet says nothing about gold in Cíbola.

The ninth account came on 9 October, a month before the Havana testimony, when an obscure friar, Gerónimo Ximénez de San Esteban, wrote a letter, parts of which he said were based on direct conversation with Marcos. This letter described Cíbola much as Marcos had in his written report but emphasized the prosperity of the Cíbolans and mentioned "silk clothing down to their feet." Marcos talked only about cotton in his relación. Ximénez wrote further, "The friar himself told me this, that he saw a temple of their idols, the walls of which, inside and out, were covered with precious stones. I think he said they were emeralds." Since Marcos publicly denied entering the city of Cíbola, he would not have claimed to describe a temple inside the city. Perhaps he was describing a smaller shrine he had seen in northern Sonora, which Ximénez conflated with the new northern lands of Cíbola. As seems common from other reports, "emeralds" may have been confused with widely traded green and blue "turquoises," which may very well have been affixed to Sonoran shrines. The overall impression is that Ximénez was caught up in the speculation about the North and came away from his Marcos conversation with the idea that Cíbola was fabulously rich, which is what Marcos heard from Indians along the way who were correctly comparing mighty Cíbola to their own villages. Ximénez said he hesitated to write some of the details: "Of the richness . . . I do not write because it is said to be so great that it does not seem possible."

The tenth and eleventh reports are the two letters to the king's treasurer in Hispaniola, which we described earlier. One was written by Mendoza himself on 16 October, and the other was written on 18 October by the financial officer, Albornoz, giving information about Marcos's new discoveries. Neither mentions gold. Mendoza spoke of "a very excellent and great land" about which he wanted to get more information. Albornoz talked about a "new land" with good architecture and turquoises. One might suppose that if Marcos had come back stating that "Cíbola has gold ripe for plunder," the viceroy and the financial officer might have at least hinted to the king's treasurer about the good prospects.

To summarize, we have eleven eyewitnesses giving evidence on what they understood Marcos was saying about his discoveries. Eight out of eleven (including a few, such as Zumárraga, Mendoza, and even Ximénez, resulting from personal conversations with Marcos) make *no mention of gold in Cíbola.* Only two reports, secondhand and thirdhand, mention gold, along with false information, such as Zunis wearing belts of the stuff and riding on animals. The latter claim is so radically false that natives of northern regions were unlikely ever to have said such a thing to Marcos, and Marcos had enough exciting information that he had no motive to concoct imaginary riders on animals. The data suggest merely an atmosphere of excited gossip in Mexico City—a city without radio, TV, telephones, or social media. In a modern court of law, this body of evidence would hardly be adequate to convict Marcos of returning to Mexico City and trumpeting false tales of golden treasure in order to motivate a grand expedition of conquest.

More Clues about What Fray Marcos Told Viceroy Mendoza: Autumn 1539

An additional story hints at the kind of information Marcos brought back to Mendoza. Bernal Díaz, who wrote the famous eyewitness account of Cortés's conquest of Tenochtitlan, produced a second, lesser-known half of his *History of the Conquest of Mexico* that gives a brief account about "how the Viceroy Don Antonio de Mendoza sent three ships in discovery of the South Coast, in search of Francisco Vázquez de Coronado." Díaz wrote his account around 1570 and was not quite sure of the sequence of exploration between Marcos and Coronado, but he adds details to Castañeda's account, saying that after Marcos had seen Cíbola,

> it appeared to the friar that he should go back to New Spain and give an account to the viceroy, don Antonio de Mendoza, in order that [Mendoza could] send ships along the south coast, with iron pieces and darts and powder and crossbows and all sorts of weapons, and wine and olive oil and biscuits. This was because Marcos had given Mendoza a relación

[about] the lands of Cíbola, which neighbors the South Coast. [The idea was] that with the ships and iron pieces, [Coronado] and his companions, who already were in these lands, would be helped. That's why he sent the three ships. . . . I was not part of this [Coronado] army; I describe it merely as I heard it. [Thanks to Michel Nallino for pointing out and translating this passage.]

This supports the idea that Marcos's conversations with Mendoza involved not just Marcos's land route to Cíbola but also the idea of sending ships to rendezvous with the land army at a port somewhere near Cíbola. Everyone from Cabeza de Vaca, Marcos, and Mendoza to Bernal Díaz as late as 1570 still seemed convinced—falsely, as it turned out—that Cíbola was near the Pacific, "South Sea" coastline.

Mendoza Plans His Expedition: Late 1539

Mendoza now felt he could not afford to wait during the several months it would take for Díaz and Zaldívar to get back with more detailed information from Cíbola, since Cortés's three ships had already sailed. Thus, he went ahead with his plan for a giant, two-pronged expedition. One half would involve armed Spaniards, their servants and support personnel, native allies from central Mexico, and livestock, traveling by land. The other half would involve ships sent up the Gulf of California to carry supplies and seek a harbor where they could rendezvous with the land party. Mendoza's friend, the governor of the new frontier, Francisco Vázquez de Coronado, would lead the land expedition. To lead the naval expedition, Mendoza chose a captain named Hernando Alarcón.

Mendoza chose not to organize the land army in Mexico City because it might alarm the region's Mexican population. Instead, he arranged for the soldiers to dribble out of Mexico City around December 1539 and to rendezvous in Compostela, some 513 trail miles to the northwest (Hallenbeck [1949] 1987, 46), roughly halfway to the frontier in Culiacán.

The famous Coronado expedition—or, to be more accurate, the Mendoza/Coronado/Alarcón expedition—was now under way.

CHAPTER SEVEN

Cortés and the Viceroy
Compete for "Country Enough
for Many Years of Conquest"

The coastal lands of the Gulf of California are a lost byway of history and geography. The east coast of the gulf is the Mexican mainland, where Marcos de Niza explored. The west side of the gulf is the spindly peninsula of Baja California. Seen from a ship, the coastal strips on both sides are mostly sunblasted desert, where afternoon temperatures can reach 100°F in the summer. Marcos had spent most of his time a few days inland in more pleasant, north-trending river valleys. At the north end of the gulf, one of the major rivers of the world, the Colorado, forms a delta where complex estuaries and mudflats cut through a wider landscape of dry dunes and craggy igneous ridges, virtually bereft of vegetation.

Northwest-trending geologic fractures, such as the famous San Andreas Fault, are seismically active in this region. They opened the trench that formed the Gulf of California five to six million years ago. The trench extends the axis of the gulf onto the continental surface, where the Salton Sea and agricultural towns of the Imperial Valley actually lie below sea level. The whole region is dotted with hot springs and is occasionally shaken by earthquakes.

The gulf itself has a rich and varied cultural history. In 1539–40 Cortés and Mendoza raced to explore its northern coasts. In the 1920s and 1930s a new race began as fishermen worked their way up the gulf in search of totoaba, a large, delectable fish that weighs up to about 150 pounds. All was well for twenty years, until overfishing collapsed the fishing economy in the 1940s. By the mid-twentieth century, movie stars, jet-setters, and college students on spring break were frequenting coastal resorts at the sixteenth-century ports of Acapulco and Guaymas. Scenes of Spanish explorations were transformed into memories of beer and beaches, sunsets and sex, charmingly recounted by New Mexico anthropologist David Stuart in his memoir, *The Guaymas Chronicles*. Meanwhile, the fishermen turned to shrimp. In a few decades, by the 1980s, their skill and enthusiasm had collapsed the shrimping economy. Establishment of a United Nations biosphere reserve, along with environmental regulations, returned the area to a more sustainable economy around 1990 to 2000. The history of the Sonoran coastland and fishermen is beautifully told from the Mexican point of view by Sonoran novelist Guillermo Munro in his prize-winning novel *Las voces vienen del mar* (The Voices Come from the Sea), which is available so far only in Spanish but deserves an English translation.

Around 2000 a new conquistadorial frenzy began. The current conquistadors are primarily land developers and sales reps. Seemingly overnight, upscale beach-front resorts and eleven-story condos appeared among the northern Sonoran coastal dunes. Promotional literature described the northern Sonoran coast as a new "gold coast." Some of the construction was rumored to be financed by drug money laundering. Sales soared. By 2008, however, boom had turned to bust, leaving the projected tourist economy in limbo. For five hundred years the story of the Sea of Cortés has been a work in progress.

Ulloa Discovers the Mouth of the Colorado River: September 1539

Cortés always insisted that the gulf was his by right as a result of his sailors' explorations from 1532 to 1535. As we saw in chapter 6, when Cortés got wind of Marcos de Niza's explorations, he dispatched one of his captains, Francisco de Ulloa, to sail north from Acapulco on 8 July 1539, only weeks before Viceroy Mendoza prohibited further unauthorized exploration on 24 August.

Two accounts of Ulloa's voyage survive. One is a journal by Ulloa himself, translated and analyzed by the historian Henry Wagner in 1925. The other is an account by a participant, Francesco Preciado, reproduced in 1600 by a pioneering English geographer named Richard Hakluyt. The accounts are similar, and to save space, my quotes below, unless marked otherwise, are paraphrases based on my synthesis of the two versions.

Ulloa's voyage got off to a shaky start. On 28 August the fickle Sea of Cortés acted up, and Ulloa lost one of his three ships in a storm. The plan, in case of a separation, was to rendezvous in the "haven of Santa Cruz," the site of Cortés's failed colony of 1535–36 at the southern tip of Baja California. The two remaining ships arrived there about 8 September, but the third ship never showed up. As for the colony site, it was "all destroyed, and without a sign of a house or anything else of what we had left, except some pieces of pottery and bottles that were lying about. Everything was burned." Natives of Baja probably gutted the site after Cortés's colonists abandoned it.

Giving up on his third ship, Ulloa returned a few days later to the gulf's east side near the mouth of the Río Sinaloa, just north of Culiacán. From there, he sailed north along the shore, with no certainty about what he would encounter. Unknown to him, Marcos had already discovered that the coast turned west and was at that moment back in Mexico, advising Mendoza on how to explore the North.

Ulloa and his crew noted various empty plains and hills along the Sonoran coast. Soon they went ashore to claim the land at a point that Wagner (1925, 19) identifies as Guaymas. Although the mariners had seen very few inhabitants on the coast, they found "certain equipment made by the Indians to catch fish, and small huts containing ceramics as well made as those of Spain." As for the landscape, Ulloa was unenthusiastic, describing "poor" land without trees except for some cacti and shrubs (Wagner 1925, 20). Perhaps Preciado was with some party that penetrated inland along the Río Mátape or the Río Yaqui, which empty into the bay near Guaymas; he said he saw "a country full of fresh and green grass [along with] great, green mountains" (Hakluyt [1600] 1904, 211–12).

Having contacted no inhabitants, the two ships departed on 19 September. Ulloa wrote that "for 60 leagues beyond this port it is a high land, all stone and sheer rocks, without any verdure or green thing." To the west, on their left, the highlands of the Baja California side were now closer and more prominent. The sailors debated whether "Baja" was an island or a peninsula.

Cortés had surely ordered Ulloa to learn whatever he could about northern cities, but Ulloa found nothing so exciting. Around 22 September they passed "six or seven white, high, sharp rocks in the sea, 4 leagues [10 to 12 miles] distant from the coast . . . which we named Los Diamantes" (see Wagner 1925, 21; Hakluyt [1600] 1904, 214). Wagner correctly related "the Diamonds" to the tiny islands, still called Los Diamantes when Wagner wrote, 10 or 12 miles off the coast near 31° latitude. Rick and Peggy Boyer, directors of the Center for the Study of Deserts and Oceans in Rocky Point, Sonora, pointed out to me that these islands, now called the Saint George or Bird Islands, consist of a handful of rocky elevations separated at high tide and visible at a distance of about 26 miles from Rocky Point. Their brilliant white color results from a coating of fresh guano from countless nesting birds.

Los Diamantes lie just in the pocket where the coastline turns west, about 95 miles from the Colorado River delta. Sure enough, a day or so after recording Los Diamantes, the explorers found themselves sailing west, and they noted the coastal bend that Marcos had already reported to Mendoza.

In the next days, Ulloa's boats came to something very strange. The date was about 23–27 September by their calendar. The first curiosity was that the sea turned "white like chalk, so that we all began to marvel." This was a common sign of the mouth of a major river, but here the view revealed only a maze of low sandbars in open water. To the west, beyond the sandbars,

the other land was full of high mountains. We searched diligently [for] any passage between two lands because, looking directly [north], we saw no land. Always we found shallower water, and the sea was thick, dark, and all reddish as if turned to mud, and 4 to 5 fathoms [24 to 30 feet] deep.

We decided to continue toward the western side, still more than 2 leagues [5 to 6 miles] away. As we crossed, we continued to measure the same depth or less, and we rode all night in five fathoms. [Presently,] we perceived the sea to run with such rage into the land that it was a marvelous thing. Later, when it ran out, it left dry land. Then, with fury, it returned again, covering more than 2 leagues between us and the mainland, and measuring 11 fathoms [66 feet] deep. The flood and ebb continued regularly on a six-hour cycle, flood and ebb, without falling off a jot.

On 28 September we wanted to continue [north], but with low tide at dawn, shoals blocked the way between the two lands. Between these two lands we could see many summits of mountains, whose bases were hidden by the earth's curvature. (Hakluyt [1600] 1904, 204, 214; Wagner 1925, 21–22)

It's interesting to read the matter-of-fact reference to Earth's curvature, given the twentieth-century legend that everybody in those days thought Earth was flat. As I witnessed during a boating expedition into the Colorado delta, the view of distant California peaks is still notable.

The mariners were not sure what to make of their strange observations. Was it a narrow strait, like Gibraltar, entering into some northern sea?

The captain and pilot went up to the top of the ship and saw the sand-filled land all around the compass. There were diverse opinions among us about this place. It seemed it might be an inlet at the mouths of some lakes by which the sea went in and out. Others thought it might be a great river that caused the currents. When we could find no passage through nor discern the country to have any inhabitants, the captain went ashore on a sandbar with several of us to take possession of it. We named this area Ancón de San Andrés and the sea Mar Bermejo—the Estuary of Saint Andrew and the Vermillion Sea. (Hakluyt [1600] 1904, 22; Wagner 1925, 22–23)

We know today that the "raging" of waters in and out was caused by a funneling of high-tide waters up the gulf, concentrating in waves that rushed *upstream* on the lower Colorado River, only to be replaced hours later by an outflowing mass of muddy water. Visitors to the Colorado River delta marveled at the effect until the river outflow was tamed by the 1936 Hoover Dam and river waters were diverted into irrigation canals supporting modern agriculture. The specific sandbar where Ulloa and his officers stepped ashore has probably been lost in the ever-shifting pattern of shoals in the delta. The men's impotent formal ceremony, dwarfed by the immensity of the coastal desert, was intended to ensure that Cortés and his man Ulloa, not Mendoza and his man Marcos, would be counted the true discoverers of the northern lands. Their name, "Vermillion Sea" (Red Sea), is still encountered in descriptions of the delta waters; it refers to the Colorado River's massive outflow of reddish-brown muddy water, which was even more vivid in the days before modern dams reduced and slowed the river's outflow.

Ulloa and his crew had discovered the mouth of the Colorado River but without full recognition of the river itself. He recorded the latitude as 34°, which (unbeknownst to him) compares well with the 35° reported by Marcos five months earlier for the latitude of the coast's westward turn at the top of the gulf. As we've mentioned, however, there's a mystery about these latitude figures. The actual latitude of the Colorado delta is about 31.8°, not 34° or 35°. Henry Wagner (1925, 14) discussed the still-unsolved puzzle of the common Spanish error of one to three degrees, noting that, curiously, Ulloa's error was near zero at the south end of the gulf and got larger the farther north he went. The problem may have had to do with errors in tables that the Spaniards used that related latitudes to observational phenomena.

A day later, Ulloa abandoned the strange, deserted inlet with its violent tides and headed south, down the Baja side of the gulf. In his journal, he remarked presciently that the entire coastal area, from Culiacán onward, was "so great a country that, if it continues inland, I suppose there is country enough for many years of conquest." As described in the opening pages of this chapter, the conquest of the gulf coastlands is, indeed, still under way.

Ulloa's voyage was not over. He rounded the south tip of the Baja California peninsula and sailed north along the Pacific Coast (see map 1). About 9 January 1540 he arrived on Cedros Island, a rocky, bird-populated island halfway up the west coast of Baja. "Isle of Cedars" may seem strange for an island that in Ulloa's words was so barren that at first approach "it seemed ... impossible that in such a poor kind of land there could be a living thing." Later, however, his men encountered a few villagers, springs, and a few pines and cedars on hilltops. He took formal possession of Cedros Island on 20 January, recording a latitude of 29.5° (actual latitude: 28.0° to 28.4°).

The documents of possession from this and several earlier sites along the way describe the process, always in the same words: Ulloa, in the name of Cortés and the king, "put his hand on his sword and stated that if any person disputed the act of possession, he was ready to defend it. [This was followed by] cutting trees with his sword, moving stones from one place to another, and then from there to another, and taking water from the sea and throwing it upon the land, all in token of said possession" (adapted from the translation by Wagner 1925, 65). This ceremonial folderol apparently satisfied a legal requirement that an act of possession must include some sort of quasi-purposeful activity or construction to create human "dominion" over the claimed land.

From January to March, Ulloa tried to push on to the north but kept being driven back by storms. In late March, he was still stuck near Cedros Island, so he decided to send his largest ship, the *Santa Agueda*, back to Mexico to give news to Mendoza. Meanwhile, he could continue trying to sail onward in his other ship, *Trinidad*. On 5 April 1540 the two ships separated. The *Santa Agueda* headed back to Mexico, and Ulloa disappeared to the north. Ulloa's remaining story is murky. According to Wagner (1925, 12), most Spanish historians of the time did not know whether Ulloa ever returned, and one "states expressly that nothing more was ever heard of him." The last lines of Preciado's account (Hakluyt [1600] 1904, 278), however, say that Ulloa finally reached a point about a degree of latitude farther north from Cedros Island but encountered more storms and began to run out of food supplies, whereupon he "returned to New Spain." The Flints say that at some point he left Mexico for Peru, leaving a wife behind, and "lived illicitly" with a Peruvian woman from Cuzco, dying "in 1553 or some time before" (2005, 652, footnote 20).

Ulloa's official relación did reach Mexico, apparently on the *Santa Agueda*. That ship reached the gulf's east coast on 18 April and Acapulco shortly thereafter. The relación—seventy handwritten pages, signed by Ulloa at Cedros Island—was finally certified in Mexico City on 29 May 1540. According to a preamble, it had been carried to "the great city of Tenochtitlan" by the chief steward of "the very illustrious señor marqués del Valle [de Oaxaca]" (Cortés). This courier, fearful lest Ulloa's pages "be torn or lost or wet or burned," requested official transcripts that he could send to Cortés—the sixteenth-century form of photocopying.

Ulloa's relación must have been too late to influence Mendoza's initial planning for his expedition, since Mendoza's naval captain, Alarcón, sailed north from Acapulco on 9 May 1540. Alarcón and his crew seem to have met up with Ulloa, however, probably in the port of Acapulco between about 20 April and 9 May. Some contact must have occurred, because Alarcón, according to his relación (Flint and Flint 2005, 185ff.), apparently knew all about Ulloa's discoveries and seems to have hired some of Ulloa's men to sail with him.

Cortés's Flanking Maneuver in Spain: 1540

Recall from chapter 6 that Cortés had taken off for Spain to outflank Mendoza and press his case directly with King Carlos V. Cortés sailed from Mexico in January 1540 (Thomas 1995, 599) and arrived in Spain in April (Wagner 1934, 220). In Madrid on 25 June he filed a legal brief to Carlos V.

This document sheds light on the venomous conflict between Cortés and Mendoza. Referring to the start of the Ulloa expedition back in the summer of 1539, Cortés's brief claimed that "after Ulloa had navigated many days at sea," Mendoza stationed men at the coastal ports with orders to intercept Ulloa or his messengers upon their return. Cortés's complaint sounds like a screenplay précis for an Errol Flynn or Johnny Depp pirate movie:

> When one of Ulloa's ships returned to the port of Colima, a sailor disembarked so that he might come to me [Cortés] and give me a report. Mendoza's man, don Rodrigo Maldonado, who was in that port as a guard, apprehended him and tortured him to learn what information he was bringing. When Maldonado was unable to extract anything useful, he took horsemen to the port to seize the ship in order to extract secrets from its men.
>
> The ship, however, had left to sail farther down the coast, so Maldonado's party followed it for more than 120 leagues [300 to 372 miles, to a point closer to Mexico City]. Ulloa's men, fearing capture, anchored

off the rugged coast. One day a storm gripped their ship, during which it lost its anchor and small boat. It struggled to the port of Guatulco, and Mendoza's men captured the pilot and sailors. The ship itself was lost. (adapted from the translation by Flint and Flint 2005, 245)

Mendoza's man, Rodrigo Maldonado, was later recorded as a member of the Coronado land expedition. The fact that Maldonado was still on the south coast when the ship arrived and that Cortés had this information suggests the arrival date of the ship being described was before January 1540, when most expeditionaries were already heading to Compostela from Mexico City and when Cortés left Mexico City for Spain. This in turn indicates that the ship in question was Ulloa's "lost ship," which almost sank in the August 1539 storm on the gulf and did not turn up at Cortés's burned-out colony of Santa Cruz. It must have limped back to Mexico. The fact that Maldonado acquired no useful information by torturing a crew member reflects merely that Ulloa's party had not yet discovered anything useful.

The View from Mexico City: January 1540

From Mendoza's perspective, the new decade held fabulous promise. The city of Tenochtitlan was now well settled by Spaniards. Stone by stone, pagan pyramids were being dismantled and transformed into Christian cathedrals. Cortés had departed, giving Mendoza a free hand to pursue the North. The land expedition to the northern empires was already under way.

As for the seaborne expedition, Mendoza was finalizing his plans. A description comes from the chronicler Pedro de Castañeda. His book 1, chapter 6, says that Mendoza "arranged that Hernando Alarcón, a naval captain, would depart with two *navios* [square-rigged, three-masted, oceangoing ships]. He would travel coastwise, behind the land expedition, because it was understood, according to the report of Fray Marcos, that the army had to traverse lands near the seacoast. Thus, by means of the rivers, the army could locate ports. . . . It was assumed that the [ships] would always have news of the land expedition" (paraphrased from the 2005 translation by Flint and Flint). Side by side, the navy and army would then invade the lands of Cíbola. All the pieces were falling into place.

CHAPTER EIGHT

To Cíbola by Land and Sea

In this chapter we'll follow the Mendoza/Coronado/Alarcón expedition as far as Cíbola, but we'll be forced to jump back and forth between the land and sea parties because the two halves of the expedition became separated.

Events departed from Mendoza's tidy plan.

Starting by Land toward Cíbola: Early 1540

Histories written in the early twentieth century pictured the Coronado expedition essentially as a land expedition with some three hundred Spanish knights in shining armor and a modest crowd of "Indian allies." This concept comes from the muster roll, recorded when the army assembled in Compostela on 22 February 1540. It listed 287 enlistees as "free men," mostly Spaniards. The Spanish chroniclers usually referred to this group as "the Christians," and they saw themselves as aristocratic gentlemen and bold soldiers. Other contemporary accounts, however, indicate that some of the rank-and-file soldiers were regarded as young ne'er-do-wells and that Mexico City was well rid of them. The "Indian allies" were mostly natives of the region around Mexico City, and they were given short shrift in the Spanish memoirs.

Historian Herbert Bolton, writing in 1949, looked into things more carefully and estimated that the expedition comprised 336 European men in total, with a few additional Spanish women and children and several hundred Indian "servants, hostlers, and herdsmen" (1949, 68). In recent years, the relentless sleuthing by New Mexico historians Richard Flint and Shirley Flint has revealed a much larger expedition. It was the Apollo expedition of its day. Richard Flint's 2008 book documented a minimum of 367 European men-at-arms (perhaps more like 400 in total), plus another 368 or more mostly unnamed European, African, and Indian wives, children, servants, and slaves, plus 1,800 or more "Indian allies." The Spanish fighting force of three to four hundred was thus outnumbered by its own military contingent of *indios amigos* by four or five to one. The latter did substantial amounts of the fighting, even though they get only occasional mention. The "Christians," or European contingent, often called "Spaniards," included at least five Portuguese, two Italians, and one each from France, Scotland, and Germany. Thanks to the Flints, who spent hours in various archives, we now know most of them by name and occupation. They included blacksmiths, tanners, herdsmen, artists, and so on. Many of their family names are still prominent in Mexico today. Then came the animals. Halfway through the expedition, Pedro de Castañeda (book 3, chapter 8) recorded a thousand horses, five hundred cattle, and five thousand sheep—food on the hoof.

The bishop of Mexico City, Zumárraga, sent along three priests and two brothers with a retinue of assistants and servants. They were, as he put it, "men of science and conscience." Zumárraga urged that "the conquest may be Christian and apostolic, and not a butchery" (Bolton 1949, 75). It's interesting that, nearly a century before the Roman Catholic Church arrested Galileo, Bishop Zumárraga could advertise his priests, not incorrectly, as the most educated "men of science" on the scene. Marcos de Niza was prominent among them. In the vanguard, Marcos would help lead the expedition back to Cíbola along the route he'd explored in 1539.

Richard and Shirley Flint have more recently emphasized a view that the Coronado party should not be called an army, because it consisted of many ordinary men (and a few women), untrained in military matters. Even the twelve appointed "captains" in many cases were twenty-something sons of the more aristocratic families, untrained in military theory. True, it was not like the familiar precision British or Prussian armies of later centuries, but my own feeling is that it does not advance understanding to argue that it was not an army. After all, the expedition was called a "conquest" and had a captain general (Coronado) who arranged the group under captains, leading men armed with crossbows, arquebuses, and small cannons, as well as a support team of blacksmiths, wranglers, tailors, and so on. As we'll see, they fought a pitched battle to get into Cíbola; they requisitioned pueblos in the Albuquerque area, laid siege to other pueblos, and carried out executions. Perhaps we might say they were an army, but not a very professional one.

The expedition was an early exercise in venture capitalism. It was funded by investors and participants, wagering against expected profits. In 2003 Shirley Cushing Flint investigated the investors. At the top of the list was Viceroy Mendoza, who put up about 14 percent of the initial money. The second biggest initial investor was Coronado, or rather Coronado's wife, Beatriz de Estrada, who put up about 12 percent of the cost. She was the wealthy daughter of the former royal treasurer (briefly governor) of New Spain, Alonso de Estrada. She and Francisco had married only three years earlier, in 1537, when she was about thirteen—an age considered reasonable for marriage in medieval New Spain. Another 15 percent share was later chipped in by Pedro de Alvarado, Cortés's officer, "the Sun," who ordered the notorious massacre in Tenochtitlan and who was now governor-for-life of Guatemala. His funds topped the Beatriz de Estrada/ Coronado contribution. The twelve captains and the men themselves purchased smaller shares. The total investment equaled about half the wealth that Pizarro had acquired in Peru, proving that the investors expected a northern empire on the scale of Peru. Gold and silver would be sent back by land and/or sea in amounts that would provide splendid profits.

Mendoza was so enthusiastic that, after a tour through still-restless Michoacán, he proceeded northwest and caught up with the expedition at Compostela. He dressed in his best clothes and made a rousing speech. As described by Castañeda, Mendoza listed the expedition's goals: (1) conversion of northern peoples to Christianity, (2) profit to the men themselves, (3) expansion of the lands of King Carlos V, and (4) favorable treatment from Mendoza to those who did their duty. The excited men-at-arms took an oath to perform well.

In the last days of February, they started northwest from Compostela toward the frontier outpost of Culiacán. Mendoza went with them two days north on the trail, then returned to his viceregal duties.

Retracing the Trail: 1540 to the Twenty-First Century

Parts of this chapter involve the scholarly adventure of retracing Coronado's long-lost route to Cíbola. And there is good reason for doing so. The 500th anniversary of the Marcos and Coronado trips is approaching in 2039–40. Back in 1940, during the 400th anniversary, keen interest arose regarding the route, and leading up to the 450th anniversary in 1990, efforts were made to create a Coronado National Trail so that hikers, horseback riders, and drivers could retrace the footsteps of the first Europeans to come north into the American West. Many western states hoped for a piece of this historic trail—or, to be more precise, a piece of the tourism action—but no one could prove where most of the route lay. During the 500th anniversary, interest will be even greater. If we can deduce more details of the route and improve the intertwined U.S.-Mexican relationship, we can perhaps look forward to a cheerful, role-model party of Native American, Spanish, Mexican, and American hikers re-creating the journey to Cíbola on the original route.

News from the North: March(?) 1540

Soon after the expedition left Compostela, who should now appear but Melchior Díaz and Juan de Zaldívar with their handful of mounted soldiers, returning from the North. Recall that soon after Marcos returned in 1539, Díaz and Zaldívar had been sent north to Cíbola by Mendoza to get better information than Marcos had been able to gather.

What news did they deliver? Alas, it was little more than Marcos had already reported, because they were stopped by winter snows fifteen days south of Cíbola in a province known as Chichilticale, the region of Marcos's "last village" in southeastern Arizona (Flint 2002, 254). They spent weeks there, interviewing local inhabitants about Cíbola.

Castañeda gives a broad view of the army's mood after Díaz and Zaldívar gave their news to Coronado:

> Despite the privacy in which it was discussed, the bad news was soon rumored. There were some statements which, although embellished, did not disguise what the news was. Fray Marcos de Niza, being aware that some [of the troops] were upset, dispelled that danger by vowing that what they had seen [so far] was excellent, and that he had gone there and would place the expedition in a land where they would fill their hands. With this [the disturbance] was quelled, and [those who were discontented] put on good faces. (translation from Flint and Flint 2005)

Richard and Shirley Flint, during their work in the archives of Seville, discovered a previously unknown document that describes the news more specifically as heard by a caballero named Diego López: "This witness [López] had no hope from the day [the army] met Melchior Díaz, from whom [the army learned] of the ruins that were found there and that there was nothing in the land" (Flint and Flint translation, private communication).

Ruins? Yes. Southeastern Arizona was dotted with multistory and single-story ruins that were about 150 years old at that time. López probably heard something to the effect that the army "covered most of Marcos's route, and the only multistory towns they saw were in ruins!"

More direct evidence exists about what Díaz and Zaldívar actually reported in secret to Coronado. Mendoza received a written report from Díaz, delivered on 20 March by Zaldívar. The original is now lost, but Mendoza wrote to the king on 17 April 1540, including what he called a "verbatim" copy of Díaz's report about the province of Cíbola: "I have inquired into it, [said Díaz], through many people who have been there for 15 [to] 20 years. I have attempted this in many different ways, making use of the Indians together and separately. They end up agreeing in what I will tell" (translation by Flint and Flint 2005, 236).

This had been Marcos's method of information gathering, too. Díaz followed with a long description of the lifestyle in Cíbola, military intelligence about Cíbola, and news about another major settlement, Totonteac. Finally, he got to the fundamental issue: Did treasure exist in the northern lands?

> [Among the people of Cíbola,] many turquoises are hung from their ears and around their necks and wrists. . . . [My informants] are unable to give me information about any metal, nor do they say that [the people of Cíbola] possess it. They do have turquoises in quantity, though not so many as the Father Provincial [Marcos] says. . . .
>
> The people of this region [Cíbola and/or the larger region, including Totonteac] are famous [among the people of Chichilticale province] because they have buildings, food, and turquoises in abundance. I have been unable to learn more than what I am telling, even though I have brought with me Indians who have been there fifteen and twenty years.

This "news" still danced frustratingly around the question of gold in Cíbola. Why? The whole point of sending Díaz and Zaldívar was to find out the prospects for financial reward from Mendoza's expedition, but instead of saying "I conclude there is no gold or silver in Cíbola," Díaz (as quoted by Mendoza) says in a roundabout way that his informants were "unable to give me information about any metal, nor do they say that [the people of Cíbola] possess it." Neither Marcos, nor Díaz and Zaldívar, nor any of the other dramatis personae wrote a clear picture of what was said specifically about gold in Cíbola. Perhaps Díaz didn't want to tell anything discouraging to

Mendoza, and Mendoza didn't want to tell the king. The soldier López was the most frank: there seemed to be no prospects for a history-making heist.

Díaz added information about Estevan's fate: "The death of Estevan, the Black, took place in the way Father Fray Marcos must have related it to Your Lordship. . . . [I add, however,] that the [people] of Cíbola sent [word to the people of the Chichilticale province] that if the Christians came, they were to consider them of no importance and were to kill them, since they were mortal. This they knew because they had the bones of [Estevan]" (translation from Flint and Flint 2005, 238). According to Díaz, the Cíbolans helpfully added that if the people of the Chichilticale province didn't dare to kill the Spaniards, they should just ask the Cíbolans, who would come and do it themselves.

How did Coronado react when Díaz showed up on the trail with such fuzzy information? In my novel, *Cities of Gold*, I imagined a tempestuous meeting in which Coronado calls Díaz and Marcos into his tent and demands a clear answer. "You talked to people who've been there! You showed them gold samples! Does Cíbola have gold or not?!" Such a meeting likely occurred . . . but we have no record of it.

The expedition marched on toward a destination where, in spite of Dorantes's copper bell, no one had clear "information about any metal." As must have been growing more obvious to all concerned, the expedition was a far cry from Cortés's 1519 march to Tenochtitlan, when the invading Spaniards received golden gifts from their target city.

Some days later, the army arrived in the outpost of Culiacán. They must not have been too depressed, because they played a cheerful game with the settlers of the Spanish outpost. As described by Castañeda (Flint and Flint 2005, 391–92), the men of Culiacán lined up and fired off seven small bronze cannons to "defend" their town, and then the expedition advanced and "captured" Culiacán. All the lads had a jolly time . . . except for one cannoneer who lost a hand because the order to fire was made before he had finished removing his ramrod.

Toward Cíbola by Sea: May–August 1540

As mentioned above, Alarcón started the seaward half of the expedition on 9 May, sailing up the coast from Acapulco with two three-masted ships. At a nearby port, he repaired damage from a storm, picked up more men, then headed northwest up the coast toward Culiacán. As I've emphasized, the naval venture was more important in the minds of the participants than has been realized before. In fact, the scattered threads of the naval story have rarely, if ever, been gathered on one page. Here they are:

* Cabeza de Vaca's group in 1535–36 concluded that a coastline of the South Sea curved north of them and that prosperous cities lay near it.
* As a result, Mendoza in 1538 ordered Marcos to "inquire always about knowledge of the coast, because . . . some arm of the sea may run into the interior of the land."
* In August 1539 Marcos returned from the North apparently thinking he had support for the existence of Mendoza's inland arm of the sea, even though he also found out that the coastline turned to the west at latitude 35°. As we've seen, according to Bernal Díaz, Mendoza sent his ships north partly as a result of Marcos's report.
* On 12 November 1539 testimony about gossip in Mexico City produced at least one story that Marcos had found good land "on the coast of the [Mar] del Sur," fitting the preconception that the good land could be reached by ships.

Following Mendoza's plan, Coronado's army left supplies in Culiacán, along with a ship loaded with food and supplies. Alarcón would pick up the ship. Castañeda in his book 1, chapter 6, refers to the supplies merely as "clothing the men-at-arms could not take" (Flint and Flint 2005), but, as noted earlier in this chapter, Bernal Díaz (writing around 1570) said that the ships also carried "all sorts of weapons, and wine and olive oil and biscuits." Everyone hoped for a later rendezvous.

Today we have direct pictorial evidence of Mendoza's preconception of the inland waterway. Joining up with Alarcón's ships at some point was a cartographer, Domingo del Castillo, who had sailed with Ulloa. Castillo went on to create a map of the gulf in 1541 at the request of Mendoza. Castillo probably tried to combine the discoveries of Ulloa, Marcos de Niza, and Alarcón. His map shows the northern end of the Gulf of California with a broad estuary (probably based on the Gila River, but much too wide) leading northeast to Cíbola, exactly as Mendoza had imagined it when Alarcón sailed north (see map 11).

Alarcón Discovers the Colorado River: August 1540

Now we shift to Alarcón's progress in searching for the expected inland arm of the sea. After picking up the army's supplies in Culiacán, Alarcón

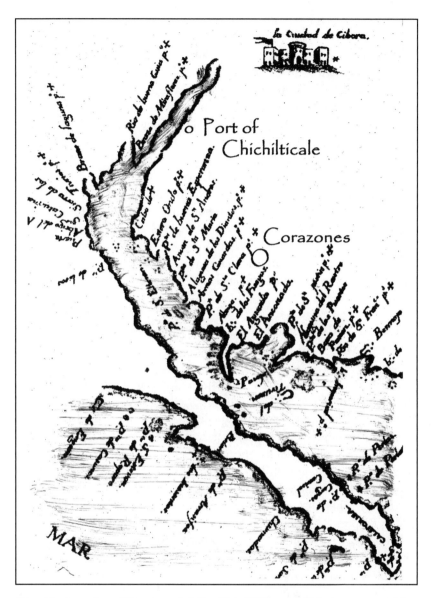

Map 11. A portion of Domingo del Castillo's 1541 map of Mexico, prepared for Viceroy Mendoza. This portion shows Mendoza's hypothetical inland waterway leading to Cíbola, based on the Cabeza de Vaca party's reports, Marcos's speculations about the Gila River, and Castillo's (exaggerated) version of Alarcón's voyage. The impressive castle-like symbol for Ciudad de Cibora [*sic*] at the top is used only one other time on the map: for Mexico City, illustrating the expectation that Cíbola rivaled Mexico City in grandeur. Minor additions by WKH include approximate positions of Corazones and the port of Chichilticale as they might have been estimated by Mendoza and Coronado (compare map 7).

continued north, all the way to the mouth of the Colorado River, confirming a barren coast as described by Ulloa but taking each opportunity to advance Mendoza's claim over Cortés's: "Traveling very close to the shore, I [discovered] some other very good anchorages that Ulloa, representing Cortés, did not locate. When I reached the shallows where [Ulloa's ships] turned back, it seemed to me and the others that it was dangerous. The shallows frightened us, and the pilots and other men wanted us to turn back as Ulloa had done. But because Your Lordship commanded that I should report about the secret of that Gulf, I determined that by no means should I avoid entering" (abridged from the translation by Flint and Flint 2005, 188). The passage confirms, incidentally, that Alarcón had already learned the detailed results of Ulloa's expedition.

During that August 1540 Alarcón began an epic exploration, upstream on the Colorado River. But now we need to return to the landward expedition.

Coronado's March from Culiacán to Corazones: 22 April–May 1540

When it came time to march north from Culiacán, Coronado was troubled by the underwhelming results reported by the Díaz/Zaldívar party. He decided, therefore, to split his expedition. Rather than lead the gigantic expedition and the livestock all the way to the gates of Cíbola without proof of gold, Coronado would race ahead, taking Marcos de Niza and Melchior Díaz as guides, along with local guides, cavalry, some foot soldiers, and most of the Indian allies but only a few livestock. They would learn, once and for all, whether Cíbola, or perhaps Totonteac beyond, was the next golden empire. They departed Culiacán on 22 April 1540 with supplies to last eighty days. Coronado ordered part of the expedition to trail them with the livestock and then establish a midway garrison when they reached Cabeza de Vaca's "gateway" settlement at Corazones. There, they should await further instructions. I'll call that group the "following" part of the expedition.

According to various accounts, the "following" expedition left Culiacán fifteen or twenty days after Coronado's lead party. The captain who'd been ordered to establish the midway garrison was the lieutenant governor of the expedition, Tristán de Arellano. (The *ll* is pronounced with a *y* sound, which means that the name was pronounced are-eh-YAH-no.) The garrison would serve as a supply depot for future shipments of goods north to Cíbola and treasure south to Mexico City.

Castañeda traveled in that following party and referred to it as the "main expedition." This attitude carried forward to twentieth-century accounts. Historian Herbert Bolton, for example, in his classic 1949 book (pp. 92ff.), pictured the advance party as a small, light, reconnaissance effort, citing the eighty horsemen and twenty-five to thirty foot soldiers, although he at least mentioned a "large number" of Indian allies. Richard and Shirley Flint, after analysis of many documents, recognized that Coronado took most of the Indian allies with him in case they had to fight their way into Cíbola (Flint 2008, 71). The advance party, based on the Flints' findings, contained about 150 Europeans and 1,500 Indian allies, making it larger than the following party. The mobility of the advance party came not from small size, but from leaving most of the livestock and support staff with the followers, perhaps explaining why Castañeda repeatedly pictured the followers as the "main expedition."

The advance party raced north. One of the most reliable Coronado chroniclers, Juan Jaramillo, was with them. (This Juan Jaramillo is not the individual who married Cortés's mistress Marina back in 1524 but a later Spaniard with the same name.) Jaramillo recorded that after they left Culiacán, he and others were sent ahead to the Arroyo Cedros (see map 9, lower right, and map 12) to see if they could find the valley where Marcos had mentioned rumors of Indians using implements of gold. Jaramillo tells the story:

> We were to go through an opening which the mountains formed to the right [east] and see what was in those [mountains] and behind them. If more days were necessary than we had been allotted, he would wait for us at the Arroyo de los Cedros.
>
> It happened just that way. All that we saw there were a few Indians in some valleys settled in something like *rancherías*—a lean land. . . . From here we went to the river called Yaquimi [Yaqui], which is probably approximately three days' travel [northward]. (translation by Flint and Flint 2005, 512)

So Marcos's eastern valley with possible gold implements was a bust, and this was a new source of discontent among the troops. Nonetheless, Marcos's reports may have had some factual basis, since significant gold mining was later established in this part of the Sierra Madre, as little as 50 air line miles east of the Arroyo Cedros. Perhaps a few gold trinkets were actually fabricated there in late prehistory.

The advance party (and soon afterward the following party) moved up the Arroyo Cedros and then across rough, mountainous country to the

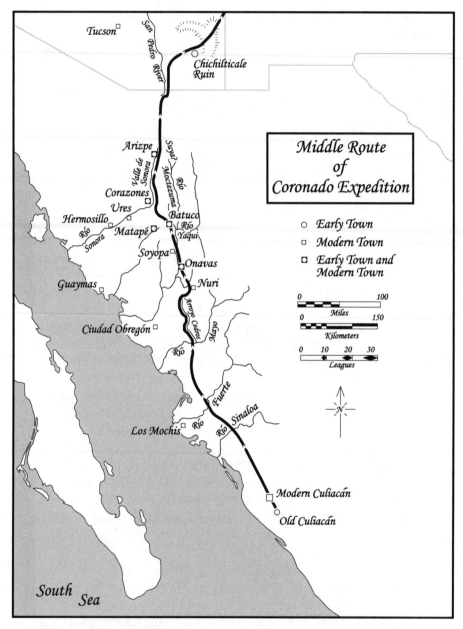

Map 12. Reconstructed middle portion of the Coronado expedition route. Locales with still-recognizable names, such as Arroyo Cedros, Batuco, Río Yaqui, Valle de Sonora, and Arizpe, are mentioned in the Coronado-era texts. Map by Ron Beckwith.

Río Yaqui (see map 9). In spite of the fact that we can recognize locales from these and other Sonoran place-names that they recorded, no camp-sites or Coronado artifacts have been located in Sonora as of this writing (mid-2013). This is surprising, because Coronado campsites may be *better* preserved in rural northern Mexico than in the United States, where urban sprawl and pot-hunting vandalism have ruined many ancient sites. As we'll see, however, such sites *have* been found in the United States.

Carl Sauer in 1932 and Herbert Bolton in 1949, pursuing their studies of the expedition, took early model cars on colorful trips into backcountry Sonora to locate traditional old trails that might mark Mexican parts of the route. The country was not much different than in Coronado's day; they bumped along dirt roads, fording streams and fixing flats. Comparing Coronado-era and modern place-names, they estimated that the expedition traveled up the Arroyo Cedros across rugged mountains and then descended into the Río Yaqui valley near the modern town of Onavas, where prehistoric village sites are known. Then the expedition continued north, upstream along the Río Yaqui. At some point they left the Río Yaqui, moving northwest to reach the Río Sonora probably near Batuco (see maps 9 and 12).

Coronado was bitter about this part of the trip. He wrote about it two or three months later, on 3 August, shortly after reaching Cíbola.

> We all traveled cheerfully, [but it was] along a very difficult way, which could not be traversed without preparing a new trail or improving the one that was there. This troubled the men-at-arms not a little when they saw that everything the friar [Marcos] had said turned out to be the opposite. Among the things that he attested was that the route was excellent and flat, with only one insignificant grade half a league long [something over a mile]. . . . [In the mountains,] even if the trail is well repaired, it can't be traversed without great danger of the horses falling. It was so bad that . . . I left behind the greater part of the horses I had brought from Culiacán at the Yaqui River, because they were unable to travel. . . . I left them with four horsemen. The rest were left dead because of that escarpment, [and] ten or twelve of our horses died from exhaustion. Because they had been carrying heavy loads and eating little, they could not endure the labor. Some of our Moors and Indians ran away for the same reason. (based on translations from Bolton 1949, 101; Flint and Flint 2005, 254–55)

Marcos, during his northern march, had written about the flat-lying trails traversed by his small party near the coast and had probed the mountains only on his return. Coronado's expedition, however, had taken the inland route toward the north. Why, then, did they blame Marcos for describing flat "routes"? This question leads to another question: How much direct contact occurred between Marcos, the troops, and the officers? The letter cited above begs the question: Didn't they talk along the way? Didn't Marcos get a chance to explain himself? Did they travel shoulder to shoulder as partners in adventure, or did they distrust each other and stay to themselves in different contingents of the larger expedition?

At Cabeza de Vaca's "Gateway," Corazones: May 1540

Recall from chapter 3 that the Cabeza de Vaca/Dorantes party, during their journey from the Houston area to Sonora, emphasized the native Sonoran community they called Corazones, calling it "the gateway [between the inland and] many provinces on the South Sea." Coronado's advance party arrived at Corazones on 26 May, and the following party arrived two or three weeks later. The various expedition memoirists clearly considered it a key point along the route. They described it as a cluster of three villages and placed it specifically on the Río Sonora drainage (see the sidebar, "Pinpointing Corazones from the Coronado Records").

SIDEBAR: Pinpointing Corazones from the Coronado Records

If we knew the location of Corazones, it would solve many problems about Coronado's route and also about Cabeza de Vaca's route. Most historians locate Corazones by citing the "gateway" description of Cabeza de Vaca and then interpret "gateway" not as a metaphor but as a physical reality, namely, an impressive narrow gorge on the Río Sonora east of Ures (fig. 7a). Carl Sauer in 1932 fathered this idea in his study "The Road to Cíbola," saying that Cabeza de Vaca's gateway "is hardly a cryptic remark to anyone who knows this famous river pass between the coast country of Sonora and the Valley of Sonora proper. It is the most significant gateway in the state. Through this canyon passed almost all the transport between the north and south of Sonora in the colonial period" (17). Indeed, a notable canyon on the Río Sonora is about 9 road miles long (depending on how one defines the endpoints) and reaches about 900 feet deep. It's locally called the Puerta del Sol, the Gateway of the Sun, colorfully indicating that it passes from the pastoral river valley at the east end to the sunburned desert

The new garrison established there was named San Gerónimo de Corazones. As for its detailed location, scholars for years placed it near the present town of Ures on the Río Sonora, but my own travels in the Río Sonora valley have led to a new suggestion that Corazones was at the modern Río Sonora crossroads village of Mazocahui (map 9), as described in the sidebar.

lands to the west. To followers of Sauer, Cabeza de Vaca's "gateway" is obviously the Puerta del Sol (see fig. 7a).

The memoir by Juan Jaramillo mentions a different feature, however, that has been brought into the discussion. Jaramillo said that going north from Corazones

continued

Figure 7. Constrictions along the Río Sonora, discussed in the text. (a) Portion of the 9-mile-long Puerto del Sol gorge, just downstream from Mazocahui (Corazones?). (b) Few-hundred-yard-long "small pass" upstream from Mazoca-hui, between Mazocahui and the Valle de Señora. Photos by the author.

Looking for Alarcón: May 1540

Once the Spaniards arrived on the Río Sonora, they hoped to make contact with Alarcón and his supply ships. Rodrigo Maldonado (the officer who had sought out one of Ulloa's ships and tortured one of the sailors) was sent five days downriver from Corazones with a small party to seek out Alarcón's ships. He found no news of the ships, but (as related by Pedro de Castañeda, book 1, chapter 9) he amazed his fellow expeditionaries by bringing back "an Indian so large and tall that the tallest man in the camp did not reach his chest." The tribal affiliation of this Indian was not reported, but many later Spaniards reported that the Yuma Indians, who lived around the head of the gulf, were much bigger and stronger than the Spaniards themselves.

to Cíbola, "we went . . . through a sort of small pass and, very near this stream, to another valley formed by the same stream, which is called [Arroyo or Valle] de Señora" (translation from Flint and Flint 2005, 513). So, according to Jaramillo, Corazones was on the "same stream" as a river segment they called Valle de Señora, but they had to go through a "sort of small pass" to get from one to the other (see fig. 7b). Castañeda, in his book 2, chapter 2, specifically confirms that Corazones was "our base downstream from the valley of Señora."

Our problem now is that Sauer in 1932, Herbert Bolton in the 1940s, the Flints, and most others equate Jaramillo's "sort of small pass" with Cabeza de Vaca's "gateway" and the Puerta del Sol gorge so that, to them, Corazones had to be downstream from the gorge, which would put it near Ures.

My own solution is different for four reasons. First, it's not clear that Jaramillo's "sort of small" pass is the same as Cabeza de Vaca's "gateway." Cabeza de Vaca's original "gateway" statement is ambiguous and hard to translate: "[Corazones] is the gateway to many provinces on the South Sea. If those traveling toward the provinces on the South Sea do not take the route through here, they will be lost, for there is no maize on the coast. . . . But along the [maize] route that we found, we believe there are more than a thousand leagues of populated country with good supplies of food" (synthesis of translations; see chapter 3). In my view, this text, especially the "thousand leagues" phrase, gives only a 2,500-mile-scale geographic travel advisory. It tells his audience of future explorers to seek Corazones as the best portal between Spanish frontier settlements (such as Culiacán) and the northern inland provinces (all the way to modern New Mexico and Kansas) and to avoid trying to get there along the barren coastal

"The Best of All Settled Places": The Río Sonora Valley, May 1540

The Coronado chroniclers are unanimous that they passed through the Valle de Señora (Valley of Sonora) just north of Corazones and that it was the most fertile and beautiful stretch along the entire route to Cíbola (see maps 9 and 12 and fig. 8). The "Relación del Suceso" says of this region: "The population is all one type of people [with] houses . . . all made of cane mats and some among them [have] low, flat roofs. They all have corn [and] melons and beans. The best of all the settled places is a valley they call Señora, which is ten leagues farther on from Los Corazones. . . . Among these [people] there is some cotton. What they dress in most is deerskins" (translation by Flint and Flint 2005, 497). In Castañeda's words,

plains. In other words, Cabeza de Vaca's "gateway" statement was never meant as a comment on a local feature such as Sauer's 9-mile Puerto del Sol gorge.

Second, in support of the above, note on our map 9 that the Río Sonora flows straight south, then angles sharply to the west through the gorge onto the coastal plains. This angle, or "corner of the Río Sonora," is the closest point to the Río Yaqui drainage. If you travel south from the modern border along the Río Sonora, as Cabeza de Vaca apparently did, you find that the last town before the river turns west is Mazocahui, nestled in a pleasant, flat pocket of land about 3 by 5 miles across. The name alone is a provocative clue. The words *mazo cahui* mean "deer mountain" in the native Opata language of the region, fitting with Cabeza de Vaca's exclamations about the feast of deer hearts. From Mazocahui, the modern road coming in from the north forks, with one branch following the Río Sonora through the gorge to Ures and the western plains, and the other branch turning northeast to a major branch of the Río Yaqui. More importantly, an additional old trail, still shown on some maps, runs 30 to 37 miles from the Mazocahui area to the southeast, joining the main portion of the south-flowing Río Yaqui. Thus, Mazocahui is the "gateway" that allows the traveler to avoid the coastal plains and continue south on the Río Yaqui (see maps 9 and 12).

From the point of view of the army marching north up the Río Yaqui (as can be followed on map 9), this trail would be the easiest, closest connection from the Yaqui (at the village of Batuco, or somewhat north) to the Río Sonora (at Mazocahui), just as Castañeda indicated. Sure enough, Jaramillo says the expedition

continued

Señora is a river and valley heavily populated by very intelligent people. The women wear petticoat-like skirts made of cured deerskin and little *sambenitos* [that reach] to the middle of the body. In the mornings [the] lords of the *pueblos* station themselves on small elevations which they have built for this purpose. In the manner of public proclamations, [like] town criers, they make announcements for the space of an hour, as though directing [the people of the pueblo] as to what they must do. They have several small buildings which serve as shrines, into which they thrust many arrows, which they put on the outside like [the bristles of] a hedgehog. They do this when they expect to have war. (Adapted from the translation by Flint and Flint 2005, 416; recall from chapters 3 and 4 that Las Casas also described small temples in this region, mostly from information attributed to Marcos de Niza.)

took two days to go from the Río Yaqui to the "stream" where Corazones was located, fitting the above-mentioned distance of 30 to 37 miles. (We should note in passing that this also fits Estevan's two-day trip from Vacapa, where Cíbola was not known, to an unnamed village where Cíbola was known.) Mazocahui is thus the logical location for Corazones as the most direct north–south "gateway" between the two rivers (map 12). Passing through Ures and the gorge, on the other hand, would involve a detour of as much as 70 miles.

A third observation beautifully explains Jaramillo's "sort of small pass" between Corazones and the Valle de Señora upstream without invoking the 9-mile gorge. About 5 miles upstream from Mazocahui, the Río Sonora goes through "a sort of small pass" a couple of hundred yards wide and a few hundred yards long (see fig. 7b). Another 4 or 5 miles upstream from the small pass, the valley opens up again into the south end of a lush, irrigated valley a few miles wide. This perfectly fits Jaramillo's account, whereas it seems dubious that Jaramillo would have referred to a 9-mile-long, 900-foot-deep winding canyon as "a sort of small pass" (see Hartmann and Hartmann 2011).

A fourth argument is the most decisive. The "Relación del Suceso," or "Anonymous Narrative," a short account by an unknown author, adds valuable information. It describes how the Spaniards eventually moved their garrison about 10 leagues (25 to 31 miles) upstream from Corazones to the valley segment that the Spaniards originally noted as a local Indian word, "Senora." Later the valley was referred to as "Valle de Señora," as shown in map 9 and discussed in more detail below. That distance fits a move from Mazocahui to the valley segment that was called Señora, but it does not fit with a move from the Ures area to that segment (see map 9).

Arizona archaeologist William Doolittle (1988) and his colleagues surveyed prehistoric village sites in the Río Sonora valley in 1977 and 1978 and found features that fit Castañeda's descriptions in terms of village spacing, irrigation, and apparent public platforms where leaders made their daily announcements.

Castañeda, acting as an early anthropologist, gave more details when he described a neaby valley (called Suya) as having a similar society:

> The people are of the same cultural level as those in the *valle de Señora* and nearby areas as far as the unsettled region beginning at Chichilticale. . . . The women are tattooed on the chin and around their eyes, like Moorish women of Barbary. The people include flagrant homosexuals.

A loose end remains (as always). Coronado-era memoirists give two inconsistent statements about Corazones's distance inland from the sea. The Cabeza de Vaca party Joint Report says that Corazones was 12 or 15 leagues (30 to 46 miles) from the coast, and Cabeza de Vaca, in his own report, mentions a 12-league distance. Coronado, however, writing from Cíbola on 3 April 1540, told Mendoza that Corazones was "a long five-days' journey from the western shore." Five long days would imply 90 to 140 trail miles inland, much farther than the Cabeza de Vaca estimate. Ures is about 110 road miles up the Río Sonora from the river's mouth, and Mazocahui is at about 129 miles. Coronado's datum, recorded in real time during his expedition, seems more reliable than the Cabeza de Vaca estimate based on sign language, and it fits a Corazones location anywhere from Ures to Mazocahui.*

To summarize, archaeological evidence of Corazones, the three-village community where Cabeza de Vaca and his friends feasted on deer hearts and where Coronado established a garrison, may lie beneath Mazocahui (Deer Mountain) or beneath its surrounding irrigated fields—if it has not been obliterated by the town or by farming.

---

* Curiously, the Cabeza de Vaca scholars Adorno and Pautz (1999) placed Corazones on the Río Yaqui near Onavas, even though Coronado documents say it was on the Río Sonora. Adorno and Pautz explained this conclusion by asserting disingenuously that the Coronado army simply misidentified the true Corazones. This is rather hard to accept, since Coronado and his men established a base at Corazones and had weeks to confirm that it was the same village where the Cabeza de Vaca/Dorantes party were given a feast of deer hearts and a gift of "emerald arrowheads," and, most importantly, where the inhabitants knew about northern trade centers.

People drink a wine made from *pitahayas* (fruits of giant cacti), and become drunk from it. They keep prickly pears in their juice, without sweetener, and make abundant preserves from them. From mesquite beans they make a bread like cheese. It keeps the entire year. They have melons so large that it requires a person to carry just one. They make strips from them, cure them in the sun, and can keep them all year. When eaten they have the flavor of dried figs. When cooked they are very good and sweet. (adapted from Flint and Flint 2005, 416)

The original Indian name of the "best of all settled places" in the Valle de Sonora was recorded by Castañeda as "Senora," an Indian root word for "corn." Flavio Molina, the modern Mexican editor of a 1730 document about the area, remarks in a footnote that the Indian root word was "Xunut (pronounced csunut)." In the nearby town of Huepac in 2006, the local *cronista*, Dr. Sigifredo Montoya, pronounced the place-name as something like "tson-ora" and also referred to it as connoting abundant corn. (The *cronista* is the official town historian, an attractive Mexican tradition we might well adopt in the United States.) All this fits perfectly with Cabeza de Vaca's testimony, which referred to his route (probably down the Río Sonora) as the "maize route." This obscure Indian district, Senora, gave its name to the whole modern state of Sonora. The process, like many historical processes, was circuitous. Castañeda (book 1, chapter 9) explains that Coronado's troops transformed the Indian name Senora into Señora, that is, the Virgin Mary. Their Valle de Señora then led to the name of the river, Río Sonora, which led to the name of the state.

Even today, it's easy to see why the Coronado-era Spaniards rhapsodized about the Río Sonora valley. It's a jewel of the beautiful Mexican state of Sonora (see fig. 8). The state itself stretches from warm beach resort towns on the southwest coast to the rugged axis of the Sierra Madre on the northeast. The Río Sonora valley is one of several bucolic, flat-floored valleys running north–south down the middle between parallel mountain ridges formed by the West's "basin and range" tectonic geology. The central stretch of the Río Sonora that runs 50 to 60 miles is dotted by quiet towns with prehistoric roots. Signposts for each town give "founding" dates in the mid-1600s; these towns were "founded" when Spanish priests established mission churches. The missions were built next to preexisting Indian communities. Lovely cottonwoods—fresh green in the spring and gold in the fall—line the river. Horses graze among agricultural fields watered by the prehistoric canal systems fed by the Río Sonora and mountain tributaries.

Figure 8. The Valle de Señora, along the Río Sonora in Sonora, Mexico. This was the area considered to be the best the Coronado expedition had seen on their journey north to Cibola. December 2005 photo by the author, showing cottonwood trees turning gold along the river.

The valley segment called the Valle de Señora was "the best of all settled places" in 1540, and it's still known that way today. During a visit to the Río Sonora in 2007, I discussed local names with Alberto Suárez, another local cronista, who casually remarked that the best part of the valley was this same stretch, namely, between the towns of Banámachi and Huepac. In a confirmation, in 2008 the mayor of Banámachi told us of an old tradition that Banámachi "has always been regarded as the part of the valley where people feel the best."

The modern towns are rather poor, however. Young men leave to try their luck looking for work across the international border to the north. Around 2000 several Americans invested in the area, renovating crumbling haciendas near the central plaza into wonderful small hotels, particularly in Banámachi. There is talk of promoting a "Coronado trail" that would attract more tourism. The main issue today is the conflict between civilization and the drug cartels, which frightens American travelers but, so far, has not contaminated this area.

In addition to the use of the Senora name, another proof that the Coronado expedition passed this way is that Castañeda and Jaramillo both refer to an Indian town that matches the name and location of a modern town in the Valle de Señora, namely, Arizpe. Castañeda (book 2, chapter 2) spells it "Arispa" in his list of Indian towns, and Jaramillo refers to it as "Ispa." It lies about 24 road miles north of Banámachi. Arizpe/Arispa/Ispa became the Spanish colonial capital and largest city of the Spanish province of Sonora by the 1700s. Juan Bautista de Anza, the Spanish officer who founded the American metropolis of San Francisco in 1776, is buried there (though there is suspicion that the body displayed as his in the local church is the wrong one and that Anza is actually buried in a nearby grave in the same church).

The Lost Spanish Garrisons of Central Sonora: 1540

Coronado knew that Corazones and the Río Sonora valley were about halfway between Culiacán and Cíbola. That's why he ordered the establishment of a garrison at Corazones under the leadership of Tristán de Arellano. Arellano and the following army arrived in Corazones two to three weeks behind the advance army, probably in mid-June. Arellano quickly established the garrison, called San Gerónimo de Corazones, probably a mile or so outside the natives' village—a typical practice to minimize friction between the Spanish soldiers and the villagers.

After a few weeks, however, Arellano realized that the resources of Corazones (the 3-by-5-mile pocket at Mazocahui?) were inadequate to supply the newcomers. He learned that the "best of all" places in the Río Sonora valley was the valley segment mentioned above, Senora, lying "10 leagues [25 to 31 miles] farther on from Los Corazones."

Where, specifically, was Gerónimo II? The 1730 document mentioned above, edited by Flavio Molina, was written by an anonymous Jesuit missionary, who stated clearly that the local name "Senora" was applied to a cluster of "Indian rancherías" near a "muddy spring half a league from Huepac." This fits Indian sites around a well-known local spring, Ojo de Agua, between Banámachi and Huepac. Ojo de Agua is the Spanish term for "spring," literally and charmingly, an "eye of water." In this area, the valley widens to several miles, and the flat floodplains are occupied today by irrigated fields (fig. 8).

The priest-historian Bartolomé de Las Casas, writing around 1560, gave additional geographic information, less precise, but consistent. He says Corazones had eight hundred houses (not crowded for a 3-by-5-mile area) and that "six leagues farther on in the valley" from Corazones was a still larger town called Agastán. But then he mentions another even bigger town.

He mentions no distance, but, given the sequence of sentences, the "bigger town" was apparently still farther on. He says it was "the principal city and government center of this region," called "Señora or Senora," and that it had "3000 very good houses" (Las Casas quoted by Riley 1976, 19–20).

In summary, the available information fits perfectly with a move of the San Gerónimo garrison from Corazones/Mazocahui 10 leagues upstream to the settlements called Senora around the spring Ojo de Agua (see Hartmann and Hartmann 2011 for more detail). As mentioned earlier, this information also supports a location for Corazones at Mazocahui instead of Ures, because, as mentioned earlier in this chapter, a distance of 10 leagues fits if measured from there but does not fit if measured from near Ures.

In terms of the archaeology of lost sites, San Gerónimo II may be the easiest of the garrison sites to find today because it had the largest total count of person-days occupied by Spanish and their allies from central Mexico. On the other hand, the site, if it is located near Ojo de Aqua in the fertile Banámachi–Huepac corridor, may have been covered by sporadic flood sediments, plowed over by farmers, or demolished by later town construction.

As we'll see in chapter 10, the garrison was moved one more time to an ill-fated location in the valley called the Suya, creating San Gerónimo III. The moves led to confusion in the Coronado documents. Castañeda and other memoirists knew San Gerónimo primarily as the garrison site at Corazones,

SIDEBAR: A "Flap" about Tribal Names

Interestingly, the Río Sonora valley as a place of abundant maize relates to a twentieth-century "flap" about Native American tribal names. Early Spaniards designated the inhabitants of present-day southern Arizona as Papagos, derived from a Spanish word for "beans," and the word stuck for three centuries. The "beans" included pods of the mesquite tree, which were harvested and ground into flour. We've already seen how Cabeza de Vaca also frequently described regions according to their available food. By the mid-twentieth century, however, the connotation of "bean eater" for an Indian nation was seen as condescending, and the tribe changed its official name back to their own term, O'odham, which means "the people." The research above, however, suggests that the "bean" reference may not have been condescending originally but started out, in prehistoric times, as a practical geographic term simply to distinguish the "dominantly bean region" from the "dominantly corn region."

and so their later records typically refer to the garrison as Corazones, even after the garrison had been moved out of that community. Scholars must be careful, therefore, because the old documents sometimes refer to events in Corazones that actually happened in one of the two later locations.

Tracing Coronado's March from Corazones to the Chichilticale Ruin: June 1540

To paraphrase John Kennedy's secretary of the interior, Arizonan Stewart Udall (in *Arizona Highways*, April 1984), most of the Coronado route through Sonora, Arizona, and New Mexico to Cíbola is surprisingly unchanged since Coronado's day. If we could lead Marcos, Coronado, and their compatriots back among those sites of their young days, they could still recognize geographic features and say, "Yes, this is where we were." The challenge for us is to discover those places. In Arizona we pick up more explicit clues.

After Coronado's advance party completed the trek up the Río Sonora valley, they crossed into what is now southern Arizona, where streams flow north and where Marcos de Niza in 1539 described the last villages prior to the final, fifteen-day despoblado that led to Cíbola. According to the chronicler Juan Jaramillo, they traveled "about four days [through] unsettled land to another stream which we understood to be called Nexpa. We went downstream along this rivulet for two days. Once we left the stream, we went to the right to the foot of the mountain range in two days, where we were told it was called Chichiltiecally. . . . We crossed the mountain chain that I had heard about even in Nueva España, more than 300 leagues away. At this pass we gave the mountains the name Chichiltecally because we were informed that they were so called by some Indians we had passed." (The preceding passage is based on the translation from Flint and Flint 2005, but I have arranged Jaramillo's sentences more chronologically. Notice how, as based on the Flints' transliteration, Jaramillo (or his scribe?) spelled the mountain name two different ways, with *ie* and *e*, testifying to the mutability of Spanish phonetic transcriptions of local words.)

This passage beautifully matches a march across the open Cananea grasslands north of Arizpe, across the modern border, and then downstream on the north-flowing San Pedro River (see map 10 and fig. 6). At this point, a two-day turn to the right (east) would bring them to the western foot of the massif known today as the Chiricahua Mountains, and a couple more days, would bring them to the pass (see route maps by Brasher 2007 and 2009).

This passage can be matched to Marcos de Niza's report. He talked about a final populated valley (the San Pedro) and then a four-day trip from the riverside villages to the beginning of the final despoblado. Jaramillo implied that the beginning of the final despoblado was marked by the mountains and the pass. Thus, Marcos's four days likely comprised two days toward the mountains, then a couple more days to Jaramillo's pass (see map 10).

Castañeda, traveling through the same area a few weeks later in the following army, gives a consistent account except for one important detail. He used the name Chichilticale to refer not to the mountains or pass but only to a famous ruin near the base of the mountains. The ruin was apparently known widely as a campsite on the Cíbola trail. Castañeda says (book 1, chapter 3) that Marcos de Niza found it first—an important clue, telling us that Marcos was exactly on this route.

The troops had heard about the ruin in advance and apparently expected a wonderful ruined castle. Castañeda described what they found in three passages, which I've rearranged here:

It grieved everyone to see that the renown of Chichilticale was reduced to a ruined roofless house, although in former times, when it was inhabited, it appeared to have been a strongly fortified building. It was well understood that the house had been built by civilized [and] warlike foreigners who had come from far away. (book 1, chapter 9, Flint and Flint 2005, 393)

Chichilticale was so called because [Marcos de Niza] found in this vicinity a building that in former times was inhabited by people who split off from Cíbola. It was made of reddish or bright red earth. The building was large and clearly seemed to have been strong. It must have been abandoned because of the [Indians] of that land, who are the most uncivilized people of those that had been seen until then. They live in rancherías, without permanent habitations. They live by hunting. (book 2, chapter 3)

At Chichilticale the land again forms a boundary and the spiny forest disappears. That is because the gulf reaches about as far as that place [and then] the coast turns [west], and the mountain [chains also turn west] likewise. There, one finally crosses the mountainous land, [which] is broken to permit passage to the land's region of plains. (book 2, chapter 2, translations by Flint and Flint 2005, 393, 417)

The mystery of the lost ruin's location has attracted many historians, both amateur and professional. As late as 1985, New Mexico Coronado scholar Carroll L. Riley recounted earlier suggested positions ranging all over the map, from Casa Grande Ruins National Monument south of Phoenix to cliff dwellings at Tonto National Monument, northeast of Phoenix. Nonetheless, a focus gradually centered on the Sulfur Springs valley in southeastern Arizona just east of the San Pedro River, which more exactly fits the Coronado chronicles. In 1932 Carl Sauer proposed a large ruin on the Haby Ranch in the northwestern Sulfur Springs valley. In 1984 respected Arizona archaeologist Emil Haury proposed a ruin on the nearby 76 Ranch in the northeastern part of that valley.

SIDEBAR: Chichilticale: A Study in Linguistics

The name Chichilticale has its own story, which I've investigated with Sonoran linguist Constantino Martínez. (Our paper has been submitted to a professional journal but is still under review at this writing.) It's another lesson in the mutability of words. The modern name, Chiricahua Mountains, comes from the name Chiricahui or Chiguicagui, recorded by Spanish priests in the late 1600s and 1700s. That name meant Turkey Mountain in the now nearly extinct Opata Indian language of the region. Going still farther back, we realized that in Opata, repetition of the first syllable, "chi," creates emphasis or a plural, and the syllable "te" often connotes a future tense. Thus, we deduced that the name Chi-chiltecally, assigned by Jaramillo to the mountains, was his rendering of something like "Chi-chiri-cahui," the name that he heard from the Indians (or from his hungry fellow troopers who had talked to the Indians) and that it meant Mountain Where You Will Find Many Turkeys. Even today, a stream flowing west out of the Chiricahuas is called Turkey Creek.

Virtually all books from the twentieth century tell a different, earlier story. They assert that the name divides into two words, *chichilti-cale*, which, to the central Mexican Nahuatl speakers in the expedition, would have sounded like Nahuatl words connoting a red building, place, or thing. Castañeda, who applied the name only to the ruin, said it was made of red earth, so the name has been translated ever since as a Nahuatl term for "red house." Our linguistic study suggests that this may have been an interpretation suggested to Castañeda by Nahuatl speakers (in 1540, during the expedition, or in the 1550s or 1560s, when he was writing his memoir). Both stories about the name could be true. The name applied to the reddish ruin could have been a pun by Nahuatl speakers traveling with the Coronado expedition, based on the local Opata name for the mountains.

Figure 9. Pueblo ruins in the Chichilticale Province. (a) The partially reconstructed Besh-ba-Goa pueblo ruin (ca. 1300–1400, in Globe, Arizona) gives some idea of the possible appearance of the Chichilticale ruin (about 160 trails miles to the south) when Coronado's expedition encountered it in 1540. Photo by the author, 1993. (b) Graph showing examples of age distribution from painted pottery sherds observed at various Salado-era pueblo ruins, including Kuykendall (Chichilticale?). Vertical "activity level" scale measures relative concentration of sherds in any age interval. Most sites were active only between 1300 and 1400. Hitherto unpublished graph from data assembled by Betty Graham Lee and the author; see the text.

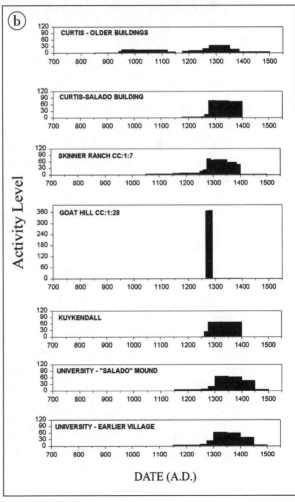

After a search of many decades, the correct ruin has probably been found. The candidate is an extensive ruin in the southeastern part of Sulfur Springs valley on the Kuykendall ranch, named for a family that ranched the land in the early 1900s. It lies near Turkey Creek, just west of the Chiricahua Mountains. It lies one or two days' march south of Apache Pass, a historic pass across the Chiricahua Mountains; that pass would thus qualify as Chichilticale Pass. The story of the discovery is recounted in the sidebar "Discovering the Chichilticale Ruin: 1540–2007."

SIDEBAR: Discovering the Chichilticale Ruin: 1540–2007

I fell under the spell of the lost Coronado ruin in the 1980s while writing a book about the Sonoran Desert, *Desert Heart.* How could such a once-famous place still be unknown?

My archaeologist wife, Gayle, and I engaged the issue more seriously in the 1990s, recognizing that southeastern Arizona is full of so-called Salado pueblo ruins, typically dating from around 1300 (fig. 9a). They had been poorly studied by archaeologists, but one of them had to be Chichilticale. We soon befriended a wonderful old-timer, Bill Duffen, the only professionally trained archaeologist to have excavated one of the many Salado-era ruins in the Sulfur Springs valley, namely the 76 Ranch Ruin, the very one that Haury had proposed as Chichilticale. In the depressed 1930s, Duffen felt lucky to get a job at the ranch, which was being run as a dude ranch for eastern tourists. In his spare time, he was allowed to excavate the mound that marked the ruin and uncovered the intact walls of a collapsed, multiroom pueblo. Unfortunately, the ranch managers allowed guests to take home the artifacts, which are now lost. Duffen published a short report in 1937 that noted affinities to late prehistoric pueblos in the Four Corners area to the north. This was intriguing because many Four Corners pueblos were abandoned between around 1150 and 1350, and many of the refugees migrated south into southeastern Arizona.

The cause of the migration has been revealed by tree-ring studies and other evidence to be primarily a broad climate shift in those days. A medieval warm period, recorded in European records and also in Greenland ice cores, lasted from about A.D. 800 to 1200 and was ended by a rapid cooling trend around 1300 to 1450, producing the "little ice age," recorded in European weather records as lasting from about 1400 to about 1850. (The climate records are well summarized in a 1997 book by Sir John Houghton, co-chair of an international scientific panel on global climate changes.) The rapid climate change around 1300 probably

The Mysterious Port of Chichilticale: Summer 1540

Chichilticale was much more important to the explorers than most modern accounts indicate. The Coronado chroniclers tended to divide their journey in terra incognita into three segments, each lasting a few weeks. The three segments can be remembered from four landmarks beginning with C: Culiacán to Corazones, Corazones to Chichilticale, and Chichilticale to Cíbola. Expectations were high for Chichilticale, and Marcos

played a role in the migration out of the Four Corners area, but also in the collapse of the mighty Cahokia metropolis on the Mississippi River east of Saint Louis and the collapse of the Viking colony in Greenland, both dated at around 1350–1400, when the Vikings' cattle died and North Atlantic routes became more dangerous for Viking supply ships due to increasing numbers of icebergs (see Houghton 1997 and numerous updated web sources).

In the mid-1990s Bill Duffen (then in his eighties) rode with me to the 76 Ranch. It was his first visit in fifty years, but we shared a laugh when he unerringly found the bathroom in the old ranch house, and, relying on his excellent memory, we found the mounds he'd excavated as a young man. Later, we located his original notes, photos, and diagrams and published a more thorough report (Duffen and Hartmann 1997). Bill died some years after that, but it felt good to help expand his early work.

Our paper together (and my other publications in 1997 and 2002) supported the idea that Marcos in 1539 and Coronado in 1540 had traveled a route from the San Pedro a few days east and north through the Sulfur Springs valley. We also remarked on the large number of candidate Chichilticale pueblo ruins that dotted southeastern Arizona, and we included floor plans of three such Salado-era candidates, one of which was the Kuykendall ruin, to which we'll return in a moment.

It's worth noting that the archaeological study of these "Salado" pueblo ruins in southeastern Arizona is a bit of a scandal for three reasons. First, twentieth-century Arizona archaeologists tended to ignore them, focusing on the more complex Hohokam ruins in the Tucson-Phoenix area, with their agricultural canals and ball courts, dating from the 900s to the 1300s.

Second, archaeologists held conferences in the late 1900s about whether the Salado ruins were built by people from the south, east, or north, but their published papers gave little weight to Duffen's 1937 evidence for a northern origin

continued

was denounced when the region did not live up to expectations. Hence Castañeda's comment that Chichilticale's appearance "grieved everyone."

Exploring the complaints made by Coronado and his troops against Marcos de Niza, I noticed a peculiar mystery. In a letter sent back to Viceroy Mendoza a few weeks after passing through Chichilticale, Coronado complained that Marcos had been telling him that they would find a "port" in that region:

> When I reached Chichilticale, I found myself fifteen days' travel from the sea. The father provincial [Marcos] had been saying that the distance was only five leagues [12 to 16 miles] and that he had seen it. We all

or the eyewitness evidence from Castañeda, who recounted local traditions that Chichilticale was built by people from the north: "It was well understood that it had been built by civilized [and] warlike foreigners who had come from far away. . . . [It was] a building that in former times was inhabited by people who split off from Cíbola" (book 1, chapter 9; book 2, chapter 3). In 1987 archaeologist Lex Lindsay argued that migration had come from the Four Corners area into southern Arizona, but he was ignored for some years. Finally, in 1995 archaeologist Michael Woodson reported evidence that the Goat Hill pueblo site, just northeast of the Sulfur Springs valley, had been established by Anasazi migrants around 1275 to 1315, confirming what the native inhabitants told Castañeda 447 years earlier (Hartmann and Flint 2001).

All of us are to blame for a third scandal. On our watch, in our generation, the ruins in question are being lost to vandalism and illegal pot hunting. When Gayle and I visited the Eureka Springs ranch with archaeologist Betty Graham Lee in the Sulfur Springs valley in 1995, the ranch manager described people sneaking in by night and tearing up ruins on his property in search of pots and other artifacts. We also learned of the bogus buyers who made a few payments on a ranch purchase in the valley, only to disappear after ravaging one of the ruins for artifacts on "their private property." Contrary to law in some other countries, American historic sites are not protected on private property, though commercial traffic in prehistoric artifacts is outlawed in the United States.

Archaeologist Betty Lee was elderly when she helped us. She had married a pharmacist and lived in the nearby small town of Safford (see map 10). Isolated from the archaeological mainstream, she began her own long-term study of the northern Sulfur Springs valley and the Marcos de Niza route. She interviewed ranchers, inventoried their collections, and visited ruins on their properties. She found everything to be contrary to what he had told Your Lordship. The Indians of Chichilticale say that whenever they travel to the sea for fish and other things they bring back, they travel cross-country and they take ten days' travel [to get] there. . . . I understood that Your Lordship's *navios* [ships] had appeared [on the coast west of Corazones], the ones that were traveling in search of the port of Chichilticale, which the father said was located at thirty-five degrees. (translation by Flint and Flint 2005, 256)

As we'll see, Coronado had reason to be dispirited when he wrote this letter to Mendoza on 3 August, but this passage goes beyond dispirited and

showed us a dozen valley ruins marked by low mounds, prehistoric wall foundations, and scatters of broken pottery sherds. We recorded statistics of the painted pottery styles, which could be dated to within a few decades by design styles. Later, she and I rooted through her several cardboard boxes of earlier interviews and records to expand our statistics. As shown in figure 9b, the data show that most of these pueblo structures were built around the 1280s and abandoned around 1400. We published a 2003 paper affirming that Chichilticale was likely to be one of the migrants' ruins in the Sulfur Springs valley. Betty died a few years later, but as with Bill Duffen, it was good to help her bring her work to fruition.

A parallel effort began in 1991–92, when archaeologist John Madsen of the Arizona State Museum distributed "wanted" flyers in rural southeastern Arizona and western New Mexico, asking ranchers to report Spanish-looking artifacts that might have Coronado affiliations (see Madsen 2003, 2005). Extending Madsen's efforts, a Tucson archaeology firm, Desert Archaeology, and a retired Tucson Public Television producer, Don Burgess, organized a group of us in 2004 to go on a "Coronado Roadshow," inspired by the Public Broadcasting System's *Antiques Roadshow*. Archaeologist Homer Thiel, in a 2005 paper, and Burgess in 2011 described how our merry band of Coronado sleuths gave presentations in various small towns where local ranchers brought in artifacts to be identified and dated.

What turned up was not Coronado material but a number of Spanish artifacts from the 1700s concentrated along an interesting route that had already been studied by Madsen. It was the route followed by a Spanish expedition in 1795, headed by José de Zúñiga, commandant of the then twenty-year-old Presidio San Agustín in Tucson. He had been assigned to discover a path that would link the two northern Spanish colonial capitals, Arizpe (in Sonora) and Santa Fé

continued

would not have seemed very coherent to Mendoza. For example, he quotes two different travel times (fifteen days from "Chichilticale," then ten days for the Chichilticale Indians) between Chichilticale and the sea coast, without seeming to recognize the discrepancy. (Perhaps he referred to ten days' travel from the villages on the San Pedro River and about fifteen days from the Chichilticale mountains, which Marcos had indicated were four days east of the villages.) More importantly, he seems unaware that his comments about what Marcos said disagree with Marcos's own, notarized relación. The relación lists at least eight days of travel from the point where Marcos investigated the coast to the point where he reached the last village

(across the Continental Divide in New Mexico). In other words, Zúñiga was trying to find a route for much the same journey Coronado made 255 years before. From old diaries, Madsen showed that Zúñiga's route crossed Apache Pass in the Chiricahuas (see map 10) and then went north along the Arizona–New Mexico border to Zuni (Cíbola) and thence to Santa Fé.

About this time, the Flints concluded that Coronado followed that same route across Apache Pass in the Chiricahuas, northeast to the Gila River, and north along the Arizona–New Mexico border. But where was Chichilticale?

An answer soon emerged with a set of discoveries by a colorful New Mexican, Nugent Brasher, who was successful in the business of petroleum exploration geology. Brasher, in a 2007 paper, described his interests as "intellectual challenges and outdoor adventures" (433). He had attended one of the Coronado Roadshow presentations in September 2004, talked with the Flints, and become fascinated by the problem of the lost ruin. He decided he'd find it. His ace in the hole was his geologic-hydrologic experience plus his extraordinary collection of geophysical data and maps—along with time and resources to pursue his goal.

A leading Arizona archaeologist, Bernard Fontana (private communication, 2011), later called Brasher perhaps the most "methodical" researcher he'd ever met. Brasher interviewed by telephone most of us who'd already been involved in Coronado research. Then he went to the original documents, mostly in Spanish transcriptions by the Flints, made his own new translations, and matched the route descriptions to his data on water sources and topography. Brasher agreed that the expedition had come north on the San Pedro and then turned east toward the Chiricahuas. He then talked with ranchers in the area, many of whom were skeptical about traditional academic scholars and federally financed research efforts but embraced Brasher's approach. Brasher investigated regional water prior to Cíbola, that is, a village on the San Pedro River on the west edge of Chichilticale province (see map 10). From there, Marcos then reported another four days to the place where he entered the despoblado (on the northeast side of Chichilticale province). That gives eight to twelve days or a few days more from the coast to "Chichilticale." Marcos's own report thus overlaps very nicely with the ten to fifteen days that Coronado reported.

Why, then, would Coronado claim that Marcos was talking about a Chichilticale "port" 12 to 16 miles away, if Marcos already reported the province to be around eight to twelve days inland? This peculiarity of Coronado's letter has been virtually ignored, but Coronado must have been

holes and local lore and then sought out likely overnight Coronado camp spots. He soon zeroed in on a route that would intersect the Kuykendall ruin. He leased excavation rights from the current owners and began surveys and excavations.

The Kuykendall ruin has its own colorful history. Like most Salado ruins, it had not been studied by professional archaeologists. However, it was one of several ruins excavated in the mid-twentieth century with professional-level care by Jack and Vera Mills, who were talented amateur archaeologists. They worked at the site from 1951 to 1961 and published their report in 1969. They commissioned archaeomagnetic dating of two fire pits, giving dates of 1375 and 1385, with uncertainties around twenty years. Combining these dates with ceramic types, they concluded that the site was abandoned between 1385 and 1450, 90 to 155 years before Coronado came through. This fits Castañeda's description of an imposing ruin with a fallen-in roof.

The climax was that Brasher and his field crew found Coronado-era artifacts at the Kuykendall site and concluded that it was probably Chichilticale (see map 10). Still, he cautioned that "evidence of the captain general's presence there in 1540 and 1542 is thin at best" (2009, 50).

The artifacts Brasher and his team found at the site are fascinating. Perhaps most important was a 13-millimeter fragment of what most experts agree is a Spanish coin issued between 1497 and 1507 and three corroded iron objects, identified (partly by X-rays) as crossbow points of a style common in the 1500s. Crossbow points are especially important because Coronado's expedition was the only large group to penetrate into the southwestern United States while armed with crossbows. Thus, crossbow points tend to be near proof that "Coronado was here."

continued

trying to say something. As a solution, I suggested in a 2011 paper that when Marcos arrived in the San Pedro villages in 1539, he followed his instructions from Mendoza, as usual, and asked about access to the coast and inland waterways. He may have learned that inhabitants of what is now southern Arizona made ten- to fifteen-day pilgrimages to the coast to collect salt in coastal salt flats (as known from later historic records), but he may also have learned that the Gila River lay only about two days north of the Chichilticale Pass, and that, as Alarcón was soon to learn, natives' trails stretched from Cíbola along the Gila River to the Yuma area just north of the Colorado River delta.

My hypothesis, then, is that Marcos, when he got back to Mexico City, speculated in private to Viceroy Mendoza and Governor Coronado that

At a nearby site where Brasher had predicted a Coronado camp, a day or two north of Apache Pass, Brasher found lead arquebus balls that gave at least rough chemical matches to lead balls collected at the Zuni village of Hawikku (Marcos de Niza's Ahacus), where, as we'll see, a battle occurred between the Coronado army and the residents of Cíbola.

Based on these and other artifacts found by the Brasher team, it seems hard to deny that the Kuykendall ruin corresponds to the long-lost Chichilticale. Still, it's prudent to consider three loose ends.

First, the overall assemblage of artifacts at Kuykendall does not quite match assemblages from any other known Coronado site. These include well-preserved "caret-head" nails (a 1500s design with an inverted-V-shaped top) and *iron* crossbow points. Why are the Kuykendall/Chichilticale points iron instead of copper? I can imagine an answer, though it is a stretch. Iron points evolved in Europe to penetrate armor. Iron, however, was scarce in the New World. Cortés found that copper points penetrated Aztec quilted cotton armor, and he solved his ammunition problem during the siege of Tenochtitlan by having his troops manufacture eight thousand copper points in only eight days (Gagné 2003, 241). This is a plausible production rate based on my observation of an El Paso blacksmith who, starting with a hot fire, proper tools, and a long quarter-inch rod of copper, turned out a spike-like nail in one to three minutes. In my reconstruction, when Viceroy Mendoza sent his parties north in 1539–40, he assumed the Cíbolans were hostile (because of the Estevan debacle) and that metalsmiths worked there. Thus, the Díaz/Zaldívar and Coronado parties may have armed themselves with iron points in case the still-mysterious Cíbolans had metal armor. They might have changed ships or small boats might be able to deliver supplies up the Gila waterway to some "port" on a significant river only a day or so from the Chichilticale province (see maps 7a and 11). This news fit Mendoza's cherished dream of an inland waterway. Mendoza kept that news and the name Chichilticale out of Marcos's relación to avoid giving Cortés any useful information, but he told Coronado to seek the "port of Chichilticale" on the nearby river. The idea seems plausible. The Gila River is the largest east–west river at this latitude. Today, much of it is usually dry, but in those days, before dams, it flowed along most of its length. For example, it helped feed a huge system of prehistoric canals near Phoenix around A.D. 1000. In the 1800s barges floated commercial goods at least partway along the Gila. Coronado, however, when he reached Chichilticale, asked about the nearest

to their supply of copper points only when they arrived at Hawikku and realized that the precious iron points were not needed.

A second loose end is that Castañeda always refers to the ruin in the singular. His Chichilticale was "a ruined roofless house . . . a strongly fortified building" (Flint and Flint 2005 translation). However, Mills and Mills (1969), as well as Brasher (2007, his map 2), documented that Kuykendall is a cluster of buildings spread over an area of about half a square mile, half a mile on a side. Figure 9a illustrates how a dilapidated Salado pueblo ruin could match Castañeda's description. We wonder if future research at Kuykendall might confirm that one building stood out as the main "fortified" complex.

The third loose end is that the artifacts might have been left by the Díaz/Zaldívar party, who were in the area for many weeks, rather than the Coronado party, who were there for only a few days on their way north and again on their way south. If Díaz's small group camped for a couple of months at the Chichilticale ruin, they could have spent about as many man-days in that area as the Coronado army (Hartmann and Martínez 2013). In this case, Kuykendall might be the main Díaz/Zaldívar site, while the true Chichilticale ruin might be another, more singular Salado-era pueblo structure in the same area.

Future work at Kuykendall may give better proof that "Coronado slept here." Perhaps by the five-hundredth anniversary of the expedition in 2040 the Kuykendall/Mills/Brasher site, or a nearby site, will be properly set aside as a national (or, more accurately, international) monument or World Heritage site—the campsite of the first trans-Atlantic explorers to penetrate north from Mexico into what is now the United States.

route to the sea and was, of course, told that the sea was ten to fifteen days away. Coronado's party then followed the ancient trade route to Cíbola. As suggested by the Flints and supported by Brasher's evidence, the route crossed the Gila River farther upstream in the hills, where it is much less impressive. Marcos was thus charged with the nonexistence of the "port of Chichilticale" and therefore for the failure to link up with Alarcón.

As the troops departed the province of Chichilticale on the last leg of their journey to Cíbola, they were in for still greater shocks.

CHAPTER NINE

Entering the Seven Cities of Cíbola

After Coronado's advance party crossed what is now the border into Arizona (see map 10), they continued along the prehistoric trade route toward Cíbola. Moving up the west edge of New Mexico, they encountered higher country, eventually entering pine forests. As mentioned in chapter 8, New Mexico researcher Nugent Brasher (2011a, 2011b) has reported Coronado-era artifacts along that route.

The First Mammoth Bones Found in the American Southwest?: June 1540

Paleontologists and archaeologists have documented several hundred remains of mammoths in Arizona dating back at least eleven thousand years. At some of the late sites, the animals were killed by some of the first Americans, whose spear points and tools were found among the animal bones. At some sites in southeastern Arizona, where the expedition was now traveling, mammoth bones have been found protruding from eroding banks of dry washes. The first such find may have been recorded by the Coronado expedition. Castañeda writes that three days after they left Chichilticale, "a horn was found on the bank of a river which is in a very deep canyon. [Flint and Flint 2005, 674–76, footnote 176, place this along the Arizona–New Mexico border, north or northeast of Virden, New Mexico.] After the general had seen it, he left it there, so that those of his expedition would see it. It was one braza in length [about 5.5 feet, according to the Flints' footnote 177]—and, at its base, as thick as a man's thigh. . . . It was something to see" (translation by Flint and Flint 2005, 395). The Spaniards thought it might be from a goat, but the dimensions more nearly match mammoth tusk fragments.

Death in the Pine Forests: June/July 1540

During the final approach through the highlands toward Cíbola, the Spanish troopers and Mexican Indians suffered from the low temperatures and lack of food. Some were driven to sample plants that turned out to be poisonous. Castañeda mentions three deaths. Coronado, in his 3 April 1540 letter to Mendoza, mentions those three and also the deaths of "some of my Indian allies" from general exhaustion. A "proof of service" document for one of the *hidalgos* (upper-class expeditionaries) says that "many Indian allies and horses were left behind and died" (translation by Flint and Flint 2005, 562).

The Battle of Cíbola: 7 July 1540

The diverse narratives from the Coronado expedition—memoirs, letters, and legal testimonies—converge climactically at the moment of the arrival at Cíbola. It was the first time that an organized European "army" confronted a relatively urban, organized opposing force in what is now the United States. In my novel, I rearranged and lightly paraphrased various passages from the various eyewitness memoirists in chronological order to create a multi-eyewitness view of what happened moment by moment. I utilize some of that material here, identifying the original eyewitness sources and giving distances in miles. Original translations of these sources can be found in Flint (2002) and in Flint and Flint (2005).

Coronado's party first saw the Cíbolan Indians at a river 20 to 25 miles from Cíbola. Castañeda says there were two of them, and they ran away, presumably to report the advancing Spaniards and Mexicans.

A cavalry captain named García López de Cárdenas, who would soon save Coronado's life, recollected the next contacts in testimony given during a 1546 judicial review.

> We arrived about 10 to 12 miles from Cíbola, without any skirmishes. I was ahead with eight or ten horsemen and noticed some Indians on a hilltop. I advanced alone, making signs of peace and offering presents

of things I carried to trade. Some of them came down and took the articles that I offered. I shook hands with them and remained calm, giving them a cross and telling them by signs to go to their town and tell their people that we wanted to be their friends. They returned to Cíbola, and I remained to await Francisco Vázquez Coronado and the others.

Here we camped for our last night before reaching Cíbola. I went ahead with a few men to guard a dangerous pass, so that we could block any hostile approach. Sure enough, at midnight many Indians attacked us at this pass. Because of their cries and arrows, the horses became frightened and ran away. Had it not been for two mounted guards, they would have killed me and my ten companions.

Castañeda added an amusing vignette: "The Indians startled the men so much that they leapt from their sleep, ready for anything. Some of the new recruits got so excited they put their saddles on backwards, but when the older veterans mounted up and rode around the camp, the Indians fled. None of them could be caught because they knew the country." As we noted earlier, they were an army but not a very good army.

Cárdenas picked up the story: "Next morning, Francisco Vázquez arrived with the rest of the men. We all set out together in order, marching toward Cíbola. About three miles from the city, we spotted four or five Indians. I again stopped my men and went ahead of the others, alone, to make demonstrations of peace. The Indians didn't wait for me, so we continued in order until we approached Cíbola. All the Indians of Cíbola, along with people from other nearby places, had gathered there to oppose us." The anonymous "Traslado de las Nuevas" emphasized the danger to Coronado's troops at this point: "Coronado reached Cíbola on Wednesday, 7 July, with all the men except for those who died from hunger some days earlier. . . . We did not approach the city as well as we should have, because we were all exhausted. Still, there was not one man in the army who would not have done his best."

Ahead of them was the hillside town that Marcos reported as Ahacus, the first large pueblo on the trade-route approach along the Zuni river from the southwest. It was a pueblo later abandoned, and twentieth-century writers called the ruins Hawikuh. It is now spelled Hawikku, based on Zuni phonetics. To the troops, the first glimpse of Hawikku indicated that the whole expedition had been a fiasco. Castañeda describes their reaction:

When they saw the first pueblo, Cíbola, such were the curses that some of them hurled at fray Marcos that may God not allow them to reach his ears [see fig. 5b and fig. 10]. It is a small pueblo, heaped up and down

Figure 10. The arrival of Coronado's army at Cíbola. The view, looking northwest, shows the pueblo of Hawikku in the distance with the Zuni inhabitants assembling to oppose the invaders. The ensuing battle was fought on the plain and around the city walls. Painting by the author, 1999, from on-site photos and visits.

the hillside. In Nueva España there are ranches that, from a distance, have a better appearance. It has three and four upper stories and with up to 200 fighting men.

People from the area had assembled there to wait for our army, drawn up in divisions in front of the villages [as shown in fig. 10].

Coronado's troopers may have thought that the first town, Hawikku, represented all of Cíbola. Modern archaeological evidence indicates that this "first pueblo" was among the three largest of the seven towns, with eight to nine hundred rooms (Mathers, Simplicio, and Kennedy 2011, fig. 10.3).

Coronado himself described what happened next, writing in his 3 August letter to Viceroy Mendoza some four weeks after the event. He gave a similar account at his trial in 1544, and I combine details of both accounts to give the clearest picture:

When I arrived within view of the first village, I noticed many smokes rising in different places around it, and I saw some Indians in warlike array, blowing a horn. I sent don García López de Cárdenas and two of the friars, Daniel and Luis, plus the notary and some horsemen, a short distance ahead to read them the Requerimiento, as prescribed by his majesty. This was to tell them that we were coming not to harm them, but to defend them in the name of the Emperor.

About 300 Indians approached Cárdenas and the friars with bows, arrows, and shields. Our side summoned them to peace three times and explained our objectives through the interpreter, yet they never consented to submit to either the Pope or the King. Being proud people, they weren't affected by our reading. Because we were few in number, they thought they would have no trouble defeating us.

As they advanced, I wanted to be present. Taking a few mounted men and some trade articles, and ordering the army to follow, I joined the small advance party. I was observing the large body of Indians arrayed in front of the city, when they advanced and began to shoot at us with their arrows. They even pierced Friar Luis's gown with an arrow, which, blessed be God, didn't harm him.

In obedience to Your Lordship's orders and those of the King, I didn't let my army attack them, even though the men were begging to begin the attack. I told them they shouldn't offend these people, that what they were doing to us was nothing.

But when the Indians saw that we did not move, they grew bolder, coming up almost to the heels of our horses to shoot their arrows. They wouldn't stop shooting arrows at us. Seeing that the Indians were wounding the horses and had pierced Friar Luis's gown, I knew there was no time to hesitate. As the priests approved of the action, I ordered an attack on them. The Indians turned their backs and ran to the pueblos, where they fortified themselves.

Cárdenas, who was out in front with the friars, described the same events and picked up the next part of the story at his judicial inquiry in 1546: "In the ensuing skirmish, the soldiers killed about ten or twelve Indians, but the others fled toward the pueblo of Cíbola. After they took refuge there, Coronado again urged them to accept peace. While this was happening, Father de Niza, the Franciscan friar who was guiding the army, arrived. Coronado explained what had happened and when the friar heard it and saw that the Indians were fortified, he said, 'Take your shields and go after them.' So Coronado and some of the others began the main attack on Cíbola."

It's intriguing that, according to Cárdenas, the priest who approved the final attack on the city was none other than Marcos de Niza. What was his mood at that moment? Was he bent on avenging the death of Estevan? Was he trying to ingratiate himself with the soldiers? Or did Cárdenas, at his trial, exaggerate Marcos's enthusiasm for the attack in an effort to escape the charges that the military men had used too much force?

Interestingly, Coronado himself did not implicate Marcos in the order to attack Hawikku but took the responsibility himself: "I gave the Indians assurances that no harm would be done to them and that they would be well treated. Seeing that they would not agree and that they continued shooting arrows from above, and considering that the army was suffering from hunger, I ordered that the city itself be attacked." A similar description of the crucial moments comes from the "Traslado de las Nuevas":

> When the captain general reached the city, he saw that it was surrounded by stone walls and high buildings, four, five, and even six stories high, with flat roofs and balconies. [The levels ranged up the slope of the hill facing the plain; it was not a free-standing building six stories high.] The Indians were inside, and would not let us near without shooting arrows at us. Since we could get nothing to eat without capturing the city, his grace decided to enter the city on foot, while surrounding it by horsemen, so that those inside could not get away. Because he stood out from the rest in his gilded armor, with a plume on his helmet, all the Indians aimed at him. They knocked him to the ground twice by stones thrown from the flat roofs, stunning him in spite of his headpiece. Besides knocking him down, they hit him many times with stones on his head, shoulders, and legs, and he received two small facial wounds plus an arrow wound in the right foot.

Coronado himself described this scene in his 3 August letter and in his 1544 testimony:

> After I dismounted with some of the gentlemen and the soldiers, I ordered the musketeers and crossbowmen to begin the attack and drive back the enemy from their defenses along the roofs so they couldn't injure us. But the crossbowmen broke all their strings, and the musketeers could do nothing because they had arrived so weak that they could scarcely stand on their feet. Therefore, the Indians up above were not impeded at all from injuring us.
> As for me, when I tried to enter through a narrow street, the people threw countless great stones from above, knocking me to the ground twice.

If I hadn't been protected by my good helmet, and if don García López de Cárdenas hadn't come to my aid, like a good cavalier, throwing his own body atop mine the second time they knocked me down, the outcome would not have been good for me! My comrades picked me up, with two small wounds in my face and an arrow in my foot, along with many bruises on my arms and legs. In this condition I retired from the battle, as if dead. When I regained consciousness they told me that the Indians had surrendered, and the city was taken. This was through God's will, and inside the city we found a sufficient supply of corn to relieve our necessities.

As for our injuries, Torres, Suárez and at least two others received arrow wounds. Cárdenas and others sustained bruises. It was because my armor was gilded and glittered that the Indians directed their attack mostly against me. That's why I was hurt more than the rest, not because I was farther in front. All the gentlemen and the soldiers bore themselves well, as expected.

Pedro Castañeda said the battle lasted about an hour, and another account indicates that it ended that afternoon.

At Coronado's trial in 1544, the judges asked him whether any cruelties were inflicted on the men and women of Cíbola after the surrender:

No, we did not inflict any cruelties. On the contrary, I ordered all of the people to be well treated, especially the women and children of the area, and I forbade anyone to touch them under severe penalties. I sent for some of the chiefs and explained through the interpreter that they had done wrong in not coming to render obedience peacefully, as they had been asked, but that I would forgive them if they would now comply. If any of them wished to stay there with their women and children, they would be accorded good treatment, and I would leave their belongings and houses undisturbed, and the wounded would be cared for.

They replied that they realized they had done wrong, and that they wanted to go to the nearby pueblo of Masaque in order to bring their neighbors to render obedience, because the larger community of Cíbola included people from all those pueblos.

Next day, or within two days, the chieftain of Masaque and the other pueblos came with presents of deer and cattle skins, yucca fiber blankets, some turquoises, and a few bows and arrows. I gave them some of the barter articles that we had. They went away very pleased, after rendering obedience to his Majesty and saying that they wanted to serve him and become Christians. . . .

Later three or four Indians came from a more distant pueblo and told us they had heard about us as strange new people, bold men who punished those who resisted them, but gave good treatment to those who submitted. They too had come to make their acquaintance and be our friends.

Cárdenas, when called to trial in 1546, confirmed that the Indians left peacefully after the battle and that no other cruelties were inflicted. Coronado's private, real-time letter on 3 August affirmed to Mendoza that there were no atrocities but gave a pithier account of the Zunis' reaction in the days after the battle:

Three days after I captured the city, some of the Indians who live here came with an offer of peace. They brought me some turquoises and poor blankets, and I received them in the King's name, with as good a speech as I could. I tried to make them understand the purpose of my coming, which is, in His Majesty's name and by the commands of Your Lordship, that they and all others in this province should become Christians and should know the true God as their Lord, and His Majesty as their King on earth. Then they returned to their houses. Suddenly, the next day,

---

SIDEBAR: Archaeological Evidence of the Battle of Cíbola

Since we know the battle between the Europeans and the Cíbolans occurred amidst the plains and walls surrounding Hawikku, we might expect to find artifacts from the battle in those locations. This evidence has recently been found.

Archaeological excavations at the Hawikku pueblo ruin were first conducted in 1917–23 by the pioneering Southwest archaeologist Frederick Hodge, but his focus was on Zuni prehistory. Ironically, what turned out to be crucial Coronado-era artifacts were filed away as random Spanish materials without being given much attention (see Smith, Woodbury, and Woodbury 1966). Wichita State University researcher Frank Gagné (2003) examined those collections and discovered a number of copper crossbow points from the Coronado era (see fig. 11a and 11b).

Since about 2000, the Zunis, inspired by such discoveries, have worked with non-Zuni archaeologists to investigate Coronado's presence at Cíbola. Careful surveys with metal detectors, reported by archaeologist Jonathon Damp and a team of coworkers in 2005, turned up numerous Coronado artifacts in the fields near Hawikku, including more copper crossbow points. New Mexico archaeologist Clay Mathers and his colleagues in 2011 described a crossbow point found years earlier in a room at one of the other Cíbola ruins.

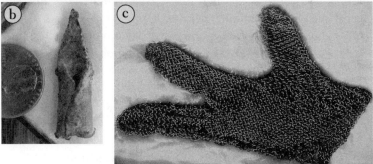

Figure 11. Artifacts from the Coronado expedition. (a) Copper crossbow bolt heads (points) and two copper awls from the Coronado site in Blanco Canyon in the lower panhandle of Texas. (b) Closeup of copper crossbow point found at the Piedras Marcadas site on the west side of Albuquerque, showing "fold-over" manufacture technique and stylistic match to the points found in Texas. (c) Chain mail glove found on the rim of Blanco Canyon, Texas. The three-fingered design was often used to protect the hand wielding a sword from blows by an opponent. (a) and (c): 1996 photos by the author, with thanks to Nancy Marble Floyd County Historical Museum, Floydada, Texas; (b): 2011 photo by the author with thanks to Matt Schmader, Albuquerque Open Space program archaeologist.

they packed up all their goods and fled to the hills! They left their towns deserted, with only a few people remaining in them.

Meanwhile, the near-starving Spaniards occupied the city in the first hours after the battle and requisitioned corn and other food supplies. In those same hours they discovered that they had marched a thousand miles to conquer a modest agricultural town with no gold or substantial metalworking facilities. Dreams of instant wealth seemed to dissipate in a cloud of dust. But what about the surrounding pueblos? The "Relación del Suceso" describes the gradual understanding of the situation: "After the Indians left their buildings, we made ourselves at home. Friar Marcos understood, or at least gave us the impression, that the area which contains seven villages was a single community, and comprises the whole settled region of seven separate towns that is called Cíbola. Most towns have from 150 to 300 dwellings, which are joined in one large structure, or, in others, divided into two or three compounds."

As we saw in chapter 5, Marcos's relación compared Cíbola to Mexico City, and an early historian named Peralta quoted Marcos as saying Cíbola was twice the size of Seville in Spain. Later writers, not to mention the soldiers themselves, rightly pointed out that none of the individual Zuni/Cíbola pueblo towns was that big. But if Marcos thought of the whole complex of towns and agricultural fields as one coherent community under the name Cíbola, then his conception of the size was perhaps justifiable.

In the days following 7 July 1540, Marcos was probably desperately trying to explain his views, or excuses, to the troops. No doubt he pointed out that he had heard about other kingdoms: Maratta, Acus, and Totonteac. Perhaps the golden empires they sought were beyond Cíbola.

Exploring the Newly Occupied Land: Late Summer 1540

By about 19 July Coronado had recovered enough from his wounds to ride out into the province to take a look around. According to the "Traslado de las Nuevas," he traveled 10 to 13 miles from Hawikku to see the great mesa that Zunis call Toyolana, some miles east of Hawikku, where the Zunis had barricaded themselves. More recently called Thunder Mountain, it is several miles across and rises a thousand feet above the plain just east of the modern town of Zuni.

A now-ruined pueblo at Toyolana's southern base faces some hills across the cultivated valley. Historian Madeleine Rodack, writing in 1981 (and private communication), suggested that this may have been the place, rather than Hawikku, that Marcos referred to in 1539, when he crept to a spot where he could see a town "situated in a plain, on the lower slope of a round hill," as Marcos described it (see chapter 5). This is plausible, but we may never know Marcos's exact location.

Coronado's letter of 3 August 1540 tells more about his exploration of Cíbola. He complains that Marcos had "not spoken the truth about anything he said," but he then grudgingly admits that, well, Marcos had been right about "the name of the settlement and the large stone houses." As he complains, he unconsciously supports Marcos's description:

> Although they may be decorated with turquoise, the buildings are neither mortar nor brick. Nevertheless, they are very good houses, of three, four, and five stories. They contain good lodgings, rooms with galleries, and some underground rooms, very excellent and paved, which have been built for winter. . . .
>
> The seven ciudades are seven small towns. They are within 10 to 12 miles of each other, each one with its own name, and no single one called Cíbola. In the one where I'm now lodged, there may be some 200 dwellings, all encircled by a wall. It seems to me that together with other houses that are not enclosed in this way, they could number 500 hearths.
>
> The population of the neighboring towns seems large and intelligent to me, but I'm not certain about it. They have the intellect to build these houses, but for the most part they go about completely naked with only their shameful parts covered. I think they have turquoises in quantity. By the time I arrived, these had disappeared along with the rest of their possessions, except for the corn.

The letter included geographical details. The people did not grow cotton, because the climate was normally too cold. Wood came from the nearest juniper forest, 10 or 12 miles away. There were no fruit trees. Food consisted of corn, beans, and game such as deer and rabbits and "the best tortillas I have seen." There were a few turkeys, larger than those in Mexico. Grass for the horses was found about half a mile away.

As for wealth, this "quarterly report" was not encouraging. Coronado sent some turquoise jewelry and raw turquoises, a bison hide, two baskets, and some other stones (although he says that he gave some of the material to an aide to send to Mendoza, but "according to what they tell me, however, he has lost them").

Coronado reported, too, on the lives of the people:

> They maintain the finest order and cleanliness in grinding corn that may be seen anywhere. One woman grinds as much corn as four among

the Mexica. They have excellent granular salt that they bring . . . from a lake one day's journey from here. . . . I cannot tell Your Lordship about the women's clothing with any certainty, because the Indians keep the women so carefully guarded that until now I have seen no more than two elderly women, and these had two long blouses hanging to their feet, open in front and belted, and fastened with some cotton cords. The women wear two earrings like the women in Spain.

As for governance, Coronado tried to understand the local system and with whom he should negotiate:

From what I can see, none of these towns seems to have a single chief. . . . I haven't seen any principal house by which any superiority of one over others could be shown. Eventually, an old man came, saying he was the governor, and wearing a mantle or blanket of many pieces. I reasoned with him so that he stayed with me. Then he said he'd go and return in three days with the rest of the leaders to arrange the terms that would exist among us. They did come, bringing some small ragged blankets and turquoises. They agreed to come down from their hilltop strongholds and return to their houses with their wives and children and to become Christians and recognize the King—but up until now, they remain in their strongholds with their wives and all their property.

I proposed they make a cloth painted with all the animals in that country. They are poor painters, but they quickly painted two for me, one with animals and the other with the birds and fishes. They also say they will bring their children so that our priests may instruct them, and that they want to know our laws. They say it was foretold among them more than 50 years ago that people like us would come, and from the direction we came, and that those people would conquer this whole land. (translations adapted and abridged from Flint and Flint 2005, 258–59, 261–62, and other translations)

The old prediction is interesting. Could it be some echo of the Tenochtitlan legend (chapter 1), transmitted along with macaw feathers from the south, that bearded Quetzalcoatl would return?

Anthropology and Ethnology: 1540–1541

The Coronado chroniclers carried out what might fairly be called the first anthropological and ethnological reports about the American Southwest. Coronado's letter continued in this vein: "As far as I can tell, these Indians worship water, because it makes the corn grow and sustains their life, and the only other reason they have for it is that their ancestors did so." This comment—that the only reason for the Zuni religion was that their ancestors had handed it down—is especially amusing. Did the Spaniards' ancient Palestinian religion, featuring a tripartite god, a virgin mother, and an infallible Rome-based authority, have a different justification?

Around 1560 Bartolomé de Las Casas compiled additional information on the religious practices of the Cíbolans from other sources. His account extends Coronado's report and foreshadows ethnographic descriptions of Zunis in the 1800s.

> The province of Cíbola is the nation which we found worshiping the sun and sources of water. When they worship toward the sun, they raise their hands and rub their faces and the rest of their bodies. In the case of the water sources, they bring many feathers of various colored birds and place them around the water sources, close to the water. They also sprinkle ground cornmeal and other yellow powders.
>
> They made the same offerings and the same ceremonies to the cross, after seeing that our Christian people venerated it. They touched it with their hands, and then they rubbed their faces and their entire bodies. After that, they made offerings to it, including many vessels, such as bowls of cornmeal.

Castañeda added his own ethnological data, describing his observations in Cíbola:

> The homes are small and not very roomy; a single patio, or open space, serves each section.
>
> They plant corn, and the ears are fat and long with about 800 kernels. They trade in turquoises, but not in the quantities stated. . . . A man has no more than one wife.
>
> There are no lords like those in New Spain. Instead, they are governed by a council of their elders. They have priests, who are elderly and advise them, and who climb to the rooftops at dawn and then make like town criers. The people sit quietly in the covered passageways, listening as they advise about how they must live and some rules they must follow. Among these people, [one sees] no drunkenness, homosexuality, sacrifices, or theft. They work in their pueblos communally. The underground *estufas* are shared, and it is a sacrilege for the women to sleep there.
>
> They burn their dead, along with personal implements of the deceased. (abridged from the translation by Flint and Flint 2005, 417–18)

Young soldiers and adventurers today are scarcely likely to return home with clearer, more concise descriptions of the foreign societies they've supported or attacked.

The Mystery of the Missing Kingdoms of Acus and Maratta: Late Summer 1540

When Viceroy Mendoza handed out the royal commission to explore the North back in January 1540, he formally appointed Coronado to be captain general not just of Cíbola but of all the lands Marcos had mentioned: "Acus, Cíbula [*sic*], the 7 Ciudades . . . , Matata [*sic*], and Totínteac [*sic*]" (translation by Flint and Flint 2005, 109; the spellings seem to come from Mendoza or his scribes).

What became of those other, supposedly important kingdoms? It's a story full of strange twists. Coronado's letter of 3 August gave a dismissive report, starting with Marcos's word "Acus." He said the name was not known in Cíbola but paradoxically admitted Marcos might have been right: "The *reino* of Acus is only one small *ciudad* called Acucu, where cotton is harvested. I say that this is a town, because Acus, with aspiration or without, is not a word [known] in [this] land and because it seems to me that [the Cíbolans] believe their word 'Acucu' is derived from 'Acus'" (translation by Flint and Flint 2005, 260). In other words, the Cíbolans knew of a town that they called Acucu and speculated that Acucu was their equivalent of Acus, the name Marcos had recorded in Sonora.*

As for Maratta/Matata, Marcos reported that in northern Sonora he talked to a man who'd been to Cíbola, and the man said that "there is a kingdom called Maratta, in which there used to be many very grand settlements. They all have multistoried houses made of stone. They have been at war with the lord of the seven cities of Cíbola. Because of this war, the kingdom of Maratta has shrunk to a great extent. It still rules

---

* Flint and Flint oddly state in their geographical appendix that "the polity to which this name (Acus) applies has not been identified" (2005, 598), and in a footnote on page 655 they dismiss the equating of Acucu with Acus as the result of a "linguistic fishing expedition" by the people of Cíbola. Interestingly, however, the Flints themselves state in their preceding entry (598) that "ak'u" was a local name for the famous mesa-top town now known as the "sky city" of Acoma, about 75 road miles east of Zuni. The same entry does not list "Acucu" but does list "Acuco, Coco, Acoco" as alternate Coronado-era spellings for the town of Acoma, or "ak'u." To summarize, it seems likely that Acus/ak'u/Acucu/Acuco/Acoco/Coco all refer to Acoma and that Marcos was correct in reporting it from his interviews in Sonora.

itself, however." Coronado, in his 3 August letter, dismissed this as another Marcos error: "There is no kingdom of Marata [Coronado's spelling] here, nor do the Indians have any information about it."

Some modern scholars associate Marcos's report with a mighty trade center that was located in Chihuahua just south of the New Mexico border. It lay about 340 air line miles south-southeast of Cíbola but only 135 air line miles due east of northern Sonora over rugged mountains. Now known as Casas Grandes, it is a massive pueblo ruin, with the main structure rising as high as six or seven stories. It was probably the biggest pueblo complex at that latitude. Thus, if Maratta was Casas Grandes, then Maratta/Matata/Marata may have been a local name used only in the realm south of the fifteen-day despoblado and was thus a name unknown (at least by the Spaniards' pronunciation) in Cíbola. Archaeological data indicate that it was abandoned as late as the early 1400s, so its legend may well have lived on among prehistoric "cosmopolitan" travelers as a place where "there used to be many very grand settlements" that had now "shrunk" in population.

The Mystery of Totonteac: Late Summer 1540

What about the fourth and most glorious kingdom reported by Marcos and reaffirmed by the Díaz/Zaldívar party, namely, Totonteac? It was the place that Marcos's informants labeled the "grandest in the world, [with] the most people and the greatest wealth," and where there were Cíbola-like buildings with "no end." Marcos considered it so important that he ended his relación by emphasizing how much better it was supposed to be than Cíbola. Díaz independently said the people of Totonteac had buildings larger than in Cíbola and were "famous because they have buildings, food, and turquoises in abundance." Yet Coronado, in his letter of 3 August 1540, reported a very different story to Mendoza about "the *reino* of Totonteac, extolled so highly by the father provincial [Marcos de Niza], who said that there were such marvelous things and such grandness. . . . The Indians say [instead] that it is a hot lake, around which there are five or six dwellings" (translation from Flint and Flint 2005, 258, 260). Coronado thus wrote off Totonteac as another Marcos bungle. That seems also to be the attitude of most modern historians. After 3 August 1540 Totonteac disappears from the thoughts of the Coronado explorers. But how could "the grandest province in the world, with no end," reported by different informants not only to Marcos but also to Díaz, be reduced to a few dwellings near a hot spring?

To investigate this mystery, let's start by collecting the references to Totonteac. (The page numbers refer to the original translations in Flint and Flint 2005.)

* Marcos, two days north of Vacapa in the first town where Estevan learned of Cíbola (central Sonora, 9 or 10 April 1539), is told that besides the seven towns of Cíbola there are three other kingdoms: Maratta, Acus, and Totonteac (70).
* In a village in north-central Sonora in April 1539, Indians examine Marcos's gray, closely woven woolen habit and tell him there is much of this material in Totonteac and that Totonteac inhabitants wear clothes made of it. It is the fur of some "small animals . . . the size of [the] two Castilian greyhounds which Estevan had with him" (71).
* In the village where he heard that the coast turns west (probably northwestern or central Sonora in mid-April 1539), Marcos receives "another report about the woolen cloth of Totonteac. They say that the houses there are like those of Cíbola, [but] better and much more numerous. It is a marvelous thing and has no end" (71).
* In a well-populated valley (north-central Sonora, April 1539), Marcos meets a native of Cíbola, who tells him about Cíbola's seven towns and who "says that to the west is the kingdom they call Totonteac. He says it is . . . the grandest thing in the world, [with] the most people and greatest wealth." The informant repeats earlier information that Totonteac inhabitants wear woolen cloth similar to what Marcos wears, obtained from the animals described in the earlier village. Marcos adds that from what he has learned, the people of Totonteac seem to be "a very civilized people and different from the people whom I have seen [so far]" (72).
* In the last populated valley before entering the final despoblado to Cíbola (probably on the San Pedro River in southern Arizona, early May 1539), Marcos finds that "they have as much information about [Cíbola] as I [have] of that which I hold in my hands. They also have [information] about the kingdoms of Maratta, Acus, and Totonteac" (72).
* On the last pages of his relación, talking with important men who came with him from the last villages of Chichilticale (ca. 24 May 1539), Marcos is observing one of the "seven cities" at a distance, and he comments on "how excellent Cíbola seemed to me." The village leaders responds that "Totonteac is much grander and better than all the seven *ciudades*" and that Totonteac "comprises so many buildings and people that it has

no end." Marcos takes formal possession of Cíbola, Totonteac, Acus, and Maratta (76).

* Melchior Díaz, stuck in Chichilticale by snow, interviews many different Indians separately and in groups (ca. December 1539–January 1540). Indians who'd been to Cíbola told him it was "short of water," so that cotton was not harvested there but rather obtained from Totonteac. "Totonteac is seven short days' travel from the *provincia* of Cíbola." It has the same sort of multistory buildings and people. Informants mention twelve pueblos there and say that each one is larger than the biggest one in Cíbola (237; the information from Díaz was quoted "verbatim," according to Mendoza, in one of his letters.

* After consulting with Marcos, Viceroy Mendoza, on 4 January 1540, appoints Coronado captain general not only of the army and Cíbola but also of "Acus, Matata, and Totínteac," indicating that he sees them as comparable in importance to Cíbola (109).

* Coronado, after his first weeks in Cíbola, writes to Mendoza on 3 August 1540 that Marcos "has not spoken the truth in anything he said" and that Totonteac is merely a few dwellings near a hot lake (258, 260).

* Hernando de Alarcón interviews natives of the lower Colorado River below Yuma in early September 1540, using information brought back by Marcos de Niza and/or the Díaz/Zaldívar party (see chapter 10). Alarcón asks one of the Indians, probably south of modern Yuma, "whether he had heard of a place called Cíbola and a river called Totonteac, and he answered no." Then Alarcón meets a man who'd actually been to Cíbola, so he "asked him whether he had information about a river called Totonteac. He replied to me no" (193, 198).

There are many clues about Totonteac here. First, we know Marcos was not making up his information, because Melchior Díaz verified it in same area where Marcos had learned it.

Second, we see that the name Totonteac/Totínteac as a province of grand cities or a major river was known only from Pima- or Opata-speaking informants in Sonora and the Chichilticale province of southeastern Arizona but not among other language groups in Cíbola or the Yuma area. Historian Carroll Riley in 1995 made an intriguing comment in this regard. He concluded that the word is "very likely . . . from the Piman root, totoni," which refers to "ant," and that it connotes "something like Ant Place." Maybe we have here a prehistoric joke in which the Sonorans, in their small villages, pictured the great, multistory pueblos, with people coming and going, as bustling anthills. (The same general rural-versus-urban attitudes are manifest throughout history, from the biblical texts of rural tribes of ancient Israel talking about Babylon, to the post–World War I song "How Ya Gonna Keep 'Em Down on the Farm (After They've Seen Par-ee)?"

A third clue is provocative: Alarcón seems to have been told to ask about Totonteac as a significant river, suggesting that the great province of Totonteac was associated with such a river. (That information could only have reached Alarcón through geographic information collected by Marcos or Díaz/Zaldívar, probably given in secret to Viceroy Mendoza and then secretly passed on to Alarcón.)

A fourth clue is that Totonteac was supposed to have been a supplier of cotton to Cíbola and also to have produced a wool-like cloth.

Fifth is a mixed bag of clues about location. Díaz said he learned that Totonteac was seven short days from Cíbola, and Marcos's report says that one man indicated it was to the west. These last clues, seven days to the west, would place it near the Hopi pueblo towns in modern Arizona—but none of their towns match the repeated descriptions of endless multistory towns larger than the Cíbola pueblos and located on a river. The Hopi province is a handful of modest-sized mesa-top communities spread mostly over about 30 miles but not along a river. They did produce some cotton, and the name of the Hopi village of Moenkopi, lying 42 road miles west of the other Hopi towns, means "place where cotton is grown" (Underhill 1944, 33; Tanner 1968, 54). The "Relación del Suceso" (Flint and Flint 2005, 498) said the Hopis were like the Indians of Cíbola, except "these [Hopis] harvest cotton." Nonetheless, in the 1540s the amount of cotton seems to have been unimpressive. Clara Lee Tanner, an expert on historic Pueblo crafts, cites one of Coronado's captains, Pedro de Tovar, who went through Hopi land (see below), as saying that his party was given only "bits of cotton cloth by the Hopis" (1968, 54). Castañeda said the Hopis wore cotton, but "not much because in that land there is not any" (Flint and Flint 2005, 397). Another problem with the "Hopi solution" is that Alarcón was talking to people who traveled in the lands west of Cíbola but knew nothing of Totonteac. Worse yet, the "Hopi solution" requires the informants in Sonora and Chichilticale to wax ecstatic about the rather poor Hopi pueblos while remaining ignorant of a more prosperous and extensive region of larger, cotton-producing pueblos along a grand river to the east. We'll come back to that "Rio Grande solution" in a moment.

Historians Carroll Riley (1995) and the Flints (2005) championed a "Hohokam solution," namely, that Totonteac referred not to a contemporaneous community but to earlier, Hohokam peoples who built imposing towns and irrigation canals, especially around modern Phoenix, southwest of Cíbola along the Gila and Salt Rivers. Several problems exist with this hypothesis. First, as both Riley (1995, 220) and the Flints (2005, 603) admit, Hohokam "high culture" collapsed around 1400, so their towns were in ruins by the 1540s. Yet the 1539–40 documents imply clearly that Totonteac was a vibrant province, currently supplying cotton to Cíbola. Such a supply line from the Hohokam heartland to Cíbola would have been around 250 trail miles over mountainous country, requiring more than "seven short days" of travel. The Flints, Cal Riley, and I maintain a cheerful disagreement on the "Hohokam solution."

Part of the solution to the Totonteac puzzle is that Marcos and Díaz, in the Pima-speaking borderlands, must have heard words different from the ones used by the Cíbolans (who still speak an isolated language different from that of the Pimas or even the Rio Grande Puebloans). Coronado confirmed this when he described how Cíbolans didn't know Marcos's word "Acus," which Marcos recorded in Sonora, but thought it might relate to the town they knew as Acucu. The same situation would explain why Cíbolans gave little useful response when asked about Totonteac. Piman slang for a province of busy "anthills" of the North might not have been recognized in Cíbola—especially as pronounced by visiting Spaniards. If Coronado had been motivated to do a little more sleuthing instead of condemning Marcos, he might have cleared up the misunderstanding and identified which province the Sonorans meant.

This leads us back to the "Rio Grande solution." The Rio Grande valley in central New Mexico was the most populous province in the American Southwest and included towns larger than the largest in Cíbola. These pueblos were spread across more than 60 miles, dotted along the river in several groups seven or eight days *east* of Cíbola. The 1583 Espejo expedition into New Mexico recorded that "a great deal of cotton is grown in these settlements" (Flint and Flint 2005, 696, footnote 86). Anthropologist Ruth Underhill (1944, 33) noted that cotton production increased as one moved south of Albuquerque due to the warmer, lower-altitude climate.

Provocatively, while the pueblos north of Albuquerque became famous under the province name Tiguex (the Spanish spelling of a local name, usually pronounced TEE-wish), the pueblo group extending at least a dozen miles south of Albuquerque was recorded a few times in the Coronado records as Tutahaco (see Flint and Flint 2005, 18, map) and then mostly forgotten. Tutahaco is an interesting name when we remember that place-names recorded by Spanish memoirists had variant spellings. Given that the name recorded by Marcos in northern Sonora as Acus turned out to be Acucu, Coco, Acoco, and Acoma and that the Cíbolan town that Marcos recorded as Ahacus was recorded later as Hawikuh or Hawikku, might not the province Tu-tah-aco be the one that Marcos recorded in Sonora with the syllables To-ton-te-ac (especially if we add an *o* sound on the end of Marcos's version—Totonteaco—as with Acoco being a version of what Marcos called Acus).

Castañeda clearly places Tutahaco on the Rio Grande south of Tiguex and modern Albuquerque. He describes how Coronado moved the army from Cíbola to the Rio Grande: "After eight days' travel they reached Tutahaco. . . . There it was learned that downstream on that river there were other pueblos. . . . They are multi-storied pueblos like those of Tiguex, with the same clothing. The general departed from there, visiting the whole provincia upstream along the river until he arrived at Tiguex" (translation by Flint and Flint 2005, 400). Castañeda refers again later to Tutahaco and large pueblos south of Albuquerque. He says: "Another captain went downriver [from Tiguex] in search of the settlements which the [people] of Tutahaco said were several days' journey from there. This captain descended [the river] for 80 leagues and found four large pueblos, which he left in peace. He traveled [on] until he found that the river sank underground" (translation by Flint and Flint 2005, 412–13). Flint and Flint (2005, 682, notes 366–67) state that the four large pueblos would have been among nine pueblo ruin sites near present-day Socorro and that the Rio Grande sometimes sinks into the gravel at Elephant Butte (close to the town of Truth or Consequences), which fits the 80-league distance.

In summary, the cotton-producing pueblos along the Rio Grande, south from Albuquerque as far as Truth or Consequences, may have been known to the natives of Sonora and Chichilticale as the "anthill" pueblos of Totonteac. Coronado, having already written to Mendoza that Marcos's and Díaz's grand Totonteac didn't exist, may have had no stomach for admitting sheepishly that, well, really it did.

There's an objection to every Totonteac theory, and the obvious objection here is the single word in Marcos's relación that says that Totonteac was *ueste*, or west, from Cíbola. (The modern spelling is *oeste*.) Strikingly, however, Flint and Flint (2005, 630, footnote 139) point out that the Spanish word *ueste* has been rendered incorrectly by some translators as *sueste*, or southeast, which would match the direction to Tutahaco. One letter in the Spanish document can make a big difference! This raises the possibility that Marcos or some sixteenth-century scribe, taking dictation or copying a letter from Marcos, misheard or misread Marcos's actual word *sueste* for *ueste*. In my mind the "Rio Grande solution" solves the Totonteac mystery with the minimum number of improbabilities and the maximum plausibility. I'm surprised it hasn't been already more widely proposed and accepted. Perhaps some future participant in our five-hundred-year-discussion will find a new document that will resolve the mystery one way or another.

Marcos de Niza Departs Cíbola in Disgrace: August 1540

Marcos, in his own lifetime, was not to be vindicated about Totonteac or anything else. As Coronado completed his letter of 3 August to Mendoza, he organized a party to take it back to Mexico City. Whether by Marcos's own decision or by being driven out by Coronado, Marcos was part of the departing group. He was fleeing from the contempt of the soldiers. Other principals in the party were an officer, Capt. Juan Gallego, who was ordered to get the report back to the viceroy, and Capt. Melchior Díaz, who had spent the preceding winter months reconnoitering Chichilticale and seeking more information about Cíbola and Totonteac. Díaz was assigned to maintain the San Gerónimo garrison and search for Alarcón's ships.

Marcos, candidate for bishop of Mexico in 1539, was now considered "the lying monk." When he reached Mexico City in 1540, he retired (under pressure from his superiors?) and disappeared from public life.

From Cíbola to the Hopi Pueblos of Arizona: July–August 1540

Coronado, meanwhile, busied himself with wider-ranging explorations from his Cíbola base. He dispatched Cíbolan couriers to various neighboring provinces to announce that "Christians had come to their land," to quote Castañeda.

By 15 July Coronado had already sent a captain, Pedro de Tovar, westward to reconnoiter the Hopi pueblos. With seventeen horsemen, about four foot soldiers, and Friar Juan de Padilla, Tovar stealthily approached one of the eastern Hopi pueblos late at night (possibly Awatovi, now in ruins; Flint and Flint 2005, 674, footnote 183). The pueblo was on a mesa. The Spaniards concealed themselves at its base, so close that they could hear the people talking in their rooms. Castañeda reports that the Hopis had confined themselves there, having already been warned that "Cíbola had been overrun by the most ferocious people, who rode on animals and ate people."

Discovering the Spaniards the next morning, the Hopis drew themselves up in military formation with bows and clubs. The Spaniards recited their requerimiento. The Hopis drew lines on the ground and forbade the Spaniards to pass. The Spaniards crossed the lines, continuing to talk to the Hopis. Tension rose to the point where, according to Castañeda, one of the Hopis struck a horse with a club. Castañeda says that "Fray Juan, angered by the time that was being wasted . . . , exclaimed to [Tovar], 'Truly, I don't know why we've come here!'" (This and translations below are by Flint and Flint 2005, 396–97.) According to Castañeda, this goaded Tovar to attack. Castañeda had already remarked that Father Juan, in his youth, "had been a combative fellow."

Numbers of Hopis were "knocked down," Castañeda says, and the Hopis retreated quickly to their pueblo but very shortly reemerged "in peace with gifts," and hostilities ended. Tovar's group soon learned that the Hopis were culturally similar to the Zunis in terms of their life in various multistory, semiautonomous communities, with agricultural and hunting economies in a land with cold winters and warm summers. The land, said Castañeda, "is governed in the same way as Cíbola, by a council of the oldest persons. They have their designated governors and captains."

The Spaniards were probing west partly to seek news of Alarcón's ships, and the Hopis told them about a large river that turned out to be about twenty days farther on. News of this river was the most exciting discovery for the Spaniards. Could it be Mendoza's inland seaway, which would allow a rendezvous with Alarcón? Tovar and his party hurried back to Cíbola with their news.

Discovering the Grand Canyon: August–October 1540

As soon as Coronado received the news of the river, he sent out a party in late August to find it, under direction of the cavalry captain who had saved his life during the battle of Cíbola, López de Cárdenas. Everyone hoped for the long-desired reunion with Alarcón's ships. Cárdenas reached the Hopi pueblos, then traveled another twenty days and discovered the most famous landmark of the American Southwest. Castañeda recounts the scene.

> Once they camped at the canyon's edge, it appeared through the air that the canyon's width was more than three or four leagues [7 to 12 miles]. It is an elevated land covered by forests of short, gnarled pines. Even in the hot season, it was not possible to live there because of the cold.

For three days they searched for the way down to the river. From that height the stream appeared to be [a few yards] across. . . . Descent was impossible. After three days the most agile men attempted to climb down at the place that seemed the least difficult. They descended a long time in view of those above, until lost from sight. They returned at four in the afternoon, but had not completed the descent. . . . What looked easy from above was very rugged. They said they'd descended a third of the way. From the position they reached, the river appeared to be very large. . . . The explorers on the rim had distinguished several small-looking blocks, broken off from the cliff, apparently the height of a man—but the men who climbed down to them swore that they were larger than the biggest church tower in Sevilla.

Cárdenas's company traveled no farther along the canyon rim because there was no water. Until that point, every day in the late afternoon, they had to make a side trip of one or two leagues [2 to 6 miles] into the interior in search of streams. For that reason, whenever the Indians traveled that way, they brought women along loaded with water in gourd jars. Along the way, they buried the jars of water for their return. The Indians commented that the distance our people traveled in two days, they traveled in one. The whole company turned around at that point, and the trip had no further result. (adapted from the translation by Flint and Flint 2005, 397–98)

From Cíbola to Pecos Pueblo, New Mexico: August 1540

Back in Cíbola, an odd event occurred in August. Along the trail from the east came a party of diplomatic visitors, led by "a tall young man," as Castañeda described him, "well disposed and with a vigorous expression." The Spaniards named the young leader Bigotes, Spanish for "mustaches," since he wore a striking example. The visitors announced they were from a pueblo that the Spaniards variously recorded as Cicuye, Cicuyc, or Cicuique. Today we know it as Pecos pueblo, some 220 trail miles northeast of Cíbola and 22 modern road miles east of modern Santa Fe (see map 13). Bigotes explained that his townspeople had heard about the events in Cíbola and wanted to be allies of the Spaniards. Gifts were exchanged. The Spaniards were given buffalo hides, shields, and a kind of Indian helmet. The Pecos ambassadors were given metal bells of European manufacture, glass beads, and glass drinking vessels. Coronado's men learned more about the mysterious "cows" of the plains from an odd source: one of the visitors

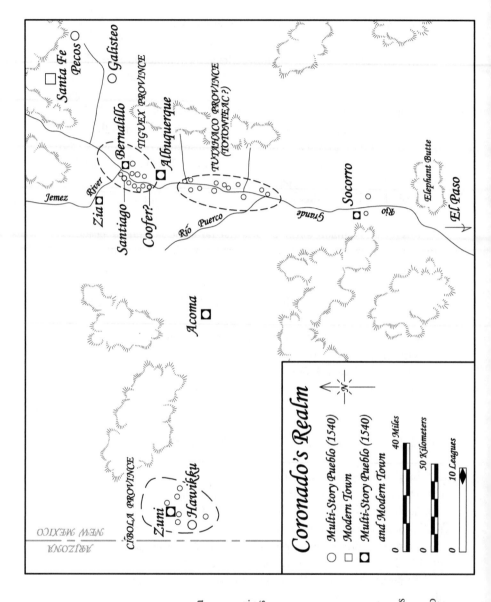

Map 13. The region of Coronado expedition activities in central New Mexico. Pueblo communities such as Cibola, Acoma, Tiguex Province, Tutahaco Province, and Pecos can be identified from Coronado-era records and/or artifacts. Tutahaco Province pueblo sites are based on Barrett (1997, map 12). Map by Ron Beckwith.

Coronado's Realm

○ Multi-Story Pueblo (1540)

□ Modern Town

◪ Multi-Story Pueblo (1540) and Modern Town

0   40 Miles

0   50 Kilometers

0   10 Leagues

from Pecos sported a buffalo tattoo, which Castañeda described as much more instructive than the hides alone.

Coronado ordered one of his captains, twenty-two-year-old Hernando de Alvarado (not to be mixed up with the notorious Pedro de Alvarado, "the Sun") to return to Cicuye/Cicuyc/Cicuique/Pecos with Bigotes and his group, taking twenty soldiers. Alvarado was to return with a report in no more than eighty days. On 29 August Alvarado, Bigotes, and their joint party set out, recording several ruins around Cíbola in the first days. Five days to the east they came to the pueblo Marcos de Niza learned about in Sonora, the one he called Acus, now known as Acoma (see map 13). Castañeda described it correctly as sitting atop an impregnable sheer rock mesa, reached only by a steep trail with steps cut into the rock. The summit included farm fields and cisterns to collect snow and rain water.

Disturbed by news of the attack on Cíbola, the men of Acoma, two hundred strong, confronted Coronado on the plain below, prepared for a fight. Provoked by their mere presence, the Spaniards rushed them. The Acoma warriors immediately surrendered. Peace was established, and the people of Acoma came out with gifts of deer hides, roosters, bread, beans, and corn.

Three days east of Acoma (eight days from Cíbola), Alvarado's party crossed the Rio Grande amidst the Tiguex province of pueblos north of Albuquerque. Alvarado described the people as having abundant food, wearing cotton, leather, and feather materials, and ruled by their elder men. People there, seeing the Spaniards traveling with the group from Pecos, came out peaceably. Five days farther on, Alvarado and his crew were in Cicuye/Cicuyc/Cicuique/Pecos (see map 13).

The next few days included events that would influence the rest of the expedition. The Spanish party acquired two "Indian slaves" who had been captured by Bigotes and the governor of Pecos (Bolton 1949, 188ff.). One was known by his Indian name, variously recorded as Ysopete or Sopete (once again, the usual variation in phonetic Spanish spellings). The other, whether by clothing or physiognomy, looked Turkish to the Spaniards, so they gave him the name El Turco. Both captives came originally from lands to the east. Ysopete, described by Castañeda as a tattooed Indian, was a native of a place called Quivira (kee-VEER-a), or, in one spelling, Quisvira. The Turk was said to be a native of the lands extending toward La Florida—eastern lands in general, but perhaps indicating the southeastern plains and gulf coastlands.

Ysopete and El Turco led Alvarado's group on a short trip onto the plains to see the buffalo. To the amazement of the Spaniards, El Turco began recounting tales of precious metals back in his Quivira homeland. To paraphrase Castañeda's next succinct sentences, "so many were the things that El Turco said about riches of gold and silver in his land that Alvarado gave up his investigation of the buffalos, having seen only a few, and turned back to give Coronado the magnificent news" (adapted from Flint and Flint 2005, 400).

Coronado's Departure from Cíbola: Autumn 1540

Back in Cíbola, Coronado had been busy. He'd ordered the discoverer of the Grand Canyon, García López de Cárdenas, eastward to the Tiguex pueblos with troops (see map 13). Cárdenas's mission in Tiguex was to negotiate—or force—his way into one of the best pueblos on the Rio Grande so the Spaniards could use it as winter headquarters for the expedition. The one he picked was referred to in the Spanish records as Coofor, Coafor, or Alcanfor. The Flints (2005, 600) relate the name to the local word for parched corn. Bolton and the Flints locate the town on the west side of the Rio Grande, somewhere near the modern town of Bernalillo, which lies about 15 road miles upstream and northwest of Albuquerque. Scholars still debate which ancient pueblo site it was and how violently it was requisitioned.

Castañeda, writing around 1560 and remembering touchy issues raised during the 1544 investigation of the expedition's relation to the northern peoples, mentions the unpleasant incident in only a few sentences. Glossing over inconvenient details, he explains that it was "important" for the pueblo communities to realize the resolve of the Spaniards and to provide them with a place to live. As a result, he says, the inhabitants "were forced to abandon one pueblo and were given shelter in the other pueblos of their friends." As the people moved out, "they did not take more than their persons and clothing." The foreign policy of the Spanish explorers was always to display a steel will to get what they wanted and to "punish the Indians" (their phrase) in case of resistance.

As Cárdenas requisitioned the pueblo, Alvarado and his party, including El Turco, were returning from Pecos (see map 13). Some days later, Alvarado and Cárdenas happily rendezvoused at Alcanfor/Coofor/Coafor and sent messages back to Coronado.

Meanwhile, back in Cíbola, Coronado was waiting for the following army from the San Gerónimo garrison in Sonora. The following party (containing chronicler Castañeda) probably straggled into Cíbola, arriving mostly sometime around September. Coronado immediately took thirty of his own well-rested men and set out to reach Coofor, his new winter headquarters, leaving the newly arrived troops in Cíbola. He told them to follow as soon as they were sufficiently rested.

Coronado's party arrived at the Rio Grande in the Tutahaco province, briefly noting multistoried pueblos but saying nothing about possible links to Totonteac. Then they headed some tens of miles north upstream to rendezvous with Cárdenas and Alvarado and begin their winter occupation of Tiguex.

The mood was celebratory as Coronado reunited with Cárdenas and Alvarado. Perhaps that very night, Coronado's men heard the tales of gold and silver from El Turco himself. Weeks later, in December, the rest of the army arrived after traveling through heavy snows from Cíbola.

The entire land expedition was finally reunited, but by this time the situation in Tiguex was a mess. Castañeda observed matter-of-factly that the day before the arrival of "the main expedition," as Castañeda calls his own group, Coronado's men had just burned one pueblo: "We encountered them as they were returning to their quarters."

Tales Told by the Turk: December 1540

As hostilities in Tiguex escalated, the troops hunkered down in their requisitioned pueblo and collected more tales from El Turco about the interior lands of North America. He told of a river in his land as much as 2 leagues (3 to 6 miles) wide, flowing through the plains. He claimed that the river contained fish the size of the Spaniards' horses and that "many exceedingly large canoes" were known that "carried sails" and had more than twenty rowers on each side. On the prow was a large eagle of gold, and the lords of these boats sat on the poop deck beneath awnings (Flint and Flint 2005, 400). The language suggests El Turco may have come from as far away as the region of the lower Mississippi or had heard about it. The Flints (2005, 676, footnote 228) note that the expedition of Hernando de Soto, who visited the Mississippi the following year, saw a giant canoe that "carried 80 Indian warriors." Alternatively, between the catastrophic 1528 expedition of Narváez/Cabeza de Vaca and 1540, when El Turco was telling his tales, unsanctioned Spanish ships may have nosed along the Gulf Coast and entered the Mississippi, leading to Indian tales of giant "canoes" with sails and lords on poop decks.

Perhaps, in addition (as also suggested by the Flints in private communication, 2012), the Turk was repeating oral traditions about the extraordinary urban complex at the Cahokia mound-builder site near modern Saint Louis. Cahokia's influence spread up and down the Mississippi River, but then the society collapsed about 150 years prior to Coronado.

El Turco said that the lord of his homeland slept during his siesta under a great tree. Small golden bells hung on the tree and chimed charmingly in the breeze. Further, he said, plates and small bowls were gold, and the common serving dishes were silver. El Turco used the word *acochis* to refer to gold.

Castañeda says the Spaniards were much impressed by the ease and candor with which the Turk talked. They believed him, because "they showed him tin jewelry and he smelled it and said that it was not gold. He was very familiar with gold and silver, and he took no notice of the other metals." The "Relación del Suceso" adds that El Turco "was in the habit of providing very detailed information about what he was saying, as if it were true and he had seen it."

Fatefully, El Turco mentioned that he had gold bracelets with him when he was brought to Cicuye/Cicuyc/Cicuique/Pecos but that the people of Pecos took them from him. As a way of testing El Turco's stories, Coronado sent Captain Alvarado back to Cicuye/Cicuyc/Cicuique/Pecos to see if he could find the gold bracelets. We'll catch up with him shortly.

CHAPTER TEN

Meanwhile . . . on the Colorado River, in Spain, and in Mexico City

As Coronado's attention shifted toward the east, chances of rendezvousing between the sea and land expeditions faded. But why had the two parties failed to link up? What had become of Alarcón and his ships? Answers can be found in the relación prepared by Alarcón about his journey. As noted earlier, the original is lost, but in this chapter, as before, I cite it by synthesizing versions published by Giovanni Ramusio in 1556 and by Richard Hakluyt in 1600.

Alarcón Discovers the Colorado River and Its Inhabitants: August–September 1540

In August 1540, as Coronado was still exploring Cíbola, Alarcón was approaching the north end of the Gulf of California. During his journey along the coast, he'd seen no signs of the land expedition nor Indians who could tell him about it. Where the coast turned west, he found Ulloa's strange outflow, the mouth of the Colorado River. In order to outperform Ulloa, he determined to penetrate it and sail inland in search of Cíbola. He sent two men out in barques (small boats with sails and oars) to lead his three larger ships through the maze of shoals and sandy islands.

At one point, Alarcón's ships all ran aground on the shoals and found themselves at the mercy of the outrushing river and the inrushing tidal surge. The surge washed over their decks but then lifted the ships. They pressed on, and "it pleased God that . . . we came to the very end of the bay, where we found a very mighty river, running with so great fury . . . that we could hardly sail against it." The date was 26 August 1540. Spain had discovered the Colorado River.

Coronado's expedition was now some 350 air miles inland to the east, though Alarcón had no way of knowing this. His hope was that the broad river would lead him inland to a rendezvous with the troops, thus fulfilling his assignment from Mendoza.

Alarcón decided to leave his three large ships and press upstream in two of his barques with twenty men and "some small pieces of artillery." On that first day, they struggled 6 leagues (15 to 19 miles) against the current as some of the crew pulled on tow ropes. On 27 August, roughly 9 leagues (23 to 29 miles) up the river, still south of the present U.S. border, the Spaniards had their first significant interaction with the local people: "Certain Indians, who happened to be approaching their shelters near the water, rose up furiously as soon as they saw us. Crying with a loud voice, they came running with about fifty companions, removing their things from the shelters . . . and making vigorous signs and threats that we should go back." Alarcón calmly approached them in a small boat. At the shore, he lay down his shield and sword in his boat and stepped on them to show peaceful intent. Cheerfully, he waved some trade items. Working mainly through such signs, he established friendly bartering with the crowd.

In the next days, farther upstream, he continued such contacts and described the people, who tried to look as fierce as possible:

> They came decked out in various fashions, some with paint covering all their faces . . . all marked with soot, each as he liked. Others carried masks before them of the same color, with the shape of faces. On their heads they wear a kind of helmet of deerskin two spans broad, and upon it were small sticks with feathers. Their weapons were bows and arrows of hardwood, and maces of wood hardened in fire.
>
> They are strong and well featured, without any fatness. They have holes in their nostrils where pendants hang. Others wear shells, and their ears are full of holes where they hang bones and shells. They all wear a band around their waist made of diverse colors, and in the middle is fastened a round bunch of feathers, hanging down like a tail. On the muscular part of the arm they

wear a straight string, which they wind around to the width of one's hand. They wear pieces of deer bone fastened to their arms, with which they strike off the sweat. . . . Women go naked but for a great wreath of feathers in front and in back. Men and women cut their hair in the front, but it hangs down their backs to the waist. Also we saw three or four men dressed as women.

These people, with simple tools and earthen houses, were hardly the kind of urban civilization that any European might have expected along the banks of one of the world's major rivers, comparable to the Nile. Still, after the friendly overtures, they grew so enthused about the visitors that they brought food and competed with each other to pull the tow ropes.

By 29 August Alarcón realized that "the thing they most esteemed and revered was the sun." Shrewdly, he made it known that (amazingly enough) he himself had come from the sun! Natives were soon swimming out to the boats, bringing gourds full of maize, which they traded for various items such as rope and small crosses fashioned by the Spaniards. On 1 September Alarcón found an Indian leader who was able to converse in a language the interpreters knew. Initially suspicious and even hostile, this individual quizzed Alarcón on his exact relationship with the sun and why the sun had not sent him earlier to help his people in their wars. Alarcón worried about sinning against Christianity by identifying himself with the sun, so this time he explained that he and his men were Christians . . . who had been sent by the sun. They'd come from far away. Alarcón said he couldn't come during their earlier wars because he had been a child. By evening the two men were friends.

Alarcón soon established that the man had not heard of a place called Cíbola or a river called Totonteac. They discussed religion, but Alarcón concluded that the riverside natives had no strong system of beliefs. He explained that there was a great lord who lived in heaven called Jesus Christ and noted in his report that "I was careful not to stretch myself farther into theology with him." Now he changed the subject and asked if the people of the region were currently in a state of war. His informant's wonderful answer resonates through the centuries: "Yes, a very great war, over trivialities." Alarcón asked for an explanation: "When they lacked a particular reason to make wars, the oldest and bravest leaders assembled and someone would say 'Let's go make war at such and such a place,' and then they all went off with their weapons. At other times, when the oldest and bravest said they should fight no more, they would stop. When I came among them, they lost interest in war and were willing to maintain peace."

News of Coronado: September 1540

During the next days, Alarcón probed upstream on the Colorado River to a point near present-day Yuma, just north of the modern border. Here, the Gila River enters the Colorado from the east (see map 7b). From the junction, the Gila leads eastward, upstream all the way across Arizona, as mentioned in our discussion of the "port of Chichilticale" in chapter 8.

Could the Gila River lead Alarcón to Coronado? Alarcón kept asking about Cíbola and news of other travelers who looked like him. In early September he hit pay dirt, probably near Yuma, Arizona. Here, from a nearby province, came an interpreter who had actually been to Cíbola. He told Alarcón all about it: "The trail to Cíbola went from his homeland along a river [the Gila?]. Using that trail, one could reach Cíbola in forty days. The Indian went there just to see it because it was a wondrous thing, with high stone houses of three and four stories and with windows on each side. The walls of the houses were one and a half times thicker than the height of a man. The people there wore fine clothes and many azure or blue stones dug out of the rock. They have one wife."

The story tells us that here, 371 air line miles from Cíbola, local travelers had good knowledge of Cíbola, matching what Marcos heard in central Sonora at a comparable distance from Cíbola. The "road mileage," if one traveled along the Gila River from Yuma to the New Mexico border and then north along the despoblado route to Cíbola/Zuni, would be roughly 590 miles. Given that the native interpreter took forty days, his average rate would have been a reasonable 15 miles per day.

It's interesting that azure turquoise was part of Alarcón's description of Cíbola, since Marcos reported similar stories at a comparable distance from Cíbola. Both Díaz and Coronado complained to Mendoza that Marcos exaggerated the news about turquoise, but Alarcón's report supports Marcos. Folks hundreds of miles from Cíbola were dazzled by the blue stones of Cíbola, just as fashionable travelers today may bring home turquoise Indian jewelry from New Mexico. Recall, too (from chapter 5), that anthropologist Frank Cushing in the 1800s confirmed Marcos's report of turquoises in Zuni doorways.

Alarcón relates additional news that surfaced during his talks with the native interpreter: "The governor of Cíbola had a dog like mine. When I called for my dinner, the interpreter saw my dishes and told me that this lord of Cíbola had plates like them, except green. Only four of these plates existed in Cíbola, and only the governor had them. He had gotten them, along with the dog, from a certain black man with a beard, who had come from an unknown region. The interpreter had heard that the governor later ordered the black man to be killed." Here was a clear account of the arrival and murder of Estevan de Dorantes in Cíbola fifteen months earlier. The story gives us an excellent demonstration of a Native American news network.

Shortly before the interpreter left, Alarcón learned about two "upriver" provinces named Quicama and Coama. The Flints (2005, 646, footnote 75) identify these names with two Yuman-speaking Maricopa tribal groups, Halyikwamai and Kahman, recorded in the 1700s as living along the lower Gila River in southwestern Arizona. Comparing spellings and phonetic sounds, we have:

Qui-ca-ma = Halyi-kwa-mai
Coa-ma = Kah-man

If the comparisons seem iffy, imagine if you were trying to record unfamiliar Chinese or African names in English characters. Based on these names, the Flints inferred that Alarcón had turned east into the Gila River. This makes sense. The Colorado takes a 7-mile bend near Yuma, where it flows from east to west (map 7b). Alarcón, moving upstream, would have encountered a fork at this point. What is now called the Colorado comes from the north, and the Gila River comes from the east. Alarcón likely perceived the Gila as the more likely path toward Coronado's land expedition. The Flints (2005, 647, footnote 110) identified certain narrows and other geographic features along the Gila that may correspond to features that Alarcón recorded 5 to 10 miles upstream from the Colorado junction near Kinter, Arizona.

Here, in the next few days, Alarcón's party met an even more exciting informant, an "old man" (Alarcón's term) who had also been to Cíbola. According to historian Herbert Bolton, writing in 1949, Yuma Indians used the term "old man" not so much for an elder as for a leader, just as soldiers might refer to their general as the "old man." Regarding Cíbola, the "old man" told Alarcón that Cíbola was

an excellent place where the governor was well obeyed. There were other lords thereabouts, with whom the governor was continually at war. I asked if the Cíbolans had silver and gold. When he saw my bell samples, he said that what they have has that color. [These may have been copper bells, such as Cabeza de Vaca had brought from the north in 1536. —WKH] I asked if they produced this metal there. He said no, but they brought it from a mountain where an old woman dwelt. I asked if he knew anything about a river called Totonteac, and he said no, but he did know of another mighty river with such large crocodiles that the people there made round shields from their hides. (abridged and adapted from the translation by Flint and Flint 2005, 198)

The "mighty river" might have been the Rio Grande, but some scholars wonder if the full description reflects knowledge of the lower Mississippi, where alligators can reach nineteen feet in length and were hunted for their hides.

Alarcón says the old man

pointed me out to the others, saying, "This is the lord, the son of the Sun," and so they came out and made me comb my beard and straighten my clothes and told me all their news and problems with each other. I asked, "Why do you tell me all your secrets?" and the old man said, "You are our superior; we should hide nothing from a master."

After we continued on our way, I asked him more about Cíbola. Had the people there seen anyone like us? No, except for the Negro, who wore on his legs and arms certain devices that ring. We knew that the Negro who went with Friar Marcos liked to wear bells and feathers on his arms and legs, and carried serving plates of different colors, and had come into those lands not much more than a year ago. I inquired about the circumstance by which he was killed, and the old man told the story he had heard: The lord of Cíbola had inquired whether he had any other brothers. The black answered that he had an infinite number, and they had many weapons and weren't very far away. Hearing this, many of the chief men there conferred with each other and resolved to kill the black, so that he might not give news to his brothers about where they dwelt. That was why they killed him. They cut his body into many pieces, which were divided among all the lords, so that they'd all know he was dead. Likewise, sometime later, the governor killed the dog like mine, which he had kept.

Here, then, was additional testimony about why the Cíbolans murdered Estevan—in this version, it was to prevent other Spaniards from learning about their city.

As Alarcón passed out crosses and recorded descriptions of buffalos from the inland plains, a man from a group onshore hailed the old man. A conference ensued, with much pointing back at Alarcón. Alarcón sent his interpreter over to listen in on the parley. The group had talked to upstream friends of theirs who had just arrived from a trip to Cíbola!

The newcomers were telling the old man that other men like us, with beards, had just invaded Cíbola and that they called themselves Christians. Therefore, we must all be from the same group. They proposed to kill us then and there so that the other Christians, the ones who were now occupying Cíbola, wouldn't learn of us and come to do them harm.

The old man answered them: "This stranger is the son of the Sun, our lord. He does good to us. He won't enter our houses even when we invite him in. He takes nothing and doesn't interfere with our women."

The other insisted we must all be one people. The old man said, "Let's go ask him."

So they came to me and said, "Other men like you are living in the country of Cíbola."

I pretended to be astonished, and said, "It's impossible!"

"No, it's true! We've talked to two of our friends who just came from there, and they say that those men have swords and things that shoot fire, like you do."

I asked if they had seen them with their own eyes. They answered no, but their friends had. Then the old man asked me if I was the son of the

---

SIDEBAR: Another Example of Long-Distance Native Communication

Coronado-era records of long-distance Native American communication from Cíbola to the Río Sonora and to the lower Colorado River (see map 7b) give fascinating insight into the original Americans' lives at the end of prehistory. To list one more example, Spanish ships under Juan Rodríguez Cabrillo in 1542 encountered Indians near present-day San Diego. These Indians told the sailors about bearded men with crossbows and swords marching through the interior (Kelsey 1986, 144–46). This presumably related to various Coronado parties marching forth and back from Sonora to Cíbola along their route roughly 560 trail miles east of San Diego. At the very least, it might have referred to a foray by Coronado's trusted captain, Melchior Díaz. As we'll see in the next pages, Díaz in 1541 reached a point about 125 road miles east of San Diego.

The impressive thing about these prehistoric "news reports" is not just the distances of up to 500 miles but their accuracy in terms of descriptions of events and the fact that they were often received only months to a year after the fact.

Sun, and I said yes. They said the Christians in Cíbola claimed the same thing, so I said maybe it's true after all.

They asked me: If those Christians from Cíbola came to join me, what would I do? I assured them they needn't be afraid, because if the others were really sons of the Sun, they would be my brothers and would offer everybody the same friendship and courtesy I had extended. At that, they seemed satisfied.

I tried again to find out how far it was from that river to Cíbola. They said it was far. The man who'd been talking described a *despoblado* ten days wide, without settlements, but he did not estimate the distance after that, though he said there were people along the way.

The man seems to have been describing the trip his friends had just made back from Cíbola: ten days south across the despoblado to a point on the Gila headwaters where a trail to the west passed various riverside villages along the way down the Gila River to the Yuma area (see map 7b): "Learning this, I wanted to notify Captain General Francisco Vásquez of my presence. I asked my own men-at-arms. I offered many rewards, but no one wanted to attempt the journey. One Negro slave finally volunteered, but he spoke only grudgingly. Still, I expected that other Indians who had been in Cíbola would soon appear, so we continued upstream on the river."

In spite of resistance from his crew, Alarcón hoped for a successful rendezvous with Coronado. He tried to get the Natives to send for the specific Indian travelers who'd come from Cíbola. They were said to be eight days' journey to the east, suggesting they were natives of the well-settled Phoenix/Maricopa area near the junction of the Gila and Salt Rivers. Alarcón pressed for more details. One of the Yuma-area locals, he was told, had just set out on a visit to Cíbola, but when he met the newly returned travelers, they said not to go there because of the fierce strangers. According to this secondhand account, the bearded strangers

argued with the people of Cíbola, because the Cíbolans had killed the black. They asked, "Why did you kill him? What did he do to you? Did he take any bread from you, or do any other harm?" The strangers were now living in one of the great houses at Cíbola, and many of them rode upon beasts which ran swiftly. . . .

One day, on the travelers' last days before leaving Cíbola, they saw more Christians streaming into Cíbola from sunrise to sunset and taking up lodgings. Two of the travelers talked to two of the Christians, who asked where they lived and whether they had fields of corn. The

Christians gave each of them a little cape and another to carry to their companions. The travelers promised to do this and then left Cíbola to return to their Gila River village.

The date of Alarcón's interview was around 10 September. Given the forty-day reported travel time, the bearded strangers streamed into Cíbola no later than late July or early August, three to four weeks after the "battle of Cíbola" on 7 July. The new arrivals might have been stragglers from Coronado's advance party or early arrivals of the following army.

Alarcón redoubled his effort to organize a party of Indian guides and Spanish couriers to make the forty-day journey to Cíbola, but his own men were still against him. They were reinforced by the old man and his villagers, who—perhaps for their own reasons—claimed "many inconveniences" and dangers along the way. The Indians had no desire for these sons-of-the-sun Christians to link up with the other sons-of-the-sun Christians, who had attacked Cíbola and moved in. They told the Spaniards that the people of an intervening province had threatened to make war because some of the Yuma-area natives had entered their country and killed a stag. The argument about traveling to Cíbola was so heated that Alarcón's friend, the old man, leader of the locals, "fell into a rage." Alarcón stalled. He tried to put a good face on the situation and announced he would now return to his ships: "I told the 'old man' and the rest that I'd come back, and I left them as satisfied as I could, though they said I was running away out of fear. The stretch of river it had taken me fifteen and a half days to ascend I covered downstream in only two and a half days because the current was so swift."

Alarcón's Second Attempt to Probe toward Cíbola: Late September 1540

Back among his own ships, Alarcón hoped the trouble would die down. His mission was to contact Coronado. Anything less would be an embarrassing failure. When he announced that he wanted to make a second journey up the river, however, his men again argued against him. He loaded some barques with provisions anyway and started a new journey back up the Colorado River on 14 September in a desperate attempt to find locals who would make the journey to Cíbola. On his way, he was given some macaw feathers, said to have come from people about sixty days away who traded with Cíbola. The travel time might refer to a round trip to Sonora, where, as Cabeza de Vaca first reported, macaw feathers were sent northward.

Alarcón said the local informants gave him a list of names of peoples and governors for many miles around. Like Marcos, he said he recorded these in a separate book that he would deliver to the viceroy. This supports our earlier suggestion that Viceroy Mendoza was keeping routing information secret. The book was probably delivered but has never been found.

As Alarcón continued up the Colorado to the Gila, he found people honoring the crosses he had left before. Some of them didn't recognize him at first because he'd donned fresh clothes from his ships and had brought along fife and drum players. He again reached the towns of Quicama and Coama (this time spelled Coano in the surviving Ramusio edition). He speaks of trying to push farther upstream to a province called Cumana, where the leader was said to be unfriendly because of the stag incident. The text indicates a couple more days of upstream travel and describes how a "wizard" tried to stop them (unsuccessfully) by placing some reeds across the river from bank to bank. However, Alarcón got only as far as the home village of the old man who had been traveling with him: "Here I ordered a very tall cross to be set up, where I engraved certain letters to signify that I had come this far. I did this so that, if by any chance envoys of the general Vásquez de Coronado should come, they might learn of my presence there."

At this point Alarcón says, "When at that point I finally understood that I would not be able to learn what I wanted to know, I decided to return to the *navios*." From two Indians who had come from Cumana, he learned that the distance to the river's source was much farther than what he had traversed so far; their knowledge of it was poor because "it came from very far away, and many other rivers entered it." On his way downstream toward his ships, he recorded one last, all-too-human drama: "A woman leapt into the water, crying to us to wait for her. She came to our boat and crept under a bench, where we couldn't get her to come out. Finally, I learned it was because her husband had taken another wife, by whom he had children. She said she no longer wanted to live near him. So she and another Indian came with me of their own accord."

How Far Inland Did Alarcón Get?: Autumn 1540

How close did Alarcón come to Cíbola? At the end of his second upriver venture, he comments that on both trips, "this time and the other, I had penetrated inland more than 30 leagues." This suggests he did not get much farther the second time than the first, perhaps thirty-five to forty days from Cíbola.

As for Alarcón's farthest penetration inland, Bolton places it not on the Gila River but on the Colorado River just north of the Colorado-Gila junction in Yuma. The Flints, as mentioned, place it a few miles up the Gila River east of Yuma, based on the match with Maricopa names.

An interesting clue about the upriver distance comes from an irrepressible Arizona pioneer named Godfrey Sykes (1944, 207–19). In the 1890s he built a boat, launched it from "the port of Needles," California, and floated down the Colorado River to the delta, where he got stuck on a sandbar and witnessed the strong tidal surge. In those days, before massive dams and irrigation projects, the flow rate may not have been too different from that in Alarcón's day. Sykes says it took his boat three or four days to go from Yuma to the sandbar. This would be a bit south of where Alarcón sheltered his ships, beyond the tidal surge. Alarcón says his barques took two and a half days to return downstream from the point where he learned about Cíbola to his ships at the port just north of the deltas. So Sykes took 20 to 60 percent longer but went farther south and probably spent more time each day ashore, camping and looking around. I speculate from the two accounts that Alarcón reached a point where the return trip was only a few days downstream, not much farther inland than the region where the Flints place him.

More information on Alarcón's farthest inland position comes from a number of sources, reporting in leagues. Alarcón himself said he penetrated inland more than 30 leagues on each of his two trips (see map 7b), but in the disjointed style of his report's final pages, a few lines later he says, "I traveled 85 leagues up the river" (translation by Flint and Flint 2005, 205). Additional numbers come from a land expedition a few months later led by Melchior Díaz, searching for Alarcón. We don't have their formal report, but Castañeda must have had it or perhaps talked to members of the group. He reports that Díaz reached the Colorado River. At that point,

> Díaz understood [from] an interpreter that the *navios* had been three days' journey downstream toward the sea. [They went downstream, and] when they reached a place where the *navios* had been [more than 15 leagues upriver from the port at its mouth] they found written on a tree, "Alarcón reached this point. At the foot of this tree there are letters." They extracted the letters, which said Alarcón's party had been there for some time waiting for news of the expedition. . . . When [Díaz] understood this, he returned upstream [without seeing the sea] in order to search for a ford by which to cross, so as to follow the other shore. (abridged from the translation by Flint and Flint 2005, 394)

The "Relación del Suceso" adds valuable information, specifying that Díaz reached the river "30 leagues from the coast" and that "Alarcón had ascended this far and as many [leagues] more upstream with his boats two months before they arrived," that is, 60 leagues in total from the coast.

At first glance, all these numbers seem confusing and inconsistent. Did Alarcón get only a bit "more than 15 leagues" inland? Or was it 30, 60, or 85 leagues? The sidebar synthesizes the reports and concludes that the Flints are probably correct and that Alarcón reached a point perhaps 5 to 20 miles east of Yuma on the Gila River and perhaps thirty-five to forty days' travel from Cíbola.

SIDEBAR: Reconciling Reports of Alarcón's Inland Travels

To reconcile the inconsistent statements about Alarcón's travel distance inland, I observe that some writers measured from the actual coastline (i.e., the entry into the shallow channels and shoals of the delta), but others measured from the place that the three navios reached, north of the shoals "in a sheltered area." That place was important to Alarcón. His relación says he called it Campaña de la Cruz (Plain of the Cross) and told his men that "in that land . . . they were to build a chapel" while he went upriver. With their chapel and sheltered ship-repair site, the men created the "port" that Castañeda mentions. Second, I observe that Alarcón's party must have left more than one cache of messages, and the cache Díaz found at the foot of a tree was not the one Alarcón left below a cross at his farthest inland point. Richard Flint (private communication, 2012) supports the idea of multiple caches, citing instructions Mendoza gave Alarcón in 1541 (for a subsequently aborted second voyage) in which he says that Alarcón should leave "markers and letters in all the ports behind you."

With these two observations, the reports begin to make sense. Castañeda says the cache found by Díaz was on the Colorado, "mas de quinçe leguas el rrio arriba de la boca del puerto" (more than 15 leagues upriver from the entrance to the port). That phrase could thus refer to the distance Alarcón traversed from the coastline to the position of the protected upstream "port" where his sailors minded the ships and built a chapel. Indeed, the straight line distance from the delta entrance to the end of the shoals (at a little settlement shown on some maps as Riíto, where the Mexican railroad bypasses the delta) is about 36 miles (12 to 14 leagues) inland through the delta channels. Alarcón's navigators would have estimated a larger distance winding through the shoals—let's say 18 leagues.

Alarcón estimated that he traveled additionally more than 30 leagues on each trip inland from the "port." If we say that he allowed 32 leagues for the first trip

Alarcón, at the end of his report, added a parting shot at Ulloa. He says he found that Ulloa's latitude measurements were "incorrect . . . by two degrees." Recall that Ulloa recorded the latitude at the outflow of the Colorado delta as 34°, whereas really it is more like 31.8°, and so Alarcón seems to be correct. But did Alarcón's pilots measure latitudes correctly? In a somewhat opaque conclusion, Alarcón implies that he reached a latitude four degrees higher than Ulloa. This seems impossibly high, requiring him to be on the Colorado River in the northwestern corner of Arizona along the southern tip of Nevada. The whole issue is confused by the mysterious Spanish errors in latitude measurements, not to mention the question

and 35 for the second, that would be a total of 60 leagues from where he left the navios. But he could estimate, truthfully (but perhaps with deliberate ambiguity to maximize Mendoza's claim), that he had logged roughly 18 + 32 + 35 = 85 leagues along the river.

When Díaz came in search of Alarcón, he traveled a historic trail (see the next section) that reached the Colorado River near or just south of present-day Yuma, about 40 air line miles and perhaps 45 trail miles (14 to 18 leagues) north of Alarcón's "port" near Riíto. The Indians told him correctly that Alarcón's ships had been seen three days downstream at the port, and Díaz thus headed downstream. Thus, it was at Alarcón's "port" and chapel that they found a sign written on a tree: "Alarcón reached this point. At the foot of this tree are letters" (Flint and Flint 2005, 394). The sign, of course, would have been unintelligible to the local inhabitants, ensuring that the buried cache was safe from curious locals. The letters indicated that the Alarcón party had been there for some time waiting for news of the expedition (fitting a message left at the "port" but not on the Gila River) and that Alarcón had decided to return south, along the Baja California coast.

The smoking gun in this case is Castañeda's statement that the Díaz party then turned around, traveling back upriver, searching for a crossing point. They finally crossed on rafts, probably at the later-named Yuma crossing. In support of this, it is clear that they were west of the Colorado River after that crossing (see the text about Díaz's expedition later in this chapter). They could not be in California after the crossing if Díaz had recovered the final set of letters that Alarcón buried at the foot of a cross left by Alarcón on the Gila River.

To sum up, it's plausible that Alarcón left messages at his farthest inland point, thirty-five to forty days from Cíbola on the Gila, but Díaz found messages that Alarcón left at his "port" just above the Colorado River delta.

of whether Alarcón (or some later hand?) might have exaggerated in his parting shot.

By late September 1540 Alarcón was on his way back to New Spain, sailing down the Baja California coast, looking for indications of Ulloa's visit. He found none. He had required nearly five months to sail north to the Colorado delta, with several stops, and so we might estimate that he didn't return to his home port until sometime around January or February 1541. His news probably did not reach Mendoza until some weeks later.

Mendoza, anxiously awaiting results from his expeditions, must have been disappointed, if not outraged, that Alarcón reached a point within forty days of Cíbola on an inland river where a "port of Chichilticale" still seemed possible—but then turned back.

Alarcón was probably unhappy, too. In those days, Spanish mariners who returned from the king's business reporting failure were sometimes imprisoned. Alarcón's discoveries, however, found their way onto Castillo's 1541 map, which places a broad inland waterway roughly in the position of the Gila River (compare maps 7b and 11).

Mendoza remained optimistic about naval contact with the troops at Cíbola. On 31 May 1541, as mentioned earlier, he proposed a second voyage north, with at least two substantial ships full of artillery, munitions, supplies, and letters for the land army. Stung by Alarcón's near miss on his first voyage, Mendoza stated in no uncertain terms that the purpose this time was specifically to find and link up with Coronado. Before Alarcón could organize his ships and leave, however, word probably arrived that Coronado was moving farther inland. Furthermore, Mendoza needed the supplies for the "Mixtón War," which was raging between the Spaniards and Indians west and northwest of Mexico City. The second Alarcón voyage was canceled.

Melchior Díaz and His Freakish Fate: August 1540–January 1541

As mentioned above, Díaz had been sent in early August from Cíbola back to the San Gerónimo garrison to seek out news of Alarcón. His higher priority was to serve as governor of what was now San Gerónimo II in the Río Sonora valley. He was to occupy it with eighty men, keeping lines of communication and supply open between Culiacán and the new northern lands.

San Gerónimo II was now a substantial enterprise (see fig. 12). Castañeda refers to it several times in its various locations as a "town" and

Figure 12. The San Gerónimo II garrison in the Valle de Señora as viewed from Ojo de Agua hill, south of Banamichi. The Río Sonora is outlined by cottonwood trees in the middle distance. Painting by the author, 2011, from on-site photos and visits.

calls the inhabitants not soldiers but "settlers" (according to the translation by Hammond and Rey 1940, 209, 268); Flint and Flint refer to the Spaniards' "settling" of a "pueblo" (midsized settlement) of San Gerónimo at Corazones in their translation and to each later incarnation of San Gerónimo as a "villa" (small settlement) (2005, 393, 394, 416, 426). Had the San Gerónimo "villa" survived, it would have been the only long-term settlement established by the Coronado expedition. Fate—more precisely, the incompetence of the "settlers"—decreed otherwise, as we'll soon see.

Bolton in 1949 portrayed Díaz as one of Coronado's most capable captains, and Arizona scholar Ronald Ives in 1936 called Díaz "a self-made man . . . not only a competent military man, but a daring and skillful leader" (90). Díaz arrived at San Gerónimo II around late August 1540. As soon as he arrived, he announced that eighty men from the following army would stay there, while most of the others would head north to join Coronado. Another party, under Capt. Juan Gallego, would continue south with disgraced Marcos de Niza to carry news to Viceroy Mendoza. In the marvelous September weather of Sonora, Díaz started organizing his search for Alarcón's supply ships. At that moment, however, Alarcón was already exploring the Colorado River.

Díaz now made one of the biggest mistakes of the Coronado expedition. Later memoirists indicate that the "settlers" of San Gerónimo were the least-reliable officers and men, purposely left behind by Coronado. From these men, Díaz had to appoint an interim governor to serve while he was gone. His mistake was to pick a soldier named Diego de Alcaráz. Alcaráz, operating out of Culiacán in 1536, had been among the slave raiders met by Cabeza de Vaca's party. He was, in Castañeda's understatement, "a man not well prepared to have people under his command." We'll return later to his story.

Díaz (fig. 13) set out with a party of twenty-five Spaniards and some local guides (and probably uncounted Indian servants), as well as some sheep to provide food. They headed northwest toward the head of the Gulf of California. Their trail was along the notorious Camino del Diablo—the Devil's Highway (Ives 1959; Hartmann 1989; Broyles et al. 2012). As we noted above, this trail delivered Díaz and his party to the Colorado River near Yuma. Castañeda tells how they reexperienced other Spaniards' surprise at the "tall and muscular" natives of that region: "Our people wanted to bring a log to the fire and six men could not bring it, [yet] one of [the Indians] came and lifted it in his arms and, by himself, placed it on his head, and carried it very easily" (Flint and Flint 2005, 394).

This is where Díaz's party went downstream and found the letters Alarcón had left at his "port," then returned upstream to build rafts and cross the river. In Castañeda's words, "In order to do this, they summoned many people of that land." The words probably sugarcoat forced labor. Spotting suspicious reactions, the Spaniards "confined" one of their guests. After the Spaniards "inflicted pain," he admitted that resentful locals planned to attack them in midriver. The Spaniards executed the informant, drove off the attackers with lances and arquebus shots, and finally reached the California side with their horses and remaining sheep.

The reconstruction of Díaz's route is an epic in itself. The most thorough scholar of Díaz's search for Alarcón was an iconoclastic geographer-historian named Ronald Ives (see the sidebar). Ives retraced much of Díaz's route on the ground. For his trouble, he got into a wonderfully grumpy argument with the other great Coronado geographer of the day, Carl Sauer.

Figure 13. What Melchior Díaz might have looked like with his fateful lance a few weeks before his death as his party traversed the Camino del Diablo (Devil's Highway) between Caborca, Sonora, and Yuma, Arizona. The photo illustrates that most of the travelers associated with the Coronado expedition did not wear the oft-depicted conquistador helmet and shining armor. Photo by the author, 1989, taken on-site in the Cabeza Prieta National Wildlife Refuge during a historically accurate reenactment.

Ives's initial article, published in 1936, favored not the Camino del Diablo but rather a route downstream on the Río Sonora and then up the desert coast, where Díaz could watch for Alarcón's ships (see map 7b). Ives followed the route on foot and noted a number of freshwater springs along the otherwise dry coast. Sauer, in keeping with his name, blasted Ives's route in 1937, calling it a "myth . . . [a] bizarre, circuitous expedition along the coast" (1937a, 146, 148). Ives fired back in the same year: "If Dr. Sauer chooses to . . . cite his own works as authorities . . . he is certainly privileged to do so [but my] conclusion was reached after . . . field work in the desert country" (1937, 149).

Thirty years later, in 1959, Ives ironically ended up favoring Sauer's inland route, as proposed also by Bolton. Ives in 1959 disingenuously cited his own 1936 coastal-route article as presenting evidence *against* his own earlier coastal route, saying that the coastal route "has been investigated and . . . found entirely practicable for one man afoot, but not for a mounted party driving sheep, as did the Díaz party" (1959, 156). The story exemplifies the perils of converting Coronado chronicles into routes.

Ives's 1959 paper analyzed the strange ending of Díaz's trip on the west side of the Colorado River. In one place, to paraphrase the account by Castañeda,

they encountered dunes of steaming cinders, which no one could enter. It was like being swamped in the sea. The land they traversed vibrated like a drumhead, as if caverns existed beneath it. It seemed an extraordinary thing that in some places the ash was steaming in a way that seemed

---

SIDEBAR: Ronald Ives—Another Colorful Coronado Scholar

Ronald Ives (1909–82) was trained as a geographer. According to his biographer, Karen Dahood (1989), he pursued his vision of a "science of environments" that would unite fields such as geography, geology, cartography, climate, archaeology, history, folklore, and so on. Dahood recounts that when Ives retired to Flagstaff, Arizona, the local rumor was that he had published more articles than most of the faculty of the local Northern Arizona University combined. It may have been true; his bibliography then listed 565 entries.

During World War II, he was the only survivor from an aircraft that "disintegrated" over the Aleutian Islands. He parachuted into the sea, swam to an island, and lived for eighty-nine days on fish and seaweed before being rescued.

After the war, he specialized in the history of the northwestern Sonoran desert. A few years before he died, I sought him out in Flagstaff. I remember him as a thin, intense fellow with wire-rimmed glasses. Like many desert rats, he seemed skeptical about the academic greenhorn in front of him, but we had a good conversation. He taught me that in the desert you should walk no faster than a speed at which you could breathe with your mouth closed.

His pleasure was to find old documents from historic travelers, such as Díaz, and then set out into the desert to determine exactly where the great figures of the past had walked and slept—and, in the case of Melchior Díaz, died. With his science of environments Ives enriched the sense of place for those who live in the Southwest.

infernal. Díaz's party detoured around this place because of the danger and because of their lack of water.

One day a whippet, owned by a man-at-arms, ran after several rams. . . . When Díaz saw it, he hurled his fighting lance at it as he was galloping. The lance, however, stuck in the ground. Unable to stop the horse, Díaz ran onto the lance, and his thigh was pierced by it, so that the tip exited at his groin and his bladder was ruptured. (adapted from Flint and Flint 2005, 406)

The Spanish lances had a sharp metal tip on the butt end called a *regatón* (not included on the lance in fig. 13), useful for sticking the lance in the ground temporarily without dulling the business end. The regatón was Díaz's undoing. The explorers "turned back with their wounded captain. Every day they skirmished with the Indians, who were still up in arms. Díaz lived about twenty days, during which his men endured great hardship, because they were carrying him. In this way they returned, in good order without losing a man, until Díaz died. At that point they were freed of their greatest hardship. They buried him on a little hill, covering him with a large mound of earth and stones, and erected a cross there."

Ives concluded that Díaz died on 18 January 1541 (Julian date). Ives used his own fieldwork, including multiday treks on foot, to interpret these intriguing passages. His 1959 paper reported: "The place that 'looked like something infernal' is easily identified as Volcano Lake, at the foot of Cerro Prieto, about 20 miles southeast of Mexicali [a border city in Baja California south of El Centro, California], about 55 miles west of the Colorado River. At this site hot mud still bubbles up from below, steam and fumes spread over the area, and numerous 'rubber meadows'—zones where hot mud is covered by an inch or so of turf—are present. A man can walk safely over much of the area, but a horse cannot" (1959, 158). Gayle and I explored Cerro Prieto in the 1970s and found the boiling mud pots still active. The area had been usefully transformed, however, by a large Mexican geothermal electric plant. This whole geothermal province is subject to occasional significant earthquakes.

The goal of Ives's 1959 article was to reconstruct the sad, twenty-day trip back to the point where Díaz died and was buried. Taking into account the terrain, nights lit by a nearly full moon, and historical military records of journeys with wounded men carried on litters, Ives proposed that the grave of Melchior Díaz lies in "a strip of desert valley floor, from three to more than 15 miles wide, extending southward from Sonoyta to, or close to, Caborca" (1959, 166). Perhaps Melchior Díaz's grave is still identifiable on some lonely hilltop in that desert area.

The Location (and Destruction) of San Gerónimo III: 1541–1542

Back at the San Gerónimo II garrison, along the middle Río Sonora (fig. 12), things went downhill after Díaz's departure and death. By early 1541 Alcaráz and his troops had outraged the local Indians with demands for food and molestations of women. At least one Spaniard was killed by a poisoned arrow, a weapon notorious throughout central Sonora. Alcaráz also faced insurrections among his own men. Castañeda remarked that "from that time on, there never failed to be quarrels and mutinies" at San Gerónimo II (Flint and Flint 2005, 394).

Coronado, still in New Mexico, learned of the problem and sent Pedro de Tovar—the captain who had reconnoitered the Hopi pueblos—to look into things and to "cull out" some of the less reliable men to take messages back to Mexico City. Tovar arrived at San Gerónimo II sometime in May 1541, carrying a letter written by Coronado to the king on 20 April (Bolton 1949, 236, 317). Tovar ordered punitive attacks on the Río Sonora natives, leading to seventeen more Spanish deaths. Tovar and Alcaráz were finally forced to move San Gerónimo II to a new location probably in June or July 1541. Castañeda mentions in two places that Tovar moved the garrison "40 leagues" closer to Cíbola, reestablishing it in the "Valley of Suya" (Flint and Flint 2005, 407, 416). The distance amounts to 100 to 124 miles, but the location of Suya remains a mystery.

San Gerónimo III was beyond easy reach by Indians who had been abused, and it had a chance for a fresh start. Once established, however, it had even greater problems than San Gerónimo II. During the 1544 investigation of Coronado's performance, a trooper named Alonso Sánchez testified about the reasons: "When [the army passed north through the region], all the towns of that valley came out in peace[, but later] they rose up in arms . . . because of the cruelty and outrages committed by . . . Alcaráz [and his men] because they seized women and girls. This happened specifically in the town and province called Señora, and in the valley of Comulpa" (Flint 2002, 65). "Señora" referred to San Gerónimo II, and "Comulpa" was probably modern Cumpas in the Río Moctezuma valley, the next valley east of the Río Sonora valley. Cumpas/Comulpa is not easy to reach from San Gerónimo II, being across high mountains. Sánchez's account suggests, instead, that the raids on Cumpas came from San Gerónimo III, closer to Cumpas/Comulpa. A later memoir by Baltasar de Obregón, who came through the area in 1565 with the next Spanish foray (led by Francisco Ibarra), says that people of that region still complained, twenty-five years later, about how Alcaráz and his men had "taken their wives and daughters to use for dishonorable purposes" and had demanded tribute, personal services, and provisions without paying (Hammond and Rey 1928, 163).

According to Castañeda, the situation grew so bad that some of the troops "mutinied" and fled south to Culiacán, leaving San Gerónimo III understaffed and with a number of sick people. One night, probably in March 1542, guards at San Gerónimo III grew careless in the predawn hours. Sonorans crept into the settlement, killing at least three Spaniards, untold servants, and more than twenty horses, and looting the premises. Survivors fled, heading for Culiacán along back-country trails (Flint and Flint 2005, 416, 427).

Obregón recorded the local Indians' version of that night. They said Alcaráz had been "lying with two Indian women" in spite of having been warned of an impending attack and that "100 men" were killed along with Alcaráz himself. In this version, "only a priest and five soldiers escaped" to

SIDEBAR: Where Was Suya?

Suya's location has long been a puzzle. Gayle and I reviewed a number of clues (Hartmann and Hartmann 2011). In addition to reporting that it was "40 leagues closer to Cíbola" than San Gerónimo II, Castañeda says that "in this [Suya] valley there are many settlements, [and] people are of the level as those of Señora." He adds that the new garrison "was established near a small river [and during the attack], a few people got out to the plain when they had the opportunity" (Flint and Flint 2005, 416, 427). These comments indicate that "Suya" was in a populated "valle" separate from the "Valle de Señora" but that San Gerónimo III itself was perhaps on a small tributary stream from which some Spaniards escaped onto the main valley floor (see map 9, top).

A move of 40 leagues (100 to 124 miles) "closer to Cíbola," if straight north along the Cíbola trail, would have put San Gerónimo III in the Chichilticale province. However, identifying Suya with Chichilticale is unlikely for several reasons. Most importantly, Castañeda distinguished Suya from Chichilticale. Second, according to Jaramillo, the occupied portion of the San Pedro River was known as Nexpa, not Suya (Hartmann 2002, 111ff.; Flint and Flint 2005, 513). Third, a move north to the Chichilticale region would put San Gerónimo III roughly 150 trail miles from Cumpas, probably inconsistent with the report that the Spaniards raided Cumpas.

continued

Culiacán. The true events are unclear, but San Gerónimo III was abandoned. Coronado learned of the debacle sometime later after a group of his soldier-messengers reached Suya, finding "the villa abandoned, with the people, horses, and livestock dead [and] the land up in arms." These troopers fled back to New Mexico to alert the general (Flint and Flint 2005, 425).

Cortés Discredits Marcos and Mendoza in Spain: 1540

In a more distant development, Cortés had arrived in Spain in the spring of 1540 on his last-ditch attempt to convince King Carlos V to revoke Mendoza's authority to explore the North. Cortés was furious—or at least he pretended to be furious. He knew how to act the role of the righteous but betrayed explorer. In the Spanish court, he filed his grievance on 25 June 1540. It started out by claiming that Mendoza and Marcos had learned nothing that Cortés hadn't already discovered: "I have come from New Spain to inform Your Majesty of the injury that don Antonio Mendoza, viceroy of New Spain, has done to me by impeding me in the conquest of a certain land that is included within the limits and confines of the territory

Castañeda gives another indication that Suya was off the main route to Cíbola: the troops complained that San Gerónimo III had been "betrayed," because communications between Cíbola and New Spain were "conducted through another area more convenient to New Spain" (Flint and Flint 2005, 426).

We suggested that Suya/San Gerónimo III was on the Río Moctezuma, the next valley to the east, paralleling the Río Sonora. Cumpas lies at that valley's south end. In this view, Alcaráz fled the turmoil by leading his "settlers" roughly 70 road miles north from San Gerónimo II to Arizpe or Bacoachi and then about 25 miles east or southeast along trails into the northern Río Moctezuma. Suya would then have been as little as 25 to 30 miles upstream from Cumpas (see map 9, upper right). This fits the above testimony that San Gerónimo III was on a drainage different from the Río Sonora valley, not too far off the Cíbola route, and within easy "molestation distance" from Cumpas.

In 1542, when Coronado was departing from the American Southwest, his southbound army seems to have detoured around the Río Sonora onto the Río Moctezuma. Castañeda says they arrived in Batuco (modern Batuc, roughly 50 trail miles south of Cumpas near the Río Yaqui [map 9]). After the army "reached

Your Majesty contracted to me in 1529. I have already taken possession of it." (This and subsequent quotes in this chapter are abridged from the translations by Flint and Flint 2005, 244–45.) Next, Cortés implied that the "certain land" he had pursued was the same as the northern land visited by Marcos. Cortés falsely claimed it had already been reconnoitered by his own captains and even by himself. The document bears Cortés's trademark: a disingenuous spinning of the facts: "The viceroy has tried to justify the harm and trouble he has caused by claiming that a friar, Marcos de Niza, reconnoitered that land anew. But what is actually happening is that I have occupied myself with the reconnaissance and conquest of that land. I've launched four armed expeditions, all at my own expense, and I went there myself on one of them and endured very great hardships and dangers."

Cortés proceeds to spin an account of his four voyages, discussed in chapter 2 (see map 5). He correctly says his "first expedition" was in 1532, but in his version, "my lieutenant [and] captain general . . . sailed along nearly the whole coast and arrived near the first and principal [place] which is populated, [but] because the ship . . . ran aground, the conquest was not completed at that time." In reality, instead of being well on the way to Cíbola, the ships were lost and were nowhere near any populated place Marcos had recorded.

Batuco . . . Indian allies from the valley of Los Corazones came to the camp in order to see the general, like [the] friends they always were." Had Coronado's army marched south down the Río Sonora, there would have been no need for the Corazones friends to travel all the way to a neighboring river valley to see him. We infer that he detoured to avoid the outraged natives of the Río Sonora and to inspect the remains of San Gerónimo III.

Can San Gerónimo III be found today? Probably, but we shouldn't expect obvious foundations of massive defensive structures. Castañeda says that Alcaráz, "being dull and obstinate," failed to establish adequate defenses. Obregón specifically supports this by saying that San Gerónimo III "had no fortress" (Hammond and Rey 1928, 168). Typical of abruptly abandoned sites, its ruins would be rich in left-behind artifacts that would reveal its identity. Possibly the place is already known to a few local Sonoran ranchers as an ancient settlement without being recognized as the final garrison of the Coronado expedition—the villa that might, in an alternate universe, have become the first permanent European settlement on a route across the present U.S.-Mexico border.

Cortés now seems to muddle or omit the 1533–34 Ximénez disaster, during which the crew mutinied and the ship was lost to Guzmán. What he calls "the next expedition" was actually the third one, in 1535.

> I reached the land of Santa Cruz and remained in it. This is very near the land that is being talked about [the northern lands reported by Marcos]. No one else had reached it. I returned to get more supplies, and I brought back some Indians from Santa Cruz, who, after they learned our language, informed me in great detail about the land—knowledge no one else was aware of. When I departed, I left nearly all the people I had taken, so that from there, they could continue the journey by land to the land that is now being talked about. Don Antonio de Mendoza, however, ordered that I remove all the people I had established in the aforesaid land. It was done, according to his order.

Cortés's text contains wondrously incredible distortions, which he surely could not have believed when he left for Spain. First, he says "Santa Cruz" was "very near" Marcos's fertile northern lands. In reality, he knew it was in the barren desert of Baja California on the *west* side of the gulf, just across from Culiacán, whereas Marcos had gone 450 to 500 leagues north of Culiacán along irrigated river valleys on the east side of the gulf.

Second, Cortés pretends that Indians at the south end of Baja told him about Marcos's Cíbola, but they could not have told him any such thing. Marcos himself didn't learn about Cíbola until he was much closer to Cíbola, about 150 leagues to the north, across the gulf in central Sonora (see map 7b).

Third, Cortés pretended that his troops, at the south end of Baja California, were in position to march to Cíbola as soon as he supplied them, and that Mendoza caused his Baja colony to fail. In reality, he established his outpost on a hostile peninsula, where some of his men nearly starved from lack of resources.

The next expedition Cortés mentions is his fourth commissioned voyage in 1539, in which Ulloa sailed northward and reported a north end to the Sea of Cortés where a mysterious outflow of water came from the interior. Cortés does not mention that it was several years after his Santa Cruz debacle but instead claims that it was only "a very few days after I had arrived from the land of Santa Cruz."

To deflect attention from his confusing claims, Cortés now applied the best defense: offense. His targets were the designated scapegoat, Marcos de Niza, and the king's representative, Viceroy Mendoza:

At the time I returned from Santa Cruz, Fray Marcos spoke with me. I gave him information about this land and its reconnaissance, because I had determined to send him in my ships to subjugate that land, since it appeared that he knew something about navigation. The friar passed that information on to the viceroy. Then, with Mendoza's license, he said he traveled by land in search of the same coast and land I had reconnoitered, which is mine to reconnoiter.

After the friar returned, it was made public that he said he had arrived within sight of the aforesaid land. I deny that he has seen or reconnoitered it. On the contrary, what the friar reports to have seen he asserts only on the basis of the report I made to him concerning the information I was receiving from the Indians of the land of Santa Cruz, whom I brought to New Spain. Everything it is said the friar is reporting is identical to what the Indians told me.

Cortés abandoned Santa Cruz in 1536, and Marcos arrived in Mexico City from Peru in April 1537, so it's believable that Cortés conferred with Marcos at that time, but the rest of Cortés's paragraph is nonsense. He claimed to have already "explored" the land that Marcos visited, but the closest he personally came to Cíbola was the south end of Baja California. And the closest his ships came was the Colorado River delta, which his captain, Ulloa, did not understand.

Cortés went on to dismiss the Coronado expedition as Mendoza's calculated attempt to rediscover lands Cortés himself had "discovered": "In order to do me greater injury and harm, he sent Francisco Vázquez de Coronado with certain people, so it is said, to penetrate inland in search of the aforesaid land discovered by me." His deposition continued with a very interesting charge: "I deny that Marcos has seen or reconnoitered that place. By behaving in this way without respect for my work, Friar Marcos has done nothing new in putting himself forward as something he is not, and relating what he neither knows nor has seen. He has done it many times before, and makes a habit of it, as is widely known in the provinces of Peru and Guatemala. More than enough information about this will be given in court soon, if necessary."

This last charge is the most interesting section of Cortés's deposition. Because he presented it in June 1540 in Spain, he was charging Marcos with exaggerating *before* knowing that Cíbola had no treasure. (It would have been easier to claim Marcos was an exaggerator *after* this was known.) If Marcos really did have a reputation for exaggerating, that would strengthen the case against Marcos. In context, however, Cortés's charge has uncertain weight. First, Cortés clearly had self-interest in discrediting and preempting any valuable discoveries by Marcos. Second, the conquistadors generally did their best to discredit the crusading priests who attacked their behavior in Mexico and Peru. Third, as we've indicated, the kind of information Marcos brought back about Cíbola could not have been known to southern Baja Indians, which proves that Cortés was purposefully stretching the truth.

Cortés was not as up-to-date as he wanted the king to believe. His deposition included at least one clear error of fact, stating that he had received news that Mendoza and Coronado had started the conquest by dispatching twelve horsemen, who had all died. In reality, Díaz, Zaldívar, and their horsemen returned safely in the spring of 1540 with reports no more definitive than Marcos's.

King Carlos V, who had greeted Cortés warmly in 1528, seems by 1540 to have been fed up with Cortés's self-promotion. Cortés, now in his fifties, was seen in court as a has-been who should retire gracefully and rest on his laurels.

Cortés, true to his nature, bulled ahead anyway, making various attempts to prove his service to the king. In one extraordinary affair, he and his son by Marina, the now eighteen-year-old Martín Cortés, joined a royal Spanish military expedition that sailed south across the Mediterranean to Algiers in 1541. King Carlos V had captured Tunis in 1535 during the aftermath of the Spanish war to drive back the Moors. Now, as recounted by Anna Lanyon (2004, 80ff.), graying Cortés and his strapping son Martín sailed off to attack Algiers as part of the seemingly eternal postcrusade confrontation between European and Islamic civilizations. Even Cortes's nine-year-old son—the second, more "legitimate" Martín Cortés—was also with them. That would prove the family loyalty to the Crown!

The expedition was a disaster. The fleet was caught in a storm, foundered on the African coast, and returned home in defeat. Cortés was heard to complain that if the soldiers who had conquered Tenochtitlan twenty years earlier had been with him, they would not have been turned back.

Cortés continued pursuing Carlos V from city to city to vent his claims of unjust treatment, but he was rowing against the tide. The king wanted his own men ruling New Spain.

CHAPTER ELEVEN

Coronado Fights a War, Reaches Kansas, and Returns to Mexico

Now we return to Coronado and his army, which had just settled into several requisitioned multistory pueblos in the Tiguex province in the winter of 1540–41 (see map 13).

As mentioned above, Pedro de Castañeda was unconsciously becoming the first European ethnologist in America. He offers a good picture of life in communities along the Rio Grande:

> Young men of marriageable age serve the pueblo as a whole. They bring the firewood and pile it in the patios, from which the women carry it to their houses. These young men live in *estufas*, which are underground in the patios of the pueblo. [These were the male-oriented meeting places known more commonly today as "kivas."—WKH] One *estufa* was so spacious that it could probably accommodate playing a ball game.
>
> When anyone needs to marry, they follow established rules. The young man must spin yarn and weave a *manta* and lay it before the woman. If she accepts it and covers herself, she is regarded as his wife. The houses belong to the women, the *estufas* to the men. The women raise the children and cook the food. If a man spurns his wife, he goes to the *estufa*. It is irreverent for a woman to sleep in the *estufa* or even enter it, except to take food to her husband or her sons. The men spin and weave.
>
> The land is so productive that in one year they harvest enough corn for seven years. A huge number of cranes, geese, ravens, and robins live

off the planted lands, but even so, when they plant again for the next year the fields have left-over corn that they haven't been able to finish storing.

The pueblos are free of waste because the residents go outside to defecate, and they urinate into clay vessels and take them outside to empty. They have very clean houses, excellently partitioned, where they cook food and grind flour. They grind it in a separate room where they have a large grinding bin with three stones set in mortar. Three women go in, each one to her own stone. One of them breaks the grain, the next grinds it, and the last grinds it again. While they grind, a man is seated at the door playing a flute. They draw their stones back and forth in time to the melody and sing in three parts. (abridged from the translation by Flint and Flint 2005, 418–19)

Now that lifestyle was being disrupted. In the summer of 1540 came news of the invaders who attacked Hawikku. Then came García López de Cárdenas and his squadron, which requisitioned the "Coofor" pueblo for the use of Coronado's army, forcing out the inhabitants. Then came the full army. The intrusion quickly turned from irritation to skirmishes and from skirmishes to what historians call the Tiguex War.

The Tiguex War: ca. December 1540

As mentioned in chapter 9, Coronado had sent Capt. Hernando de Alvarado back to Cicuye/Cicuyc/Cicuique/Pecos (see map 13) to confirm the existence of El Turco's golden bracelets. Alvarado was welcomed in Pecos, but the people denied the existence of the bracelets, claiming that El Turco was lying. Alvarado's reaction was hardly diplomatic. He set up an audience with the Spaniards' friend, the young leader Bigotes. When Bigotes and his party arrived, Alvarado threw them into chains, demanding verifiable information. The citizenry of Pecos stormed out to the Spanish tents on the plain below the ridge-top pueblo. (All these places are still visible today at Pecos National Historical Park.) Castañeda says the people came out ready for war, shooting arrows and hurling insults. Alvarado hightailed it with his prisoners back to Tiguex, where they were held and questioned for the next six months. Castañeda says dryly, "This was the beginning of discredit about the troops' word whenever they offered peace from then on."

Hostilities in central New Mexico escalated because of the gradual accumulation of such outrages. For example, Coronado decided to requisition some native clothing from the pueblos to protect his expeditionaries from the winter cold. He summoned a Tiguex leader and proposed that the man should organize a donation of at least three hundred items of warm clothing. The leader protested that he wasn't authorized to do this, that the idea needed consultation among the governors of the pueblos of Tiguex so they could plan how to distribute the burden among the towns.

Coronado agreed but sent out his officers to visit each pueblo. As the weather grew colder, these envoys arrived without warning and demanded clothing on the spot. The Puebloans, says Castañeda, barely had time "to take off their outer fur robes and hand them over." The process continued until the required number was reached, and the items were dispatched to the army's headquarters. The couriers, however, made matters worse. Castañeda says, in his disingenuous way, that whenever they came upon an Indian with a better garment, "they exchanged with him without showing respect and without ascertaining the rank of the man they were despoiling. As a result, the people of Tiguex were not a little angry" (abridged from the translation by Flint and Flint 2005, 402).

An additional outrage was that the Spanish horses were grazing in the cornfields of Tiguex. Harvesting was over, but the Puebloans relied on the cornstalks for fuel for winter hearth fires. They responded by killing some of the horses (Flint 2002; and private communication).

Another insult was more personal. A Spanish officer sexually attacked a Pueblo woman. Castañeda starts the story with a line that shows the Spanish self-image of nobility and aristocracy. The perpetrator, he says, was "a notable individual (who, in consideration of his honor, I will not name)." In other words, yes, the officer committed an outrage and got the whole army in trouble, but he was high-born, so let's not sully such an honorable gentleman by mentioning his name.

> What happened was that the honorable gentleman, a horseman, set out one day from the pueblo where he was quartered and arrived at a nearby pueblo. Seeing a beautiful woman, he called to her husband to hold his horse by the reins. Then he climbed up to a rooftop level. Because communications were typically along the rooftops, the Indian assumed the Spaniard's purpose was legitimate. As the Indian waited, he heard a certain vague noise. When the Spaniard came down and rode away, the Indian climbed up to discover that the man had raped or tried to rape his wife. (adapted from the translation by Flint and Flint 2005, 402)

The husband, with leaders from his pueblo, promptly showed up at the Spaniards' pueblo to complain. Coronado called out his troops into a sixteenth-century lineup, but the husband was unable to identify the criminal "either because he had changed clothes or for some other reason." The husband pointed out, however, that he could identify the horse, since he had held the reins. When he was taken to the stable area, he pointed to a blanketed, peach-colored horse. The owner denied the crime. The husband was sent away on the grounds that he had not identified the perpetrator and might have been in error about the horse.

Next day, according to Castañeda's account, one of the Mexican Indian allies who'd been guarding Spanish horses showed up at Spanish headquarters, wounded, to report that a party of angry Puebloans had killed his fellow guard and taken many of the horses. The day after that, Captain Cárdenas went out to "inspect the pueblos" and found them barricaded. Inside the pueblo where the outrage had occurred, the residents were "all up in arms" and conducting mock battles with the horses, slaughtering them with arrows.

Coronado ordered Cárdenas to attack, because "this pueblo was where the most harm had been done." The Spaniards caught the Puebloans off guard, broke in, and got to the roofs in spite of casualties from Puebloan arrows shot through "loopholes" in the pueblo walls. The Spaniards occupied the rooftops during the night. On the next day additional Spanish troops and Mexican allies broke into the ground-floor rooms and set smoky fires.

The citizens of the pueblo came out asking for peace, making the shape of the cross. The Spaniards answered in kind. The Indians dropped their weapons, and the Spaniards took them prisoner. An uneasy peace was arranged. Then another ugliness occurred. During the heat of the attack, Coronado had ordered that to make an example to the surrounding country, Puebloan "rebels" should not be taken alive. The soldiers in charge of the prisoners, however, did not know that peace had been arranged, "and those who made the peace agreement kept their mouths shut" (Castañeda's words). As a result, Cárdenas approved a mass execution, ordering two hundred stakes to be erected to burn the prisoners alive. About one hundred prisoners were being held nearby in a large tent, and when they saw the soldiers tying their friends to the stakes and "beginning to burn them," they made a desperate attempt to gather sticks to defend themselves and break out: "Our footmen attacked the tent from all sides. Sword thrusts forced them to abandon the tent. Then the horsemen attacked them. Since the land was flat, no man remained alive, except some who had remained hidden in the pueblo and fled that night. They spread the word throughout the land that [the Spaniards] did not keep the promise of peace that had been given to them" (translation of Castañeda's memoir by Flint and Flint 2005, 403).

The actual order of some of these outrages is uncertain, due to differences among accounts, but it's clear that they led to a coordinated uprising involving multiple pueblos in the Albuquerque area. Before the uprising went very far, heavy snow ensued for two months. Hostilities were put on hold, and Coronado sent emissaries along icy trails to urge peace and to promise that the pueblos would be pardoned. Not surprisingly, the Puebloans responded skeptically, as Castañeda recounts: "They couldn't trust people who didn't know how to keep a promise. . . . They pointed out that the Spaniards were holding Bigotes prisoner, and that, at the pueblo that had been burned, the Spaniards broke their promise of peace" (abridged from the translation in Flint and Flint 2005, 403–4).

The Tiguex War Escalates: January–March 1541

One day, possibly in January, Captain Cárdenas was on a mission with about thirty men-at-arms at one of the major Tiguex pueblos. A leader of the pueblo agreed to come out and talk peace if Cárdenas would dismount and put his horsemen off to one side. The Puebloans would then put their own fighters aside. The agreement was made, and the Puebloan leader and two aides approached Cárdenas, saying that since they were unarmed, Cárdenas should remove his weapons. According to Castañeda, Cárdenas did so. The leader came forward to embrace him, whereupon the other two Puebloans pulled out hidden clubs and struck Cárdenas so hard on his helmet that he was almost knocked out. Two nearby Spanish horsemen rushed in and pulled Cárdenas away. Other Spanish horsemen rushed forward. A shower of arrows fell, and many Spanish soldiers and horses were badly wounded.

As this unfolded, some of the people of that pueblo fled to another pueblo a mile or two away. Cárdenas's response was to gather some of his forces and pursue them, demanding that the inhabitants of the second pueblo surrender. This was met by arrows from the rooftops, so Cárdenas returned to the first pueblo, where fighters poured out to attack. Cárdenas organized a fake retreat, drawing the Puebloans after him. The Spaniards turned on them, and "some of the most notable were thrown to the ground." (Castañeda leaves it ambiguous whether they were dead.) The others fled back to the pueblo, mounting the rooftops. The Spaniards retired to their headquarters.

Coronado now ordered a siege. Cárdenas was sent to establish a camp adjacent to the first pueblo. The Spaniards brought ladders to scale the walls, but on the first day, roughly a hundred Spaniards were felled by stones thrown from above.

The siege continued for fifty to eighty days, but the Puebloans had anticipated the attack and had laid in supplies. Finally, after many skirmishes, the Puebloans began to run short of water. They lived close enough to the Rio Grande that they attempted to dig a deep well and reach groundwater inside their walls. The pit collapsed, killing thirty people. By the end of the siege, some two hundred Puebloans had died along with a much smaller number of Spaniards.

The Puebloans finally proposed a talk. They said they noticed that when the Spaniards made war they did not harm women and children. Thus, the Puebloans asked if the women and children could leave, as the water was running so short. Then the warfare between the men could continue. They would not negotiate for peace, however, because the Spaniards would not keep their word. In the end, the Puebloans came forth with about a hundred children and women who wanted to leave. The transfer was made as the Spaniards drew up in line in front of the pueblo. Castañeda recounts what happened next.

> A respected soldier, Lope de Urrea, removed his helmet and received the boys and girls in his arms. When no more wanted to come out, don Lope pleaded that the Indians give up peacefully, promising security. The Indians told him to move away, since they didn't trust people who betrayed friendships.
>
> When Urrea refused to move away, a man came forth with a bow and arrow, indicating that he'd shoot unless Urrea withdrew. Urrea's friends shouted for him to put on his helmet, but he predicted that the Indians would do him no harm. At this, the Indian fired a warning arrow that struck the ground between his horse's front feet. The Indian immediately nocked another arrow and threatened Urrea with a more serious shot. Don Lope put on his helmet and returned, step by step, to his place among the horsemen.
>
> When the Indians saw that he was out of danger, they raised a war cry and let loose a rain of arrows. Coronado elected not to fight further that day. He backed off, hoping to achieve peace by some means. (adapted from the translation by Flint and Flint 2005, 405)

Fifteen days later, the Indians attempted to flee the pueblo during the predawn hours. They tried to cross the nearby river, shielding the remaining women in the middle of their group. Forty Spanish horsemen, keeping watch, raised an alarm, and Spanish troops poured from their nearby camp. Castañeda says that the Indians managed to kill one of the Spaniards and a horse. He reports this as a notable event, just as our media, in the 2000s, reported each single American casualty in southwest Asia. Outraged at a Spaniard's death, the troops "worked slaughter among them," killing many of the Indians in the frigid waters. "Those who escaped death or injury were few." For good measure, the soldiers crossed the river the next day, tracked down the survivors, many of whom had collapsed in the extreme cold, and "brought them back in order to heal them and to be served by them."

Meanwhile, other Indians had elected to stay in the pueblo and make a last stand. In a few days, they, too, were captured. The nearby large pueblo, to which some of the citizens had fled, was similarly subdued in a few days, most of the men being killed and about a hundred women and children being added to the captives.

The date was near the end of March 1541, and the Tiguex War was over.

SIDEBAR: Identifying the Pueblo Sites of the Tiguex War

Historians have struggled to identify the sites of the embattled pueblos mentioned in the Coronado records. Occasional names match up with existing modern pueblos. Coronado's Chía, for example, is an old site of Zia (but several miles from modern Zia). The pueblos that were attacked during the Coronado era, however, are mostly in ruins, and some have been lost entirely to urban sprawl. Usually it's unclear whether a Spanish name applies to one of the ruins or perhaps to a pueblo that is now completely lost.

Bolton (1949, 229) concluded that Coronado's first requisitioned pueblo was near the modern town of Bernalillo (see map 13) and remarked that the whole area around Bernalillo "should be a fertile field for archaeologists." His prediction was correct. Archaeologists are now finding physical traces of the Coronado expedition. In 1986 road construction just southwest of Bernalillo revealed a campsite lying under about two feet of windblown sandy soil. It was about a quarter of a mile upslope from a pueblo ruin known as the Santiago site (see map 13). As a result of provident historic preservation laws, road construction was delayed, and a team from the Museum of New Mexico was brought in, headed by archaeologist Bradley Vierra, who published the findings in 1997 with colleague Stanley Hordes. Careful excavations revealed unusual depressions about four inches deep and several yards across, along with seventeen metal artifacts, including hook-and-eye assemblies and sixteenth-century nails; thousands of fragments of native ceramics of styles dating from 1525 to 1625; sheep bones;

continued

Departure from Tiguex: April–May 1541

As warmer weather arrived in April, Coronado prepared to depart the Rio Grande toward the eastern plains. He had sent reports to Mendoza, putting a good face on the situation by citing the stories of riches beyond Cíbola. He sent another letter dated 20 April 1541 to be passed on to the king. The original has been lost, but we can suspect that Mendoza read it with a sinking feeling, because he wouldn't tell even his own staff what it said (Bolton 1949, 237). The northern riches always lay just over the horizon.

To begin the 1541 summer campaign, Coronado sent emissaries to pueblos beyond Tiguex, hoping to establish peaceful relations. He also left instructions for the Cíbolans to host any reinforcements that arrived from San Gerónimo and to send them on to the eastward trail taken by the main expedition.

Just as the army was preparing to follow their guides, El Turco and Ysopete, the native of Quivira, eastward onto the plains, doubts surfaced about the

and stone artifacts, including a blade fragment of Pachuca obsidian chemically matched to obsidian from the Valley of Mexico. The depressions were probably sites of temporary shelters. The archaeologists had found the first definitively identified campsite of the Coronado army and/or their Mexica allies. (This was two decades before the work at Chichilticale, described in chapter 5.)

Archaeologists such as Gordon Vivian in 1932 and Carroll Riley in 1981 had already proposed that the nearby Santiago pueblo was Coofor/Coafor/Alcanfor, the pueblo that López de Cárdenas forcibly requisitioned in the autumn of 1541 as winter headquarters for Coronado's expedition. Informal interviews revealed that amateur archaeologists had already recovered many copper crossbow points (see fig. 11a and 11b) and lead arquebus balls from Santiago, some flattened by impact on walls. Further information on the Santiago finds can be found in papers by National Park Service archaeologist Diane Rhodes (1997); by New Mexican avocational archaeologist Dee Brecheisen (2003); and by Flint and Flint (2005, 600). More vividly, during a 1939 excavation, the Santiago site yielded the skeleton of a man apparently killed by a crossbow bolt; the point was still embedded in his breastbone (Gagné 2003, 243–44). In summary, Santiago was certainly one of the pueblos occupied by Coronado's army—but which one?

A few miles south of Santiago, in the 1950s, a family bought land on the west bank of the Rio Grande and placed their dream house on a large mound, the site

Turk. An amusing (or is it disturbing?) medieval minidrama ensued. A Spaniard named Cervantes had been assigned to guard El Turco. Cervantes tried to prevent El Turco from learning about the fifty-day siege mentioned above, but one day El Turco stated correctly that "five Christians and one captain have died." Had someone secretly told him? Under questioning, El Turco denied it. Cervantes then started spying on El Turco and saw him talking to Satan by means of speaking into a jar of water. El Turco was in league with the devil! In that case, how could the expedition onto the plains succeed?

In spite of such serious concerns, the expedition left Tiguex in late April 1541 (Bolton 1949, 238). The first stop was Cicuye/Cicuyc/Cicuique/Pecos pueblo, about 85 trail miles northeast of the Albuquerque pueblos. Bigotes was returned to his people, and celebrations ensued. The Pecos governor and Bigotes provided Coronado with another young man called Xabe, also said to be a native of Quivira. Xabe confirmed that Quivira had gold and silver, but not as much as El Turco had been saying. Was this really an independent

of an ancient pueblo. They bulldozed segments of prehistoric walls to build their house. In the 1990s the city of Albuquerque acquired the site as part of its exemplary Open Space program, which preserves some of the beautiful and historic, cottonwood-lined landscapes along the Rio Grande. By the early 2000s, program archaeologist Matt Schmader had begun careful investigations. In the growing spirit of intercultural respect, he called elders from a nearby pueblo to ask their advice about research on the ruins. "We've seen what you archaeologists do," they said. They asked that the no-longer-lived-in town of their ancestors not be peeled away in traditional spade-and-backhoe fashion. In response, Schmader took a noninvasive approach and began an electromagnetic survey that detected outlines of walls and room floors from subtle differences in electrical conductivity. Within a few years, his map revealed one of the largest sites in the Tiguex area, now known as the Piedras Marcadas site. Roughly a thousand ground-floor rooms were divided into three pueblo structures, probably multistory, each surrounding a central plaza (Schmader, 2011, and private communication, 2011). Schmader continued noninvasive work with metal detectors. By 2011 he'd found some nine hundred Coronado-era artifacts, the largest number from a Coronado site to date. They included twenty copper crossbow points (fig. 11b), lead balls from arquebuses, many "caret-head" nails, buckles, and other items. The data suggest a Spanish attack, but was it one of the attacks mentioned in the chronicles? Or were some additional attacks not even mentioned in the memoirs and court hearings?

story of gold on the plains . . . or was Xabe merely a "plant" coached by the people of Pecos in order to get the strange, food-consuming visitors to move on? Certainly the locals now knew very well what the Spaniards were after. El Turco, for his part, reaffirmed his original descriptions of eastern treasures and remained the primary guide to the wonders of the American plains.

The expedition set out from Pecos, eastward into the Texas Panhandle (see map 14). All they had to do now was locate Quivira and determine just how much gold and silver was really there. After a couple of weeks they reached "bedouins" (Castañeda's term), known locally as Querechos. These were the nomadic Indians who ranged over the plains after the endless buffalo herds. Coronado himself parleyed with them. They affirmed El Turco's tales . . . but as canny Castañeda remarks, "since they had already talked with El Turco, they confirmed everything he said." The buffalo herds were "unbelievable," says Castañeda. "At first, there was not a horse that looked them in the face that did not flee from their gaze."

The troops had now reached the flat highlands of northern Texas, known by the Spanish name Llano Estacado (YAWN-o es-ta-KAH-do), which means "Palisaded Plains," probably referring to the cliffs that border it (see map 14). The name is more commonly translated, but less meaningfully, as "Staked Plains." The featureless, plateau-like plain was easy for travel but a hard place in which to get one's bearings.

Ysopete, who was from Quivira, now raised an alarm. He said El Turco was leading them in the wrong direction. Which guide was telling the truth? At this point, the Spaniards sided with El Turco.

A Camp in a Texas Canyon: Late May 1541

One day, Coronado sent out scouts; they came to a *barranca*, or canyon, cutting into the east edge of the seemingly featureless plain. Richard Flint, in his 2003 reconstruction of the expedition calendar, put the (Julian) date at 26 May. As mentioned in chapter 3, this is where the Spaniards were told that the Cabeza de Vaca party had passed "this way" and where the Indians presented the pile of gifts that was plundered in a matter of minutes by Coronado's avaricious soldiers.

At this point, Castañeda tells an interesting tale that had ramifications 450 years later.

> One afternoon, while the expedition was resting in the *barranca*, a whirling storm arose with strong winds and hail. Torrents of hailstones came

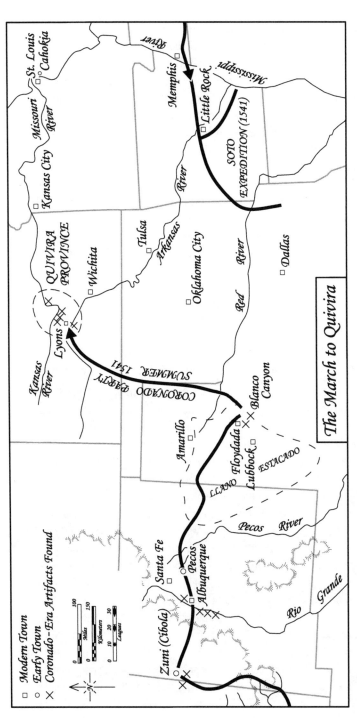

Map 14. Coronado's expedition to Quivira. After wintering in the Albuquerque area, Coronado crossed the plains to Quivira and back in 1541. The route is only estimated, but Coronado-era artifacts have been found in areas shown approximately by X's, as discussed in the text. Heavy lines at right indicate the estimated route of the Soto expedition. In the summer of 1541 the main Soto party was probably in west-central Arkansas but may have sent scouting parties west into Texas or along the Red River. Map by Ron Beckwith.

down, as large as small bowls and as dense as rain. They soon covered the ground, reaching a depth in one place of two and three *palmos* [a total of one and a half to two feet]. All the horses got loose, except for two or three which the Blacks protected with helmets and round shields. The other horses fled before the storm until it drove them against the canyon wall. Some climbed the slopes to where they were brought down only with great effort. If the storm had caught them on the plains, the expedition would have been imperiled, since many horses would not have been recovered.

The hail tore through many tents, dented many helmets, and hurt many horses. It also broke all the expedition's pottery—no small predicament because neither pottery nor gourd containers are made in that region. The people there eat only raw or partly roasted meat, as well as fruits. (adapted from the translation by Flint and Flint 2005, 409)

The probable location of this site is now known, thanks to discoveries of Coronado artifacts primarily since 1995 (see the sidebar).

SIDEBAR: Blanco Canyon, Texas: The First Known Texas Campsite

In 1995 Gayle and I participated in the first systematic survey of Blanco Canyon, which is believed to be the canyon where the hailstorm occurred, or perhaps a second nearby canyon that was also mentioned by the expedition, as reviewed by the survey organizer, Wichita State University archaeologist Don Blakeslee (2011). The canyon lies near the small town of Floydada, Texas, in the Texas Panhandle between Amarillo and Lubbock (see map 14).

The discoveries in Blanco Canyon involved detective work by amateur and professional scholars working together, and to get the story, I reviewed documents in the Floydada County Historical Museum and interviewed the helpful museum director, Nancy Marble, as well as Blanco Canyon lead investigator Blakeslee and the Flints. The first important artifact was found between 1957 and 1959, when local farmer Burl Daniel picked up an odd object while plowing his field a few hundred yards from the north rim. As he threw this item into his truck, it "sort of unfurled," and he recognized that it was something curious, a glove or "gauntlet" made of metal (fig. 11c). It languished in his artifact collection for some years until the local newspaper, the *Floyd County Hesperian*, got interested in the collection and publicized the strange gauntlet. By 1966 experts at the Texas Memorial Museum in Austin had identified it as medieval chain mail dating from

Figure 14. The Coronado campsite at Blanco Canyon, Texas. Tent designs are based on surviving examples from the 1500s. Painting by the author, 1996, on-site during the first Coronado team survey.

the mid-1500s to the early 1600s. Its design protected the hand during sword fighting. Well-known Texas archaeologist Jack Hughes urged further investigation, but interest apparently subsided.

Around the 450th anniversary of Coronado's expedition, in 1990 and 1991, Blakeslee, the Flints, and other scholars convened to discuss the location of the Coronado route in Texas and began a more professional examination of which canyons might match the Coronado descriptions. Inspired by their discussions, Floydada County Historical Museum director Nancy Marble tracked down Burl Daniel (who'd retired to New Mexico) and acquired the gauntlet for the museum's collection. Local interest mushroomed. Archaeologists Hughes and Blakeslee came to town and gave public talks in May and July 1992. Local metal detector buff Jimmy Owens listened with interest to descriptions of Coronado-era artifacts, such as Vierra's then-recent campsite discovery near Albuquerque. Jimmy told me in a 1996 interview that this was when he decided to start looking around Blanco Canyon with some friends.

In August 1992, when Richard and Shirley Flint organized the first international Coronado conference at New Mexico Highlands University in Las Vegas, New Mexico, Nancy Marble displayed the gauntlet. A year later, Nancy informed

continued

Castañeda called the people of this region Teyas, from which the name Texas was later derived. The Teyas provided guides for the next part of the journey. By this time the Spaniards were dubious about El Turco's stories, so they didn't allow him to talk to the new guides. The Turk had led them eastward for thirty-seven days (for an estimated total of 550 to 820 trail miles at the usual rate of 15 to 22 miles per day). Now they were told that Quivira was 250 leagues (625 to 775 miles) to the north! Why hadn't they been moving directly toward Quivira?

Coronado finally concluded that El Turco had been deliberately leading them in the wrong direction and, worse yet, into an area with no resources. He called his captains together for a meeting. The outcome: El Turco was arrested. A reconnaissance party under Coronado would turn north toward Quivira with thirty horsemen and six footmen (and the unmentioned-as-usual Indian allies). The rest of the army would return to Tiguex and amass new food supplies. Many of these soldiers objected. They wanted to participate in the conquest of mighty Quivira. They were overruled and ordered back to Tiguex. Coronado's group set out with Ysopete as the new guide. El Turco was brought along in chains.

Richard Flint that Jimmy Owens had just come forward with what looked like an iron crossbow point. A problem was that known southwestern points until that time were all copper and of a somewhat different shape, and Jimmy had found a broken Indian arrowhead "in the same hole" where he dug out the iron point. Thus, an ironic possibility remains that this first point—which inspired further searching—was not Coronado material but perhaps an Indian trade item. Jimmy kept looking, and eight or nine months later he came forward with a second metal point. This time it was copper (see fig. 11a), and it beautifully matched the style of Coronado expedition points already found in New Mexico.

As a result of these finds, Blakeslee organized a formal survey with his students along with the Flints, Gayle and myself, and other volunteers on Labor Day weekend of 1995. We were hosted by rancher Q. D. Williams, who owned this part of the canyon floor. Local interest, along with afternoon temperatures, ran high. One late afternoon, a procession of local ranchers' cars and trucks suddenly appeared on the dirt road into the canyon. We found ourselves being treated to a wonderful Texas barbeque dinner, after which it was marvelous to fall asleep in our tent on the very ground where Coronado might have slept. The nighttime noises of crickets and wind in the trees had not changed in four hundred years.

The trip north across the featureless plains was difficult. Some of the Teyas deserted in the first few days, and Coronado had to send troopers back for new Teya assistants. The expedition waited fifteen days, passing the time by killing five hundred buffalos and preparing their dried meat for the coming journey. Another problem involved coordinates. As the sun rose in the east or set in the west, or the stars came out at night, directions were obvious . . . but if one tracked game too far in midday, with the sun high during the approaching summer solstice season, it was easy to become disoriented. Castañeda notes that during this period, numbers of Spanish hunters lost their bearings, "foolishly traveling from one place to another without knowing how to return to the place from which they had departed." Only some of them made it back after efforts were made to attract them back to camp by the use of drums, trumpets, gunshots, and, at night, giant bonfires. Meanwhile, the Spaniards learned to establish their path by firing arrows in the desired direction of travel, starting as the solstice sun rose in the east-northeast. Then they establish straight-line travel by firing a second set of arrows, leapfrogging over the first arrows and moving forward to collect the first set, and so on.

A third crossbow point, also copper, was soon found. Jimmy told me it had been found barely embedded in one of the ranch's dirt roads, and we joked about an imaginary scenario in which a crossbow point dropped in the sixteenth century might have punctured a tire in the twentieth century. Most of the Coronado material, however, turned out to be buried five to ten inches deep in flood sediments from the nearby creek. This made it hard to test whether Blanco Canyon was the site containing the broken pottery from the hailstorm, because metal detectors couldn't detect ceramics. A further look at Jimmy's "junk box" and items from some of his friends (who did not publicly come forward) turned up a characteristic sixteenth-century nail and a probable Coronado-era horseshoe. By October 1995 about sixteen copper crossbow points were known. In honor of Jimmy's willingness to come forward with his historic material, the site was named the Jimmy Owens site.

Blakeslee organized a second survey in January 1996. This time, the temperature barely cleared 25°F on the first day, but we were warmed by our enthusiasm. The enthusiasm ran so high that my "scientific diligence" side kicked in, and I began to wonder . . . could the Blanco Canyon crossbow points be a hoax? Could

continued

Figure 15. Texas ranch road on the Llano Estacado plains adjacent to Blanco Canyon, illustrating the featureless landscape in which some Coronado expedition members became lost. Photo by the author, 1995.

the Texas boys, having been exposed to the design of crossbow points from New Mexico's Santiago site, be having a bit of fun, seeing how far we naive academics could be pushed before catching on to the joke? My concern was not helped one day when Jimmy reached in his pocket and fished out something to show me: he and some of his friends had experimented in their workshop, he said, and had produced a good facsimile of a Coronado crossbow point! My mental gears were spinning. Was this one last tweak of the scholars' noses? "Hey, did you fellas realize we can turn these things out in my garage?"

I was much relieved when Wichita State University researcher Frank Gagné compared the Blanco points with points found in New Mexico, including materials that Jimmy and his friends hadn't seen. Frank found such precise stylistic similarities that he felt certain points from both collections had been made by the same sixteenth-century craftsman. (A similar comparison is shown in fig. 11a and 11b.) Back in Blanco Canyon, the professionals carefully excavated individual points lying horizontally on ancient surfaces, finding no indication that they had been recently pushed into the ground. The site was the real thing.

As we wondered why so many points were strewn around the campsite, it began to seem plausible that as frightened horses scattered in the hailstorm, some saddlebag full of extra points might have burst open and dispersed points in the mud. Or had some skirmish been fought with the Indians, conveniently left out of the later chronicles? The answer is still unclear.

Quivira: Late Summer 1541

After forty-eight days crossing the Texas and Oklahoma Panhandles and part of Kansas, Coronado's party reached the area called Quivira. They were welcomed peacefully. They investigated. Quivira turned out to be another letdown.

Quivira was a collection of modest villages, probably along the Arkansas River in what is now central Kansas. Castañeda, still chafing twenty years later when he wrote his memoir, is terse about Quivira. He says that the local leader wore a copper medallion suspended from his neck, but this was his most valuable metal object: "Neither gold nor silver was seen among these people." What was the source of the rumors of treasure in Quivira? The usual theory is that it was a plot by the people of Pecos to get rid of the invaders. Still, Quivira was a real place and seems to have been well known to the Puebloans and on the plains. As mentioned earlier, El Turco might have been repeating older oral traditions about Quivira as a contact point for the much more impressive Cahokia urban complex, about 470 modern road miles to the east on the Mississippi River (see map 14). This does not explain the rumors of gold, however, and no substantial gold use is known in Cahokia or mid–North America, though some mound-builder sites in Ohio have yielded a few gold trinkets.

SIDEBAR: Finding Traces of Coronado in Kansas

Around 1800, settlers in Kansas began turning up pieces of European chain mail. The pieces ranged from few-inch fragments to most of a crude "shirt," now preserved in the Smithsonian (Wedel 1990, 1995). By the 1890s, some of the great pioneers of American archaeology, such as Hubert Bancroft (1899) and Frederick Hodge (1898), had concluded that the Kansas sites related to Coronado's Quivira. In 1900 a Swedish-born teacher, Johan Udden, wrote a scholarly article about witnessing the excavation of a piece of chain mail from an Indian mound in Lindsborg, Kansas. Such finds created a Coronado craze in Kansas in the early decades of the twentieth century, as described by the noted archaeologist of the plains, Waldo R. Wedel (1990, 1995).

Wedel acquired a small grant and excavated Indian mounds and pits on various Kansas farms in 1940 and also between 1965 and 1971, finding sixteenth-century European materials mixed with Native American artifacts (see the rough

continued

In exasperation, the Spaniards grilled El Turco about why he had lied about the directions and the gold. He claimed that his homeland was in the general direction in which he'd been leading them and that, besides, leaders at Cicuye/Cicuyc/Cicuique/Pecos had urged him to get the Spaniards and their horses lost on the plains so they would run out of food. Then, even if a few Spaniards came straggling back, the people at Pecos could kill them in revenge for what they had done. Regarding gold, he reportedly admitted that he did not know where any could be found, supporting the idea that gold was merely tacked onto the Quivira rumor to entice the Spaniards onward.

Castañeda describes the Turk at this point as ashamed that the expedition had believed Ysopete instead of him. In medieval tones, Castañeda matter-of-factly recounts that the troops strangled El Turco with a garrote because they were concerned that he might escape and spread harmful information about

indications of locations as X's on map 14). The finds didn't prove that Coronado slept in Kansas, because at least one other Spanish expedition reached Quivira between 1540 and 1601. Obscure documents studied by historians George Hammond and Agapito Rey (1966, 48ff., 323ff.) related that two Spaniards, Francisco Leyva and Gutiérrez de Jumana, led a disastrous expedition from the Tiguex area through Pecos onto the plains in 1593, seeking Quivira. They described Quivira as a densely populated zone extending over 10 leagues (25 to 31 miles) along a river, with a width of about 2 leagues (5 to 6 miles). Jumana, however, murdered Leyva during an argument, and most of the party was then apparently massacred by the Quivirans. Only a few escaped, and no known formal report was produced from the expedition.

Items of chain mail and Tiguex ceramics from the 1593 party were, however, probably traded among the local villages, diluting evidence for Coronado being at any specific site (Wedel 1990, 148). Wedel worried amusingly about the effects of such dilution on his conclusions about Coronado. "I am not arguing the infallibility of archaeology," he said. "No matter how flowery the rhetoric or how snowy the beard, our pronouncements are based on possibly fallible interpretations" (1990, 149). Still, Wedel documented a number of sites with Coronado-era artifacts in central Kansas a few miles northeast of Lyons. Map 14 indicates where European chain mail and other artifacts were found with pottery from central New Mexico. The finds support the idea that Quivira was in central Kansas and was visited by both expeditions.

them. "Ysopete was pleased about that," says Castañeda, since El Turco had always portrayed him as a scoundrel, and now he was vindicated.

Castañeda, reflecting on the story two decades later, opined that the Coronado expedition could have been a success if only they had never met El Turco. As the army first reached Tiguex, said Castañeda, they got information about additional pueblos toward the north. According to his Monday-morning quarterbacking, they might have succeeded had they moved north rather than following El Turco eastward out onto the plains. El Turco "was the cause of all the poor results [we] had" (Flint and Flint 2005, 400). We know today, however, that the road north would not have yielded any grander riches.

What Might Have Been: Summer 1541

Oddly enough, another Spanish expedition was now approaching the Coronado army from the east. Hernando de Soto, though known today mainly as an explorer of the southeastern United States, had crossed the Mississippi and was leading his own expedition westward. Soto had been in Peru with Pizarro and then returned to Spain, where he got a new commission to explore La Florida. He landed near modern Tampa in May 1539 just as Marcos de Niza was approaching Cíbola. Led by local guides, Soto traveled through Georgia, the Carolinas, and Tennessee, then suffered losses during an Indian attack in Alabama in the fall of 1540, a few months after Coronado reached Cíbola. He regrouped and headed west, arriving at the Mississippi River in May 1541 as Coronado was heading east from the Rio Grande. Soto then crossed the Mississippi, and the two expeditions were unknowingly heading toward each other (see maps 1 and 14).

How close did they come to each other? Two authoritative investigations of Soto's expedition route by the United States De Soto Expedition Commission in 1939 and by Georgia archaeologist Charles Hudson and colleagues, who uncovered new data in the 1980s, place Soto's party in west-central Arkansas during the crucial summer of 1541.

The potential rendezvous was not to be. During those very weeks, Coronado decided to turn back from Quivira toward Tiguex. By May 1542 Hernando de Soto had fallen ill and died along the Mississippi River. In the summer of 1542, the Soto survivors probed into east Texas (see map 14), but the Coronado party had already departed, as we'll soon see.

After wintering on the Mississippi, the Soto survivors built rafts, set out down the Mississippi in June 1543, worked their way south along the Gulf Coast, and reached Mexico City in the fall of 1543, a year after the Coronado expedition had already returned to the same destination. Members of the two expeditions met up and reminisced in Mexico City rather than in Texas.

How might American history have been different if the two parties had learned of each other and met up in the fateful summer of 1541? Europe would then have had its first hard data on the actual east–west width of North America and the size of La Florida relative to the lands of Mexico, Cíbola, Totonteac, Tiguex, and Quivira. Recall that in those days it was very difficult to measure such longitudinal distances (see chapter 3 and Sobel 1995). If the parties had linked up, the Spaniards would have finally understood the possibilities for colonization between La Florida and Mexico and would probably have established fortified presidio outposts all the way across what is now the southern United States (as they did from California to Texas in the 1700s). The northern border of "Mexico" might thus have extended from South Carolina to California, with an English- and French-speaking realm to the north. With a Coronado/Soto linkup, might North America have evolved into Canada and Mexico, with no United States in the middle?

According to an incident related by Castañeda, such a linkup almost happened through an unknown Indian woman. Castañeda says that during the eastbound journey onto the plains in the spring of 1541, Capt. Juan de Zaldívar (explorer of Chichilticale with Díaz) had brought with him "a tattooed Indian woman" who had been a slave in Tiguex. Like El Turco, she'd grown up in the eastern plains. When the army arrived at the Texas Panhandle canyons, she recognized the land and fled from Zaldívar "downstream through the canyons." This was likely in the Blanco Canyon area, where the canyons drain east and where Coronado's party arrived in late May. Traveling in that direction, she met up with Soto's party. Castañeda relates what happened based on information he gathered years later in Mexico.

> [Soto's party], who penetrated that region from La Florida, met this Indian woman and had her in their possession. After they returned to New Spain, I heard them say that she had told them how, nine days earlier, she had fled from other Spaniards (our group). She even gave the names of the captains. This means that our group had penetrated almost to where the Soto expedition informants reconnoitered. They said that at that time they were more than 200 leagues inland. Thus, we infer that the land must be more than 600 leagues across in that region, from sea to sea. (adapted and abridged from Flint and Flint 2005, 412)

Castañeda's estimate of the continent's width at that latitude amounts to at least 1,500 to 1,860 miles. The actual distance from Tampa to the west coast of Sonora is about 1,700 air line miles and even more by ground travel, so Castañeda was in the right ballpark.

Especially intriguing is the woman's reported nine-day linkup between Coronado's party and the Soto expedition. The distance from Blanco Canyon to west-central Arkansas (the reputed position of Soto's troops at the relevant time) is about 450 air line miles, or perhaps 500 trail miles on the plains. We know, however, that Soto's party sent cavalry detachments ahead on surveys, so it's plausible that such a scouting party was in northeast Texas only 260 to 350 miles away in northeast Texas, perhaps having heard regional native grapevine rumors of an escapee from Spanish strangers to the west (see map 14 for estimated routes of the two parties). If the lone woman fled for her life downstream at 30 miles per day (the rate at which Marcos said he fled from Cíbola), a nine-day trip would be a distance of 270 miles. Native people, however, were commonly said to achieve considerably higher travel rates than Europeans. Thus, it seems plausible that a Soto scouting party found her and brought her back to the main Soto party. By the time they returned to Soto, Coronado's location was unknown to them. From the data at hand, it seems that Spain came within a few weeks and one woman's odyssey of a history-changing linkup across North America.

The Coronado Expedition's Return to Tiguex: Summer and Autumn 1541

The disgruntled portion of Coronado's army, sent back from Texas, arrived in Tiguex in July and began requisitioning food supplies for the coming winter in expectation of Coronado's return from Quivira. Puebloans had reoccupied some of the pueblos while the expedition had been away, and hostilities arose once again over the Spanish presence. By winter the Spaniards were afraid to go out singly or in pairs for fear of attack. Meanwhile, larger parties explored as far northward as Taos (132 road miles north of Albuquerque) and identified two new provinces within that interval. One, called Hemes or Jemez (modern Jemez), had seven pueblos, whose inhabitants "came out in peace and provided food." The second, "called Yuque Yunque," is thought to have been farther north, near the modern town of Española. While the Spanish were setting up their camp, these people fled to the mountains. Castañeda tells us that "in the two abandoned pueblos were very beautiful pottery, glazed, intricately worked, in many shapes. Many jars were found full of choice shiny metal, with which [the Indians] glaze their pottery. This was an indication that their land had sources of silver, if only they had been sought" (abridged from the translation by Flint and Flint 2005, 412).

Did the "shiny metal" really imply silver, as Castañeda surmised? According to archaeologists Ann Ramenofsky and David Vaughn (2008, 127), Rio Grande pottery had a metallic, shiny luster because it was glazed with lead compounds. The most easily smelted of these is galena, a lead sulfide mineral frequently associated with silver in geological deposits. Thus, according to the most straightforward interpretation, advanced by archaeologist Albert Schroeder (1979, 250), the jars of "shiny metal" were filled with galena. Since galena can be a sign of silver deposits, Castañeda seems justified in his inference that valuable material might be found in the vicinity (if Coronado's expedition had paid attention to minerals and ores).

These explorations have fascinating ramifications, because Castañeda insisted, twenty years later, that mineral riches lay just beyond the regions that Coronado's expedition actually explored. Indeed, the entire Sonora/ Arizona/New Mexico region contains significant gold and silver ore deposits. The problem was the get-rich-quick motivation of capitalist ventures. Coronado's troops failed to recognize their opportunity because they sought Tenochtitlan-style gold and silver artifacts that they could ship back to Mexico to pay off their investors and acquire short-term riches for themselves.

Since Coronado himself was expected soon, Capt. Tristán de Arellano, the captain who'd been left in charge of Corazones back in 1540, set out to Cicuye/Cicuyc/Cicuique/Pecos to welcome him. The residents came out ready for a fight. Castañeda says that Arellano responded by killing two important men and "several" other people.

Coronado finally returned to Tiguex in September 1541.

Describing this period, Castañeda buttresses his case for undiscovered riches with another intriguing story. With Arellano was the young Indian named Xabe who had been "provided" to the army by Bigotes and the governor at Cicuye/Cicuyc/Cicuique/Pecos before the departure for Quivira: "When [Xabe] was aware that the general was coming he . . . was pleased. He said, 'Now that the general is coming, you will see that in Quivira there are gold and silver, although not as much as El Turco said.' When the general arrived and [Xabe] understood that [they] had found nothing, he became sad and dumbfounded, insisting, in such a way that he convinced many [people], that [this result was merely] because the general had not penetrated the land farther into the interior" (translation in Flint and Flint 2005, 413–14). Xabe claimed that the expedition's failure was merely because the late-summer rainy season was beginning, and Coronado had been too timid to pursue the populated lands beyond Quivira. Castañeda agreed. He says that even Coronado wanted to gather the entire army and explore beyond Kansas once the winter was over.

Belief in treasure beyond Quivira may have been widespread. Castañeda claims that Coronado had received "news of great settlements and . . . powerful rivers, and that the land was very similar to that of Spain in its fruits, grasses, and weather. Further, the travelers to Quivira were not content to think there was no gold. They suspected that treasure lay in the land farther into the interior, since [the Indians] did not deny it and understood what [gold] was, and [even] had a name for it—'acochis.'" (This was the name used by El Turco; the quotes are abridged from the translation by Flint and Flint 2005, 414).

According to Castañeda, grumbling about the failure to find distant gold began during the winter of 1541–42. Meanwhile, he says, the most noble-born members of the expedition appropriated the warmest clothing and arranged the least work for themselves. In response, Coronado made a grand announcement that when the weather warmed, the expedition would return to Quivira and find the rich lands beyond it. Castañeda, in a reflective mood, wrote that

> nothing in this life is under the control of humans. It's under the direction of almighty God. His will was that our plans did not come to fruition. On a day of celebration of the new plan, the general went out to enjoy himself on horseback, as he was in the habit of doing. He was on a strong horse, and his aides had put on a new cinch which, with the passage of time, must have been rotten. While he raced alongside Captain Rodrigo Maldonado, it burst, and the general fell toward Rodrigo, who ran over him. The horse struck him in the head with its hoof. The general came to the brink of death from this blow. His convalescence was long and fearful. (adapted from Flint and Flint 2005, 425)

A Radical Change in Plan: ca. March 1542

While Coronado was bedridden, things went from bad to worse. Coronado, now about thirty-two years old, may have had some personality change as the result of the fall. He seemed more prone to discouragement. Feeding this, the news was not good. Ever-reliable Cárdenas had been sent back down the trail to the San Gerónimo III garrison, located in the lost valley of Suya. He returned with the horrifying news that San Gerónimo had been destroyed, "and the people, horses, and livestock were dead." This news was so bad that no one wanted to tell Coronado. When he began to recover, they passed on the news, and he had a relapse. He spoke about an astrologer friend back in Salamanca who had predicted that he'd be important in some foreign land but would have a fall from which he could not recover. From that point on, his thoughts were dominated by a return to Mexico and his family, namely, his eighteen-year-old wife, Beatriz, to whom he'd been married only three years when he left in 1540, and the two children they'd had before he left. (A third had died.)

Castañeda gives a confused account of what happened next. Coronado apparently pretended to plan the return to Quivira while at the same time sending trusted intimates to collect signatures from some of the caballeros (high-ranking horsemen), saying that they preferred to return to Mexico. As soon as enough signatures were available, Coronado announced that the expedition must give up on Quivira and return home since the caballeros wanted it, and since they had found neither wealth nor the right kinds of lands to divide among the soldiers as encomiendas, the baronial estates given to conquerors of new lands.

The announcement caused consternation among the expeditionaries. Many critics said Coronado's behavior was duplicitous, so that some caballeros tried to rescind or physically retrieve their signatures. Coronado, in response, sequestered himself in his quarters, pretending (according to Castañeda) that his condition was worse, hiding the signed documents, and posting guards. At one point, Coronado's trunk was stolen. Some said the signatures had been recovered, but others said Coronado had kept them hidden under his mattress. Either way, the retreat was still on.

Some of the caballeros now petitioned Coronado to consider alternatives. What about letting seventy chosen men stay in Tiguex to hold the land until Viceroy Mendoza could either send reinforcements or confirm the abandonment? Or perhaps the main part of the expedition could stay, and Coronado could take his own choice of seventy men back to Mexico. Other troopers balked at both of these plans, however, since Coronado's announcement had set them dreaming of home. Many warned of conflict over command if Coronado's plan was disobeyed. Coronado stuck to his plan. They would depart on 1 April 1542. The caballeros gave in, but from then on, says Castañeda, they disavowed Coronado's leadership.

Brave (or Foolhardy?) Priests: April 1542

Seeing the collapse of the expedition, two priests chose to stay in the new lands with their assistants to pursue the grand goal of converting the Native

Americans, thus facilitating the Second Coming of Jesus of Nazareth. Fray Juan de Padilla wanted to go all the way to Quivira to pursue conversions, and Fray Luis, a lay brother, proposed to go as far as Pecos. Coronado agreed and sent a detachment to take them back as far as Pecos.

Fray Luis arrived at Pecos, but some days later, before Coronado left New Mexico, Luis reported that the Pecos elders were abandoning him, and he predicted that he'd eventually be killed. Castañeda, writing twenty years later, reported that "nothing has been learned about him to this day," but he speculated that Luis was safe, because "the people of that area are merciful, keep their pledge, and maintain loyalty to their friends." Castañeda also tells Juan de Padilla's story:

> Fray Padilla stayed in Quivira, along with a Portuguese Spaniard, a Black, a *mestizo*, and certain Indians from Nueva España. The people of Quivira eventually killed him because he wanted to go to a *provincia* populated by their enemies. Indian allies from Nueva España buried the friar with the consent of his murderers. The Spaniard escaped on a mare, and the allies who buried Padilla also fled and caught up with him. They all reached safety in Nueva España, by way of Pánuco. Fray Padilla died truly a martyr, since his devotion was holy and complete. (abridged from the translation in Flint and Flint 2005, 423–24, 427)

As the army left Tiguex, Coronado freed the Indians who had been taken from that area as servants and slaves. Castañeda felt that "this was incorrect, because it would have been better for them to have been educated among the Christians."

Coronado brightened as the expedition retraced their trail through Cíbola toward Chichilticale and the Río Sonora valley. Natives from Cíbola followed along for two or three days, picking up cast-off baggage and urging the Spaniards' servants to abandon the expedition and stay with them. Some of the Mexican allies did so, and Castañeda indicates they were desirable as interpreters for Cíbola. This observation, that natives of one province would engage natives of other provinces as interpreters, clarifies how a network of interpreters allowed prehistoric travelers to communicate from one province to another.

Help Is on the Way: Spring 1542

Unbeknownst to Coronado and his troops, reinforcements were heading north under Capt. Juan Gallego, the messenger who had been sent south from Cíbola in 1540 with Marcos and Díaz. Gallego had delivered messages to Viceroy Mendoza, who sent him back with a small party to support Coronado. On the way, Gallego had his own adventures. Castañeda recounts them in conquistadorial terms:

> Captain Juan Gallego left Culiacán with only 22 Spaniards [and non-Spanish allies and servants]. The party traveled north for 200 leagues [to the mid–Río Sonora]. That province had turned into a land of war. People who had originally been on good terms with Coronado were now up in arms due to the outrages by the San Gerónimo settlers. Along the way, Gallego had gathered as many San Gerónimo many refugees as he could.
>
> Nearly every day Gallego's band skirmished with the enemies. Gallego would leave the baggage behind with two thirds of his people, and then lead the advance guard with six or seven Spaniards—without any of the Indian allies. They entered the native towns by force, killing, laying waste, setting fires. They attacked so suddenly and with such speed and boldness, that the Indians had no opportunity to come together or understand what had befallen them.
>
> As a result, not one town dared wait for them to appear. Instead, the Indians [presumably along the Río Sonora] fled from the seven-member advance guard as if from a powerful armed force. The Spaniards struck for 10 days through the settled land without having an hour's rest. When the baggage handlers arrived with all the rest of the troop, they had nothing to do except despoil those whom the advance guard had already killed, as well as whatever locals they were able to catch. This was especially true in that area where the *villa* of San Gerónimo had been. There, they killed and hung a considerable number of people in punishment for their rebellion. (this and the next two Castañeda passages are adapted and abridged from the translation by Flint and Flint 2005, 431)

Notice that, as usual, when local populations reacted against rape and exploitation, the Spaniards called it "rebellion." It's easy to find language that will categorize your opponent (or victim) as an evildoer. Gallego's savagery was probably encouraged by the members of his party who had barely escaped the final, bloody night at San Gerónimo III. Castañeda seems more enthralled than repulsed by this carnage.

In all of this Gallego did not lose a single companion, though one was wounded. He was tearing a hide from an Indian who was nearly dead, when that man turned and wounded him in the eyelid with the natives' poisonous herb. He would have died, except that he was treated with quince juice. Even then, he lost the eye.

Such were the mighty deeds [of Gallego's troops], that they will live in memory for as long as the participants are alive. Four or five Indian allies, especially, who came with them from Los Corazones, were so amazed that they considered the deeds as supernatural, rather than human. If our own south-traveling party had not run into Gallego and his company, Gallego would surely have charged all the way to Quivira, judging by his excellent leadership, and by how well trained and practiced his troops were in warfare. That was their intended destination.

Two days south of Chichilticale (see map 12), Gallego's northbound blitzkrieg met the southbound dejected army. Gallego's men, enraptured by their treasure-seeking adventure, were shocked to find Coronado abandoning the northern lands. Coronado's rebellious caballero faction thus found allies among Gallego's troops and instigated a new round of dissent, some of which Castañeda called seditious. Gallego's group included "mutineers" who had rebelled against Alcaráz's corrupt management of San Gerónimo III in Suya and had saved their own lives by escaping *before* the garrison was overrun. Agitators argued that the whole army should return to the North and find the treasures that waited for them in the heartland of the new continent. As a compromise, they offered to reestablish San Gerónimo with a large force and occupy it until Viceroy Mendoza issued new instructions.

In the end, however, the Coronado troops and Gallego's group headed south on a miserable march across Sonora, the troops completely polarized. The caballero faction openly disobeyed Coronado, who withdrew into seclusion (exaggerating his illness, according to Castañeda) and who traveled with guards to protect him from some of his own officers.

To make matters worse, the natives of central Sonora were hostile because of the outrages committed by Alcaráz and his men at San Gerónimo II and III and then by Gallego's men. Skirmishes and ambushes occurred nearly every day. Castañeda describes daily cries of pain, "some from Indians, some from wounded Spaniards, and some from dying horses."

As mentioned in the sidebar "Where Was Suya?" in chapter 10, about San Gerónimo III, the returning army probably detoured around the bellicose Río Sonora villages, moving one valley to the east (maps 9 and 12). There, in the Río Moctezuma valley, they passed the ruins of San Gerónimo III at Suya. This would explain why Castañeda witnessed "negotiations about establishing a settlement somewhere around there." Hostilities continued, since they were passing Cumpas, where some of Alcaráz's outrages had occurred. Castañeda says the cries of pain continued until they reached Batuco, which lies at the south end of the Río Moctezuma, where it joins the Río Yaqui. Now, finally, they were past the worst of the fighting. As described in chapter 10, their old friends from Corazones came for a visit (see map 9). Did they sense defeat among the Europeans? We don't know. The Spaniards headed on down the Río Yaqui toward New Spain and home. The expedition continued to fall apart, even as it crossed the Guzman/Spanish frontier.

When the conquistadors finally entered the valley of Culiacán, the residents came out to welcome their injured governor, and Coronado happily rushed ahead toward his own home and hearth, 25 or 30 miles farther on. The majority of the troops halted, however, to consider their own futures.

Once established on his own turf, Coronado adopted his role as governor and wooed his officers with meat and other food supplies from Culiacán. At the same time, according to Castañeda, he also "made a show of being incapacitated and taking to bed" in order to create a private setting where he could talk with selected men. His goal was to convince the troops to follow him back to Mexico City. Many of the expeditionaries, however, bailed out in Culiacán, perhaps fearing a reputation as failures.

Coronado and the remaining party set off to Mexico City from Culiacán at the end of June 1542 in bad weather as the rainy season began. His health was so poor that he had to be carried on a litter part of the way, though he was able to ride partway on a gentle horse. More troopers bailed out in towns along the way.

Coronado finally arrived in Mexico City, probably in the late summer of 1542, reporting to the viceroy with fewer than one hundred of the four hundred or so Spanish compatriots who had joyously launched the expedition from Compostela two years earlier. Castañeda says Coronado was "not very cordially welcomed" by Mendoza, who, as investor as well as viceroy, was understandably irritated at the outcome. Coronado's reputation sank. Still, as noted by Bolton (1949, 352–53), a continuing Coronado/Mendoza alliance was soon indicated when Coronado was invited to Mendoza's palace for his sister's wedding. Coronado attended. In the next years, the two men strongly defended each other in the later judicial reviews of their performance in their two offices.

After a month or two of rest in Mexico City, Coronado resumed his governorship of the northwestern province, Nueva Galicia. With doña Beatriz and their two daughters he moved to headquarters in Guadalajara, now grander than Compostela. He continued his duties for two years, settling local squabbles, dealing with occasional Indian unrest, and, as Bolton reports, "promoting public works and playing cards with his friends" (1949, 363–64). Within some months, the legal system began to take up his "performance review" as captain general of the expedition and also as governor of Nueva Galicia. We'll see the outcome shortly.

Operatic Doings in Mexico City: 1542

Cortés, still trying to get the king's attention in Spain, was now a minor part of the Mexican political picture, but his long arm reached back across the ocean to another 1542 wedding that connects many of the players in our earlier chapters.

An eighteenth-century opera librettist could hardly have produced a more melodramatic story. Recall that Marina, Cortés's translator and mistress and mother of his first son, had been married off by Cortés in 1524 to one of his officers, Juan Jaramillo. Juan and Marina had a daughter, María, in 1526. The bride in the 1542 marriage was none other than this now-sixteen-year-old daughter of Cortés's onetime lover. The groom was a nephew of Cortés's archenemy, Viceroy Antonio Mendoza! The wealthy nephew was named Luis de Quesada, and he had recently returned from the Coronado expedition.

A brilliant match, but that's just the first act.

In the second act, the young couple began legal proceedings in 1542 against María's own father, Juan Jaramillo, Cortés's onetime officer, on the grounds that Jaramillo planned to bequeath only a third of his estate to young María and the other two-thirds to his second, post-Marina wife. The legal argument alleged that Cortés, back in 1524, had given lands to Marina and Juan Jaramillo as part of their sudden marriage settlement and, furthermore, that Jaramillo had had no other children; therefore, the inheritance should pass to María.

But wait! The third act gets still more twisty. As recounted by Marina's biographer (Lanyon 1999, 161–62), Cortés, in Spain, produced a legal brief against Luis and María, stating that their marriage was clouded because Mendoza's young nephew had not courted Marina's daughter properly but had climbed the walls of Jaramillo's estate and—oh, romantic escapade!—abducted María (who seems to have been a willing abductee). In Cortés's version of the story, so many outrages followed between Luis and María that María was forced to marry the young scoundrel against the wishes of her father, Cortés's own trusted officer, Juan Jaramillo, who was now the object of her lawsuit!

The story was recorded in typical bureaucratic Spanish style as part of the legal proceedings. Perhaps it was all true. On the other hand, the abduction seems to have been reported primarily by Cortés. Perhaps it was yet another attempt by ever-competitive Cortés to discredit the family of Viceroy Mendoza. Lanyon (1999, 168) goes so far as to suggest that María might have been Cortés's own daughter, not Jaramillo's, thus explaining Jaramillo's seeming lack of regard for her. As I say, the opera has yet to be written.

The outcome of the lawsuit appears to be uncertain, but it was too late to be historically relevant. Mendoza was now the "winner" in the ill-fated race to conquer the North.

A Mysterious Expedition: Juan Cabrillo Discovers the Coast of California, 1542–1543

Early explorations in California tie together some of our other characters. A naval captain named João Rodrigues Cabrillo, probably born in Portugal and better known by the Spanish form of his name, Juan, seems to have been part of the 1520 expedition in which Pánfilo de Narváez tried to attack Cortés in Mexico (losing an eye for his trouble and then going on to invade Florida with Cabeza de Vaca in tow). Cabrillo survived the skirmish with Cortés and apparently participated in the follow-up conquest of lands that comprise Guatemala, El Salvador, and Nicaragua. He may have served briefly as a governor in Guatemala. June 1542 found him departing from a Mexican port to extend Ulloa's explorations of the California coastline. It's believed that he entered the bays of San Diego and Monterey but died of complications after breaking a leg during one of the landings.

Cabrillo is often categorized as the "discoverer of California," but Coronado's officer Melchior Díaz had already entered southeastern California in the last days of 1540 or the first days of 1541 on his fateful journey in search of Alarcón's ships.

The Decline of Cortés: 1542–1547

Cortés, the great conqueror, never returned to his New World. He'd written a unique chapter in human history, overseeing the violent first merger of urban civilizations from the eastern and western branches of humanity, but like many a celebrity, he was never able to recapture his youthful days of glory.

History marched on, and Cortés's battle to gain title to the North became moot. After a few years in Spain, he planned a return to the gardens of Tenochtitlan as the respected marqués del Valle de Oaxaca (Lanyon 2004, 88), but he fell ill in Seville and died near there in December 1547.

He left a fascinating will. It pays off various loans, makes provisions for his progeny, and then endows hospitals in Mexico and civic buildings in Coyoacán. Buried in the will is a less predictable item, numbered XXXIX. It expresses concern about the ownership of slaves: "Because there have been many doubts and opinions as to whether it is permitted with good conscience to hold the natives as slaves, whether as captives of war or by purchase, and because this has not as yet been determined, I direct my son and successor Don Martín, and those who may follow him, to use all diligence to settle this point for the peace of my conscience and theirs" (MacNutt 1908; Lanyon 2004, 91, 93).

In an interesting twist, the final version of the will disinherited Cortés's second, legitimate son. The second Martín would have become the new marqués del Valle de Oaxaca but apparently showed signs of becoming a playboy.

How strange Cortés's last months must have been! The man who had conquered an empire was hardly even recognized in Spain. His dreams must have been haunted by the fantastic scenes that the humdrum people around him could never imagine: now-vanished palaces and pyramids; the bustling Tenochtitlan market; the enigmatic emperor Motezuma, murdered while Cortés's prisoner; and Marina, his lover and aide with whom he produced his beloved first son, Mexico's first known mestizo, the child whose DNA, after at least 100,000 years, reunited the "western" and "eastern" halves of the human species.*

The Trial of Coronado: 1544–1546

A common practice in New Spain, mentioned above, was a legal hearing to assess the actions of high officials. In Coronado's case, the issues included possible mistreatment of northern peoples during the expedition as well as a review of his performance as governor of Nueva Galicia. The case was

---

* Or had this blessed molecular event already happened, unrecorded, between the Vikings and "Skraelings" in Greenland or Vinland/Newfoundland around A.D. 1000?

taken up in 1544 and is described in numerous documents translated by Richard Flint (2002). A judge from the royal audiencia of Mexico, Lorenzo de Tejada, acted as a kind of special prosecutor and took testimony. By this point, Coronado seemed a figure of pathos, though he was only thirty-four or thirty-five years old, according to his estimated birth date. In February 1545 he was called back to Mexico City and ordered to remain there under a kind of loose house arrest. His family came with him. That March, Judge Tejada wrote to the king that Coronado was more fit to be governed than to govern, because he was not the same man who left on the great expedition: "They say this change was caused by the fall from a horse." These years had clearly been hard on Coronado, but one wonders: Was this an early example of the tendency for accused high officials to be conveniently ill as they come to trial? As noted by Richard Flint (2002), the testimony of army members at the trial seems full of convenient lapses of memory. In February 1546 the judges essentially acquitted Coronado of the charges. He then spent the late 1540s still restricted to Mexico City but serving on the city council. In 1547 he testified on Mendoza's behalf during Mendoza's legal review. By 1553, still in poor health, Coronado was allowed to move out of Mexico City to retire in a more healthful spot in the country, but he lived only for another year.

Coronado had been acquitted in the 1546 trial, but that trial left it clear that violence against Native Americans had occurred and that it should be punished as a warning to future conquistadors. Capt. García López de Cárdenas, the very man who saved Coronado's life during the battle at Cíbola, discovered the Grand Canyon, and lined up Puebloans at Albuquerque to be burned at the stake for "revolting" after a Puebloan woman had been raped, took the fall. Still, his sentence was moderate. He was ordered to serve in the army for thirty more months, banished from the Indies for ten years, and required to pay a fine of eight hundred gold ducats to be used to finance religious and charitable works.

Most of the other expeditionaries who returned to Mexico slipped back into normal lives with varying degrees of obscurity. The Flints tracked down historical records of many of them in Mexico City, Seville, and Culiacán. In Bolton's words, many of the officers, as after most wars, "spent the rest of their lives begging the government for pensions or other rewards for their services" (1949, 353).

CHAPTER TWELVE

Aftermath

How can we sum up the adventures and misadventures of the colorful characters we've met: Hernán Cortés, Motezuma, Marina, Álvar Núñez Cabeza de Vaca, Marcos de Niza, Estevan de Dorantes, Francisco Vázquez de Coronado, and Antonio Mendoza? For a start, let's wrap up some loose ends by summarizing what became of them.

The End of a Generation

Many members of that generation died around the 1550s. Cortés died in 1547, Andrés Dorantes in the 1550s, Mendoza (and possibly Marina) in 1552, Ulloa in 1553 or shortly before that, Coronado in 1554, Cabeza de Vaca in 1556, and Marcos de Niza in 1558. It's as if history itself wanted to sweep away the whole dramatic era of unbridled conquest and begin a new, more prosaic story of colonization, urbanization, and cultural assimilation.

The following obituarial postscripts provide selected details about these and other players in alphabetical order:

Alarcón, Hernando: Birth year uncertain. Surprisingly little is known about this discoverer and first explorer of the Colorado River. The year of his death is also uncertain.

Alvarado, Pedro de: Born ca. 1485. Cortés's officer who slaughtered Aztecs in Mexico City in 1520, ruining the chance of rapprochement between the

Aztecs and Spain. Competed with Pizarro in the 1530s for the gold of Peru. Officially honored later as the "conqueror" and governor of Honduras and Guatemala. Died in 1541, crushed accidentally by a horse in Michoacán. His remains were later interred with official respect in 1568 in the cathedral at Antigua, Guatemala.

Cabeza de Vaca, Álvar Núñez: Born ca. 1490. Survivor of the ill-fated Narváez expedition to Florida. Returned to Spain in 1537 to request a grant to explore Florida but instead was commissioned to develop a colony at Buenos Aires. Served as governor of a region in Argentina and Paraguay about 1540 to 1544. After political wrangles with a competitor, he was arrested for poor administration and jailed in Spain in 1545. A trial dragged on until 1551. Wrote a famous memoir of his journey across America, published in various editions between 1542 and 1555. Released from jail but died in poverty and obscurity around 1556 (*Encyclopedia Britannica*; Bolton 1949, 406–7).

Castañeda, Pedro de: Born ca. 1515. Wrote the most extensive memoir of the Coronado expedition. Settled in Culiacán after the expedition and wrote his account in the early 1560s in support of a proposed new expedition to the North. The new expedition did not materialize, but he continued to believe that riches in the North had been lost by a timid, premature end to the expedition. He apparently died in obscurity at some unknown time after 1566 (Flint and Flint 2005, 378–79).

Coronado, Francisco Vázquez de: Born ca. 1510, according to his biographer, Herbert Bolton. Explorer of North America from Sonora to Kansas between 1540 and 1542. In spite of failing health, he was active in government affairs for the next decade. Charged with crimes against Native Americans during the expedition but acquitted. Died in September 1554. He was buried in a church called Santo Domingo a few blocks north of the main cathedral in Mexico City, and his wife, Beatriz, was later buried with him. Bolton reported that the location of the crypt was rediscovered by "a Kansas country editor and a Mexico City building contractor" apparently in the 1940s (1949, 405). However, according to investigations by Richard and Shirley Flint (private communication, October 2011), the church was moved twice since Coronado's death, and, according to the Flints' information, bones from the crypts were also moved and reburied en masse, probably at least hundreds of feet from the original location, so that the precise Coronado burial site is now unknown.

Cortés, Hernan: Born ca. 1484. Invader of Tenochtitlan, his reputation was tarnished by the loss (or his own theft?) of much of the reported Aztec gold and the destruction of the city as he recaptured it. Less widely known are his explorations of the Gulf of California (or Sea of Cortés). Chafing under rules set by Viceroy Mendoza, he returned to Spain in 1540 to seek royal support for stronger claims to Mexico but died in the obscure village of Castillejo de la Cuestra, near Seville, in the last weeks of 1547. His body was interred in Seville, then moved to Mexico, but it was subsequently moved several times and even hidden and temporarily lost, partly due to threats of desecration by political factions seeking revenge for the conquest. The bones are reportedly now in the National Institute for Anthropology and History in Mexico City. As recently as 1981, according to Wikipedia and other web-based sources, there was a politically motivated attempt to destroy the bones.

Díaz, Bernal: Born 1492. Served with Cortés during the conquest of Mexico and, as a reward, became governor of the city now called Antigua in Guatemala. Author of a still-in-print eyewitness memoir of the conquest of Tenochtitlan. Reportedly died in 1585 and is interred in the cathedral of Antigua. Ironically, his remains lie near those of Pedro de Alvarado, whom he criticized as the destroyer of the possibility of rapprochement between the Aztecs and the Spanish invaders.

Dorantes, Andrés: Birth date uncertain; probably ca. 1508. Survivor of the ill-fated Narváez expedition to Florida. Turned down Mendoza's request to lead an expedition north in 1537. Returned to Spain. He is said to have married well, lived prosperously, and is thought to have died in the 1550s.

Estevan (aka Estevan de Dorantes, Estevan the Moor): Born in Africa, probably Morocco, year uncertain. A servant of Andrés Dorantes, he survived the trek with Cabeza de Vaca and was chosen to guide Marcos de Niza to the northern lands. He reached Cíbola before Marcos but was killed by the Cíbolans in 1539 possibly because of reported transgressions against Indian women on the way, and/or because of the Cíbolan desire to prevent him from reporting information about Cíbola to additional Spaniards.

Estrada, Beatriz de: Born 1524 or 1525. Wealthy daughter of the former royal treasurer, married to Coronado in 1537 when she was about thirteen. She and Francisco supplied major funding for the Coronado expedition. Died 1590 (Shirley Cushing Flint 2013; and private communication).

Jaramillo, Juan: Born 1510. Important chronicler and participant in the Coronado expedition. Married and lived in Mexico City after the expedition. Probably in the 1560s, he wrote one of the best accounts of the Coronado expedition. Died at an uncertain time after 1578 (see Flint and Flint 2005, 508, 694, footnote 2).

Marcos de Niza: Born ca. 1495(?). Reportedly orphaned, grew up in Nice, France, and arrived as a Franciscan priest in Mexico City probably in 1535 or 1536. Remarkable for his connections with all three major conquests of the Americas; he was involved with Cortés after the Aztec conquest, served in Peru and criticized Pizarro's Inca conquest, first reported the seven cities of Cíbola in 1539, guiding the Coronado expedition there in 1540. Once expected to become second bishop of Mexico, he returned from Cíbola to Mexico City in disgrace in late 1540, blamed by his contemporaries for the failure of the Coronado expedition. He disappeared from public life but resurfaced in historical records now and then. Wagner (1934, 225) reproduces a plaintive letter that Marcos wrote to Bishop Zumárraga in 1546. As for his location, Marcos says: "On account of having left the hot country my health has become very bad. On this account the padre provincial orders me to return to it at Zuchimilco" (presumably Xochimilco; see fig. 2). Marcos became a celebrity of Mexico City and was the first European to write about Cíbola. He went on to say, "I, an orphan, have no father and mother, friend nor refuge except your lordship." He petitioned Bishop Zumárraga for "a donation of a little wine. I am in great need of it, because my illness is a lack of blood and natural heat" (Wagner 1934, 225).

Zumárraga supplied the wine, but Marcos's health declined. By the 1550s he was reported by the early historian Mendieta to be living in Jalapa, a warmer town near the coast, inland from Veracruz, "crippled by the hardships through which he had passed" (Wagner 1934, 225). In his remarkable life, he traveled the world from Nice to Mexico City, Peru, and Cíbola, but he died in obscurity. Wagner cites Mendieta's account: "Thinking that the hour of his death was drawing near he was taken to Mexico [City—WKH] to be interred with the ancient holy ones" (1934, 225). Another early source says that Marcos died on 25 March 1558 (Wagner 1934, 225).

Marina (aka Malinche): Born ca. 1500(?). Translator, confidante, and lover of Cortés during and after the conquest of Tenochtitlan. Mother of Cortés's first son, Martín, the first known mestizo. Married in 1524 (at the instigation of Cortés) to a soldier, Juan Jaramillo (not the same man as the later Coronado chronicler). She was well liked by Cortés's troops and well respected in Mexico City in her later life. It's unclear whether she died at a young age, ca. 1528 or 1529, or as late as 1552 (Lanyon 1999, 220).

Mendoza, Antonio: Born 1490 or 1491. Viceroy of Mexico, 1535–1551. Appointed viceroy of Peru in 1551, went there, and died in Lima in July 1552. He was buried in the main cathedral of Lima, next to Francisco Pizarro (Flint and Flint 2005, 89; Bolton 1949, 406).

Motezuma (Motezuma II): Birth date is estimated to be between 1466 and 1470. Succeeded his uncle as emperor in 1502 at the height of the Mexican (Aztec) empire. Hesitated about how to respond to Cortés's march toward Tenochtitlan. "Befriended" Cortés, but was assassinated in late June 1520 either by his own disgruntled people or by Cortés's troops.

Pizarro, Francisco: Born in the 1470s. He was a distant cousin of Cortés. Poorly educated and illiterate, he arrived in the New World in 1509. After unsuccessful expeditions to Peru in the 1520s, he went back in 1530 and attacked the gold-rich Inca Empire. He captured the leader, Atahualpa, in 1532, executed him in 1533, and was known for other outrages against the Peruvians. He was assassinated by rival Spaniards in 1541 and buried with honor in the Lima cathedral.

Ulloa, Francisco de: Born ca. 1500(?), arrived in Mexico 1528. Naval captain for Cortés. Led the first party to reach the mouth of the Colorado River, but did not fully recognize its nature. Proved that Baja California is a peninsula. Moved to Peru and died in 1553 or sometime before that (Flint and Flint 2005, 652). According to apocryphal web-based sources, he was stabbed by a sailor.

Zumárraga, Bishop Juan de: Born 1468. Bishop of Mexico City, 1528–48. Backed Marcos de Niza and the Coronado expedition. Known as a protector of the Indians, sponsor of schools for young native men and women, and sponsor of the first printing press in the New World. In 1546 the pope decreed Mexico as a jurisdiction independent from Seville and appointed Zumárraga as the first archbishop of Mexico, but Zumárraga died in 1548, weeks before the appointment could take effect (Bolton 1949, 407; *Catholic Encyclopedia* online edition, 2012).

These capsule biographies remind us that, to paraphrase Shakespeare, we're all players who strut and fret our hour on the stage and then are heard no more. It does not take much cynicism to make a case that respect in later life did not correlate with these individuals' actual contributions to the "big picture" of history. Those who gave us beautiful literary accounts of that era or otherwise tried to serve longer-term ideals—Bernal Díaz, Cabeza de Vaca, Castañeda, and Marcos de Niza—tended to die in obscurity. Those who acquired the most wealth and transferred it to their own ethnic group (Spain)—Cortés, Alvarado, and Pizarro—died as heroes within their flawed cultural framework and were buried in elaborate crypts.

Were Riches Missed in the Northern Lands?: The View from the 1550s

One of the fascinations of the Coronado expedition is that some participants returned to Mexico still convinced that treasures lay north or east of Tiguex or even beyond Quivira (map 14). Pedro de Castañeda, writing some twenty years later, opened his memoir with a poignant prologue:

> When we have something precious within our grasp, we don't value it. However, when we've lost it and need its benefits, then we have great pain in our hearts, and imagine other outcomes, searching for ways we might recover it. It seems to me this happened to all or most of those who went on the expedition. Although they didn't find the wealth of which they had been told, they did find the beginning of a good land to settle and they had the wherewithal to search for riches that lay within their grasp. Today, their hearts weep because they lost the opportunity of a lifetime. Some of them would today be happy to go back, in order to explore farther, so as to recover what was lost. (abridged and adapted from the translation by Flint and Flint 2005, 385–86)

In Castañeda's view, they would have succeeded if only they had looked harder for the riches of what he called "Greater India" and East Asia. Flint and Flint comment that Castañeda spent his later years living a difficult life in hardscrabble, frontier Culiacán, yearning for "the prosperous life that might have been" (2005, 379).

Other wildcat expeditions took up his challenge and headed north in the later 1500s. They left poor documentation but may have left their own Spanish artifacts along the way. Chapter 5 describes the 1556 expedition by Ibarra, Obregón, and their troops, who followed part of Coronado's route through Sonora and apparently reached the impressive ruins now known as Casas Grandes in Chihuahua. Chapter 11 describes the expedition of Francisco Leyva and Gutiérrez de Jumana, which reached Quivira in 1593 or 1594, only to lose most of its members in conflict with the Quivirans, thus leaving artifacts in Kansas. The fact that expeditions as much as fifty years later could easily find sites that had been visited by earlier Spaniards testifies that the Native American trail networks persisted and knowledgeable guides could be found.

During those later decades, however, the Europeans' emphasis shifted from the ancient Cíbola trade route through Sonora and Arizona to an eastern route through Chihuahua and north along the Rio Grande into central New Mexico. Around 1598 Juan de Oñate followed that route with a group of colonists, claiming what is now northern New Mexico for Spain and establishing the province of Santa Fe (originally Santa Fé, meaning "Sacred Faith"). Here, recently arrived official Pedro de Peralta, about twenty-six years old, founded the town Santa Fe as the new capital of the province in 1610. That city remains the earliest continuously inhabited state capital in the United States.

What Can Be Learned?: The View from the Twenty-First Century

Many ruminations follow from our still-emerging knowledge of American exploration in the 1500s. One thought, perhaps encouraging, is that even when a given generation is largely forgotten, historians can enter the picture centuries later, identify episodes of long-term interest, and recover their story. Thanks to many dozens of sleuths—amateur, professional, and in-between—knowledge of the Coronado era has expanded from near zero in 1800 to discoveries of actual campsites and routes today.

That process allows practical application of the observation by George Santayana (who, interestingly, was Spanish). Those who cannot remember the past, he said, are condemned to repeat it. To take one example from the Spanish story, we see repeated later examples that sincere patriotism and/ or sincere religious zeal is not necessarily correlated with good behavior or a better life among human beings. Belief in nationalistic, religious, or ideological exceptionalism, once out of control, easily morphs into excuses for oppression, murder, warfare, and mass misery, with disruption of families and societies. Examples abound throughout history, whether Spanish operations in Mexico and New Mexico or the more recent examples: Nazi obsession with racial exceptionalism; Soviet Communist Marxism as the one true exceptionalist economic theory; fundamentalist views of Islam and Christianity as exceptionalist religions. In our era, the negative consequences of ethnoideological exceptionalism are dismissed by apologists as "collateral damage." We humans, it seems, need to be constantly on guard: religio-political theories, ideologies, and economic models have not been adequate to replace empirical knowledge and practical problem solving. The subject, of course, is a touchy one.

A less-touchy application utilizes the eyewitness accounts of what I call "the last day of prehistory" to clarify prehistoric life, and perhaps even prehistoric influences on our own time. I'm struck by the disconnect between contemporary archaeologists' literature on protohistoric sites from the 1400s to the 1500s and the eyewitnesses' down-to-earth accounts of how those people actually lived. I'm happy to count myself as an academic scholar, but I sense that our generation has wandered into a detached land of academic semantic games, far removed from actual ancient life as perceived by those who lived it. We twenty-first-century scholars seem to feel that we can't experience reality without transforming it into barely testable "models," theoretical constructs, and fancy language. A respected book, which I quoted earlier, concludes with paragraphs containing the following prose (here I beg the reader's permission to criticize the paradigm, not the person).

> Freedom, agency, and equality were transformed or "corrupted" into the inequalities of subalterity and *"ignorancia invenciple."* But this transformation was not merely an objectification of the other that enabled the self to protect itself from a threatening difference. In other words, the posited recalcitrant alterity of the Nahua by Bautista . . . [etc., etc.]

This opaque language reflects a choice of words and style of writing now popular in some circles. But do the word choices expand the short-term or long-term human knowledge or merely obfuscate it?

Perhaps we can learn how to transform potsherds and statistics into plainer language that communicates our findings about our forerunners, and helps us all understand our unexamined underpinnings. Here's my own chapter-by-chapter review of the historical eyewitness information we've gained about the last days of prehistory in North America.

* Aztec culture: Roughly consistent, if sketchy, eyewitness descriptions, from both Mexican and Spanish sides, about basic Aztec culture, religion, language, technology. We learn, for example, of Motezuma's view of the world, and of interviews between the Mexican and Spanish

priests regarding their ideas about deities and human existence (Bernal Díaz and others, chapters 1 and 2).

* Late prehistoric life in the southwestern United States and borderlands: Eyewitness descriptions of village life and social practices in west Texas, southern New Mexico, southeastern Arizona, and Sonora (Cabeza de Vaca, chapter 3).

* Prehistoric personal life: Multiple, consistent eyewitness descriptions of Sonoran villages, including religious sacrifices, deerskin and cotton clothing, buffalo hides from Cíbola, jewelry, tattooing, sexual behavior, diets, irrigation, and names of geographic features and villages (in some cases recognizable today)—not to mention later-confirmed rumors about rudimentary metal resources in the Sierra Madre (Las Casas, chapter 3; Marcos de Niza, chapters 5, 6; Castañeda, chapter 9).

* Records of practical culture: Indications that the well-dressed people with flat-roofed "permanent" houses whom the Spaniards saw along the Río Sonora were copying styles of dress and housing that they had seen 500 miles away in the grander northern pueblos (chapter 3).

* Records of religion/science/"natural philosophy": A report that natives of the Río Sonora valley scheduled certain annual ceremonies according to calendric observations by priests in Cíbola/Zuni. Also, firsthand and secondhand accounts of Sonoran village political and religious practices: leaders addressing the people from platforms, small war temples, and animal sacrifices (Castañeda, chapters 8 and 9; Las Casas, chapter 3).

* Similar detailed descriptions of lifeways in the multistory pueblos of New Mexico in the 1500s, consistent with accounts by American ethnographers in the 1800s (chapters 5, 9, 10).

* Similar, less-detailed descriptions of village life along the Colorado River and in central Kansas (chapters 10, 11).

* Travel and trade networks: Consistent, independent eyewitness reports of Native American journeys and travel times, including weeks-old news transmitted over distances of 300 to 500 miles, including the Cíbola to Sonora and Cíbola to Yuma trade networks (Marcos de Niza, chapter 5; Coronado, chapter 9; Alarcón, chapter 10).

* Regional economic frameworks: First-person interviews about trade routes and dealings in macaw feathers, turquoise, buffalo products, cotton, and personal labor over regions covering 300 to 500 miles in Sonora, Arizona, and New Mexico, and trade-based dispersal of copper bells over distances more than 1,000 miles, as confirmed by archaeological evidence (Cabeza de Vaca, chapter 3; Marcos de Niza,

chapter 5; Castañeda, Díaz/Zaldívar, and others, chapter 9; Alarcón, chapter 10).

* Clarification of earlier prehistoric events (ca. 1300–1400): Eyewitness reports that the ruin called Chichilticale in southeastern Arizona was built by "civilized [and] warlike foreigners who had come from far away [and] who split off from Cíbola" (Castañeda, chapter 5). Archaeologists (traditionally separated into different university departments from historians) questioned who built these structures until Michael Woodson (1995) confirmed that a nearby example of these ruins had been built by northern people from the Four Corners area—just as reported four hundred years earlier by natives of southern Arizona, talking to Castañeda (Hartmann and Flint 2001).

* Clarification of human linguistic evolution: Eyewitness comments that indigenous people from one region would urge travelers to stay behind with them so as to become interpreters for future visitors. This helps to explain why prehistoric and early historic peoples could travel widely and still communicate (Castañeda, chapter 11).

Intriguingly, all these eyewitness observations were made during a period that archaeologists identify as a cultural nadir in Arizona and northern Sonora, citing low population and virtual absence of painted ceramics. If this was a prehistoric dark age, then how much richer may have been geographic awareness and culture during the 1200s and 1300s, when Indians as far north as Arizona lived in populous towns with irrigation canals, beautiful ceramic wares, and ball courts derived from the game played in southern Mexico?

A beguiling connection is that the whole period that we discuss in America (say, 1100–1550) resembles not just the biblical epoch, as discussed above, but the even earlier period in the "Fertile Crescent," four to six thousand years ago, when the roots of Mediterranean/European/American "Atlantic civilization" were established on landscapes from present-day Egypt to Iran. The early Asian roots are hard to reconstruct, but the same processes were happening in North America only four to nine hundred years ago on the soil beneath our feet. From Mexico City to New Mexico, the 1100s to 1500s were a period when scattered provinces had irrigated towns, impressive ceremonial centers, multistory stone structures (in a few cases), early attempts at written records, and stories of drama and courage to match those of the Egyptians, Sumerians, Israelites, and Greeks.

In the desert region of Arizona and Sonora, where I live, Native Americans of the last four hundred years created "calendar sticks"—wooden rods three to five feet long, an inch or two wide, divided into roughly inch-sized divisions, with odd symbols in each division. The concept was that the stick recorded historical events, and each symbol was a reminder to the original carver about a certain historical event. These meanings and stories were then passed on to the next-generation tribal guardian of the stick, who added new symbols (sometimes combining several uneventful years) and passed it on. By looking at the esoteric symbols, the keeper of the stick used it as a "quasi-written record," a memory aid to remember the events and recount the history of the community. One symbol might represent a great earthquake, another an attack by nomadic Apaches. It was not quite written language, but it was a first step, a fascinating missing link in the development of writing. Another step is seen in Mexican/Aztec "books," which recorded important events in pages of pictorial glyphs bound together. One example, discussed by Flint and Flint (2005, 169), recorded Aztec/Mexican events such as early usage of the Spaniards' metal coins (1542), discovery of a cave (1543), and a year-long pestilence (1545).

These American stories resemble primordial European and Asian stories such as those in the Old Testament—plagues, earthquakes, invasions, floods, national captivities, holy commandments. We see all the usual human foibles: hostilities, negotiations, trade, king making, empire building, complaints about alleged evils of Sodom, tribal/nationalistic exceptionalism, and great urban centers regarded with envy and contempt by provincials (think Babylon or Cíbola, Rome or Tenochtitlan). Among the resemblances are refugee migrations (from Egypt, from Aztlán), promised lands (Zion, Mexico), mighty kings (Solomon, Motezuma), animal or human sacrifices (Abraham, pyramidal temples), stupendous gods (Quetzalcoatl, Baal, Yahweh), famed banquets (Belshazzar, Corazones), urban wonders (eponymous Ur, Babylon, Cíbola), and great, tragic love affairs (David and Bathsheba, Antony and Cleopatra, Cortés and Marina).

Traces of these stories remain buried in Native American oral traditions. For better or worse, our "American Old Testament" began to be transformed into written words by the fascinating, tarnished generation from Cortés to Coronado. The conquest of Mexico by Cortés, the competition over northern lands, and the final march to Cíbola and Quivira is, like the Old Testament, a tale of extraordinary deeds by fallible human beings. It proves that we humans—whether primarily aggressive or primarily philosophic—can carry out amazing travels, adventures, discoveries, and observations, even when we are motivated by oppressive social principles or fallacious views of reality.

We can all learn from these adventures. All of us are children of history, captives of what we've absorbed from our cultures. How easily we convince ourselves to invade a foreign land in search of mythical gold, souls to be saved, lebensraum, revenge, or (less explicitly) a chance to control resources or spread our own socioeconomic system. The conquistadors repeatedly expressed shock that the Aztecs would capture enemies and sacrifice them to the Aztec gods to ensure the continuation of Earth, but the Spaniards went about their own righteous business of destroying towns and casting "rebellious" inhabitants into fire or slavery if they resisted the requerimiento's offer of rights under the Spanish medieval geopolitical framework. A bit of credit can be salvaged by the fact that scholars back in Europe debated (ineffectually?) whether the natives of the New World might be human beings like themselves.

Four centuries later, in spite of Santayana's admonition, we are still shocked—shocked!—by modern examples of cultural collision. Few of us humans, from southeast Asian prelates to Atlantic nation politicians, seem to understand why the rest of the world isn't enthralled by our own wonderful ideas about how to organize society, whether based on Islamic Sharia law or laissez-faire marketing schemes. History suggests that a few hundred years later, our descendants may not care about our burning issues. The forgotten concept that we can't seem to apply in ordinary life is that *Homo sapiens* finished spreading around the planet only within the last five to ten centuries, that a century is just a blink of the eye in terms of the collision of cultures, and that we humans are all in this together.

I grew up in the 1950s Cold War era, when we and the Russians threatened each other with mutual annihilation over ideological issues. Forty years later, since the 1990s, I've been collaborating with Russian friends on scientific projects about the ongoing exploration of our shared solar system. I have come to admire the Russians' thoughtful and dark sense of humor with which they address the most serious issues.

They asked me: "What is the difference between a realist and a dreamer?"

The answer? "The realist thinks that aliens will arrive in their flying saucers and hover over our capitals and offer to share their knowledge and technology with us and solve all our problems. This, mind you, is the realist. The dreamer thinks that maybe we can get our act together and solve our problems and do it ourselves."

Additional Reading and References

Adorno, Rolena, and Patrick Charles Pautz. 1999. *Álvar Núñez Cabeza de Vaca: His Account, His Life, and the Expedition of Pánfilo de Narváez.* 3 vols. Lincoln: University of Nebraska Press.

Aiton, Arthur Scott. 1927. *Antonio Mendoza: First Viceroy to New Spain.* Durham, NC: Duke University Press.

Anderson, Arthur J. O., and Charles E. Dibble, trans. 1978. *The War of Conquest: How It Was Waged Here in Mexico (as Given to Fr. Bernardino de Sahagún).* Salt Lake City: University of Utah Press.

Bancroft, Hubert H. 1899. *History of Arizona and New Mexico, 1530–1888.* San Francisco: History Company.

Bandelier, Adolph. (1886) 1981. *The Discovery of New Mexico by the Franciscan Monk, Friar Marcos de Niza in 1539.* Translated and edited by Madeleine Turrell Rodack. Tucson: University of Arizona Press.

———. (1890) 1976. *Investigations among the Indians of the Southwestern United States, Carried on Mainly in the Years from 1880 to 1885.* Papers of the Archaeological Institute of America, American Series III. Cambridge: Cambridge University Press. Reprint, Milwood, NY: Kraus Reprint Co.

Baptiste, Victor N. 1990. *Bartolomé de Las Casas and Thomas More's "Utopia."* Culver City, CA: Labyrinthos.

Barrett, Elinore M. 1997. "The Geography of Middle Rio Grande Pueblos Revealed by Spanish Explorers, 1540–1598." In *The Coronado Expedition to Tierra Nueva,* edited by Richard Flint and Shirley Cushing Flint, 234–48. Niwot: University Press of Colorado.

Bartlett, Katharine, and Harold S. Colton. 1940. "A Note on the Marcos de Niza Inscription near Phoenix, Arizona." *Plateau* 12(4): 53–59.

Blakeslee, Donald J. 2011. "Ysopete's Tantrum, or New Light on the Coronado Expedition's Route to the Jimmy Owens Site." In *The Latest Word from 1540: People, Places, and Portrayals of the Coronado Expedition,* edited by Richard Flint and Shirley Cushing Flint, 398–422. Albuquerque: University of New Mexico Press.

Blakeslee, Donald J., and Jay C. Blaine. 2003. "The Jimmy Owens Site: New Perspectives on the Coronado Expedition." In *The Coronado Expedition: From the Distance of 460 Years,* edited by Richard Flint and Shirley Cushing Flint, 203–18. Albuquerque: University of New Mexico Press.

Blakeslee, Donald J., Richard Flint, and Jack Hughes. 1997. "Una Barranca Grande: Recent Archaeological Evidence and a Discussion of Its Place in the Coronado Route." In *The Coronado Expedition to Tierra Nueva*, edited by Richard Flint and Shirley Cushing Flint, 370–83. Niwot: University Press of Colorado.

Bloom, Lansing B. 1940. "Who Discovered New Mexico?" *New Mexico Historical Review* 16:101, 102.

———. 1941. "Was Fray Marcos a Liar?" *New Mexico Historical Review* 16:244, 246.

Bolton, Herbert E. 1949. *Coronado: Knight of Pueblos and Plains*. Albuquerque: University of New Mexico Press.

———. 1960. *The Rim of Christendom*. New York: Russell and Russell.

Bonaventure, Oblasser. 1939. *Arizona Discovered 1539*. Pamphlet, Topawa, AZ.

Braniff, Beatriz. 1978. "Preliminary Interpretations Regarding the Role of the San Miguel River, Sonora, Mexico." In *Across the Chichimec Sea*, edited by C. Riley and B. Hedrick, 67–82. London: Feffer and Simons.

Brasher, Nugent. 2007. "The Chichilticale Camp of Francisco Vázquez de Coronado." *New Mexico Historical Review* 82:433–68.

———. 2009. "The Red House Camp and the Captain General: The 2009 Report on the Coronado Expedition Campsite of Chichilticale." *New Mexico Historical Review* 84:1–64.

———. 2011a. "The Coronado Expedition Program: A Narrative of the Search for the Captain General." In *The Latest Word from 1540: People, Places, and Portrayals of the Coronado Expedition*, edited by Richard Flint and Shirley Cushing Flint, 229–61. Albuquerque: University of New Mexico Press.

———. 2011b. "Francisco Vásquez de Coronado at Doubtful Canyon and on the Trail." *New Mexico Historical Review* 86:325–75.

Brecheisen, Dee. 2003. "Looking at a Mule She: Sixteenth-Century Spanish Artifacts in Panama." In *The Coronado Expedition: From the Distance of 460 Years*, edited by Richard Flint and Shirley Cushing Flint, 253–64. Albuquerque: University of New Mexico Press.

Brinton, Crane. (1938) 1965. *The Anatomy of Revolution*. Rev. ed. New York: Vintage Books.

Broyles, Bill, Gayle H. Hartmann, Thomas E. Sheridian, Gary Paul Nabhan, and Mary Charlotte Thurtle. 2012. *Last Water on the Devil's Highway: A Cultural and Natural History of Tinajas Altas*. Tucson: University of Arizona Press.

Burgess, Don. 2011. "Coronado Roadshows: In Search of the Coronado Trail." In *The Latest Word from 1540*, edited by Richard Flint and Shirley Cushing Flint. Albuquerque: University of New Mexico Press.

Chambers, George W. 1975. "How Long Is a Piece of String?" *Journal of Arizona History* 16:195–96.

Chardon, Roland. 1980. "The Linear League in North America." *Annals of the Association of American Geographers* 70:129–53.

Childs, Craig. 2002. "A Gilded Wrinkle in Time." *High Country News*, 23 December.

Cortés, Hernán. (1519–26) 1991. *Five Letters: 1519–1526*. Translated by J. Bayard Morris. Reprint, New York: W. W. Norton.

Covey, Cyclone. 1961. *Adventures in the Unknown Interior of America*. Albuquerque: University of New Mexico Press.

Craine, Eugene R., and Reginald C. Reindorp, eds. and trans. 1970. *The Chronicles of Michoacán*. Norman: University of Oklahoma Press.

Dahood, Karen. 1989. "Biographical Sketch of Ronald Ives." In *Land of Lava, Ash, and Sand: Writings of Ronald Ives*, edited by James W. Byrkit, 1–12. Tucson: Arizona Historical Society.

Damp, Jonathan E., Don Blakeslee, Jay Blaine, and Jeffrey Waseta. 2005. The Battle of Hawikku: Archaeological Investigation of the Zuni-Coronado Encounter at Hawikku, the Ensuing Battle, and the Aftermath during the Summer of 1540. Zuni Cultural Resource Enterprise Report no. 884, Research Series 13, Zuni, NM.

Day, A. Grove. 1940. *Coronado's Quest*. Berkeley: University of California Press.

Diamond, Jared. 1997. *Guns, Germs, and Steel: The Fate of Human Societies*. New York: W. W. Norton.

Díaz, Bernal. (ca. 1570) 1956. *The Bernal Díaz Chronicles: The True Story of the Conquest of Mexico*. Written 1568–1576. Translated by Albert Idell. Garden City, NY: Dolphin Books, Doubleday.

Díaz Balsera, Viviana. 2005. *The Pyramid under the Cross*. Tucson: University of Arizona Press.

Di Peso, Charles C., J. B. Rinaldo, and G. J. Fenner. 1974. *Casas Grandes: A Fallen Trading Center of the Gran Chichimeca*, vol. 7. Dragoon, AZ: Amerind Foundation Publications 9.

Dobyns, Henry. 1983. *Their Numbers Became Thinned*. Knoxville: University of Tennessee Press.

Doolittle, William E. 1988. *Pre-Hispanic Occupance in the Valley of Sonora, Mexico: Archaeological Confirmation of Early Spanish Reports*. Anthropological Papers of the University of Arizona no. 48. Tucson: University of Arizona Press.

Dorn, R. I., et al. 2012. "Assessing Early Spanish Explorer Routes through Authentifications of Rock Inscriptions." *Professional Geographer* 64:415–29.

Duffen, William. 1937. "Some Notes on a Summer's Work near Bonita, Arizona." *Kiva* 2(4): 13–16.

Duffen, William A., and William K. Hartmann. 1997. "The 76 Ranch Ruin and the Location of Chichilticale." In *The Coronado Expedition to Tierra Nueva*, edited by Richard Flint and Shirley Cushing Flint, 190–211. Niwot: University Press of Colorado.

Duran, Fray Diego. (ca. 1580) 1867–80. *Historia de Las Yndias de Nueva España y Yslas de la Tierra Firme*. 2 vols. and atlas. Mexico City: José F. Ramírez.

Favata, Martin S., and José B. Fernández. 1993. *The Account: Álvar Núñez Cabeza de Vaca's "Relación."* Houston: Arte Público Press.

Felger, R. S., M. B. Johnson, and M. F. Wilson. 2001. *The Trees of Sonora, Mexico*. Oxford: Oxford University Press.

Fernández, Zarina Estrada, C. B. Valenzuela, A. E. Camacho, M. E. C. Celaya, and A. C. Flores. 2004. *Diccionario Yaqui–Español y textos: Obra de preservación lingüística*. Hermosillo, Sonora: Universidad de Sonora; Mexico City: Plaza y Valdés Editores.

Flint, Richard. 2002. *Great Cruelties Have Been Reported: The 1544 Investigation of the Coronado Expedition*. Dallas: Southern Methodist University Press.

———. 2003. "Reconciling the Calendars of the Coronado Expedition: Tiguex to the Second Barranca, April and May 1541." In *The Coronado Expedition: From the Distance of 460 Years*, edited by Richard Flint and Shirley Cushing Flint, 151–63. Albuquerque: University of New Mexico Press.

———. 2008. *No Settlement, No Conquest: A History of the Coronado Entrada*. Albuquerque: University of New Mexico Press.

———. 2011. "When East Was West: The Oriental Aim of the Coronado Expedition." In *The Latest Word from 1540: People, Places, and Portrayals of the Coronado Expedition*, edited by Richard Flint and Shirley Cushing Flint, 105–16. Albuquerque: University of New Mexico Press.

Flint, Richard, and Shirley Cushing Flint. 2005. *Documents of the Coronado Expedition, 1539–1542*. Dallas: Southern Methodist University Press.

———. 2013. "Catch as Catch Can: The Evolving History of the Contact Period Southwest, 1938–Present." In *Native and Spanish New Worlds*, edited by Clay Mathers, J. M. Mitchem, and Charles M. Haeker, 47–62. Tucson: University of Arizona Press.

Flint, Shirley Cushing. 2003. "The Financing and Provisioning of the Coronado Expedition." In *The Coronado Expedition: From the Distance of 460 Years*, edited by Richard Flint and Shirley Cushing Flint, 13–38. Albuquerque: University of New Mexico Press.

———. 2013. No Mere Shadows: Faces of Widowhood in Early Colonial Mexico. Albuquerque: University of New Mexico Press.

Gagné, Frank. 2003. "Spanish Crossbow Boltheads of Sixteenth-Century North America: A Comparative Analysis." In *The Coronado Expedition: From the Distance of 460 Years*, edited by Richard Flint and Shirley Cushing Flint, 240–53. Albuquerque: University of New Mexico Press.

Gibson, Charles. 1964. *The Aztecs under Spanish Rule*. Stanford, CA: Stanford University Press.

Gómara, Francisco López de. (1552) 1964. *Cortés: The Life of the Conqueror*. Berkeley: University of California Press.

Hakluyt, Richard. (1600) 1904. The Principal Navigations, Voyages, Traffiques, and Discoveries of the English Nation. Vol. 9. Glasgow: James MacLehose and Sons.

Hallenbeck, Cleve. (1949) 1987. *The Journey of Fray Marcos*. Dallas: University Press in Dallas. Reprint, Dallas: Southern Methodist University Press.

Hammond, George P., and Agapito Rey. 1928. *Obregon's History of 16th Century Explorations in Western America*. Los Angeles: Wetzel Publishing Co.

———. 1940. *Narratives of the Coronado Expedition 1540–1542*. Albuquerque: University of New Mexico Press.

———. 1966. *The Rediscovery of New Mexico 1580–1594*. Albuquerque: University of New Mexico Press.

Hartmann, William K. 1989. *Desert Heart*. Tucson: Fisher Books.

———. 1997. "Pathfinder for Coronado." In *The Coronado Expedition to Tierra Nueva: The 1540–1542 Route across the Southwest*, edited by Richard Flint and Shirley Cushing Flint, 73–101. Niwot: University Press of Colorado.

———. 2002. *Cities of Gold: A Novel of the Ancient and Modern Southwest*. New York: Forge Books.

———. 2011. "The Mystery of the 'Port of Chichilticale.'" In *The Latest Word from 1540: People, Places, and Portrayals of the Coronado Expedition*, edited by Richard Flint and Shirley Cushing Flint, 194–213. Albuquerque: University of New Mexico Press.

Hartmann, William K., and Richard Flint. 2001. "Migrations in Late Anasazi Prehistory: 'Eyewitness' Testimony." *Kiva* 66:375–85.

———. 2003. "Before the Coronado Expedition: Who Knew What and When Did They Know It?" *The Coronado Expedition: From the Distance of 460 Years*, edited by Richard Flint and Shirley Cushing Flint, 20–41. Albuquerque: University of New Mexico Press.

Hartmann, William K., Heidi Harley, and Constantino Martínez Fabián. 2014. "Coronado-Era Place Names I: Marcos de Niza in Sonora, and the Occurrence of Yaqui Names in His *Relación*." Manuscript submitted for publication and under review.

Hartmann, William K., and Gayle Harrison Hartmann. 2011. "Locating the Lost Coronado Garrisons of 'San Gerónimo I, II, and III.'" In *The Latest Word from 1540: People, Places, and Portrayals of the Coronado Expedition*, edited by Richard Flint and Shirley Cushing Flint, 117–53. Albuquerque: University of New Mexico Press.

Hartmann, William K., and Betty Graham Lee. 2003. "Chichilticale: A Survey of Candidate Ruins in Southeastern Arizona." In *The Coronado Expedition: From the Distance of 460 Years*, edited by Richard Flint and Shirley Cushing Flint, 81–108. Albuquerque: University of New Mexico Press.

Hartmann, William K., and Constantino Martínez Fabián. 2014. "Coronado-Era Place Names II: 'Chichilticale' and the Origin of the Name of the 'Chiricahua' Mountains." Manuscript submitted for publication and under review.

Haury, Emil W. 1947. "A Large Pre-Columbian Copper Bell from the Southwest." *American Antiquity* 13(1): 80–82.

Hedrick, Basil C., and Carroll L. Riley. 1974. *The Journey of the Vaca Party*. University Museum Studies 2. Carbondale: University Museum of Southern Illinois University.

Hodge, Frederick W. 1898. *Coronado's March to Quivira, an Historical Sketch*. Printed also in J. W. Brower, Memoirs of Explorations in the Basin of the Mississippi, 1:29–73. St. Paul, MN.

———. 1910. *Handbook of American Indians North of Mexico*. Washington, DC: U.S. Government Printing Office.

Hornaday, William. (1908) 1983. *Camp-Fires on Desert and Lava*. New York: Scribner's. Reprint, Tucson: University of Arizona Press.

Houghton, John. 1997. *Global Warming: The Complete Briefing*. 2nd ed. Cambridge: Cambridge University Press.

Hudson, Charles, C. B. DePratter, and M. T. Smith. 1989. "Hernando de Soto's Expedition through the Southern United States." In *First Encounters: Spanish Explorations in the Caribbean and the United States, 1492–1570*, edited by J. T. Milanich and S. Milbrath, 119–34. Gainesville: University of Florida Press.

Ives, Ronald. 1936. "Melchior Díaz—the Forgotten Explorer." *Hispanic American Historical Review* 16:86–90.

———. 1937. "Reply to Critique by Sauer." *Hispanic American Historical Review* 17:149.

———. 1959. "The Grave of Melchior Díaz, a Problem in Historical Sleuthing." *Kiva* 25:31–40.

———. 1975. "How Tall Is a Man?" *Journal of Arizona History* 16:197–98.

———. 1989. *Land of Lava, Ash, and Sand*. Tucson: Arizona Historical Society.

Kelsey, Harry. 1986. *Cabrillo*. San Marino, CA: Huntington Library.

Kino, Eusebio Francisco. (ca. 1711) 1948. *Kino's Historical Memoir of Pimeria Alta*. Translated, edited, and annotated by Herbert Eugene Bolton. Berkeley: University of California Press.

Krauss, Clifford. 1997. "A Historic Figure Is Still Hated by Many in Mexico." *New York Times*, 26 March.

Krieger, Alex D. 2002. *We Came Naked and Barefoot: The Journey of Cabeza de Vaca across North America*. Austin: University of Texas Press.

Kronk, Gary. 1999. *Cometography: A Catalog of Comets, Vol. 1, Ancient–1799*. Cambridge: Cambridge University Press.

Lanyon, Anna. 1999. *Malinche's Conquest*. Crow's Nest, NSW, Australia: Allen & Unwin.
——. 2004. *The New World of Martín Cortés*. Cambridge, MA: Da Capo Press; first edition, Crow's Nest, NSW, Australia: Allen & Unwin, 2003.
Las Casas, Bartolomé de. (1552) 1992. *The Devastation of the Indies: A Brief Account*. Baltimore, MD: Johns Hopkins University Press.
León-Portilla, Miguel. 1962. *The Broken Spears: The Aztec Account of the Conquest of Mexico*. Boston: Beacon Press.
Lindsay, Alexander, Jr. 1987. "Anasazi Population Movements to Southern Arizona." *American Archaeology* 6:190–98.
Lumholtz, Carl. (1912) 1971. *New Trails in Mexico*. Glorieta, NM: Rio Grande Press.
MacNutt, F. A. 1908. *The Letters of Fernando Cortez*. New York: Putnam's Sons.
Madsen, John. 2003. "Spanish Artifacts, a Trail, and a Diary: An Eighteenth-Century Trail from Sonora to Zuni, New Mexico." In *The Coronado Expedition to Tierra Nueva: The 1540–1542 Route across the Southwest*, edited by Richard Flint and Shirley Cushing Flint, 109–15. Niwot: University Press of Colorado.
——. 2005. "In Search of the Coronado Trail." *Archaeology Southwest* 19(1): 6–7.
Manje, Juan Mateo. (ca. 1701) 1952. *Luz de Tierra Incognita*. Translated and edited by Harry J. Karns. Tucson: Arizona Silhouettes.
Marston, Betsy. 2011. "Heard around the West." *High Country News*, 14 November, 28.
Mathers, Clay, Dan Simplicio, and Tom Kennedy. 2011. "Everywhere They Told Us He Had Been There: Evidence of the Vázquez de Coronado Entrada at the Ancestral Zuni Pueblo of Kechiba:wa, New Mexico." In *The Latest Word from 1540: People, Places, and Portrayals of the Coronado Expedition*, edited by Richard and Shirley Cushing Flint, 262–85. Albuquerque: University of New Mexico Press.
Mathes, W. Michael. 2000. "Murder, Mayhem, and Discovery: The Mutiny of Fortún Ximénez." *Mainsail Haul* 36(4): 4–13. San Diego: Maritime Museum Association.
Mecham, J. Lloyd. 1927. *Francisco de Ibarra and Nuevo Vizcaya*. Durham, NC: Duke University Press.
Mills, Jack P., and Vera M. Mills. 1969. *The Kuykendall Site*. El Paso Archaeological Society, Special Report no. 6. El Paso, TX.
Molina, Felipe, and David Leedom Shaul. 1993. *A Concise Yoeme and English Dictionary*. Tucson, AZ: Tucson Unified School District.
Molina, Flavio Molina. ca. 1979. "Estado de la Provincia de Sonora 1730. La Diócese de Hermosillo, En memoria del 2° Centenario de la erección de la Diócese de Sonora (1779–1979)." Released on the Web, 2010.
Morris, J. Bayard, trans. 1991. *Five Letters of Cortés to the Emperor*. New York: W. W. Norton.
Nallino, Michel. 2012. *Fray Marcos de Niza 1495–1558. Frère Marc de Nice. À la poursuite de l'utopie franciscaine aux Indes Occidentales*. Édition intégral. The book is available in a privately printed version but also online at http://archive .org/details/FrayMarcosDeNizaInt; http://openlibrary.org/books/OL25414922M/ FRAY_MARCOS_DE_NIZA_1495_-_1558._FRERE_MARC_DE_NICE_A_ LA_POURSUITE_DE_L%E2%80%99UTOPIE_FRANCISCAINE_AUX_INDE.
Nallino, Michel, and W. K. Hartmann. 2003. "A Supposed Franciscan Exploration of Arizona in 1538: The Origins of a Myth." *Kiva* 68:283–303.
Nentvig, Juan. (ca. 1763) 1980. *Rudo Ensayo: A Description of Sonora and Arizona in 1764*. Translated, clarified, and annotated by Alberto F. Pradeau and Robert R. Rasmussen. Tucson: University of Arizona Press.

Pagden, Anthony. 1986. *Letters from Mexico*. New Haven, CT: Yale University Press.

Payne, Bob. 1987. "Walking to New York." *Walking Magazine*, October–November, 60–68.

Pfefferkorn, Ignaz. (1794–95) 1989. *Sonora: A Description of the Province, Written ca. 1778–1794*. Translated by T. E. Treutlein. Tucson: University of Arizona Press.

Poole, Stafford. 1995. *Our Lady of Guadalupe*. Tucson: University of Arizona Press.

Prescott, William H. (1843) 1943. *Conquest of Mexico*. Garden City, NY: Blue Ribbon Books.

Pupo-Walker, Enrique. 1993. *Castaways*. Berkeley: University of California Press.

Ramenofsky, Ann F., and C. D. Vaughn. 2008. "Seventeenth-Century Metal Production at San Marcos Pueblo in North-Central New Mexico." *Historical Archaeology* 42:105–31.

Reff, Daniel. 1991. *Disease, Depopulation, and Culture Change in Northwestern New Spain, 1518–1764*. Salt Lake City: University of Utah Press.

———. 1996. "Text and Context: Cures, Miracles, and Fear in the *Relación* of Álvar Núñez Cabeza de Vaca." *Journal of the Southwest* 38:115–38.

Rhodes, Diane Lee. 1997. "Coronado Fought Here: Crossbow Boltheads as Possible Indicators of the 1540–1542 Expedition." In *The Coronado Expedition to Tierra Nueva*, edited by Richard Flint and Shirley Cushing Flint, 44–56. Niwot: University Press of Colorado.

Riley, Carroll L. 1976. "Las Casas and the Golden Cities." *Ethnohistory* 23:19–30.

———. 1985. "The Location of Chichilticale." In *Southwestern Culture History: Collected Papers in Honor of Albert H. Schroeder*. Papers of the Archeological Society New Mexico 10. Santa Fe: Ancient City Press.

———. 1995. "Marata and Its Neighbors." In *The Gran Chichimeca: Essays on the Archaeology and Ethnohistory of Northern Mesoamerica*, edited by Jonathan E. Reyman. Worldwide Archaeology Series 12. Aldershot, UK: Avebury Publishing.

Rodack, Madeleine Turrell. 1981. *Adolph F. Bandelier's "The Discovery of New Mexico" by the Franciscan Monk, Friar Marcos de Niza in 1539*. Tucson: University of Arizona Press.

Sahagún, Fray Bernardino de. (ca. 1555) 1978. *The War of Conquest: How It Was Waged Here in Mexico (as Given to Fr. Bernardino de Sahagún)*. Translated by Arthur J. O. Anderson and Charles E. Dibble. Salt Lake City: University of Utah Press.

Sauer, Carl. 1932. "The Road to Cíbola." *Ibero-Americana* 3:1–58.

———. 1934. "The Road to Cíbola." *Ibero-Americana* 3:1–50.

———. 1937a. "Communication" [critique of an article by Ronald Ives]. *Hispanic American Historical Review* 12:146–49.

———. 1937b. "The Discovery of New Mexico Reconsidered." *New Mexico Historical Review* 12:270–87.

———. 1941. "The Credibility of the Fray Marcos Account." *New Mexico Historical Review* 16:233–43.

Saxton, Dean, Lucille Saxton, and Suzie Enos 1983. *Dictionary: Tohono O'odham/Pima to English, English to Tohono O'odham/Pima*. Tucson: University of Arizona Press.

Schmader, Matt. 2011. "Thundersticks and Coats of Iron." In *The Latest Word from 1540: People, Places, and Portrayals of the Coronado Expedition*, edited by Richard Flint and Shirley Cushing Flint, 117–53. Albuquerque: University of New Mexico Press.

Schroeder, Albert H. 1979. "Pueblos Abandoned in Historic Times." In *Handbook of North American Indians*, vol. 9, *Southwest*, edited by Alfonso Ortiz, 236–54. Washington, DC: Smithsonian Institution Press.

Seymour, Deni J. 2011. *Where the Earth and Sky Are Sewn Together: Sobaípuri-O'odham Contexts of Contact and Colonialism*. Salt Lake City: University of Utah Press.

Smith, Watson, Richard Woodbury, and Nathalie Woodbury. 1966. *The Excavation of Hawikuh by Frederick Webb Hodge*. New York: Museum of the American Indian, Heye Foundation.

Sobel, Dava. 1995. *Longitude*. New York: Walker and Co.

Spicer, Edward H. 1980. *The Yaquis: A Cultural History*. Tucson: University of Arizona Press.

Stuart, David E. 2003. *The Guaymas Chronicles*. Albuquerque: University of New Mexico Press.

Sykes, Godfrey. 1944. *A Westerly Trend*. Tucson: Arizona Pioneers Historical Society.

Tanner, Clara Lee. 1968. *Southwest Indian Arts and Crafts*. Tucson: University of Arizona Press.

Thiel, J. Homer. 2005. "The Coronado Roadshow." *Archaeology Southwest* 19(1): 7–8.

Thomas, Hugh. 1995. *Conquest: Montezuma, Cortés, and the Fall of Old Mexico*. New York: Simon and Schuster.

Turner, R. E., J. E. Bowers, and T. L. Burgess. 1995. *Sonoran Desert Plants, an Ecological Atlas*. Tucson: University of Arizona Press.

Underhill, Ruth. 1944. *Pueblo Crafts*. Washington, DC: Department of the Interior, Bureau of Indian Affairs, Branch of Education.

Undreiner, George J. 1947. "Fray Marcos de Niza and His Journey to Cibola." *Americas* 3:425–86.

Vargas, Victoria. 1995. *Copper Bell Trade Patterns in the Prehispanic U.S. Southwest and Northwest Mexico*. Archaeological Series 187, Arizona State Museum.

Vierra, Bradley J. 1992. "A Sixteenth-Century Spanish Campsite in the Tiguex Province: An Archaeologist's Perspective." In *Current Research on the Late Prehistory and Early History of New Mexico*. Archaeological Council, Special Publication 1, Albuquerque, NM.

Vierra, Bradley J., and Stanley M. Hordes. 1997. "Let the Dust Settle: A Review of the Coronado Campsite in the Tiguex Province." In *The Coronado Expedition to Tierra Nueva*, edited by Richard Flint and Shirley Cushing Flint, 259–61. Niwot: University Press of Colorado.

Wagner, Henry R., trans. and ed. 1925. *California Voyages*. San Francisco: John Howell.

———. 1934. "Fray Marcos de Niza." *New Mexico Historical Review* 9:184–227.

———. 1942. *The Discovery of New Spain*. Berkeley: University of California Press.

Wagner, Henry R., and Helen Rand Parish. 1967. *The Life and Writings of Bartolomé de Las Casas*. Albuquerque: University of New Mexico Press.

Walsh, Jane. 1993. "Myth and Imagination in the American Story: The Coronado Expedition, 1540–1542." Ph.D. diss., Catholic University of America.

Wedel, Waldo R. 1990. "Coronado, Quivira, and Kansas: An Archaeologist's View." *Great Plains Quarterly*, Summer, 139–51.

———. 1995. "Coronado and Quivira." In *Spain and the Plains*, edited by R. H. Vigil, F. W. Kaye, and J. R. Wunder, 45–66. Niwot: University Press of Colorado.

Winship, George Parker. (1896) 1990. *The Journey of Coronado, 1540–1542*. Golden, CO: Fulcrum Publishing.

Woodson, Michael K. 1995. "The Goat Hill Site: A Western Anasazi Pueblo in the Safford Valley of Southeastern Arizona." *Kiva* 65:63–84.

Index

Page numbers in *italics* indicate photo-illustrations. Page numbers in **bold** indicate maps.

Acapulco, **23**, 63, 88, 215, 219–20, 227

Acoma, New Mexico, 270, 276, **280**, 281. *See also* Acus

Acus (town recorded by Marcos de Niza), 172, 195, 266, 272; identified as Acoma, 275–76, 279, 281

Ahacus (town recorded by Marcos de Niza), 184, 254, 259, 276

Alarcón, Hernando, 137, 213, 220–22, 227–30, 236, 254, 256, 277–78; enters Colorado River, 285–87; interviews natives of Yuma area, 273–74, 287–94; establishes port on lower Colorado River, 286, 295–97; inland distance reached by, 289, 295–97; route of, **6**, **229**

Albornoz, Rodrigo de (official in Mexico City, 1539), 204, 211

Albuquerque, New Mexico: Cabeza de Vaca party passes south of, 113, 117; Coronado party at, 223, *265*, 275–76, **280**, 281–82, 311–20, 323, 331–32; post-Coronado explorations, 119, 348–49; pre-Coronado rumors, 81, 84

Alcanfor (pueblo in Albuquerque area). *See* Coofor

Alcaráz, Diego de (captain under slave raider, member of Coronado expedition): in charge at San Geronimo II, 300, 304; meets Cabeza de Vaca party and mistreats their native companions, 128–30; mismanagement and death at San Geronimo III, 304–7, 337–38

Alvarado, Hernando de (member of Coronado expedition), 281–84, 312

Alvarado, Pedro de (member of Cortés army, aka "the Sun"), 70; death and burial of, 343, 345; as governor of Guatemala (1534), 150; invests in Coronado expedition, 224; during Night of Sorrows, 51; and slaughter of Aztecs in Tenochtitlan (1520), 44–45, 58, 61, 72

Amazons (rumors of), 80, 90, **135**

Antilia, 80

Anza, Juan Bautista de (founder of San Francisco, 1776), 242

Apache Pass, Arizona, on route of Marcos de Niza and Coronado (?), 188, 248, 252, 254

archaeology, and role of eyewitness reports, 53, 85, 101–2, *110*, 111, 116, 121, 136, 176, 239, 243, 248–53, 260, 264–65, 271, 317–19, 322–29, 350–53

arches, as simple of celebration in Sonora, 159

Arellano, Tristán de (captain with Coronado expedition): at Pecos, 332; establishes San Geronimo I, 230, 242

Arispe, Sonora, **233**, 242, 244, 251, 306

Arroyo Cedros, Senora, 197, 231, **232**, 233, 236

Atahualpa (leader of Incas), 87, 149, 347

audiencia, 85, 132, 203–4, 342

Aztecs (Mexica), 4, 15–44, **30**, 47–49;
Aztec descriptions of Spaniards, 19–20,
25, 32; colloquium of Aztec priests
with Spanish priest, 72–79; origins and
history of, 21–22, 79–80
Aztlán (legends of), 79, 353

Baja California, (Mexican State), 204, 303;
Alarcón's explorations of, 298; explorations by Cortés's ships, 6, **89**, 92–93,
214–19, 308–9, 347; loss of information
about, 182–83; rumors and conceptions
about, 90, **135**, **229**
Balboa, Vasco Núñez de (discoverer of
Pacific), 63, 79
Banamachi, Sonora (town in Río Sonora
valley), **164**, 299, 241
Bandelier, Adolph (explorer-scholar), 100,
121, 146, 159, 170, 174–75, 355
Batuc, Sonora ("Batuco"), **164**, **232**, 233,
237, 306–7, 338
bells (prehistoric copper), 37, 81, 109–12,
110, 136–37, 189, 289–90; origins of,
110–11, 136–37, 362; role in Spanish
exploration history, 109–12, *110*,
136–37, 289–90, 351
Bigotes (native of Pecos), 279–81, 312,
315, 319, 332
bison, 172, 176, 267. *See also* buffalo
Blakeslee, Don (scholar), 322–25, 355–56
Blanco Canyon, Texas, 107–8, 264, **321**,
322–26, 232, 326, 330–31
Bloom, Lansing (scholar), 199, 207, 356
Bolton, Herbert (scholar), 86, 144, 174,
182, 222–23, 231, 233, 236, 281–82,
289, 295, 299, 302, 305, 317–19,
338–39, 342, 344, 346–47, 356
Brasher, Nugent (scholar), **180**, 188, 244,
252–57, 356
buffalo, 110, 113, 116–18, 172–73, 176, 185,
267, 279, 281–82, 290, 320, 325, 351

Cabeza de Vaca, Alvar Núñez, 7, 95. *See
also* Cabeza de Vaca party
Cabeza de Vaca party, 94–130; dealings
with Viceroy Mendoza (1536–1538),
131–39; and healings of native people,
103–6, 129; role as shamans, 103–6,

126; route of, 106–8, 111–27, **114**; trek
from Florida to Galveston (1528–1534),
95–99; trek from Galveston to Culiacán
(1534–1536), 99–130, **114**
Caborca, Sonora, 171, **181**, 185, *301*
Cabrillo, Juan Rodríguez, and naval
expedition in San Diego area (1542),
291, 240, 359
Cahokia (prehistoric mound-builder urban
center near modern St. Louis), 249,
284, 327
California (U.S. state), 80, 217, 295, 297,
300, 303, 330; loss of knowledge about,
in 1500s vs. 1600s, 182–83; origin of
name of, 80; Spanish entradas in 1500s
in, 217, 297, 300, 340
calendar: Julian vs. Gregorian, 7–8, 47–48,
55, 153, 165, 183, 217, 320; Native
American, 17, 21, 125, 352, 357
Carlos V (originally Carlos I), 12, 39, 44,
56, 58, 64, 85–85, 132, 138, 140, 142,
220, 224, 306, 310
Cárdenas, García López de (member
of Coronado expedition): involved
in battle at Cíbola, 258–59, 261–64;
involved in massacres in Albuquerque
area, 314–15; reaches Hopi pueblos
and Grand Canyon, 278–79; reports
destruction of San Gerónimo III
garrison, 333; requisitions pueblos in
Albuquerque area, 282–83, 312, 318;
saves Coronado's life at Cíbola, 263;
searches for Alarcón, 278; trial and
conviction of, 242, 262, 342
Cárdenas, Luis (naval pilot), and 1527
reports of metal-using northern cities,
81, 85
Casas Grandes, Chihuahua (ruin), 112,
136–37, 271, 349, 357
Castañeda Nájera, Pedro de (Coronado
expedition memoirist), 157; accounts of
Alarcón and Díaz explorations around
Colorado River, 295–307; accounts
relating to Marcos de Niza trip and early
plans for Coronado expedition, 136,
169, 173, 176, 178, 199, 201, 205, 212,
221; as ethnologist, 268–69, 311; belief
that riches lay beyond Quivira, 331–34,

348–49; correcting dates in manuscript of, 8; death of, 334; descriptions of Coronado expedition in Albuquerque-Pecos area, 311–16; descriptions of Coronado expedition from Albuquerque through Texas to Quivira (Kansas), 107, 320, 324–33; descriptions of Coronado expedition in Cíbola and surroundings, 257–59, 263, 269, 274–79; descriptions of Coronado expedition from Mexico to Chichilticale, 223–28, 231, 236–46, 250, 253–55; descriptions of return to Mexico, 334–38; and estimate of width of North America, 330–31; writing by and oldest surviving copies of memoir of, 8, 246

Castillo, Alonso (member of Cabeza de Vaca party), 101–4, 113,119, 126, 131

Castillo, Domingo (cartographer), 228; 1541 map of gulf and coastal lands by, 228, **229**, 298

Cathay. *See* China

Cedros Arroyo. *See* Arroyo Cedros

Cedros Island, 218–19

Chichilticale (Chichiltiecally), **181**, 226–28, **232**, 256–57; date of, 244–47, **248**; Kuykendall ruin as, 248–55; linguistic relation of name to "Chiricahua" mountains, Arizona, 246; location of, 244–45, 248–55; location as confused by possible artifacts from Díaz-Zaldivar expedition, 255; as mountains, 244–46; as port, **229**, 249–56; as province, 225–26, 239, 272–77; as ruin, 244–47, **248**

China, and belief in location of "Cathay" as just northwest of Mexico, 9, 11, 13, 52, 58, 64, 80, 90, 112, 119, **135**, 180

Chiricahua Mountains, Arizona, 185, 188, 244, 252; and relation of name to "Chichilticale," 246, 248, 399

Cíbola (Zuni, NM), 5, *168*, 199–200, *260*, **280**, **321**; battle with Coronado army at (1540), 258–66, *260*; and conflict with Estevan party (1539), 189–93; early rumors of, 125, 134, **135**, **154**, **164**, 174; gold in, 197, 203, 205–6, 209–13, 224, 226–27, 266; life and religious practices in, 125, 167–76, 184, 263–69, 288; location of, 125, 159, **164**; maps of, 1, 7, 10, 11, 12, 13; as reported by Marcos de Niza (1539), 145–47, 160–61, 167–75, 177, **181**, 196, 199–208; turquoises usage in (and modern confirmation thereof), 145, 167, 172–75, 204–6, 210–12, 226, 263–64, 267–69, 288

Cicuye. *See* Pecos

climate change, as driver of social changes ca. 1200–1300, 74, 248–49

colloquium of Aztec and Spanish priests, 72–79

Colorado River, 183, 254, 300, 302–3; Alarcón exploration of (1540), 228–30, 285–298, 343; Díaz party crossing, 300–301; discovery of (1539–1540), 9, **229**, 285–86, 343, 347; Native American life on, 273, 286–98, 351; Ulloa at mouth of (1539), 215–20, **229**, 309, 347

Colón, Cristóbol. *See* Columbus, Christopher

Columbus, Christopher, 3, 8–9, 11, 13, 64, 70, 75, 83

Coofor, location of, **280**, 282–83, 312, 318

Compostela, 131–32, 144, 153, 161, 198–202, 206–7, 213, 221–25, 338–39

copper bells. *See* bells

Corazones, Sonora, 123, 127, 249, 251, 299, 307, 353; connections with Cibola, 125, 172–73; Coronado garrison at (San Geronimo I), 230, 235, 242–44, 332; first Spanish records of (1535), 122–23; as "gateway," 122–23, 176–78, 234–39, 235; location of, 123–24, 172–74, 176–78, **229**, 234–39; Native American life in, 122–26, 134, 172–73, 307, 337–38

Coronado, Francisco Vazquez de, 3–8; birth and background (ca. 1510–1538), 144; death and burial of (1554), 344–45; injury from horseback fall during expedition (1542), 333; life after expedition (1542–1546), 338–42; trial of (1544–1546), 341–42. *See also* Coronado expedition

Coronado expedition: as "army," 223–24; artifacts from, 156, 233, 251, 253–55,

257, 264–65, 307, 317–19, **321**, 322–23, 327–28, 332, 348–49, 356; bases in Albuquerque area, 224, *264*, 275–76, **280**, 281–83, 312, 311–20, **321**, 331–33; belief in riches beyond Tiquex and Quivira, 331–34, 348–49; in Blanco Canyon, Texas (1541), 107, **321**, 322, 323, 324–25, 325; at Chichilticale, **180**, 225, **229**, 244–57, 273–74, 276–77, 288, 298; at Cíbola, 257–70, *260*; from Corazones to Cíbola (1540), **232**, 244–70, **321**; from Culiacán to Corazones (1540), 230–35, **232**; 500th anniversary of (2039–2042), 224–25; at Grand Canyon, 278–79; at Hopi pueblos (northern Arizona), 274, 277–78, 304; importance of, 3–4, 329–31, 349–54; Indian allies of, 222–23, 230–31, 243, 258, 307, 314, 318, 324, 335–36; in Kansas (1541), **321**, 327–29; from Mexico City to Culiacán (1539–40), **154**, 213, 222–27; near encounter with Soto expedition, 329–31; and race with Cortés, 5, 86, 90, 144, 177, 197, 205, 214, 306–10; return from Albuquerque area to Mexico City (1542), 333–39; return from Kansas to Albuquerque area (1541), 331–33; route of, 6, **23**, 124, 154, 164, 181, 229, **232**, **280**, 320, **321**; size of, 222–23; as venture capitalism, 24; and warfare in Tiguex (Albuquerque area, 1540–1541), 312–19. *See also* San Geronimo I; San Geronimo II; San Geronimo III

Coronado Road Show, 251–52, 356

Cortés, Hernán: early life of (1505–1518), 11–13; expedition into Honduras by (1524–1526), 81–82; and explorations of "Sea of Cortés" and Baja California (1522–1535, 1539), 63–64, 79–81, 88–93, **89**, 214–20, 306–10; and journey to Spain (1528–1530), 83–85; and later journey to and death in Spain (1540–1547), 205, 220–21, 306–10, 339–41, 345; and meeting with Motezuma, 29–33; motto of, 12, 26, 28, 56, 81; personality of, 12–13, 26–27, 69–72, 341; relationship with governor of Cuba, 12–14; relationship

with Marina (Malinche), 14–16, 26, 31–32, 35, 41–42, 46, 57, 65–66, 69–71, 81–84, 84, 231, 310, 339–41, 346, 353; relationship with Marcos de Niza, 199, 203–4, 215, 307–9; relationship with Motezuma, 34–43, 49; relationship with Viceroy Mendoza, 133, 142–44, 177, 199–201, 308–9, 339–40; route from Cuba, **23**; sequesters gold for himself (?), 56, 59, 61, 68, 133

Cortés, Martín (Martín Cortés Nezahualzolotl, son of Motezuma), 72, 87

Cortés, Martín (son of Hernán by Malinche), 65–66, 70, 81, 83–86, 310, 341

Cortés, Martín (son of Hernán by wife Catalina), 86–87, 341, 346

Council of the Indies, 58, 74, 204

Coyoacán, Mexico, 30; as Cortés's headquarters, 57, 59, 61, 65–71; as modern "house of Malinche and Cortés," 66–71; as "Paris of the New World," 69

cronista (Mexican town historian), 240–41

Cuauhtémoc, 55, 57, 70, 72, 82,

Culiacán, Sinoloa: Cabeza de Vaca party and (1536), 128, 130–31; Coronado expedition and (1539–1542), 205–6, 224, 227–28, 230, **232**, 233, 236, 242, 249, 305–6, 336, 338, 342; as Guzman headquarters (ca. 1536), 86; Melchior Díaz and, 130, 298, 300; as outpost of Coronado and Marcos de Niza (1538–1539), 144, 152, **154**, 155–60, 162, 165–66, 170, 172, 176, 198, 201–2; present vs. initial location of, 86, **89**

Cuba: and gold rush (1512), 10; mistaken for China or island off China, 9, 112; Spanish operations associated with (1506–), 12–14, 26–27, 43–44, 60, 66, 94–96, 210

Cushing, Frank Hamilton (scholar), 174–75, 288

Cumaripa, Sonora, **164**

Cumpas, Sonora ("Comulpa"), **164**, 304–6, 338

despoblado: examples of, 161–62, 179–81, 185–90, 193, 196, 200, 208, 244–45,

253, 271–72, 288, 292; meaning of Spanish term, 161

Díaz, Bernal (chronicler of Cortés in Mexico): account of conquest of Mexico, 15, 22, 29–51, 82; account of origins of Coronado expedition, 212–13, 228; background of, 7, 15

Díaz, Melchior: death of (1541) 298–303; and exploration into Arizona and California (1540–1541), 6, 291, 295–300, 301, 302–3; as explorer in Chichilticale province (1539–1540), 209, 225–27, 230, 254–55, 273; as mayor of Culiacan (ca. 1536), 130, 205; as member of Coronado expedition (1540–1542), 230, 277, 288, 301; personality of, 299–300, 301; as reporter of Totonteac, 271–77

Di Peso, Charles, 136–37, 357

diseases, interchange of between Old and New Worlds, 52, 82, 104–6, 361

Dorantes, Andrés: with Cabeza de Vaca party crossing America, 100–110, 119, 123, 126; copper bell given to, 109–10, 227; death of, 347; and interaction with Viceroy Mendoza, 131, 134–39, 143–44

Duffen, Bill (scholar), 248–51, 357

El Centro, California, 303

El Turco (Native guide from east of Pecos), 281–84, 312, 318–20, 324, 327–30, 332–33; death of, 328–29

encomienda, 60, 64–65, 334

Española (island). *See* Hispaniola

Espejo, Antonio, and expedition of 1583, 118–19, 275

Estevan the Moor (aka Estevan the Black, Estevan Dorantes): alleged misdeeds of, 169, 192–93, 290, 345; birth and background of, 101–2, 345; and Cortés's version of Estevan's role with Marcos de Niza, 198–99, 201; death of, 189–93, 227, 238, 262, 288–91, 345; and departure from Marcos and trip to Cíbola with his own party, 178–80, 185, 189–94, 288–89; and interaction with Viceroy Mendoza, 131, 143–44, 150–51, 155; and knowledge of Corazones (while with Marcos),

176–77; as member of Cabeza de Vaca party (1535–1536), 101, 104–5, 113, 122, 126; as member of Marcos de Niza party (1538–1539) 151, 155–56, 165–72, 176–78, 206–7, 272

Estrada, Beatriz de (wife of Coronado), 334, 338, 344; death and burial of, 344–45; as investor in Coronado expedition, 224

Flint, Richard and Shirley Cushing (scholars), 8, 139, 147, 165, **181**, 182, 188, 208, 219, 223–25, 231, 236, 244, 252, 256, 258, 270, 274–75, 282–84, 289, 295–96, 322–24, 342, 344, 357–58

Florida: exploration of, 10, 94–98, 178, 210; and "La Florida" (concepts and extent of), 79, 112, 210, 281, 329–30

frontiers: Cíbola, **154**, 160, 167; Guzmán, 89, **154**, 160, 162; Spanish settlement, 127, 153, **154**, 160; Yaqui vs. Opata, 175

Gagné, Frank (scholar), and research on crossbow bolt heads, 254, 264, 318, 326, 358

Gallego, Juan (captain in Coronado expedition), 277, 300, 335–37; and depredations in Valle de Señora, 336–37

Galveston, Texas, as landing place of Cabeza de Vaca party, 99–102, 108

Gila River, Arizona and New Mexico, 208, 228, **229**, 252–56, 275, 288–98

gold: claims that Marcos de Niza reported gold at Cíbola, 4, 147, 153, 190, 197–203, 205–6, 209–12, 224–27, 332; discovered in Cuba, 10; discovered in Mexico City area, 11–12, 16, 22–60, 70, 72, 83; discovered in Michoacán, Mexico, 61–63; discovered in Peru, 87, 149, 344, 347; expectations of, in northern lands (United States), 3, 93–95, 111, 134–38, 148, 178, 190, 230–31, 266, 289, 332–33, 354; expectations of, in Quivira area, 282–84, 312, 319–20, 327–28, 332–33; expectations of, in Topira area, 176; in and around Gulf of California, 81, 86, 92–93;

in "La Florida," 96–97; lost during Cortés's Mexico City campaign, 56, 59, 61, 68, 133, 144, 345; missed during northern explorations, 332–33, 348–49; Marco Polo and, 9; reported by Columbus, 9, 83; in valley east of Marcos de Niza's route, 153, 197, 231

Grand Canyon, as discovered by Coronado side-party under Cárdenas, 278–79, 282, 354

Guaymas, Sonora, 215–16, 362

Gulf of California (Sea of Cortés), 86, 88, **89**, 90–91, 101, 109, 133, 182–83, 203, 213–16, 228, **229**, 285, 300, 308, 345

Guzmán, Diego de, 88, **89**, 90, 101, 142, 156, 159–60, 204

Guzmán, Nuño de, 85–88, **89**, 90, 92, 112, 126–31, 133–34, 142, 144, 153, 156, 160–62, 177, 202, 205, 308, 338

Hallenbeck, Cleve (scholar), 100, 131, 146, 152–53, 156, 159–60, 170, 179, 189, 200, 205–9, 213, 258

Hartmann, Gayle Harrison (scholar), ix, 67–68, 248, 250, 303, 305

Hawikku (first of "Seven Cites" encountered on Cíbola trade route), *168*, 254–55, 259, *260*, 262, 264, 266–67, 276, 287

Hispaniola (island), as a Spanish base of operations in the Caribbean, 13, 59, 94, 211

houses: permanent vs. temporary (in southwest United States and Sonora), 97, 110–11, 113–25, *115*, 134, 149–53, 157–62, 167, *168*, 171, 174, 184, 193–94, 264, 267–68, 270, 272, 311–12; and reed mats, *115*, 157; in Rio Sonora valley, 237, 242–43; in Tenochtilan, 36, 40, 46, 53

Huepac, Sonora, **164**, 240–43

Ibarra, Francisco, 1565 expedition of, 304–5, 348–49, 360

Indian, and origin and use of word to mean resident of the Indies, 9

Ives, Ronald (scholar-explorer), 299–300, 302, 357

Jaramillo, Juan (member and chronicler of Coronado party), 157, 197, 231, *235*, 235–38, 241–46, 305, 346

Jaramillo, Juan (member of Cortés army and husband of Malinche), 82–83, 339–40

Jemez pueblo, New Mexico, *280*, 331

Jumana, Gutiéra de. *See* Leyva-Jumana expedition to Quivira

Kino, Eusebio (explorer-priest in Sonora, ca. 1690s), 159, 170–71, 174, 182–83, 359

kivas (aka *estufas*), 175, 269, 311

La Noche Triste. *See* Night of Sorrows

Lanyon, Anna (scholar), 15, 65, 70, 82–83, 87, 310, 339–41, 347, 360

Las Casas, Bartolomé de, 13, 60, 75, 94, 124–26, 134, 142, 149–50, 238, 242–43, 269, 351, 355, 360–61

latitude: Greek knowledge of, 9; puzzling errors in, 146, 182, 188, 207, 218–19, 297

league, length of, 8–9, 96, 100, 356

Lee, Betty Graham, 247, 250

Leyva-Jumana expedition to Quivira (1593), 328, 349

Llano Estacado, Texas, 320, 326

longitude, difficulty of measuring, 94, 103, 262, 330–31, 362

Luis (friar with Coronado expedition), 261, 335

Luther, Martin (1517), 58

Madsen, John (scholar), 251

maize road, *115*, 120–23, 236, 240

Maldonado, Rodrigo (member of Coronado party), 220–21, 236, 333

Malinche (Marina), 14–16, 26, 31–32, 35, 41–42, 46, 57, 65–66, 69–71, 81–84, 84, 231, 310, 339–41, 346, 353; childhood and homeland of, 14; with Cortés to Tenochtilan (1519–1520), 14–37; and daughter María (b. 1526), 339–40; late life and death of (mid-1500s?), 83; life and son with Cortés (1519–1524), 65–66, 82–83; and marriage to Juan

Jaramillo (1524), 82; origin of name of, 15; and reputation in modern times, 16, 71; and reputation with Cortés troops, 14–16, 41, 83

mammoth bones, found by Coronado expedition, 257–58

Marata (town recorded by Marcos de Niza). *See* Marrata

Marble, Nancy, 265, 322–23

Marcos de Niza: arrival date of, in Mexico City on return from Cíbola (1539), 201–3; arrival of, in New World (1531), 149; attacks on veracity of (early), 145, 199, 259, 266–67, 270–71, 281, 288, 306–10; attacks on veracity of (modern), 4, 146–47, 205–13; birth and early history of, 148–49; with Coronado to Cíbola, 223–234, 238, 244–45, 249–56, 259, 262, 266–67, 270–73, 277; interaction with Cortés, 203–5, 215, 255, 308–9; interaction with and instructions from Viceroy Mendoza, 143, 150–53, 177, 201–5, 211–13, 228, **229**, 255–56, 308–9; and journey and route north to Cíbola, 144, 153–95, **154**, **164**, **181**, *186*, *241*; and journey and route south from Cíbola (1539), 196–205; letters sent back during northward journey as clues to arrival time in Mexico City, 158, 188, 198–99, 201, 207; in Peru, 149; in Phoenix (?), 187; place in history of, 147–48; return of, from Cibola in disgrace (1540), 277, 300, 336; return of, from Cibola in haste (1539), 195–97; in Río Sonora valley and Corazones, 124–25, 134, 176–77; and testimony about his statements in Mexico City, 199–205, 209–13; and Totonteac, 270–77; and Vacapa and Sayota (location and identification of terms recorded by Marcos), 162–63, 170–75; and whether he viewed Cíbola, 192–96

Marina. *See* Malinche

Marrata (town recorded by Marcos de Niza), 172, 195, 266, 270–73

Matape (modern town and river), 126, 163–66, **164**, 172–75, 216, **232**

Mazocahui (Sonoran town), as location of Corazones, 235, 237–39, 242, 243

Mendoza, Antonio, Viceroy of Mexico (1535–1551), 18, 142–44; background of, 132–33; and conception of the north, 133–37, **135**, **229**; interaction with Cabeza de Vaca Party, 134–39, 177; interaction with Cortés, 133–37, 199–205, 220–21, 230, 267, 306–10, 339–40; interaction with Marcos de Niza, 143, 150–53, 177–78, 201–5, 211–13, 228–29, 255–56, 308–9; and involvement with Coronado expedition, 176, 213–15, 220–21, 224, 228, **229**, 269–74, 276–77, 288, 298, 300, 318, 336–40, 342

Mexica. *See* Aztecs

Mexico City. *See* Tenochtitlan

migrations, of pueblo peoples (ca. 1200–1300), 247, 248–50, 358

Michoacán, **23**, 61, 87, 91, 93–94, 112, 136, 224, 344, 356

Mills, Jack P. and Vera M. (amateur scholars of Salado pueblo ruins), 253, 255, 360

Mississippi River: rumors about, in Southwest, 249, 283–84, 290, 327; Soto expedition on, 329; Spanish discovery of, as recorded by Cabeza de Vaca, 98

Moors, 11, 35, 80, 95, 101–2, 131–32, 140, 143, 155, 178, 191, 233, 239, 310, 345

Motezuma (Montezuma): as co-"regent" with Cortés, 42–43, 49, 72; birth and background of, 22, 347; death of, 46–49, 347; and meeting with Cortés (1518), 29–43, **33**; and news of strangers on the coast (1518–1519), 19–22, **23**, 24–28; personality of, 22, 28–29, 36–37, 41–45, 350; pronunciation of name, 18

Montezuma. *See* Motezuma

More, Thomas (*Utopia*), 75, 355

Munro, Guillermo (Sonoran novelist), 255

Nahuatl language, 15–17, 34, 73–74, 76–77, 82, 246

nails: caret-head, 254; embedded in horseshoe, 126, 317–19, 325

Nallino, Michel, ix, 144, 147–50, 166, 171–72, 208, 213, 360

Narváez, Pánfilo, 178, 283, 340, 344–45, 355; attempt of, to arrest Cortés, 44–45, 51; disappearance at sea by, 98, 100–102; leads expedition into Florida, 94–98
Needles, California, "port of," 295
Night of Sorrows, 49–56, 59, 61, 68, 93
novels, as a tool for understanding history, 55, 148, 171, 182, 215, 227, 258, 358

Obregón, Baltasar de (member of Ibarra expedition), 304, 305, 307, 348
Onavas, Sonora, **232**, 233, 239
Onorato (member of Marcos de Niza party), 143–44, 156–58, 165, 169, 204
Opata people and language, 237, 246, 273
Owens, Jimmy (amateur first reporter of Blanco Canyon site), 323–26, 355

Padilla, Juan de (friar with Coronado expedition), 277, 335
Pánuco (port), **6**, **23**, 61, 81, 85, 97, 99–100, 103, 107, 112, 134, 335
Passion Sunday, date of, 163, 165–66
Pecos, New Mexico (Cicuye pueblo), 112, 279, **280**, 281–84, 312–20, **321**, 327–28, 332, 335
Petatlán (river and village), location of, 128, 130, 153, 156–58, 165, 172
Polo, Marco, 9, 13, 52, 62, 80, **134**
Ponce de Léon, 10, 79
Pizarro, Francisco, 70, 87, 132, 147, 149, 177, 224, 329, 344, 346–48
prehistoric daily life, evidence in Spanish documents, 350–52; as reported by Alarcon along Rio Grande and Gila River, 286–94; as reported by Cabeza de Vaca party in Sonora, 121–30; as reported by Cabeza de Vaca party in southern United States, 95, 97–121, 136–37; as reported by Coronado expedition in Arizona, Texas, Kansas, 277–70, 320–29; as reported by Coronado expedition at Cíbola and Albuquerque region, 237–40, 267–70, 279–83, 311–17, 331–33; reported by Coronado expedition in Sonora and border region, 237–40, 245; as reported by Marcos de Niza in New Mexico, 166–77; as

reported by Marcos de Niza in Sonora and border region, 155–65, 184–92
printing press (first in North America, located in Mexico City), 62, 133
private property rights, in collision with national and global archeological heritage, 250
Puerto Peñasco. *See* Rocky Point

Quetzalcoatl, 4, 20–21, 24, 28, 30, 34, 75, 268, 353
Quivira, Kansas, **321**; archaeology of, 327–28; Coronado and associates' plan to return to, 332–35, 337, 348–49; reached by Coronado party (1541), 327–31; reached by Leyva-Jumana expedition (1593), 328, 349; rumors of wealth in, 281–84, 318–20, 324, 332–33

requerimiento, 139–42, 261, 278, 354
Riíto, Sonora, 296–97
Riley, Carroll L., iv, 95, 102, 111, 124–25, 178, 243, 246, 273–75, 318, 356, 359, 361
Río Sonora, Sonora, **114**, 120–21, 125, **135**, **154**, **164**, 171–77, **181**, 185, 196, **232**, 233–44, *235*, *241*, 291, 298–301, 304–7, 335–37, 351
Río Yaqui, Sonora, 88, **89**, **114**, 126–27, **154**, 157, 162–63, **164**, 173–75, 216, 231, **232**, 233, 237–39, 306, 338
Rocky Point (Puerto Peñasco), Sonora, **181**, 217
Rodríguez, Agustín, and expedition of 1581, 117–18

Sahagún, Bernardino de, 17–21, 28–29, 42, 47–48, 73–74, 77–78, 355, 361
Salado-era pueblos, 136, **246**, 248–49, 253, 255
San Geronimo I (de Corazones), 235, 242–43, 299–300, 359
San Geronimo II (Valle de Senora), 243, 282, 298, 299, 300, 318, 336–37, 359
San Geronimo III (Valle de Suya), 243, 272, 300, 304–6, 318, 333, 336–37, 359
San Pedro River, Arizona, 110, 120, **135**, 136, **181**, 185–88, *186*, 193, 196,

200–201, **232**, 244–46, 249, 252–54, 272, 305

Santa Cruz (Cortés colony in Baja California), **89**, 92, 216, 221, 308–9

Santa Fe, New Mexico, 55, 251, 252, **280**, **321**, 349

Santiago (Coronado-era pueblo site in Albuquerque area), **280**, 317–18, 326

Sauer, Carl (scholar), 81, 146, 152, 170, 174–75, 177, 205–9, 233–37, 246, 300–302, 359, 361

Sea of Cortés. *See* Gulf of California

seven bishops, legend of, 79–80, 111

Seven Cities (seven towns), 4–5, 80, 85, 147, 167, 171–72, 184, 189, 257, 260, 270, 272, 346

silver, 9, 30, 36–37, 58, 60, 83, 87, 112, 134, 143, 149, 197–98, 210, 224, 226, 289; and possible resources north of Albuquerque area, 332; rumors of, in Quivira, 282–84, 319–20, 327

Socorro, New Mexico, 118, 226, **280**

Sonora (Mexican state and river) 5, 88, 103, 111–12, **114**, *115*, 140, **164**, **181**, 215–17, **232**, 248, 251, 288, 291, 293, 331–32, 349, 351–52, 356–62; origin of name of, 240; and relation to Cabeza de Vaca route, **114**, 120–26; and relation to Coronado route, **164**, **232**, 233–46, *241*, 282, 298–308, *299*, 335–37, 344, 349; and relation to Marcos de Niza route, 147, 159, 162, **164**, *168*, 170–85, **181**, 191, 196–97, 205–11, 270, 281; and relation to reports of Totonteac and other "missing kingdoms," 270–77, 281

Sopete. *See* Ysopete

Soto, Hernando (leader of expedition west from Florida, 1539–1543), 100, 210, 281; and near encounter with Coronado expedition (1541?), 329; route of, 6, **321**, 329–31, 359

South Sea (Pacific Ocean), **23**, 63, 84, 86, **89**, 90, 112, 136, 152, **154**, 211, 213, 219, 228, **232**, 234, 236; Spaniards' discovery of, 63

Soyopa, Sonora, 162–66, 172–75, **232**; and relation to term used by Marcos de Niza, 162

Spaniards, descriptions of, by Native peoples, 25–26, 32, 36, 48, 127, 129, 162, 291; as children of the sun, 105, 287, 290–94; as coming from heaven, 122, 126–27, 162; as Quetzelcoatl, 4, 20–21, 24, 28, 30, 34, 75, 268

Sulfur Springs Valley, as region of Coronado-era exploration in Chichilticale Province, **181**, 246, 247, 248–52

Stuart, David (scholar and writer), 215, 362

Suya. *See* San Geronimo III

Tenochtitlan, **23**, **33**, 38, **62**, 63; conquest of, as a unique moment in human history, 3, 29, 73–75, 340–41; description of city, 22, 29–32, **33**, 37–41, 38, 46–51, 53–55, **62**, 63; and Night of Sorrows, 49–51, 57, 59, 93; second assault on (1520–1521), 52–56; and urban warfare (June 1520), 44–49

Teyas people, as origin of name "Texas," 324

Tiguex (province around Albuquerque), 275–76, **280**, 281–83, 311–19, 324–25, 329–35, 348, 357, 362

Tonantzin (Aztec goddess as model for Virgin of Guadalupe), 78

Toscanelli, Paulo (geographer), 9

Totonteac (wealthiest northern settlement, as recorded by Marcos de Niza), 330; possible locations of, 230, 266, 271–77, 283; testimony about, from native peoples, 172, 184, 195, 204, 209, 226, 287, 290; turquoise in, 271

Tovar, Pedro de (member of Coronado expedition at Hopi pueblos), 274, 277–78, 304

trade routes, among Native Americans in 1500s. *See* prehistoric daily life

translation and interpreters: as accomplished from one native group to another, 129, 169, 246, 335, 352; as accomplished by Spanish explorers, 15–16, 20, 35, 41, 119, 124, 129, 139–40, 194, 249, 261, 263, 287–91, 196, 200–201, 295, 339, 346; of Aztec manuscripts, 73; and modern problems of translating 1500s documents, 5, 96, 104, 147, 167, 182, 236, 246, 276, 303, 324, 331

travel rates, and plausible number of miles per day, 120, 131–32, 157–63, 166, 173, 185, 187, 202, 206–7, 288

Turco. *See* El Turco

turquoise: among Aztecs, 24, 76, 83; in Cíbola, 145, 147, 167, 173–75, 177, 189, 204, 206, 210–12, 226, 263–64, 267–69, 288; prehistoric trade in, 121, 125, 169, 172–73, 288, 351; in Sonora and Chichilticale provinces, 121, 125, 185, 188; in Totonteac, 271

Ulloa, Francisco (naval explorer of Gulf of California and Baja California coastline, 1539–1540), 182, 188, 198, 215–21, 228, 230, 236, 285, 297–98, 308–9, 340, 347; Cortés's claims about, 308–9; route of, 6, 215–20

Ures, Sonora, **164**, 175, **232**, 234–39, 243

Utopia (More's book based on Las Casas's ideas?), 75, 355

Vacapa (village): location of, 169–75; meaning of name of, 175; as recorded by Marcos, 163–67, 169–71, 179–80, 192, 196, 238, 272

Valle de Señora, **164**, **233**, 237–44, 240

Valley de Suya. *See* San Geronimo III

Vásquez, Francisco. *See* Coronado, Francisco Vazquez de

Veracruz (port), 18–19, **23**, 24, 26–27, 82, 86, 138, **154**, 202, 346

Vespucci, Amerigo, 9

Vierra, Bradley (archaeologist), discovers Coronado site in Albuquerque area, 317, 323, 362

Vikings, in America, 3, 73–75, 249, 341

Virgin of Guadalupe, 78–79, 361

Wagner, Henry (scholar), 65, 124, 144–46, 148, 150, 170, 199, 201–8, 211, 215–20, 346, 362

Waldseemüller, Martin (cartographer), 9

Wedel, Waldo (archaeologist), 327–28, 362

Xabe (alleged native of Quivira), 319–20, 332

Xochimilco (gardens), 63, 346

Yaqui people and language, 88, 157, 162–63, 175, 231–33, 257, 359

Yaqui River. *See* Río Yaqui

Ysopete (guide, native of plains east of Pecos), 281, 318, 320, 324, 328–29, 355

Yucatan, 6, 10, 13–14, 16, 18, **23**, 81–82; Spanish discovery of, 10

Yuma, Arizona, 254, 273, 288–89, 292

Yuman peoples and language, 236, 289, 292–93; reached by Alarcón, 288–89, 292–93, 295–96; reached by Melchior Díaz, 295–97, 300–301

Zacatula, **23**, 63–64

Zaldívar, Juan de: and exploration of Chichilticale province, 205, 209, 213, 225–26, 230, 254–55, 271, 273–74; and role in near link-up with Soto expedition, 330, 352

Zia, New Mexico ("Chía"), **280**, 317

Zumárraga, Juan de (Mexico's first bishop), 79, 142; interaction with Marcos de Niza, 145, 150, 202–3, 206, 208, 211–12, 223, 346–47; role of, in Virgin of Guadalupe legend, 79; supports first American printing press, 133

Zúñiga expedition (southern Arizona to Zuni and Santa Fe, 1795), 251–52

Zunis and Zuni, New Mexico, 125, 159, *168*, 174–75, 189, 208–12, 252, 254, 259, 260, 264–70, **280**, 288, **321**, 351. *See also* Cíbola

About the Author

William K. Hartmann is internationally known as a scientist, writer, and painter. He was the first recipient of the Carl Sagan Medal from the American Astronomical Society for his popular science writing and artwork, an award from the European Geophysical Union, and lifetime achievement awards from the International Association of Astronomical Artists and NASA's Lunar Science Institute. Asteroid 3341 is named "Hartmann" in recognition of his work on solar system history.

Hartmann has published widely on aspects of the Southwest. His book *Desert Heart* (Tucson: Fisher Books) describes the natural history and social history of the Sonoran desert, and his novel *Cities of Gold* (New York: Forge) is based on his studies of Coronado's pathfinder, the priest Marcos de Niza, as well as modern issues of urban development in the Southwest. Editions of several of his books have been published in England, France, Spain, Sweden, and Japan. His scholarly papers on the Coronado era have appeared in professional journals and in all three Coronado anthologies edited by Coronado scholars Richard and Shirley Flint.

Hartmann received a Ph.D. in astronomy and M.S. in geology from the University of Arizona and a B.S. in physics from Pennsylvania State University. He lives in Tucson with archaeologist Gayle Harrison Hartmann.